D1602054

The Dead Rabbit
Grocery and Grog

MIXOLOGY & MAYHEM

THE STORY OF JOHN MORRISSEY AND THE WORLD'S BEST COCKTAIL MENU

SEAN MULDOON, JACK McGARRY
& JILLIAN VOSE

HOUGHTON MIFFLIN HARCOURT | BOSTON | NEW YORK | 2018

COPYRIGHT © 2018 BY SEAN MULDOON, JACK MCGARRY, AND JILLIAN VOSE

COCKTAIL PHOTOGRAPHY © 2018 BY
BRENT HERRIG PHOTOGRAPHY
PORTRAIT AND BAR PHOTOGRAPHY © 2018 BY GREGORY J. BUDA
PHOTOGRAPHS ON PAGE 17: STUDIO 54 © AP STUDIO/
RICHARD DREW, AND 42ND STREET © NEW YORK TIMES/
JACK MANNING.

ALL RIGHTS RESERVED.

For information about permission to reproduce selections from this book,
write to trade.permissions@hmhco.com or to Permissions,
Houghton Mifflin Harcourt Publishing Company,
3 Park Avenue, 19th Floor, New York, New York 10016.

hmhco.com

Library of Congress Cataloging-in-Publication Data
Names: Muldoon, Sean, author. | McGarry, Jack, author. | Vose, Jillian author.
Title: The Dead Rabbit mixology & mayhem : the story of John Morrissey and
the worlds best cocktail menu / Sean Muldoon, Jack McGarry and Jillian Vose.
Description: New York, New York : Houghton Mifflin Harcourt, 2018. | Includes
bibliographical references and index.
Identifiers: LCCN 2018012252 (print) | LCCN 2018019987 (ebook) |
ISBN 9781328453334 (ebook) | ISBN 9781328451873 (paper over board)
Subjects: LCSH: Cocktails—Comic books, strips, etc. | Morrissey, John, 1831-1878—
Biography—Comic books, strips, etc. | Dead Rabbit Grocery and Grog (New York,
N.Y.)—Comic books, strips, etc. | LCGFT: Cookbooks.
Classification: LCC TX951 (ebook) | LCC TX951 .M828 2018 (print) |
DDC 641.87/4—dc23
LC record available at https://lccn.loc.gov/2018012252

Book design by Drinksology

Printed in China
TOP 10 9 8 7 6 5 4 3 2 1

AT A GLANCE

MISE EN PLACE: INTRODUCTION

PERFECT SERVE: THE COMICS & THE COCKTAILS

ANOTHER ROUND: EXTRAS, INSIGHTS, TIPS & MORE

MISE EN

INTRODU

PLACE:
CTION

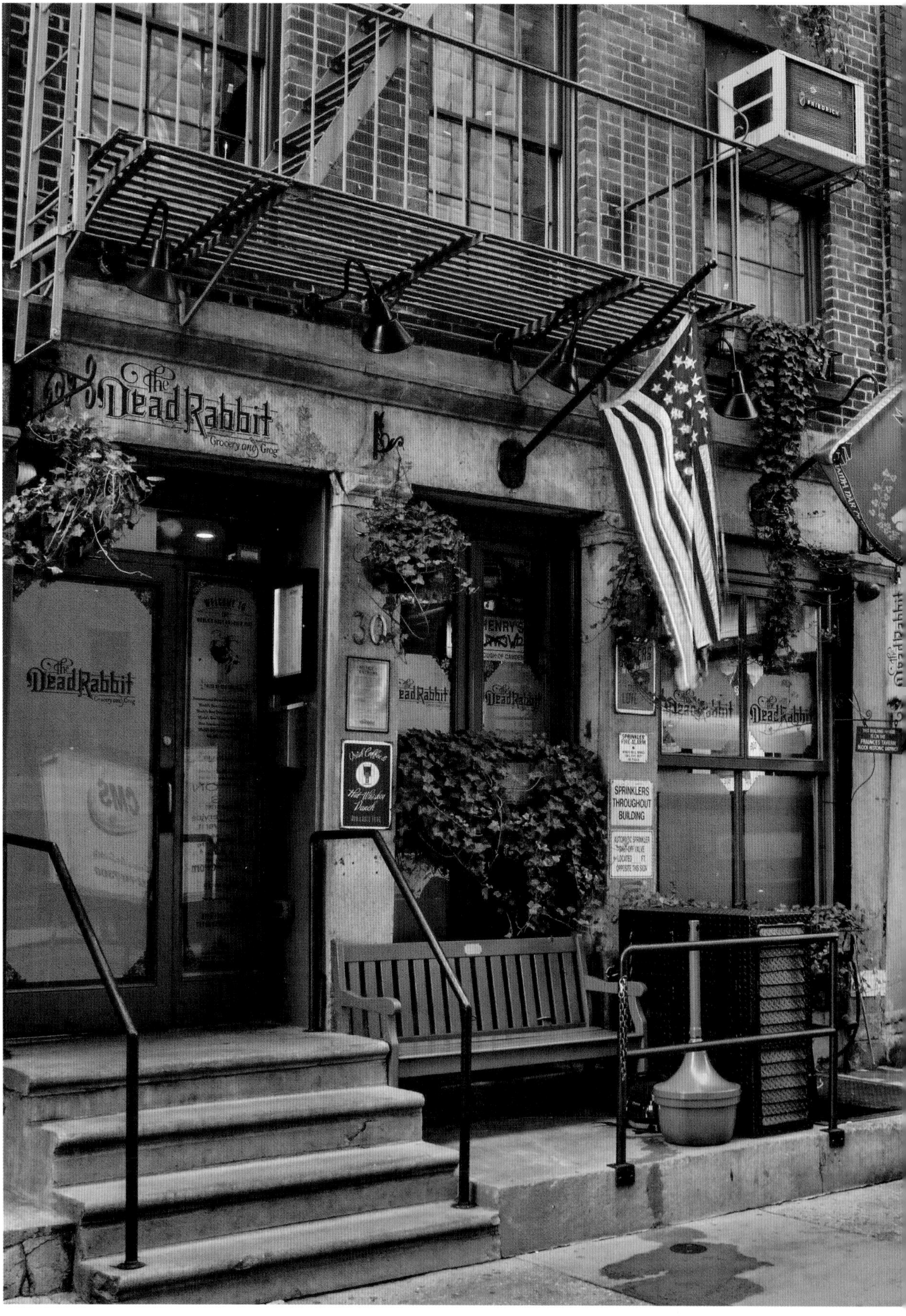

The Dead Rabbit
Grocery and Grog
SPRINKLERS THROUGHOUT BUILDING

INTRODUCTION

WELCOME, WHAT'LL YOU HAVE?

THE DEAD RABBIT IS THE BRAINCHILD OF SEAN MULDOON AND JACK McGARRY.

They'd already created the World's Best Bar back home in Belfast, Northern Ireland, and they wanted to do it again in New York. But they had a very specific goal in mind: to take the best of the traditional Irish bar into the twenty-first century, and add world-beating cocktails.

In all, it took two and a half long years to find, secure and launch the Dead Rabbit. Everyone advised them not to do it. Everyone was wrong. The bar was a runaway success from the start, winning major awards (including two World's Best titles to date) and setting new standards within the industry.

A major part of that success has been a genuinely revolutionary approach to menu creation and design. These documents continue to excite extraordinary word-of-mouth interest in the bar throughout the world.

AND HERE'S HOW IT'S DONE...

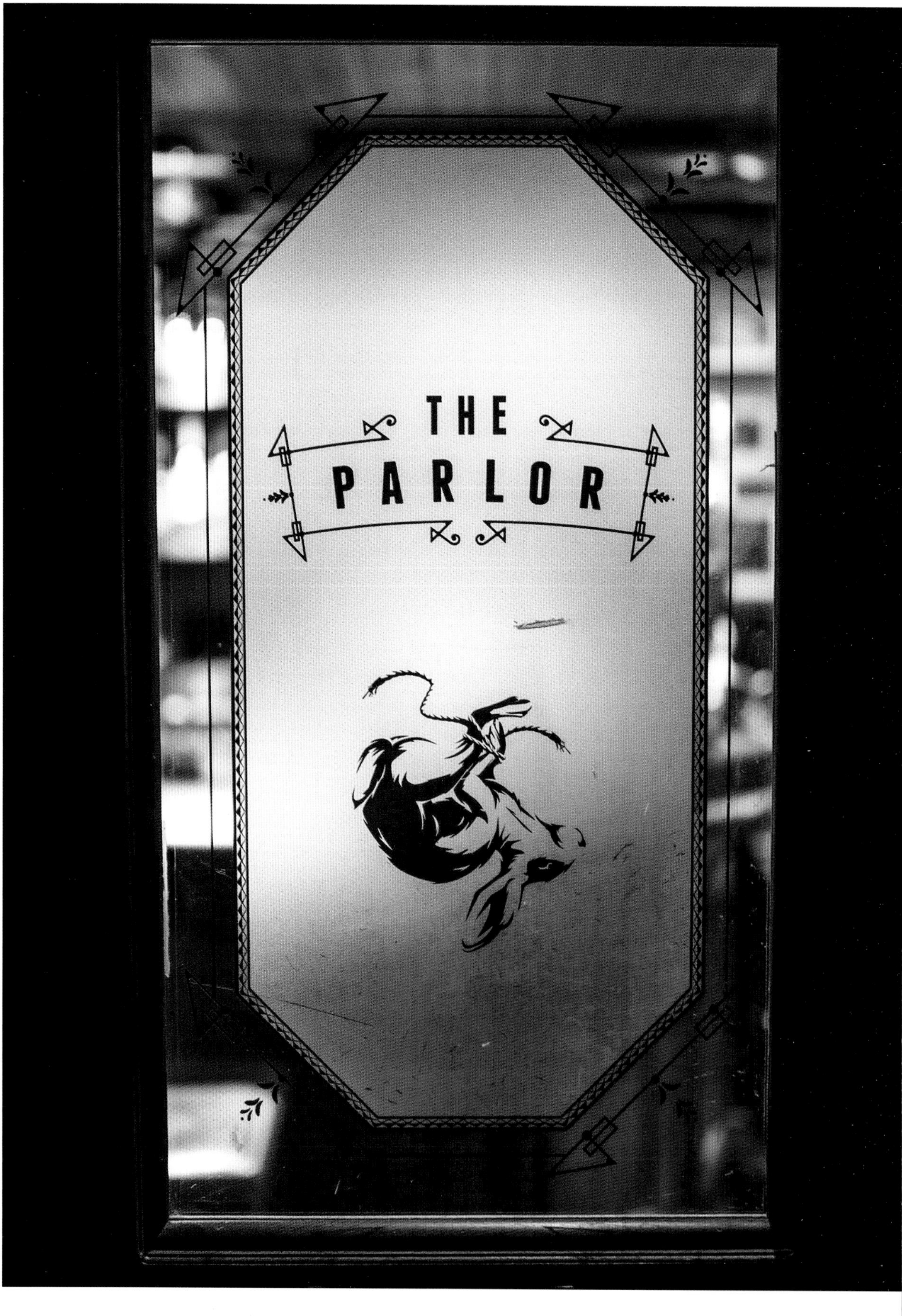
THE
PARLOR

OF METHODS & MADNESS
THERE IS METHOD
IN THE MADNESS

It's a familiar phrase that means, 'Hey, this isn't actually as crazy as it looks. Some thought has gone into it. Go figure.'

Of course, in our world, there are many colors of crazy. There's crazy-intense, crazy-strict, crazy-focused, crazy-tough, crazy-good. And there's plain old crazy-crazy.

WE'VE HEARD 'EM ALL, AND THEN SOME.

Yes, our methods are unorthodox, we admit. And maybe we do make things harder for ourselves than they have to be. We're ridiculously and relentlessly demanding of ourselves and others. Because we're driven – like maniacs – to do more, get better, stay ahead.

People say we have nothing to prove, that we should slow down, kick back.

BUT WE SAY THAT'S JUST CRAZY TALK.

9.

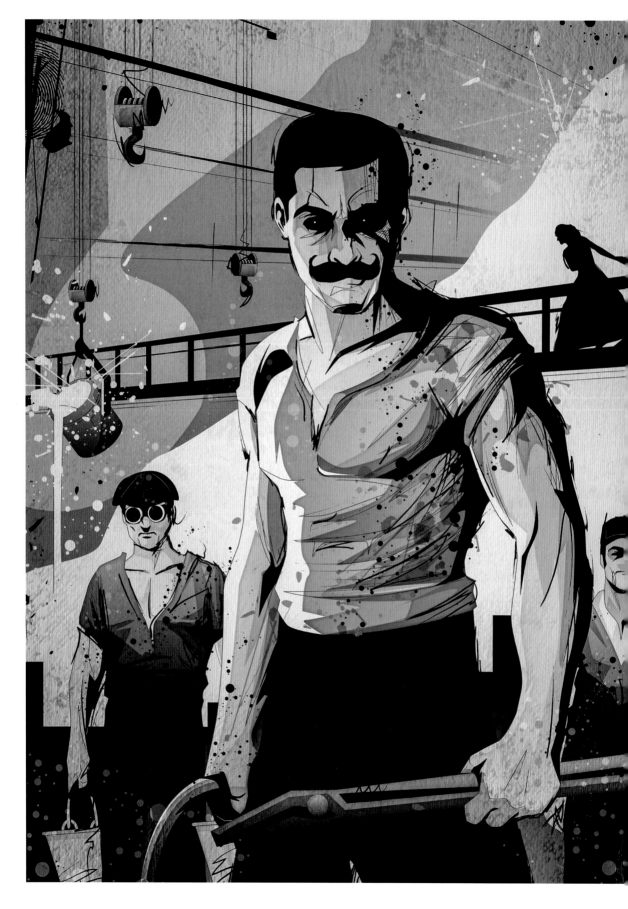

INTRODUCTION
CREATING THE WORLD'S BEST DRINKS MENUS

Well, that's an ambitious claim right from the start. Some might even say arrogant. We say, just think of it as a statement of intent. Because our menus have won the highest accolades in the business. We aim for a superlative standard in all things. It's the only thing we're after – menu after menu, drink after drink.

In this book we show how we've done what we've done, revealing our unique methodology for creating world-beating cocktails and incorporating them into equally extraordinary menus of originality and inventiveness.

In these pages you'll find history, booze and tale-telling on a vast scale. There's also evidence of some very dedicated and singular talents on display. So mix yourself a fine cocktail (instructions provided, of course) and make yourself comfortable.

READY? THEN WE'LL BEGIN.

11.

A QUESTION OF QUESTIONABLE CHARACTERS
FROM JOHN MORRISSEY TO THE RABBIT

In the rough-and-tumble Five Points quarter of lower Manhattan back in the mid-nineteenth century, nationalist and ethnic gangs fought bitterly for power and territory. Among these gangs, the most notorious was an Irish mob known as the Dead Rabbits. Their leader was John Morrissey.

Morrissey lived an extraordinary life, from street thug to champion prize-fighter, from Tammany Hall arm-twister to U.S. congressman and eventually New York senator. When he died in 1878, aged just 47, the entire state senate attended his funeral. Possibly just to be sure he was really dead.

For rumor, myth and legend trailed Morrissey just as surely as fact. His nickname, Old Smoke, was reputedly acquired when he was pinned to burning coals from an overturned stove during a fight. Despite the pain, Morrissey battled on, won the fight – and a reputation.

We liked that. We also liked his fierce devotion to the impoverished immigrant Irish he came from and whom he defended tooth and nail. For all his faults – and they were many – Morrissey had a code of honor. For him, betrayal of the tribe was the ultimate sin, and loyalty the true measure of a man.

We told this story in our second menu, 'Warren Warrior', and showed the world of the Five Points at that time in its squalor and poverty and violence and corruption. Morrissey's nature, his ruthlessness and his rage, resonated through the pages. This set the template for how we would work in the future – in how we approach drink creation, how we envision and design the menus themselves. And how we learned to intertwine the two strands inextricably.

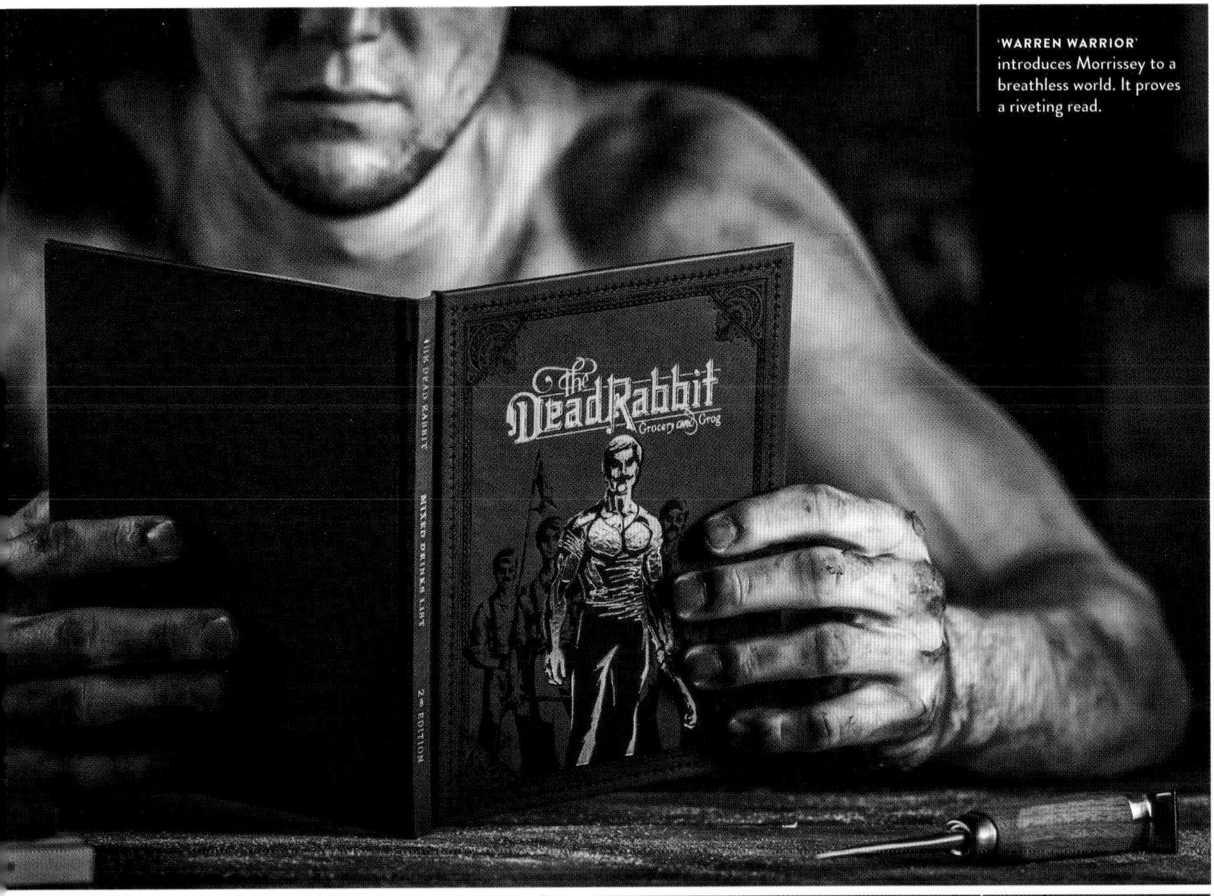
The Dead Rabbit
Grocery and Grog
THE DEAD RABBIT
MIXED DRINKS LIST
2ND EDITION

'WARREN WARRIOR' introduces Morrissey to a breathless world. It proves a riveting read.

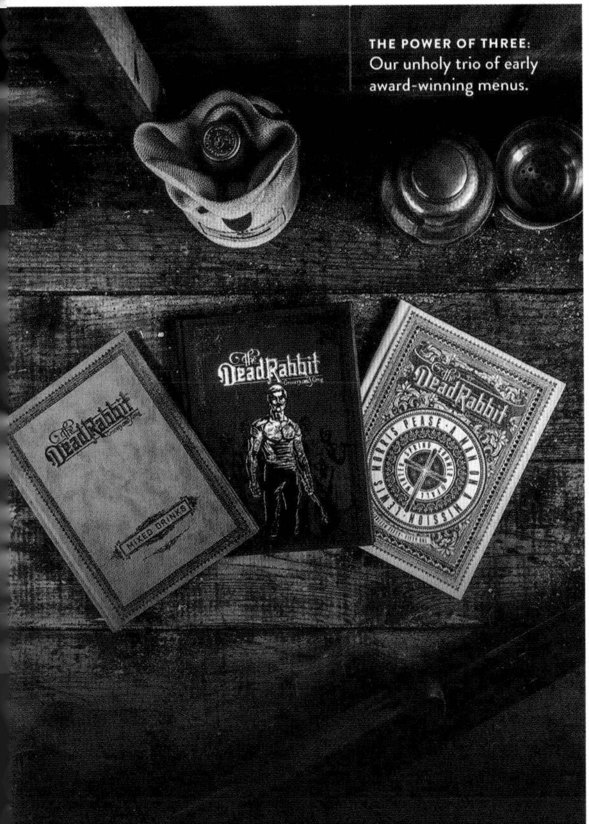
The Dead Rabbit
Grocery and Grog
The Dead Rabbit
MIXED DRINKS
The Dead Rabbit

THE POWER OF THREE: Our unholy trio of early award-winning menus.

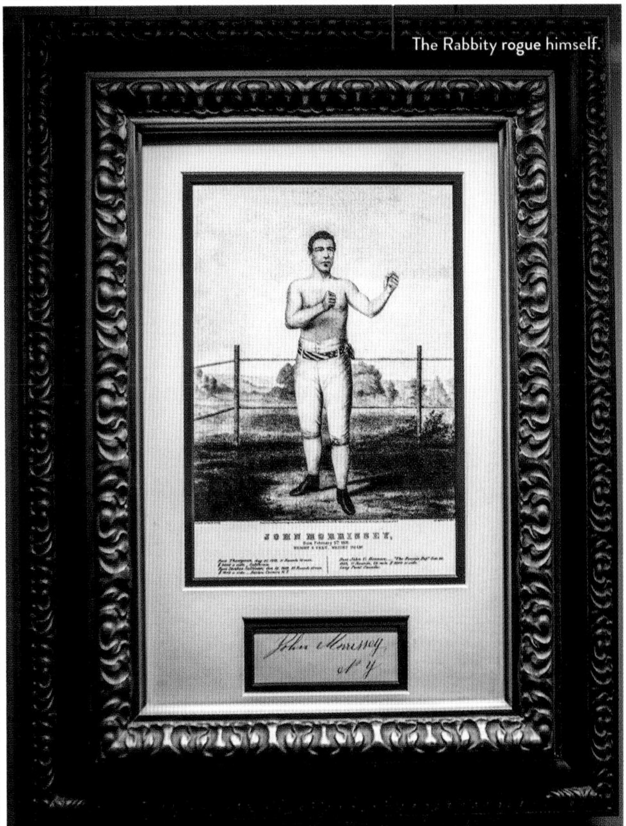
JOHN MORRISSEY,

The Rabbity rogue himself.

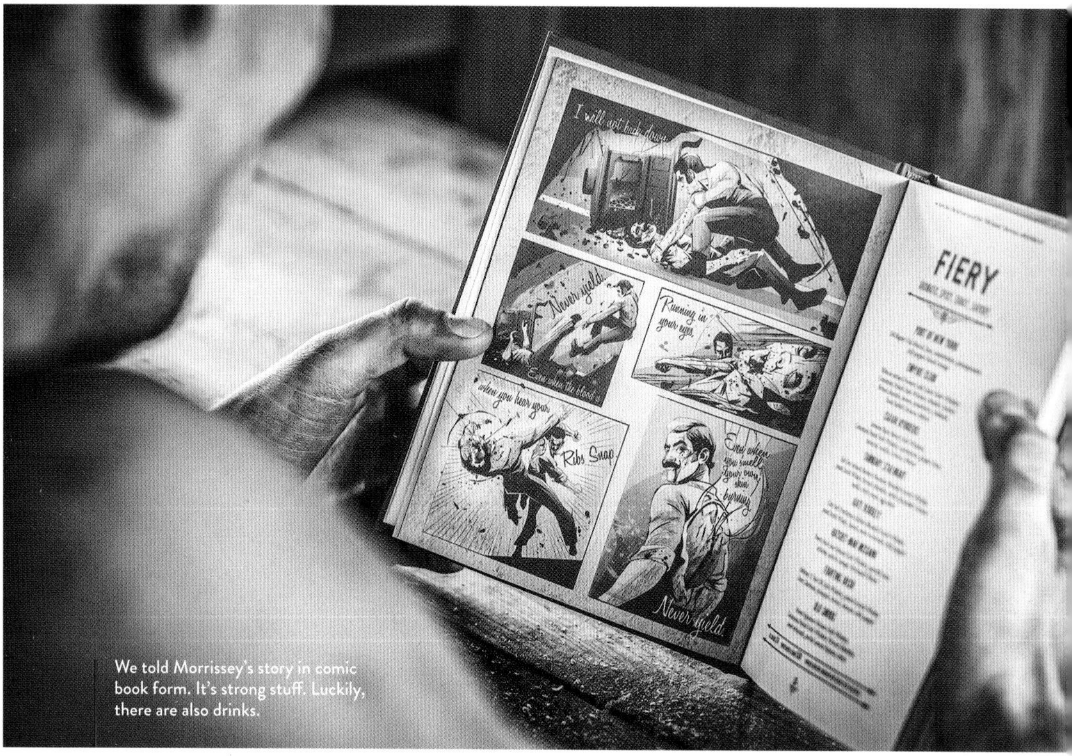
I will not back down
Never yield.
Running in your eyes
Ribs Snap
Never yield.
FIERY

We told Morrissey's story in comic book form. It's strong stuff. Luckily, there are also drinks.

Our third menu, 'Man on a Mission', stayed within the same historical and geographical framework, while the focus shifted to an evangelical crusader and social reformer, Lewis Morris Pease. He was a kind of anti-Morrissey – a man driven by altruism and by faith, battling with a Bible in one hand and pen in the other to dismantle the degenerate world in which men like Old Smoke flourished.

And he did flourish. For Morrissey would not die. Not, as some of his erstwhile senate colleagues feared, but as a presiding presence in our own story. His rage burned on and continued to cast a long shadow. Two separate mythologies – John Morrissey and the Dead Rabbit bar – began to merge.

But when we came to consider our next menu (number 4), we knew we didn't want to stay within the historical confines of the nineteenth century. That had run its course. By this point we had begun playing with a Rabbit character, creating promotional posters for special events, casting him variously as a DJ, rockstar and even a female singer-songwriter. Right from the start, he (or she) always wore the historically accurate red flannel shirt favored by the Bowery B'hoys.

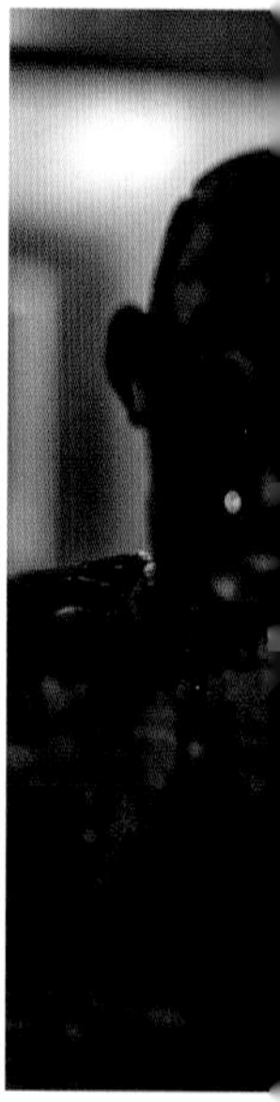

The Rabbit character appeared quite early, often to promote special events. He — and sometimes she — always wore the red flannel shirt of the Bowery B'hoys.

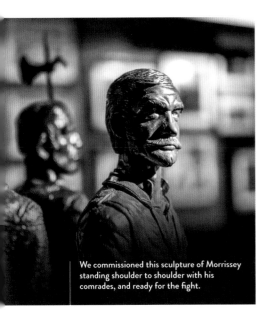

We commissioned this sculpture of Morrissey standing shoulder to shoulder with his comrades, and ready for the fight.

Perhaps the idea we'd been looking for had been looking back at us.

With our creative team we began to think about bringing back the spirit of Morrissey – seeing him reborn as a hybrid man-rabbit antihero. A character who was one badass bunny.

Discussions between the bar team in New York and creative team in Belfast quickly got intense. In what period should we set the next story? Can people see The Rabbit as he is, or do they simply accept him? How should he speak? Where has he come from? Does he know where he is? What does he remember of his past? Are there others like him?

And so on. And on.

In the meantime, our illustrator was quietly working up visuals of The Rabbit. When we saw them, they instantly settled many of the questions. But one remained: What era should his story be set in, and why?

We did what we often do. We began talking about movies. Someone on the team mentioned Woody Allen's Zelig, a human chameleon who moves seamlessly between historical contexts and situations, and who is present at key moments in history. (*Forrest Gump* is another example.)

It made sense for The Rabbit to have the same capacity to move between events. It's an idea we would flesh out more particularly towards the end of the storyline, when we began to tie together the threads we had laid down earlier. His past crimes and misdemeanors flash past, and we realize: That renegade, ruthless spirit has always been there, if we had eyes to see it.

And so we began.

HISTORY & HINDSIGHT

We plunged our new antihero into the modern era, starting with New York in the 1970s – a city on the brink of implosion, caught in a tailspin of social turmoil, economic collapse and crime. The imagery is familiar: it's the world of *Taxi Driver*, *Mean Streets*, *The Warriors*, *The Godfather*, *Serpico* and a hundred more movies and TV shows like them.

Why that period? For a start, gangs were everywhere, organized by ethnic group as well as location. These two elements led to turf wars; some minor, some protracted and deadly.

And so, a century on from the death of John Morrissey, many aspects of his world were still evident: gangs, corruption, violence, poverty. Many things had changed, too, of course. In Morrissey's day, gut-rot booze and bathtub gin were the intoxicants of choice, and where the money lay. In this new world, it was hard drugs and extortion. New York was riven with neglect and decay. The gulf between the haves and the have-nots never seemed greater. While the beautiful people cavorted in Studio 54 in the dying days of disco, out on the streets and in the projects, hip-hop culture was being born.

The more we looked, the more parallels we found. Jimmy Coonan, of the notoriously violent Westies Irish gang, was involved in a bitter struggle with overall Irish boss Mickey Spillane. Coonan wanted to work with the Italian Mob and expand operations, specifically around the Javits Convention Center, near the former Madison Square Garden site. This was on Spillane's turf, and he naturally refused to split the action. The Mob backed Coonan, and as an expression of their bona fides, had Spillane taken out. With Coonan now in place, the unholy allegiance went ahead.

Such a betrayal would have outraged Morrissey, we thought, and called out to his spirit. And so it did. The resurrection of the leader of the Dead Rabbits was to be the story.

Structurally, this menu had also been our most ambitious to date, conceived as a series of six comic books. Spanning the 1970s and 1980s, together they tell the story of the clash between a brutal, old-world code of honor and a pragmatic, modern attitude to money, violence and power. It follows the arrival of The Rabbit – called forth from the underworld – to avenge his own demons, and others'. He starts at the lowest rung, back on the street. Using his fists and his cunning, he works his way up to trusted lieutenant, via prison, and then eventually kingpin. Then politics offers a new direction, which turns out to be the old direction. It's a good, gory, gripping tale. With a twist and, of course, killer cocktails.

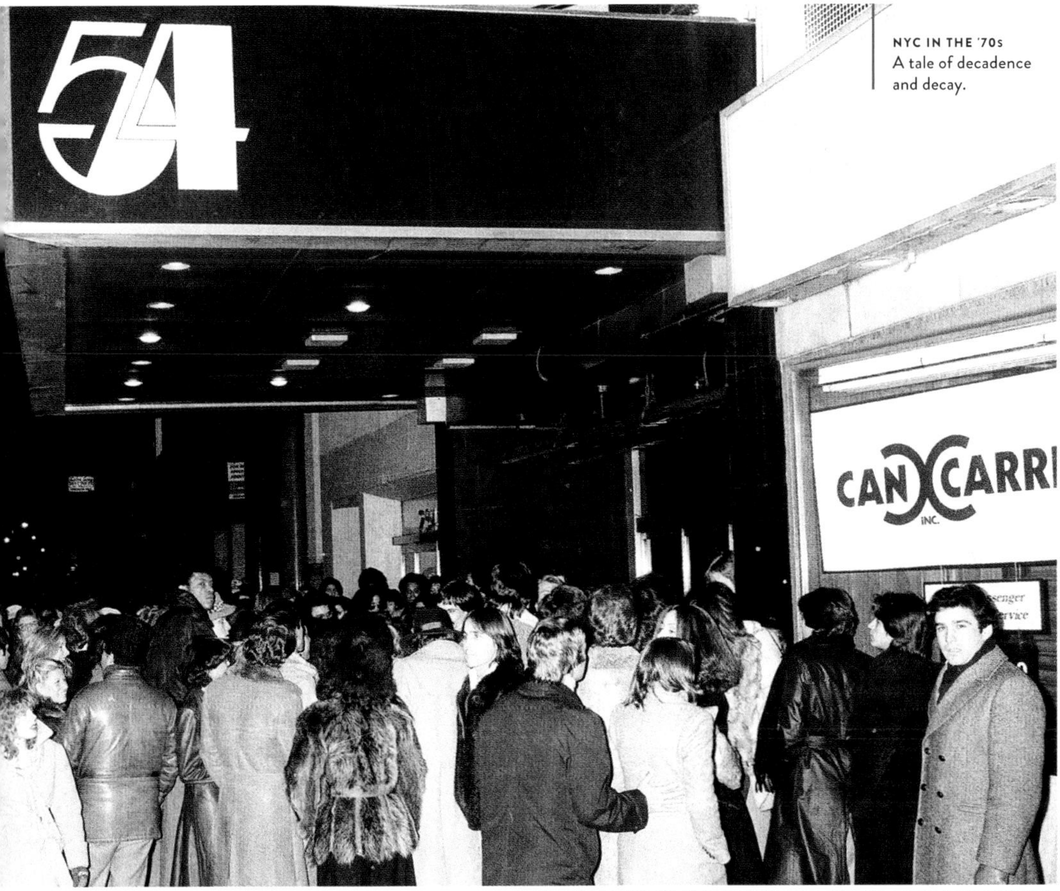
54

NYC IN THE '70s
A tale of decadence and decay.

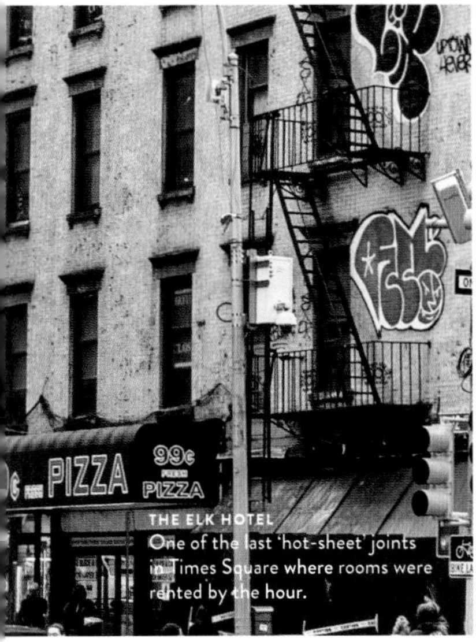
PIZZA
99¢
PIZZA

THE ELK HOTEL
One of the last 'hot-sheet' joints in Times Square where rooms were rented by the hour.

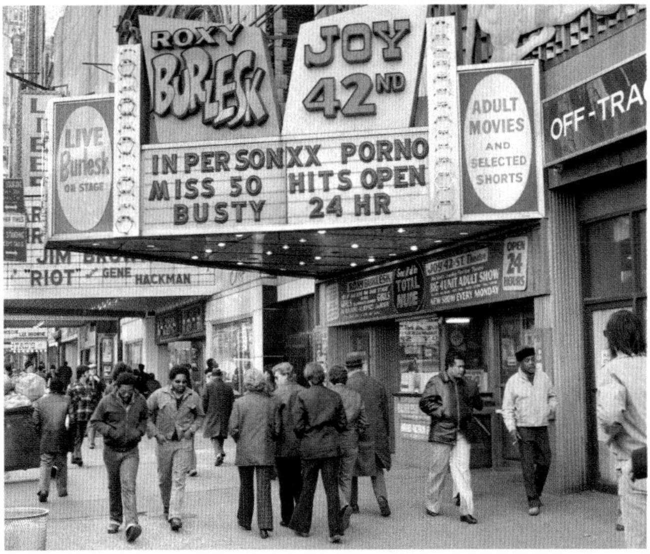
ROXY
BURLESK
JOY
42ND
LIVE
Burlesk
ON STAGE
IN PER SON
MISS 50
BUSTY
XX PORNO
HITS OPEN
24 HR
ADULT
MOVIES
AND
SELECTED
SHORTS
OFF-TRA
"RIOT"
GENE
HACKMAN
OPEN
24
HOURS

SHAPING THE TALE

— RESURRECTION —

The reborn spirit of Morrissey appears in 1970s New York. Bewildered and unsure at first, The Rabbit begins to find his way, fists first, in a gang world that is eerily familiar.

— BETRAYAL —

By now a trusted lieutenant in the Irish Mob, he encounters the power of the drug world, and the treachery that lies beneath. For The Rabbit, this is the ultimate sin.

— INCARCERATION —

The Rabbit finds himself in prison, and starting on the lowest rung. It's a violent world ruled by factions and contraband. He sees loyalties broken, and decides to act.

— RETRIBUTION —

Back on the streets, The Rabbit has scores to settle and an empire to build, quickly. This means finding money, allies and opportunities. It also means a bloody, bloody turf war.

— DOMINATION —

Here, power is hiding in plain sight. The Rabbit moves into a corrupt world of politics and big-money influence. It's as brutal as ever, and enemies are everywhere.

— ENDGAME —

The net is closing in around The Rabbit. His time is nearly up, and a new history is already calling. But first, there are some loose ends to be tidied up. It doesn't take long.

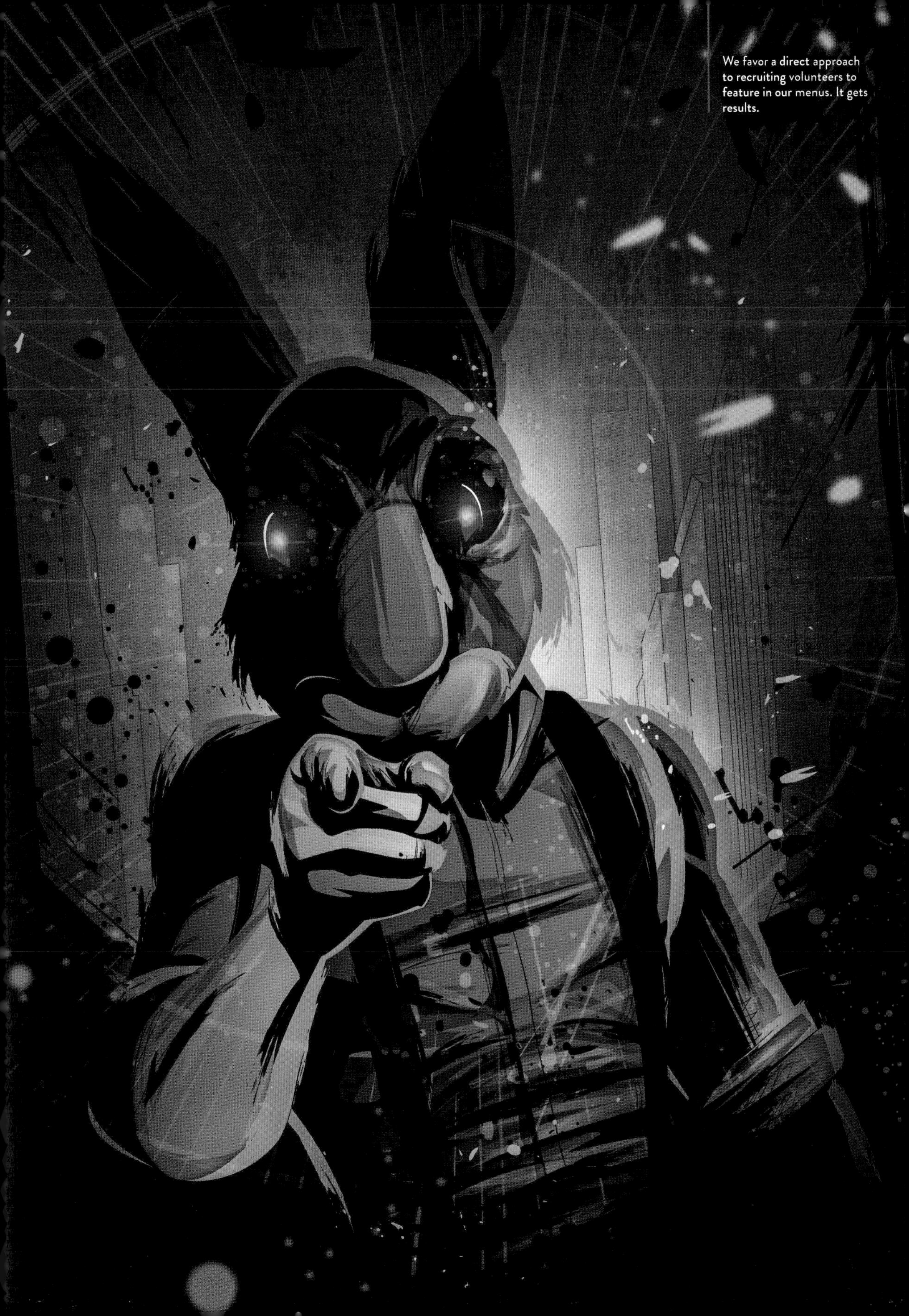

We favor a direct approach to recruiting volunteers to feature in our menus. It gets results.

FACTS, MEET FICTION

We've always done an inordinate amount of research for every menu. The story of The Rabbit is no exception. In each chapter, we knew the streets and dives that were there. We learned the names of the players, we knew what they wore and ate and drank, the cars they drove, the music they listened to, the way they spent their money and other people's. We learned what prison life was like then, what tensions were in the air. We gathered hundreds of documents and books, watched movie after movie. We kept digging.

Together with the design team, writer and illustrator, we began with a bare scenario. We binned it. We tried another. Better, but also binned. Finally a starting point was reached. We roughed out a chapter and storylined it. There were disagreements. We resolved them, and replaced them with others. Long email chains developed out of equally long and occasionally heated discussions. Along the way, voices and blood pressure were raised, and raised some more. But we progressed, word by word, scene by scene.

Here's a typical exchange:

CONOR KELLY
I sent the new storyline. What do you think?

RICHARD RYAN
Love it. Just like we discussed.

SEAN MULDOON
I've been thinking about this. Nah, let's start again.

CONOR KELLY
Um, er, OK . . . [days later] Well, how's this?

SEAN MULDOON
Better. But instead of the fistfight on p. 3, let's get a bit knifey-knifey.

RICHARD RYAN
[days later] Here, that's brutal. I near lost my lunch.

MARK REIHILL
I've never tried to draw that before.

RICHARD RYAN
Funny, it seemed to come naturally to you. Got something to tell us, Mark?

MARK REIHILL
Reminds me, I must get some fava beans and a nice chianti . . .

SEAN MULDOON
You're one sick puppy, Mark. Class.

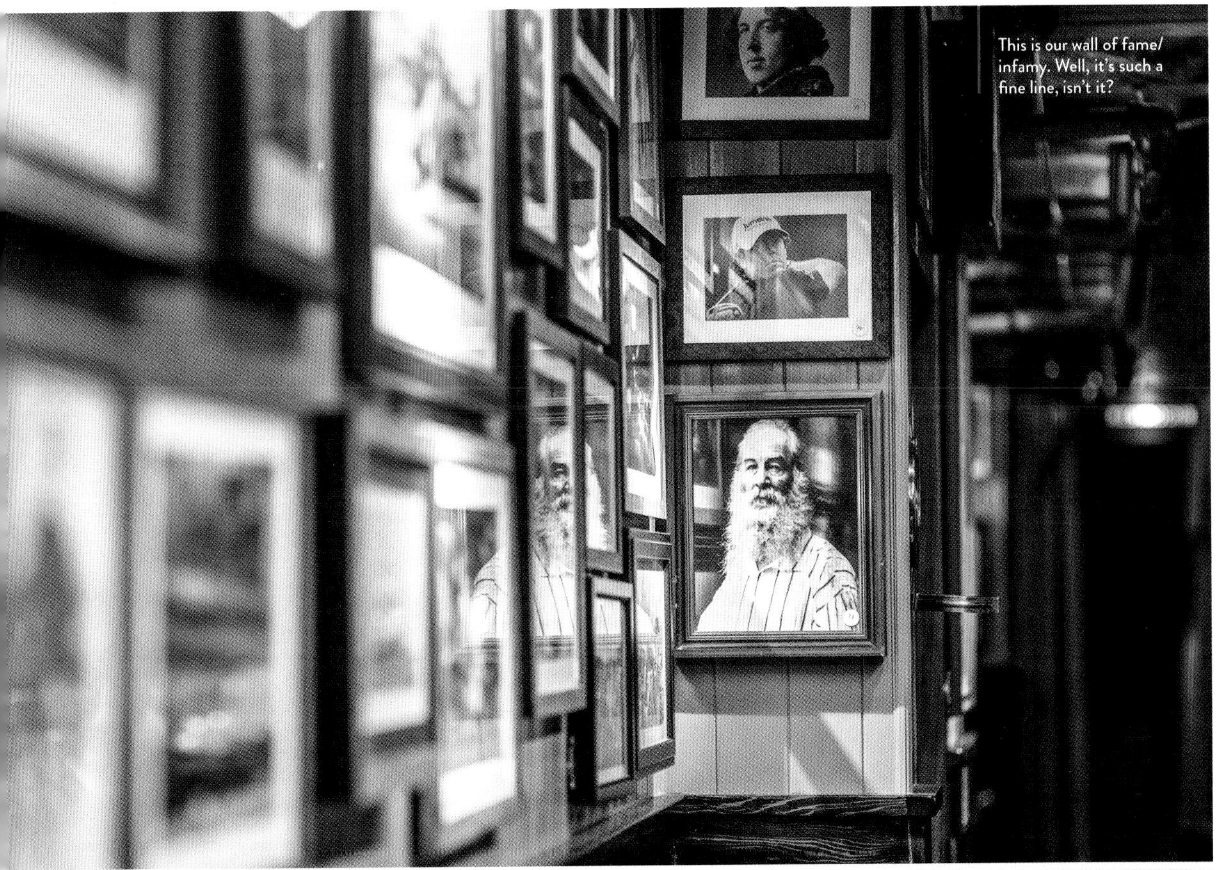

This is our wall of fame/ infamy. Well, it's such a fine line, isn't it?

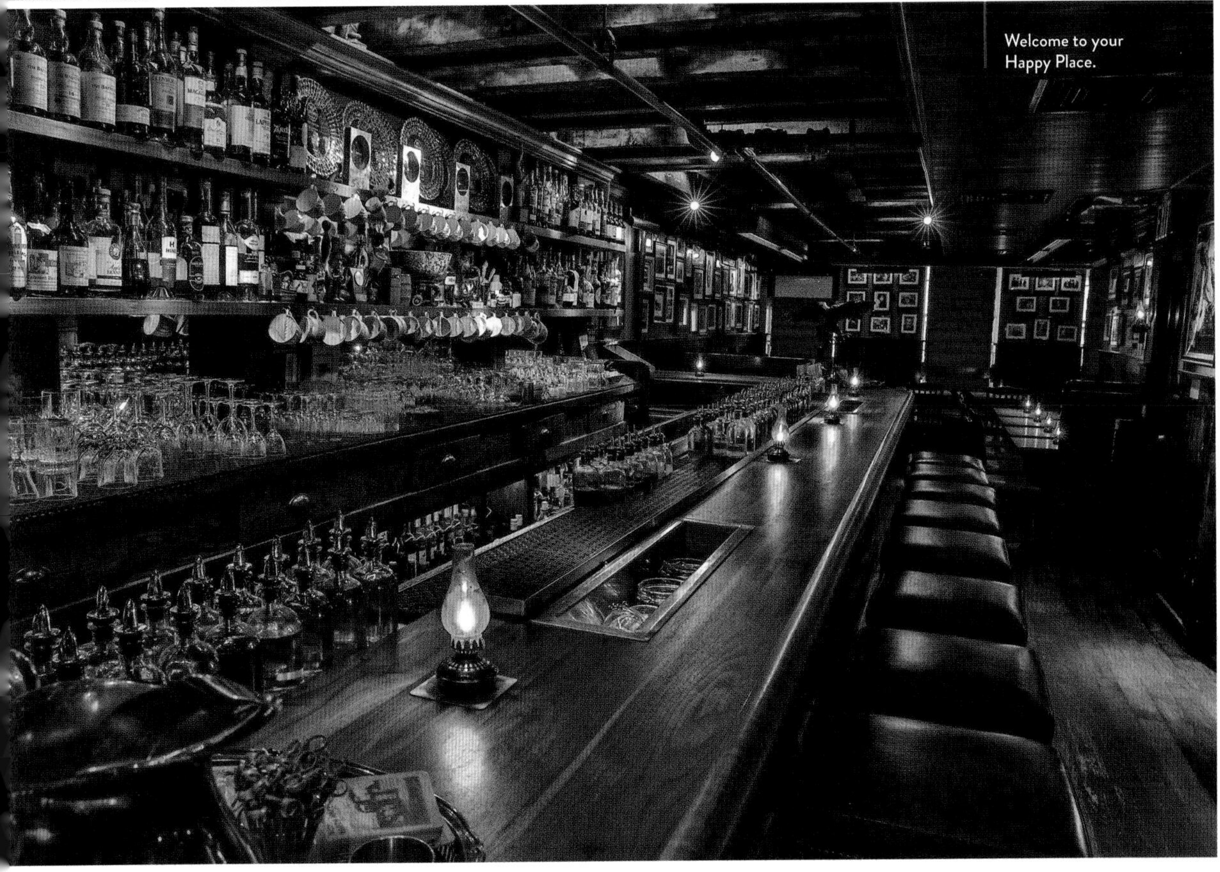

Welcome to your Happy Place.

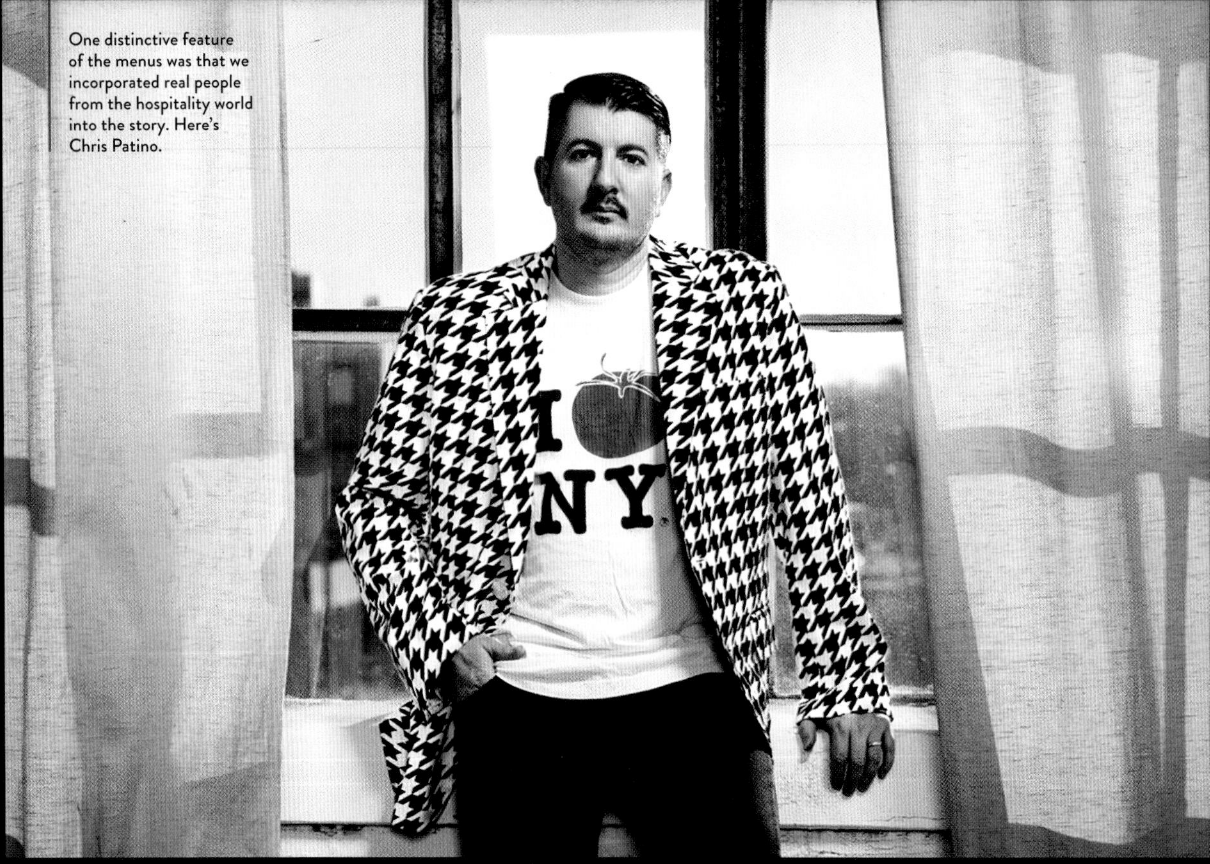
I
NY

One distinctive feature of the menus was that we incorporated real people from the hospitality world into the story. Here's Chris Patino.

Illustrator Mark Reihill gets to work on Chris.

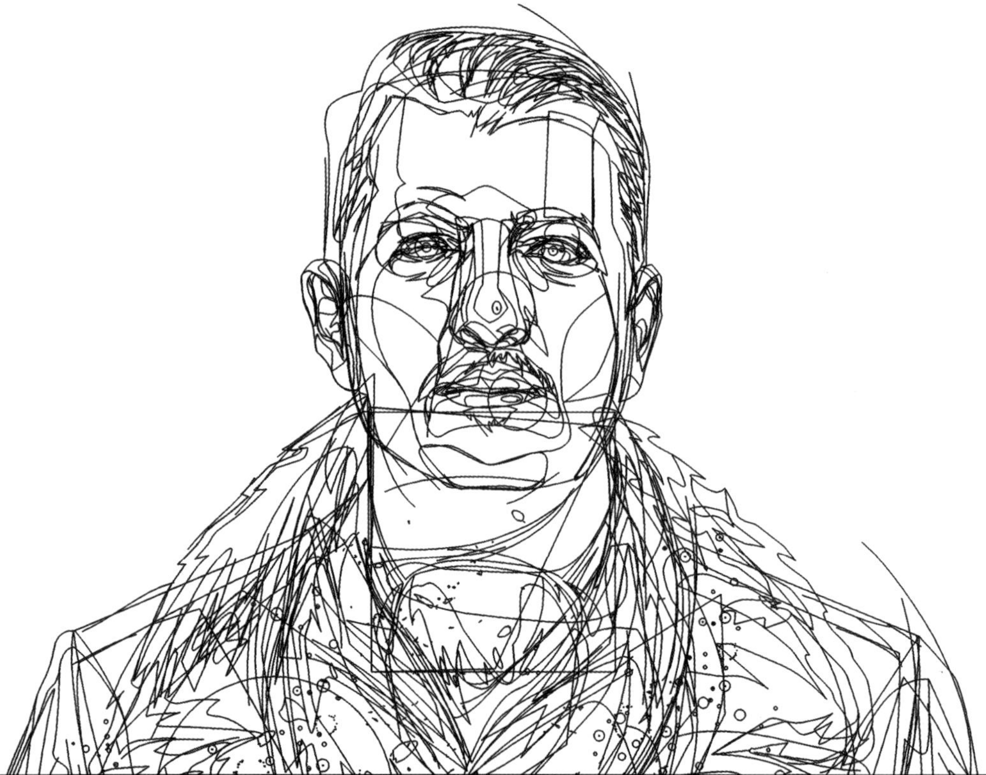

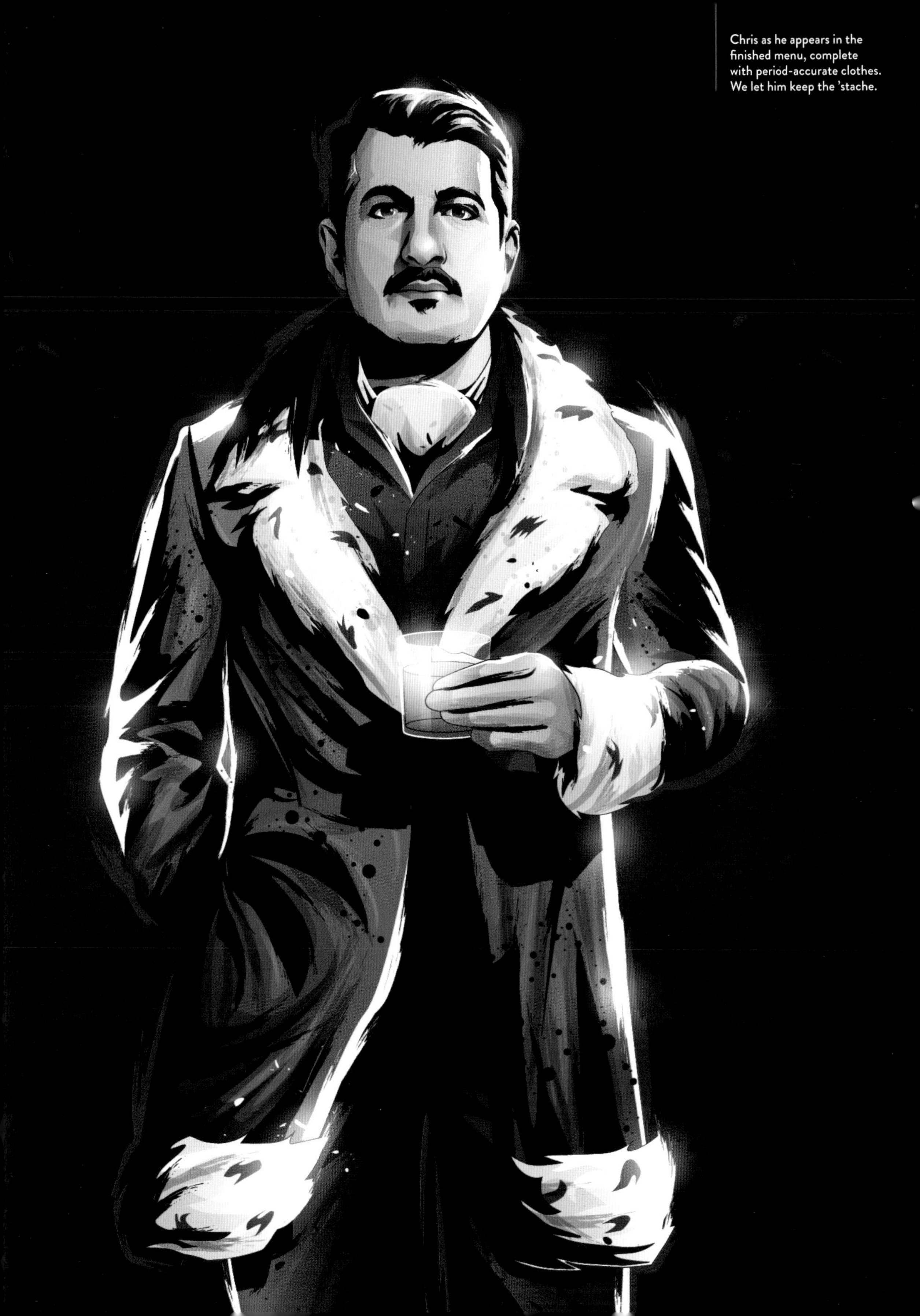

Chris as he appears in the finished menu, complete with period-accurate clothes. We let him keep the 'stache.

FAMILIAR FACES IN UNFAMILIAR PLACES

One of the more intriguing aspects of the fourth menu is that many of the characters who appear are well-known personalities in drinks and hospitality circles. When we first asked, the response was overwhelming: People weren't just happy to get involved. They loved the idea. It was very flattering – and a responsibility too. Would these people really be OK about being represented as thugs, crooks, hitmen, hookers, pimps, junkies? Oh, were they ever. Well, even the good guys enjoy a shot at being bad once in a while, don't they?

NAMING THE NAMES

While the storyline was developing and being illustrated, so, too, of course were the all-important drinks. (In fact, that work goes on all the time.) In previous menus, we've used ingredients or style of drinks as the single organizing principle. In this case, we used the narrative.

The names emerge from what is going on in the story – names like Gangsta's Paradise from 'Betrayal'; or Fun Lovin' Criminal, Sucker Punch and Switchblade from 'Incarceration'. They begin lighter and progress with the narrative towards stronger and heavier styles. They're a story in themselves.

The Dead Rabbit team extends far beyond the walls of Water Street and NYC. Our creative and design partners are back in Ireland, and work with us on a daily basis. What you can see here is some of the development work for the menus – preliminary sketches, how they develop, the evolving storyline, etc. It's an intensely collaborative process.

During that process we may disagree, argue, swear, seethe, roll our eyes. That kind of thing. There may also be some random shouting. A bit more swearing. Someone digs their heels in. Someone else digs them out. And we get on with it, because we're all focused on exactly same thing: making this the best it can possibly be. We have a principle: Egos can be bruised, but no corners can be cut.

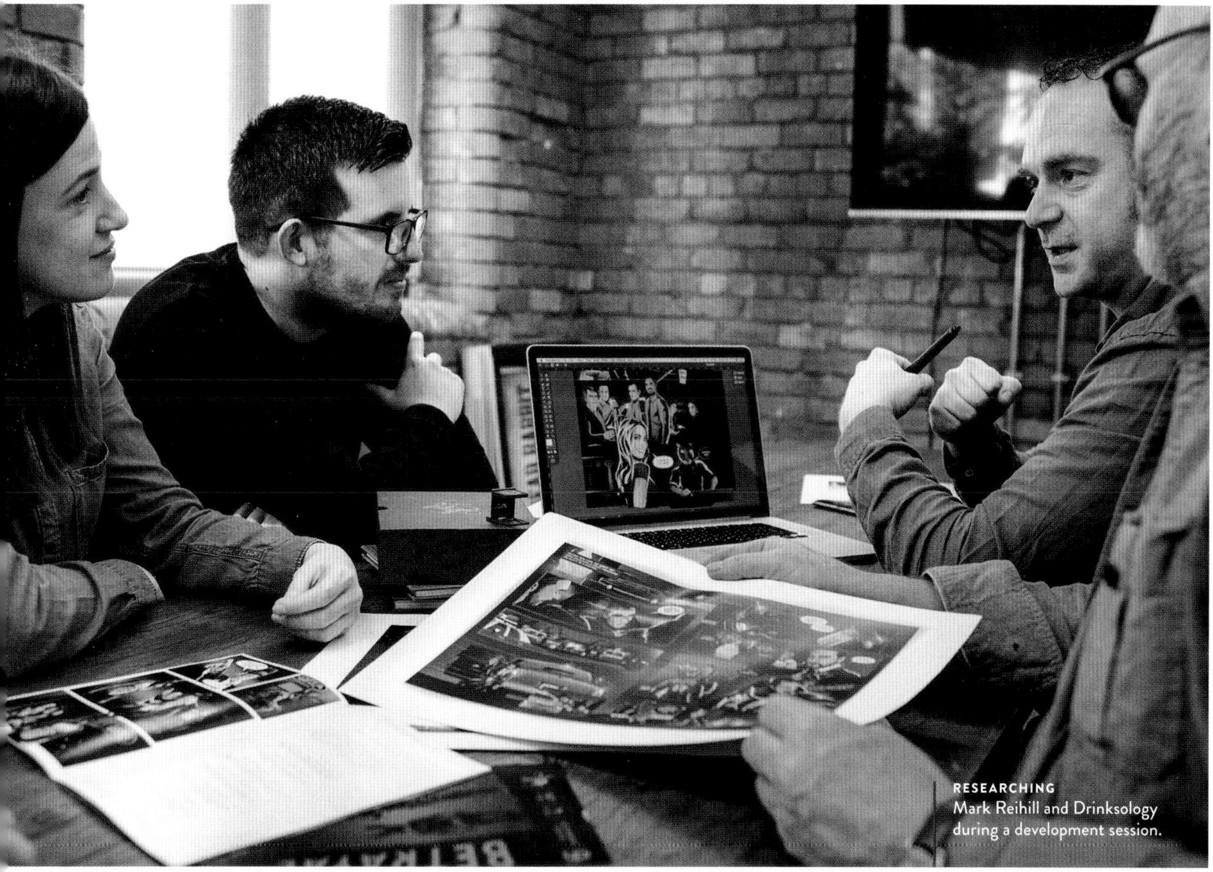

RESEARCHING
Mark Reihill and Drinksology during a development session.

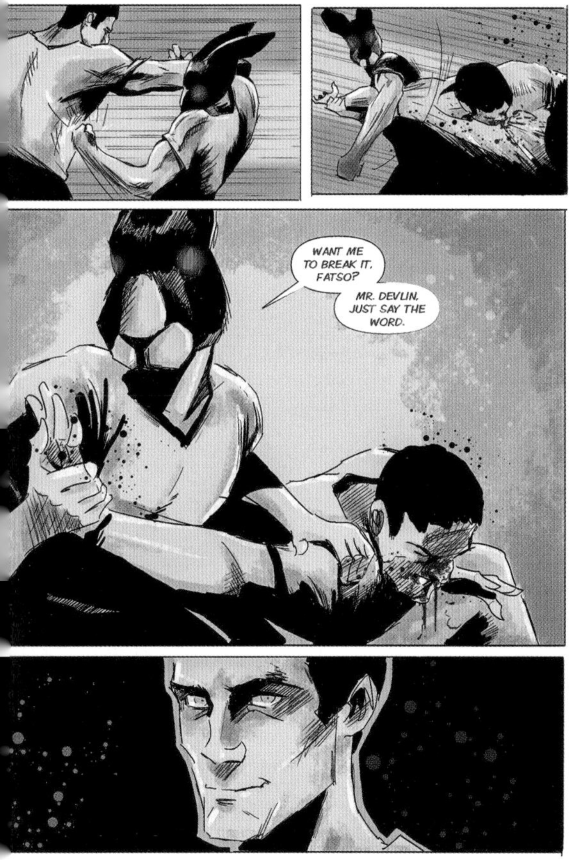
WANT ME TO BREAK IT, FATSO?
MR. DEVLIN, JUST SAY THE WORD.

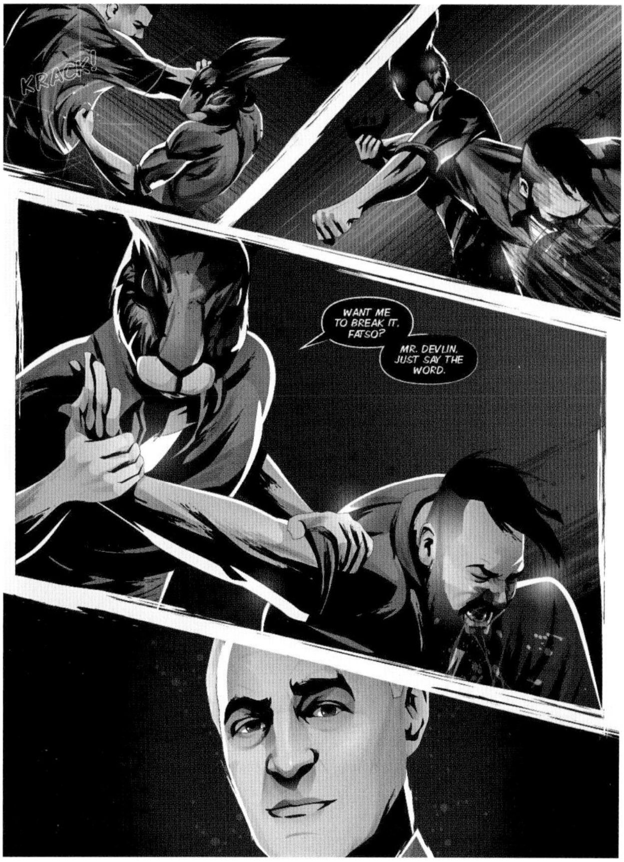
KRACK!
WANT ME TO BREAK IT, FATSO?
MR. DEVLIN, JUST SAY THE WORD.

JILLIAN SAYS
Let it rain.

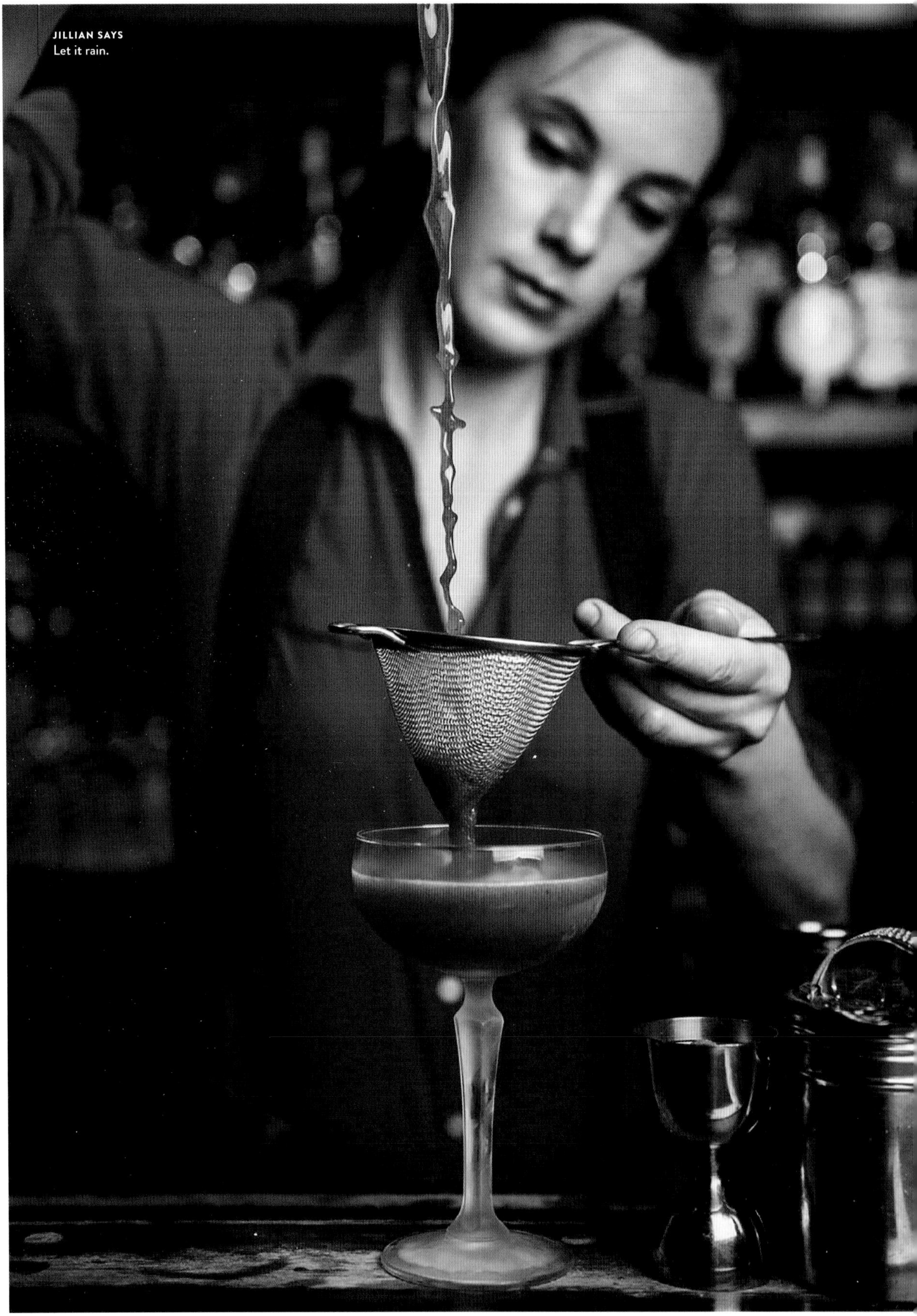

JILLIAN VOSE
DEVELOPING A MENU

FIRST OF ALL, THE DRINKS:
WHERE DO THEY COME FROM?

At the Dead Rabbit, ideas are welcome from everyone. No, that's not quite right. They're expected from everyone. So you've got an idea for a new drink? 'Course you do. OK, let's taste it at the next R&D session.

The sessions take place twice a month. We use Evernote software during and after to remember stuff, collate feedback, share ideas and eliminate repetition. At this stage, those putting forward a new drink are responsible for sourcing ingredients (we give them an allowance). They must also make any new syrups or tinctures they need. And there are no passengers: Everyone tastes everything, and everyone provides feedback.

A new recipe can be presented, tweaked and re-presented up to four, maybe five times tops. If it's still not quite there, then it's not quite anywhere, and we move on. It happens to all of us. You get over it.

(By the way, getting your drink on a menu always feels like an achievement, whether it's your first or your twenty-first. So you're allowed to treat yourself to a little air punch. Then, hey – it's back to work.)

'EVERYBODY LOVES MY NEW DRINK,
SO WHY ISN'T IT ON THE MENU?'

Even if a drink tastes great, it still has to fit the menu. Sometimes a new drink isn't right for the season, or there may be too much of the same style or a particular ingredient already on the menu. So a fabulous new cocktail may be banked until the next menu, when it will be considered again. But no promises, mind.

STRUCTURING THE MENU

Menus are all about balance. This means making sure there's a style of drink for different palates – Old Fashioned, Sazerac, Manhattan, martini-style, and so on. But within each of those categories, of course there's a world of possibilities. And we're really rigorous about the whole process. I encourage staff to think about how each drink will actually be read by the guest, and what assumptions they might make about the way the cocktail will taste. Having a structure helps the guest navigate a large menu like ours. Organization can be by: Cocktail Style; Shaken vs. Stirred vs. Build; Seasonality; or Lightest/Most Delicate to Heaviest/Most Intense.

Work on this begins without any drinks having been created.

Before a new menu is due, I'll put together a wireframe of what it will look like. This sets out Shaken vs. Stirred vs. Built etc., and includes a checklist of drink qualities – Boozy, Sour, Sweet, Low ABV, Fruity, Creamy, Vegetal, Spicy, Sparkling and so on. I might also include a checklist of ingredients – for example, whiskey, gin, vodka, agave, egg white, hot peppers, berries, etc. I circulate this well ahead of the development sessions.

I recommend that once you have an idea, you put an outline recipe down on paper before you start mixing anything. This may sound daunting, but the more research you've done on flavor pairings, the easier this gets. It also means that when you physically make the drink, you're pretty much fine-tuning proportions; perhaps an ingredient or two. It's a very practical (and cost-effective) way to work.

THE SECRET INGREDIENTS
BEHIND EVERY MENU

OK, here it is. To create a new menu you need: a poster board, marker pens (several colors) and a lot of sticky notes. And I mean really a lot. After all the potential new drinks have been presented, I'll lay them out on paper and start putting the puzzle together of where each will sit on the menu. I get the big poster board and those sticky notes and move things around until everything makes sense.

Then I take all the drinks that have made it and transfer those drinks from the Evernote developmental folder to the final folder with their assigned names. That way the staff can start to study them before the menu launches.

From there, I map out the mise en place and make labels for everything, plus an inventory of what ingredients are being taken off and what new ones will be going on. With the space we have available, we sometimes have to mix some small ingredients together into small batches to make everything fit. This makes for a much smoother menu flip. The flips take a lot of time and effort to get everything switched in one day, so you've got to be as organized as possible.

Once a new menu is finally ready, the entire staff needs to taste it and understand it so they can speak knowledgeably to guests about each drink and its ingredients.

After the menu has been in use for a couple of weeks, everyone gets a refresher test on the drinks, ingredients, service steps and techniques. Over this period, Jack, Sean and I will also do spot checks, ordering drinks from each bartender to ensure that consistency is being maintained – day after day, shift after shift. It's the only way. And we get free drinks.

29.

JESSICA
Showing how it's done. Again.

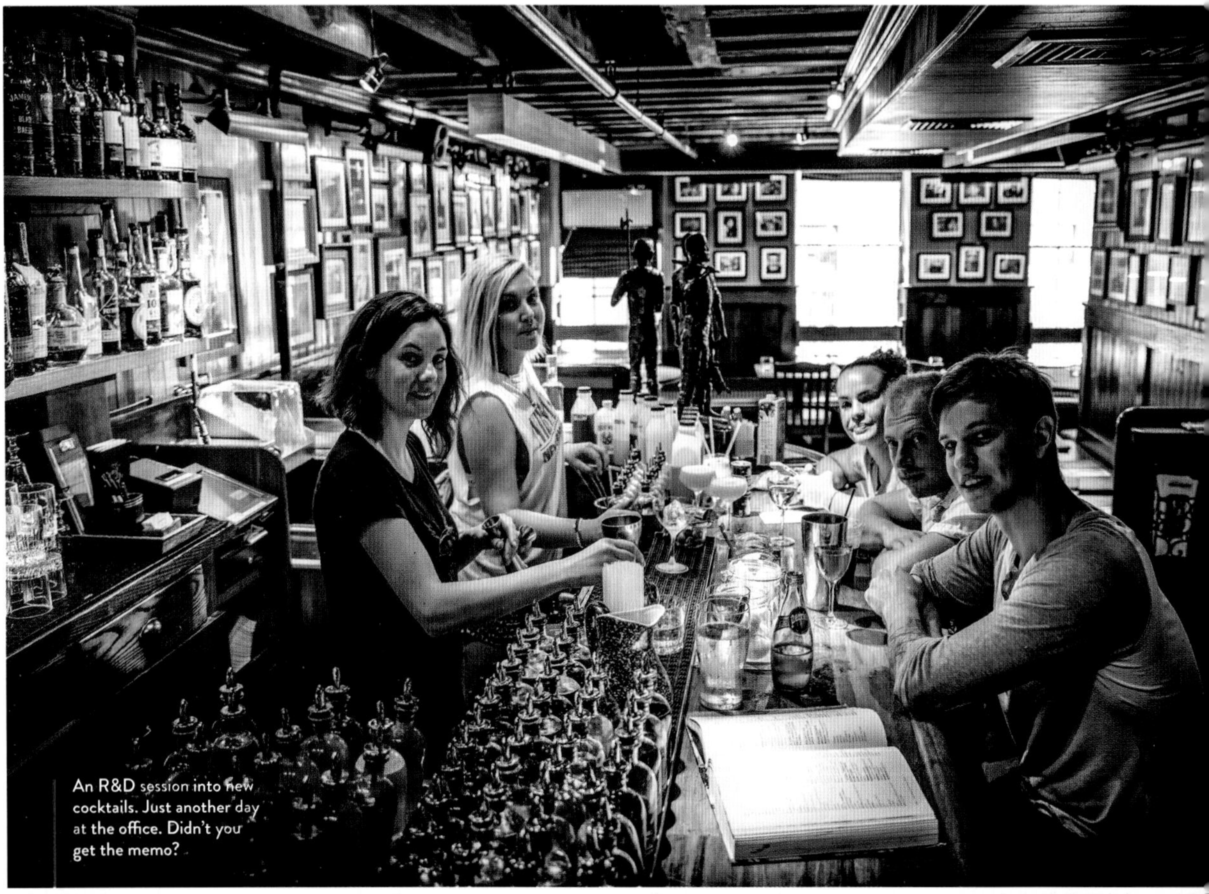

An R&D session into new cocktails. Just another day at the office. Didn't you get the memo?

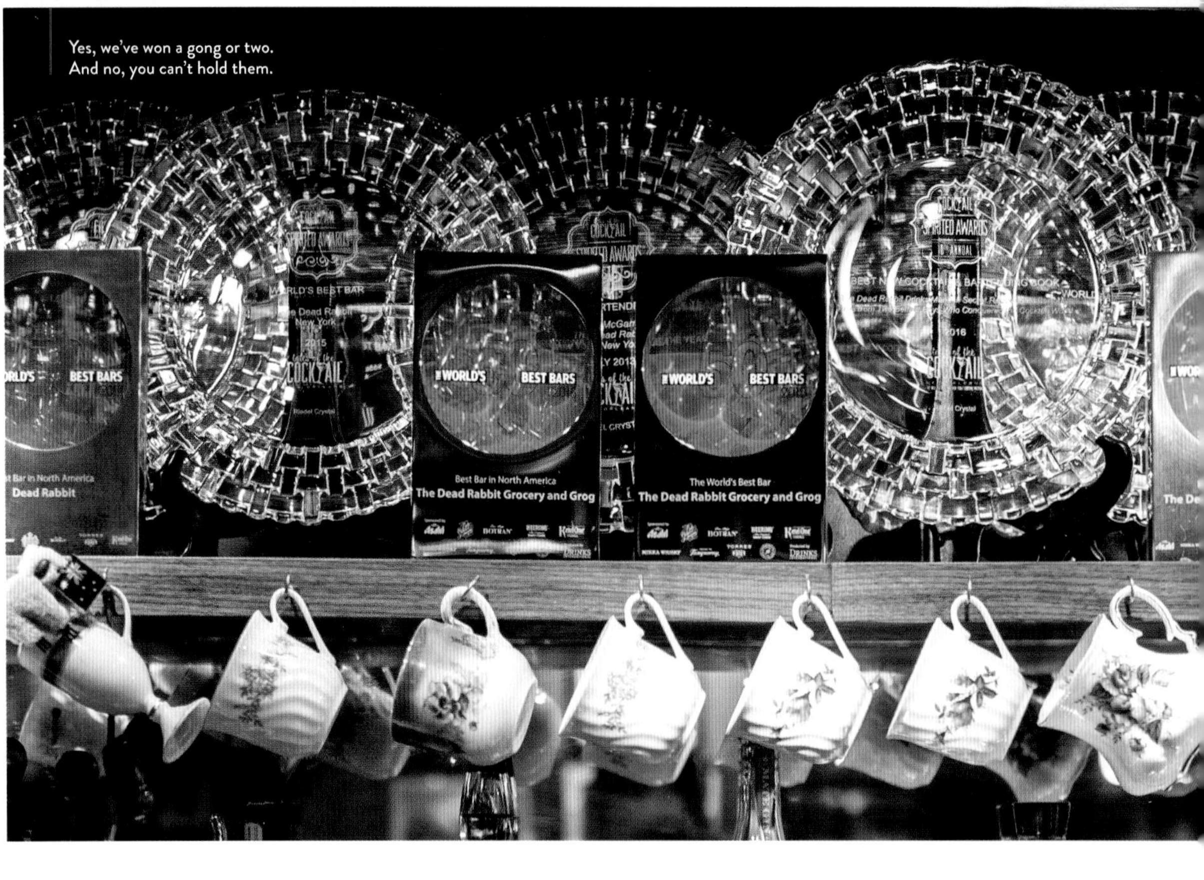
WORLD'S BEST BAR
BEST BARS
Best Bar in North America
The Dead Rabbit Grocery and Grog
The World's Best Bar
The Dead Rabbit Grocery and Grog
Dead Rabbit

Yes, we've won a gong or two. And no, you can't hold them.

THE METHOD BEHIND THE MAYHEM
MAKING COCKTAILS FROM THE WORLD'S BEST MENU

This is where we spill the beans and tell you the how, what and who behind all ninety original cocktails from our first three menus. You'll see the ingredients that go into each drink, the tools we use to make it, the glassware we serve it in, the style of ice involved (and there are lots of those), even the garnishes for that final professional flourish.

Why are we revealing all this? Well, believe it or not, there are no secrets at The Dead Rabbit. Ask us and we'll tell you: That's our attitude. Want to know exactly what's in your cocktail, how we make it, how you can too, what inspired it? No problem. We know that other bars resist doing this, preferring to keep a touch of smoke-and-mirrors mystery about it all. We don't go in for any of that malarkey. We love to make great drinks that people really enjoy, and we're happy to talk about it.

But telling you how we make these isn't our way of showing how easy it all is. Oh, no. Frankly, a lot of it is pretty tricky. Some of these recipes involve rare or unusual spirits, or ingredients such as bespoke bitters, tinctures and syrups that just aren't easily available. They have to be made. Then there are bar tools and techniques that only the most dedicated of cocktail enthusiasts/nerds will have acquired and mastered.

But, all that being the case, follow the instructions here, and you'll get pretty close to the authentic Dead Rabbit version. And pretty close is still quite something, right? As for the 100% real deal, well, you know where the answer to that is to be found, don't you?

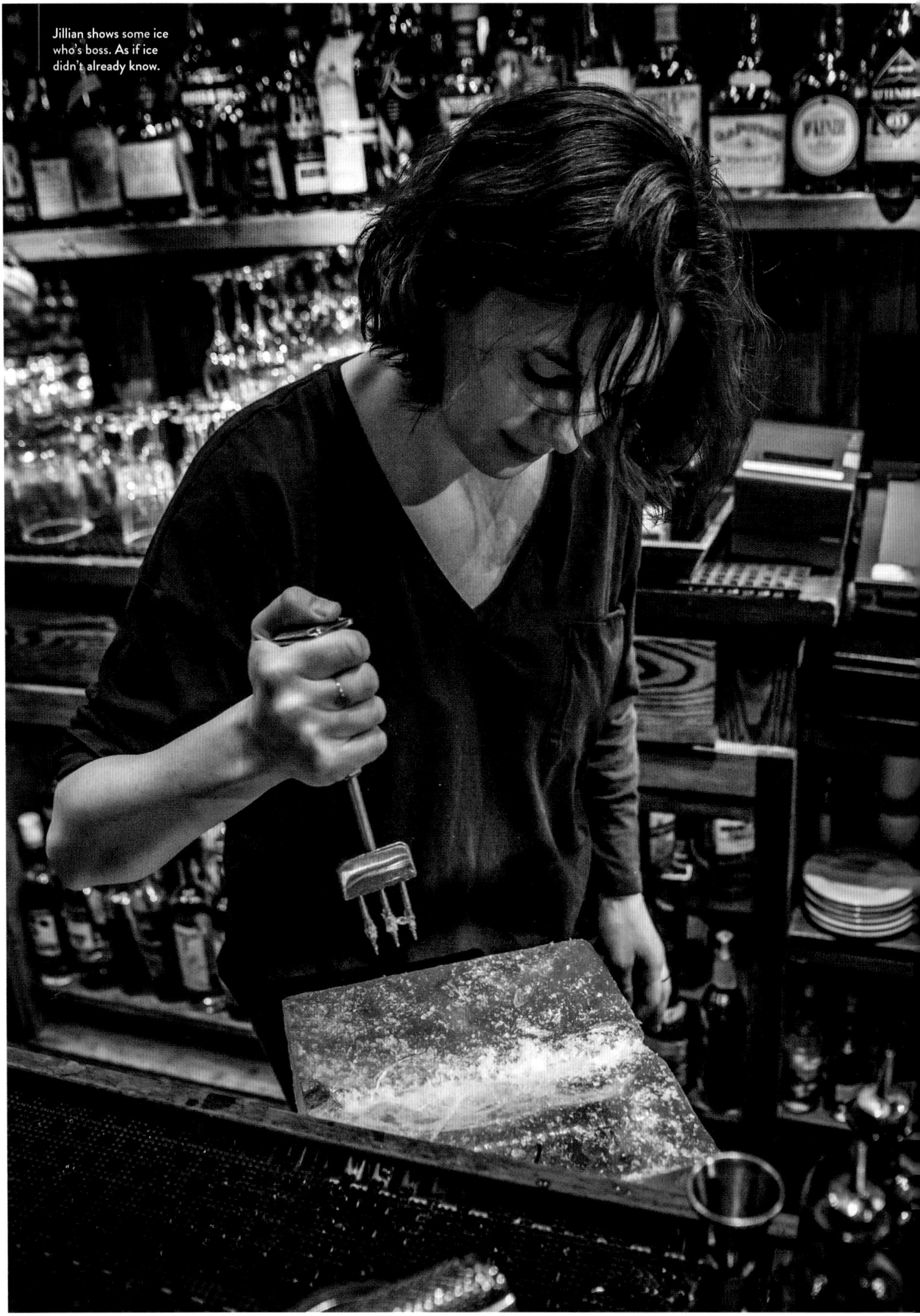

Jillian shows some ice who's boss. As if ice didn't already know.

THE HOW-TO &
THE WITH-WHAT

Let's get something straight (up). Not on the rocks. Not with a twist. Not any of that stuff. If you're expecting to be able to bartend after reading this book, well, you're reading the wrong book. Oops.

There are many other – some not altogether terrible – volumes out there that will teach you that. Go get 'em, tiger. But that's not our intention here. What we want to do is show you in detail how we make our drinks, so that you can make them correctly yourself. (If you want to: It's not compulsory or anything.)

Let's start with a list of the exact tools you'll need. Note: This doesn't include any extra bells and whistles, like pour spouts or dasher tops, your fancy-dan crystal mixing glass, fragrance-free mustache wax, limited edition blowtorch, topiary shears, Aqua-Lung or double-reverse flange-gapper. Maybe for the next edition. But probably not.

HEY, IT'S TOOL TIME

JIGGERS
You'll need these in five sizes – 0.25 oz, 0.5 oz, 0.75 oz, 1 oz and 2 oz. They're accurate, fit easily in the hand and, fortunately, are pretty much indestructible.

SPOONS
In addition to your basic teaspoon set, get a barspoon – the one with the long spiral shaft. It looks like that for a reason, which is that the spiral does a lot of the work for you.

JULEP STRAINER
Looks a bit like a large, shallow spoon with large perforations. It works well over a cocktail glass.

HAWTHORNE STRAINER
The weird one with the spring; looks like maybe something to do with horses. (It isn't.) Use it over a shaker.

FINE MESH STRAINER
It's a strainer with, spoiler, a fine mesh. You'll know when you see it.

SHAKER TINS
Ah, the signature bartending tool. It's that thing you've always seen people shaking when they're pretending to make a cocktail like in that Tom Cruise movie in the '80s. You'll need two sizes: a 28 to 30 oz and an 18 oz.

MIXING GLASS
You'll probably be using one of these with your barspoon. It often looks a bit like a beaker from chemistry class, with a lip for easy pouring. Wish you'd paid more attention in chemistry now?

ICE PICK
You'll use this for chunking off pieces of ice from a larger block. It usually has just a single spike, occasionally three. The first time you use it, you will hear the music from *Psycho* in your head. That's just a fact.

NUTMEG GRATER
Yes, it's sharp and abrasive, but think of it this way: Maybe the nutmeg likes it.

METHODS: A BRIEF EXPLANATION

STIRRED

Build the drink in the mixing glass in the order the recipe calls for. Add ice and use your barspoon to stir the drink until it's extremely cold. Getting a drink to the right dilution and extremely cold temperature will take some practice. The key is the ice. Or rather, quality ice – dry and in cube or block form. We use Kold-Draft at the bar for shaking and stirring, and custom block ice that we break down with ice picks throughout the night for 'garnish' ice. (All the pretty clear ice you see in the pictures.) You can make a drink with poorer quality ice, but you'll have to adjust how long you stir. The wetter the ice, the faster it dilutes, and the more surface area, the faster it melts. Balancing the two is what makes for a properly stirred cocktail.

When stirring a drink that will be served over ice like an Old Fashioned, we recommend stirring to 60% of what you would for a drink like a martini or Manhattan that's served without ice. The point of stirring a drink is to get it cold and dilute it down to a pleasant balance. That being said, to perfectly stir a drink and then do this extravagant long pour – which adds bubbles – completely defeats the purpose of stirring the damn thing in the first place, right? Right?

SHAKEN

Here, you'll build the drink in order of the recipe, using the smaller of the shaker tins (or a Boston shaker glass if that's what you have). Add ice to fill to the top of the small tin, then drop the larger tin over the smaller tin and give it a tap to seal them together. Pick up the tins and flip it so that your dominant hand is at the top of the smaller tin, and your other hand is at the bottom of the larger shaker tin. Now shake it. No, like you really mean it. Shake it towards your ear and then away from your body. Use a good amount of force. Imagine the ice in the shaker moving as in a tornado, in a turning circular motion. If the ice just goes up and down, hitting the bottom and top of the tins, you're going to get a pretty flat drink. The whole point of shaking a drink is to provide texture. Meaning: incorporate air. When you shake a drink correctly, the top should have a beautiful froth and make your taste buds happy. It should be very cold the whole way through as you enjoy it.

Also, the same goes for a shaken drink if you're going to be putting it over ice: You'll need to adjust your shakedown and/or change the ice you'll be shaking with. If you're making a margarita on a large ice cube, you'll shake it 60% of what you would a daiquiri-style drink.

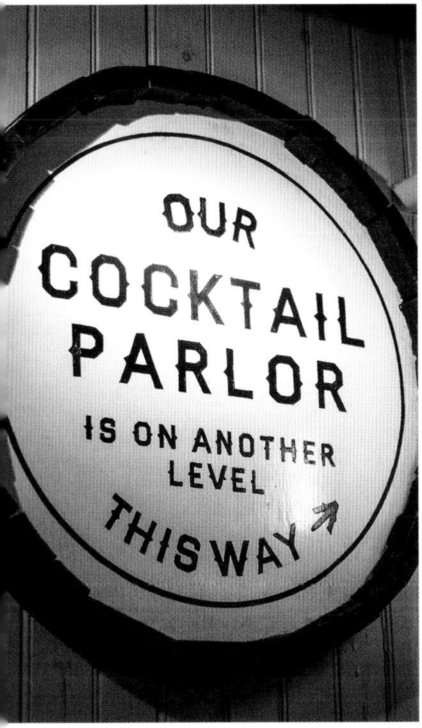
OUR
COCKTAIL
PARLOR
IS ON ANOTHER
LEVEL
THIS WAY

WHIP SHAKE

When you see this, it means take a small handful of pebble ice, roughly fifteen pebbles (or crushed ice if that's all you have) and add that to your built drink in the small tin. Seal your small tin with the large tin, and then shake the drink in a whipping motion until the ice has completely melted and you can't hear it anymore. This will typically be a drink that is being served over cracked ice or served with pebble ice. If there is a drink that says 'Whip Shake with Kold-Draft', then you're to do the same thing, except instead of pebble ice, use Kold-Draft/cube ice, shake it five or six times and then fine strain into the glassware. Why? Good question. Because the drink most likely has an herb component, and the Kold-Draft in the tin will help extract the flavor without bruising the herb too much. See? Science.

DRY SHAKE

This method is used when there's an egg component involved. Always use the freshest eggs you can find; it'll make for a much better froth. It's always wise to build your drink first in the small tin and then crack your egg into the larger tin, especially if using just the white. (That way, if you mess up by getting shell or part of the yolk in there, you can simply throw out the egg rather than ruin your perfectly good drink. Live and learn.) If the drink calls for egg white, crack the egg on the side of your larger tin, break the egg in half and gently toss the egg yolk back and forth until you've got all the egg white out. If the drink calls for a whole egg, do the same, except you can add the yolk and white into the tin and just discard the shell. After some practice, you can do this with one hand if you're the flashy type (and you know you are). Now for the shaking part.

You're going to want to seal your tins now, but without ice first, and you're going to whip-shake it for 20 to 30 seconds. Then, break the seal, add ice to the top of your small tin, then reseal it and shake it like you normally would, though for slightly longer, as egg white drinks, especially fizzes, will need some extra love to get the right texture.

Thoughts on some other details . . .

GLASSWARE

Obviously we don't expect you to use the exact glassware we do. But bear in mind that we've chosen these particular glasses because of the style of the drink, the size of the drink – oh, and because they look pretty beautiful. So there's that. The pictures in the book show you the ones we actually use at the bar, so you could use that as a guide when picking out your own glassware. Just a thought. (But a damn good one.)

GARNISHES

As a rule, we take a pretty minimal approach to garnishes. That's just how we roll. Our view is that if a garnish doesn't enhance the taste of the drink, it ain't going in the glass. We've found that nutmeg works really well on many of our shaken drinks. So we go through a lot of that. (*Hey, Indonesia: You're welcome.*) Be sure to grate it fresh with a proper nutmeg grater. Don't use a kitchen Microplane – the perforations are too large and will produce chunks rather than a fine dust.

As for citrus oils, we recommend cutting large coin-shaped swaths from the fruit, being sure not to get the flesh of the fruit. You are only looking to get the oil from the skin. To express that effectively, you'll have to get enough of the pith so that the coin is sturdy. You're going to use the coins in most cases after you've poured the drink into its proper glassware. Take the citrus coin and hold it about five inches above the glass, skin facing down towards the drink. Then, with your thumb and index finger, pinch the coin. This will express the oil onto your drink, giving it a beautiful aromatic note, with the oil contributing to the flavor of the drink. A lot of bars then rim the edge of the glass with the coin after they've expressed it. We think this actually adds an unpleasant bitterness, so we recommend you just discard the coin after you've expressed the oil. Also, a coin left in the drink would continue to release oils, changing the taste of the drink throughout. Plus it would be trying to get in your mouth the whole time, which is annoying. So it's farewell, coin. It was good what we once had, but now we're done.

DASHES

We use cork dasher tops and 200 ml bottles filled halfway with bitters for consistency. (This probably isn't realistic for a home bar, but for regular bar use it's recommended.) Every bottle of bitters has its own dasher top or dropper vial, but they're all different. A dash from an angostura bottle is going to be different from a dropper of Bittermens and it won't be consistent each time you use it.

JUICES

All the juices specified in the book are freshly squeezed or extracted and unpasteurized. If you're using juices that are store-bought or are more than 12 hours old, the drinks will not taste quite as close to what they're supposed to. Sad but true. If you don't have an electric citrus juicer or you're not making drinks in volume, use a hand juicer. You can even find large manual juicers. For juices that need to be extracted – like cucumber, Granny Smith apple, red bell pepper, pineapple, etc. – you will need an extractor. If you don't have one, you can buy freshly extracted cold-pressed juices at a deli or juice bar.

Ah, so pretty. Our mise en place is neat, organized and ready to rock. What are you having?

37.

PERFECT
THE COM
THE COC

SERVE:
ICS &
KTAILS

HE'S HERE. THE SPIRIT MADE FLESH.

The deathless Dead Rabbit incarnate: John Morrissey,
trailing a whiff of smoke and sulphur.

He's here, back amongst us with all his unquenchable
rage of old intact – for the fight, for money, for
respect, for pleasure. And for revenge.

Morrissey led the Dead Rabbits from the front, always first in
with a fist or a club or a knife. His warrior spirit, with its twisted
moral code, shaped the very spirit of the gang. Somewhere in
time, man and essence fused together. And now he flits between
death and life in a world of eternal half-light, forever ravening
after what is his.

In 1858 Morrissey had said, 'I shall have to fight to vindicate my
character for honor and manhood, and to relieve myself from the
persecution and assaults of my foes'.

More than a century later, every slight, every knockdown, every
jibe has stayed salt-in-the-wound fresh. Every
wager is still to be won. Again and again.

So beware, all you blackguards, wretches and rogues.

THE KING IS UNDEAD.

LONG LIVE THE KING.

RESURRECTION

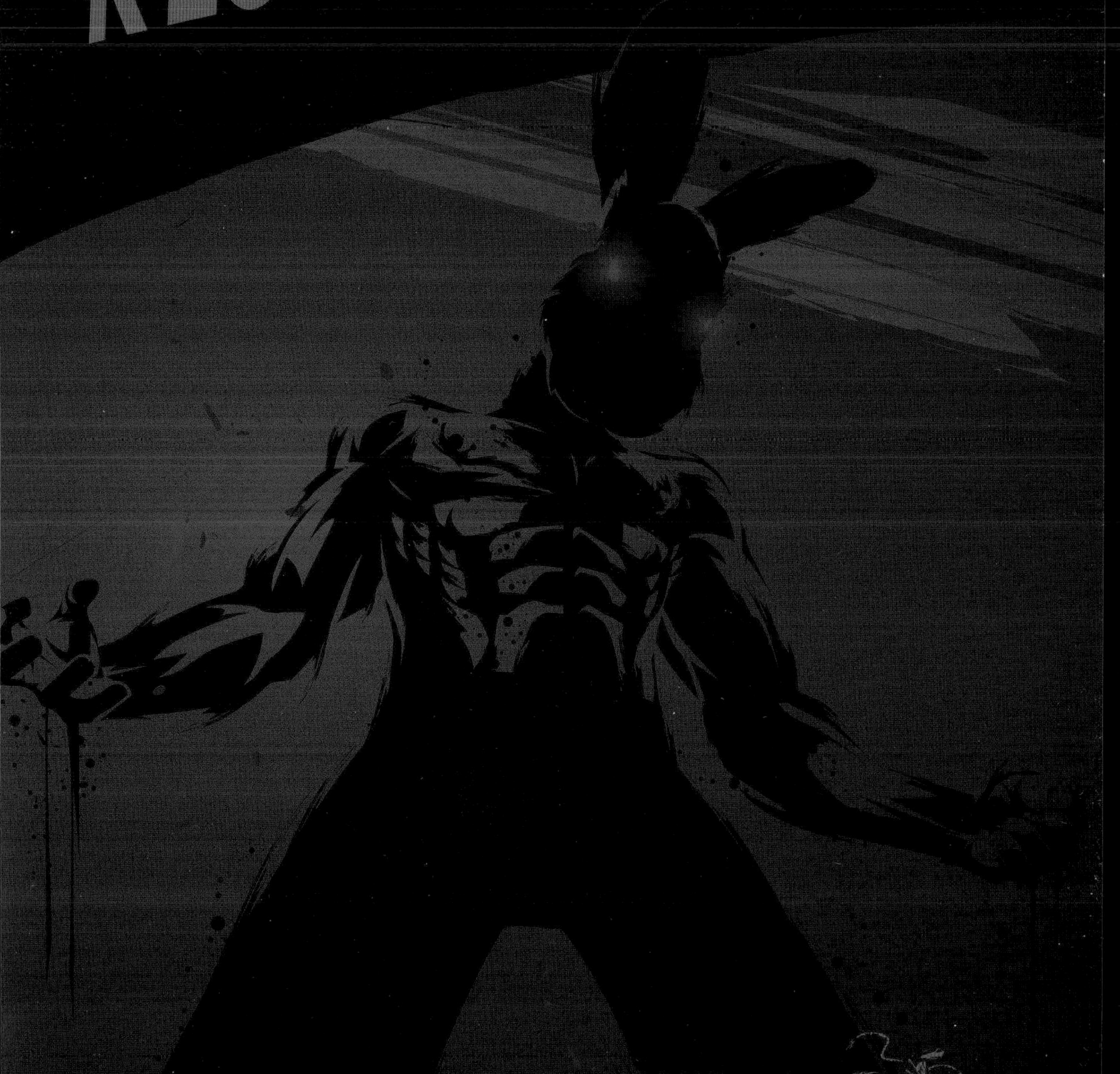

MIXED DRINKS LIST | VOL 4 | ISSUE 1/6

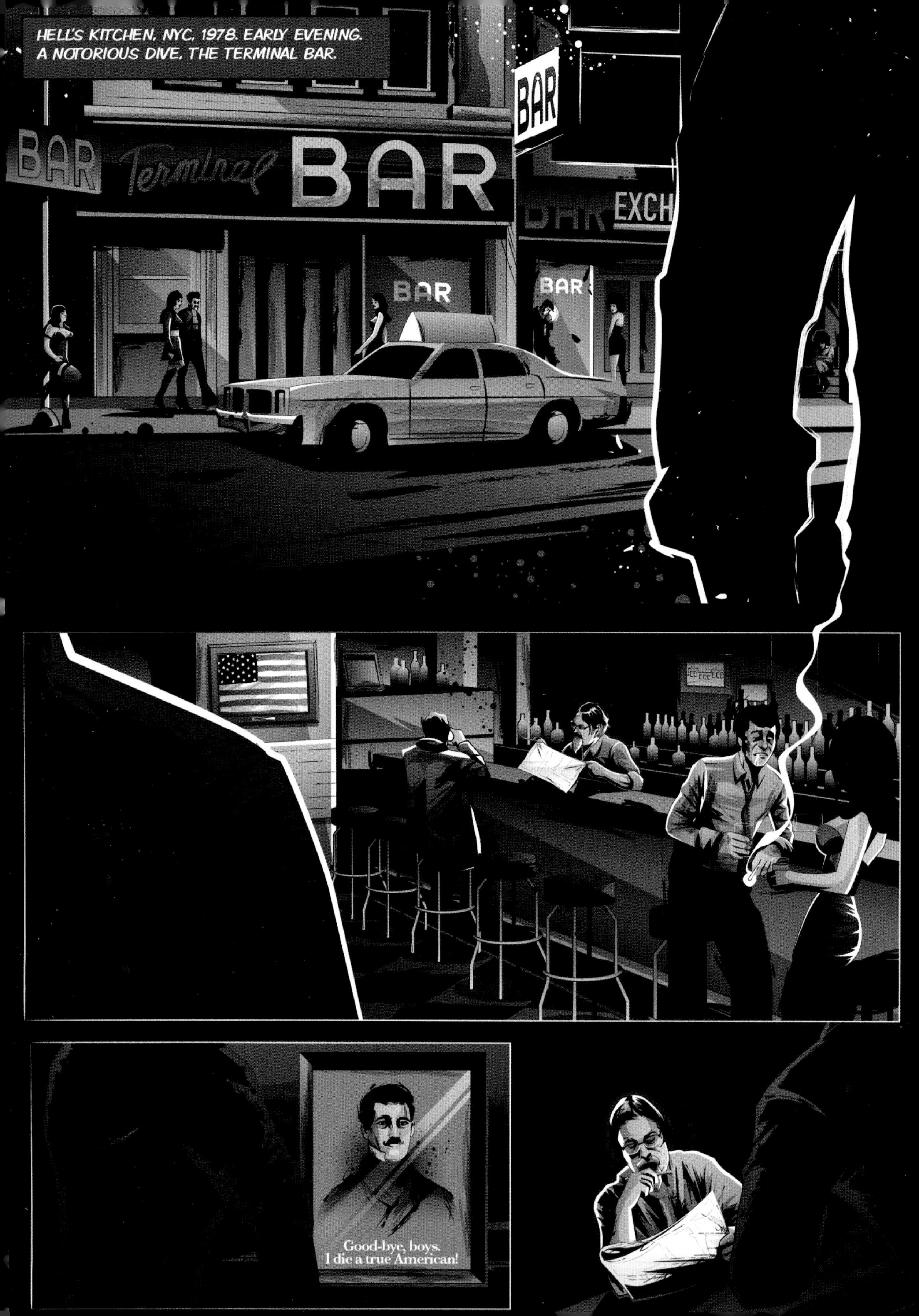
HELL'S KITCHEN, NYC, 1978. EARLY EVENING.
A NOTORIOUS DIVE, THE TERMINAL BAR.
BAR
Terminal BAR
BAR
BAR
BAR
EXCH
Good-bye, boys.
I die a true American!

EIDOLON

INGREDIENTS

1	Egg white
2 DASHES	Mace Tincture (page 263)
2 DASHES	House Cardamom Bitters (page 261)
0.75 OZ	Lemon juice
0.5 OZ	Orgeat (page 265)
0.75 OZ	Alvear Pale Cream Sherry
0.75 OZ	Plantation 3 Stars Rum
0.75 OZ	Perry's Tot Navy Strength Gin

TOOLS
Jiggers, shaker tins, fine strainer, Hawthorne strainer

METHOD
Dry shake, shake with ice; fine strain and serve up without ice

GLASSWARE
Punch glass

GARNISH
Lemon oil (discard peel)

ORIGIN
Gregory Buda

GREGORY'S INSPIRATION

INITIALLY INSPIRED BY THE ARMY & NAVY COCKTAIL.

This ended up being the template for many drinks to come.

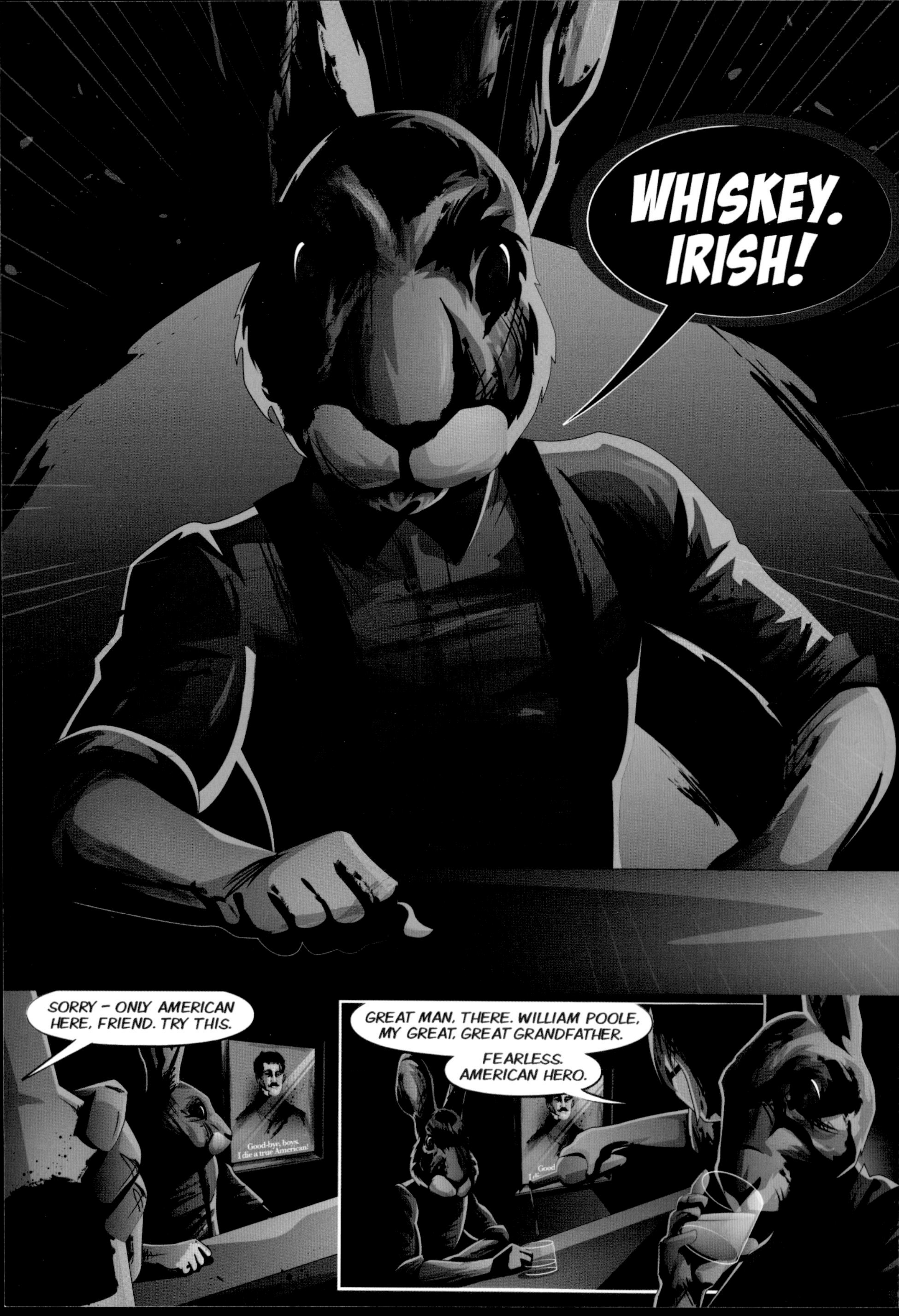
WHISKEY. IRISH!
SORRY - ONLY AMERICAN HERE, FRIEND. TRY THIS.
Good-bye, boys. I die a true American!
GREAT MAN, THERE. WILLIAM POOLE, MY GREAT, GREAT GRANDFATHER.
FEARLESS. AMERICAN HERO.

LUCKY BREAK

INGREDIENTS

1 DASH	Peychaud's Bitters
1 TSP	Cinnamon Bark Syrup (page 255)
0.5 OZ	Campari
0.25 OZ	Koval Rose Hip Liqueur
0.25 OZ	Blume Marillen Apricot Eau-de-Vie
0.5 OZ	Plymouth Gin
1 OZ	Lillet Rosé
1.5 OZ	Martini & Rossi Bianca Vermouth

TOOLS
Jiggers, mixing glass, barspoon, teaspoon, julep strainer

METHOD
Stir with ice; strain with julep strainer and serve up without ice

GLASSWARE
Nick & Nora

GARNISH
Grapefruit oil (discard peel)

ORIGIN
Jillian Vose

45.

JILLIAN'S INSPIRATION

THIS IS A LOW-ABV NEGRONI VARIATION WITH A DISTINCTIVE FLORAL ELEMENT.

Apricot and cinnamon offer a great accent pairing with rosé, while rose hip and Campari are the bittersweet components.

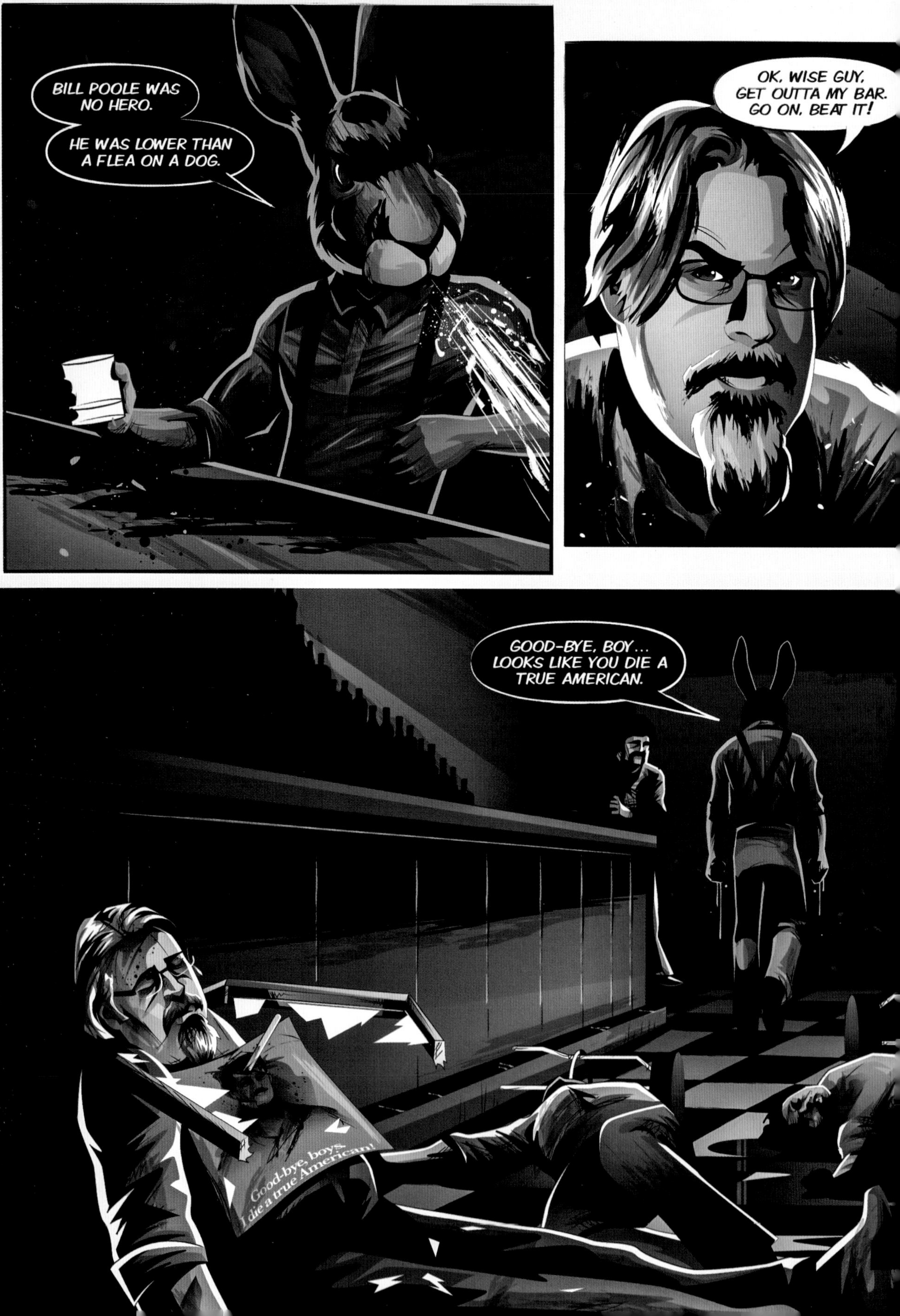
BILL POOLE WAS NO HERO.
HE WAS LOWER THAN A FLEA ON A DOG.
OK, WISE GUY, GET OUTTA MY BAR. GO ON, BEAT IT!
GOOD-BYE, BOY... LOOKS LIKE YOU DIE A TRUE AMERICAN.
Good-bye, boys, I die a true American!

TINDERBOX

INGREDIENTS

2 DASHES	Bittermens Boston Bittahs (page 239)
0.75 OZ	Lemon juice
0.5 OZ	Granny Smith Apple Juice (page 259)
0.75 OZ	Macadamia Orgeat (page 263)
0.5 OZ	Noilly Prat Dry Vermouth
1.5 OZ	Waqar Pisco

TOOLS

Jiggers, shaker tins, fine strainer, Hawthorne strainer, ice pick

METHOD

Shake with ice; fine strain and serve with ice nugget

GLASSWARE

Coupette

ORIGIN

Jillian Vose

47.

JILLIAN'S INSPIRATION

PISCO IS IDEAL FOR A JUICY, FRESH SOUR.

I like dry vermouth for herbaceousness, green apple for brightness, Boston Bittahs for a high note. Macadamia syrup subtly balances the acidity and lends a silky texture.

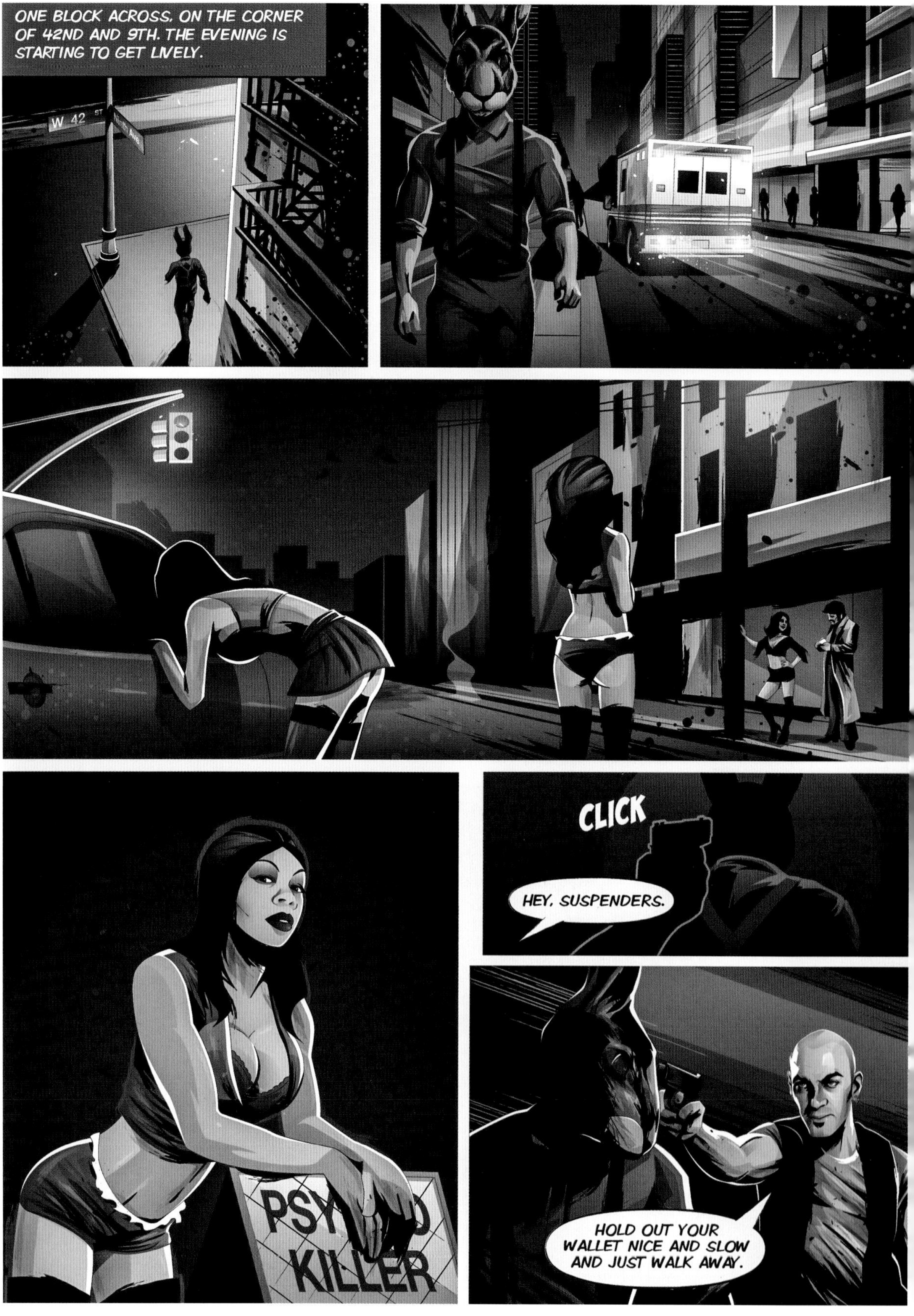
ONE BLOCK ACROSS. ON THE CORNER OF 42ND AND 9TH. THE EVENING IS STARTING TO GET LIVELY.
W 42 ST
CLICK
HEY, SUSPENDERS.
HOLD OUT YOUR WALLET NICE AND SLOW AND JUST WALK AWAY.

KERB CRAWLER

INGREDIENTS

1	Muddled ripe strawberry
1 DASH	Bitter Truth Creole Bitters
0.75 OZ	Lemon juice
0.5 OZ	Vanilla Syrup (page 275)
0.25 OZ	Giffard Abricot Brandy
0.25 OZ	Combier Crème de Pamplemousse Rose Liqueur
1.5 OZ	Tequila Cabeza

TOOLS
Jiggers, shaker tins, fine strainer, Hawthorne strainer, ice pick, nutmeg grater, muddler

METHOD
Shake with ice; fine strain and serve with ice nugget

GLASSWARE
Coupette

GARNISH
Nutmeg

ORIGIN
Madeleine Solo Rapp

49.

MADELEINE'S INSPIRATION

I LOVE AGAVE AND WANTED TO MAKE A BRIGHT, FRUITY AND REFRESHING TEQUILA DRINK.

So pairing it with strawberries, apricot and grapefruit was what came first to my mind. The inspiration here was actually the Pirate Queen – the first drink I learned when I started here.

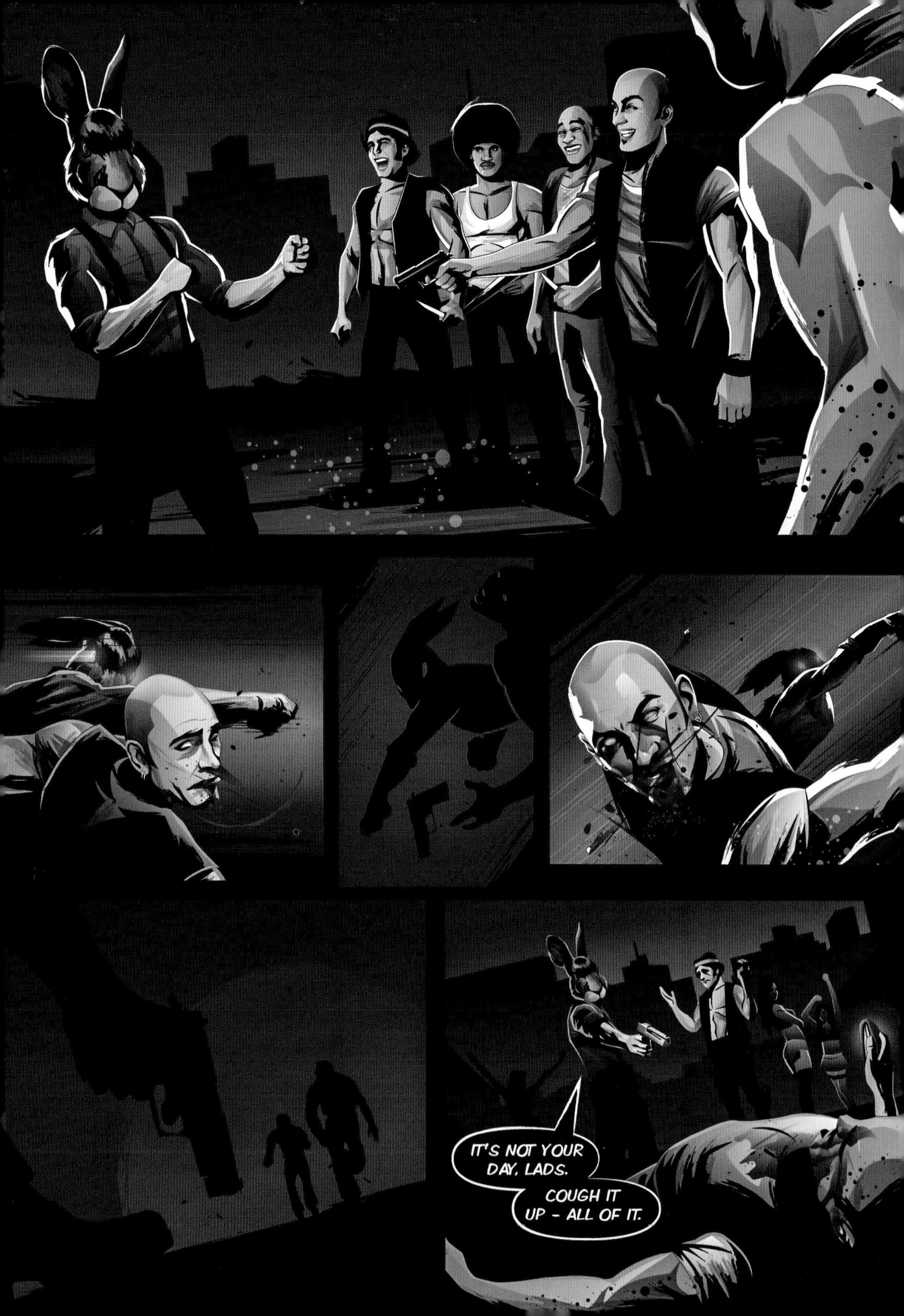
IT'S NOT YOUR DAY, LADS.
COUGH IT UP - ALL OF IT.

GADABOUT

INGREDIENTS

1 DASH	House Orange Bitters (page 261)
3 DASHES	Chipotle Tincture (page 255)
1 OZ	Lime juice
0.75 OZ	Orgeat (page 265)
1 OZ	Pierre Ferrand Dry Curaçao
1.5 OZ	Ketel One Vodka

TOOLS
Jiggers, shaker tins, fine strainer, Hawthorne strainer, nutmeg grater
METHOD
Shake with ice; fine strain and serve up without ice
GLASSWARE
Sour glass
GARNISH
Nutmeg
ORIGIN
Jillian Vose

JILLIAN'S INSPIRATION

A DEPARTURE FROM THE TYPICAL JUICY FRUITY VODKA DRINK.

This is something more 'mature', with subtle flavors from a classic template.

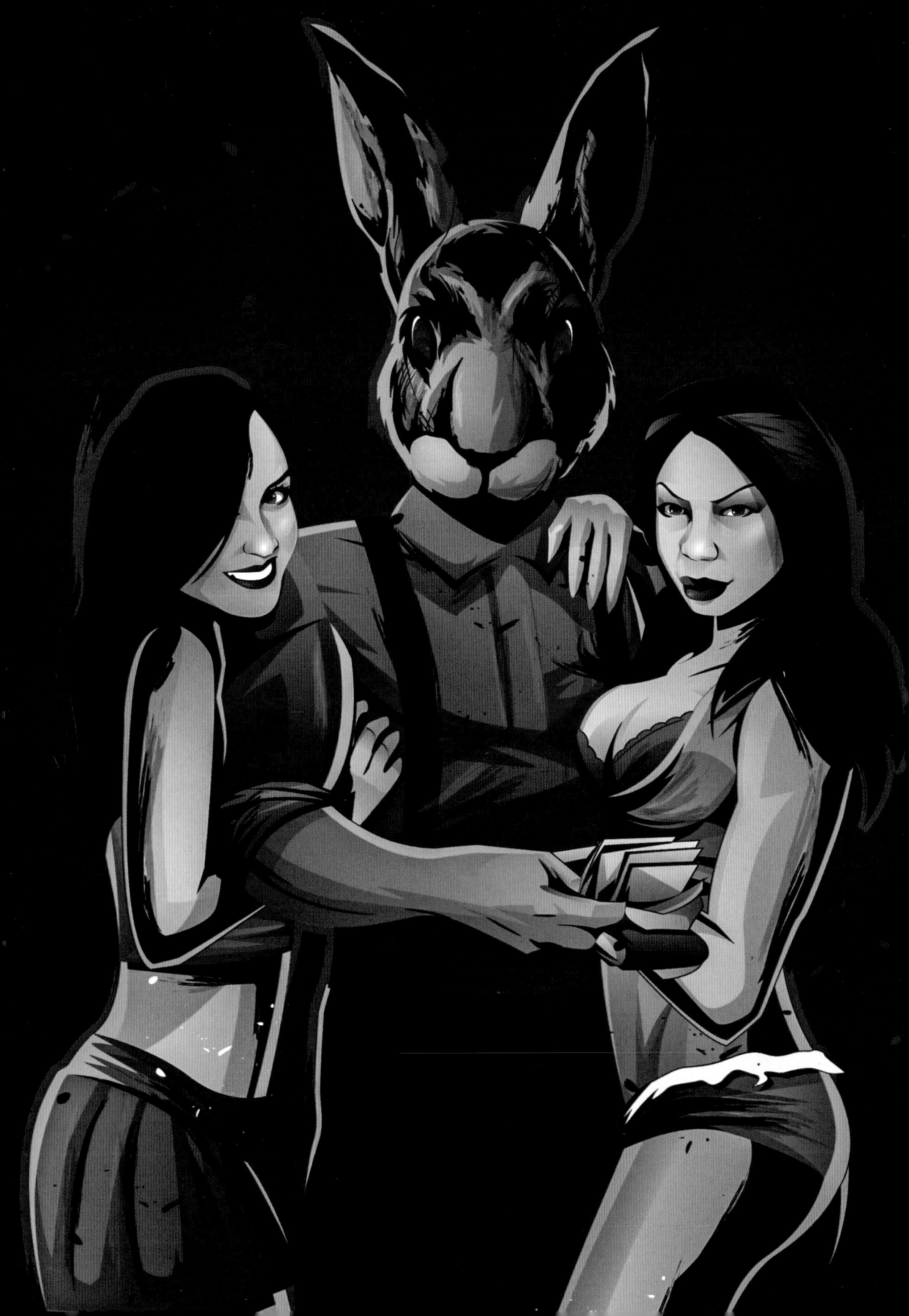

LADY KILLER

INGREDIENTS

1 OZ	Champagne (not to be shaken with other ingredients)
1 TSP	Honey Syrup (page 260)
0.5 OZ	Suze
0.75 OZ	Lemon juice
0.75 OZ	Orange Sherbet (page 265)
0.5 OZ	Sesame-Infused Powers Gold Irish Whiskey (page 270)
1.5 OZ	Hibiki Japanese Harmony Whisky

TOOLS
Jiggers, teaspoon, shaker tins, fine strainer, Hawthorne strainer

METHOD
Add Champagne to glass. Shake with ice; fine strain into glass with Champagne and serve up without ice

GLASSWARE
Champagne glass

ORIGIN
Jillian Vose

JILLIAN'S INSPIRATION

THIS IS A COCKTAIL WITH A SPIRIT BASE THAT MIMICS A MIMOSA.

The light, citrusy Hibiki and sherbet complement the Asian note of the sesame-infused Irish whiskey. I added lemon to boost the acidic citrus. Suze is for complexity and bitterness and adds an almost marmalade quality.

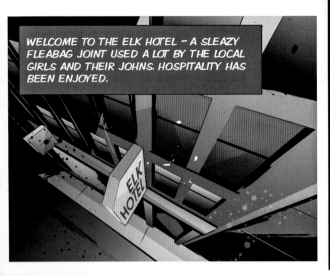

WELCOME TO THE ELK HOTEL — A SLEAZY FLEABAG JOINT USED A LOT BY THE LOCAL GIRLS AND THEIR JOHNS. HOSPITALITY HAS BEEN ENJOYED.

KNEW A SWEET THING LIKE YOU ONCE IN FRISCO.

LOLITA FERNANDEZ BY NAME. TOM MAGUIRE WAGERED ME FOR HER IN A HORSE RACE.

I WON, BUT I LET HIM HAVE HER ANYWAY.

HOW 'BOUT THAT — A HORSE FOR A WHORE.

MAN, YOU SURE TALK FUNNY! WHERE YOU FROM?

SOLDIER BOY

INGREDIENTS

0.75 OZ	Lime juice
0.5 OZ	Grapefruit juice
0.5 OZ	Don's Spices (1:1 Vanilla Syrup, St. Elizabeth Allspice Dram)
0.5 OZ	Cinnamon Bark Syrup (page 255)
0.5 OZ	Combier Crème de Pamplemousse Rose
0.5 OZ	Laird's Straight Apple Brandy
1.5 OZ	Old Forester 100 Proof Bourbon

TOOLS
Jiggers, shaker tins, fine strainer, Hawthorne strainer, ice pick, nutmeg grater

METHOD
Shake with ice; fine strain and serve with ice nugget

GLASSWARE
Punch glass

GARNISH
Nutmeg

ORIGIN
Jillian Vose

JILLIAN'S INSPIRATION

A STRONG BOURBON SOUR THAT'S ALSO BRIGHT AND REFRESHING.

Cinnamon, grapefruit, vanilla, allspice and apple all go so well together. This one tastes like fall in a glass.

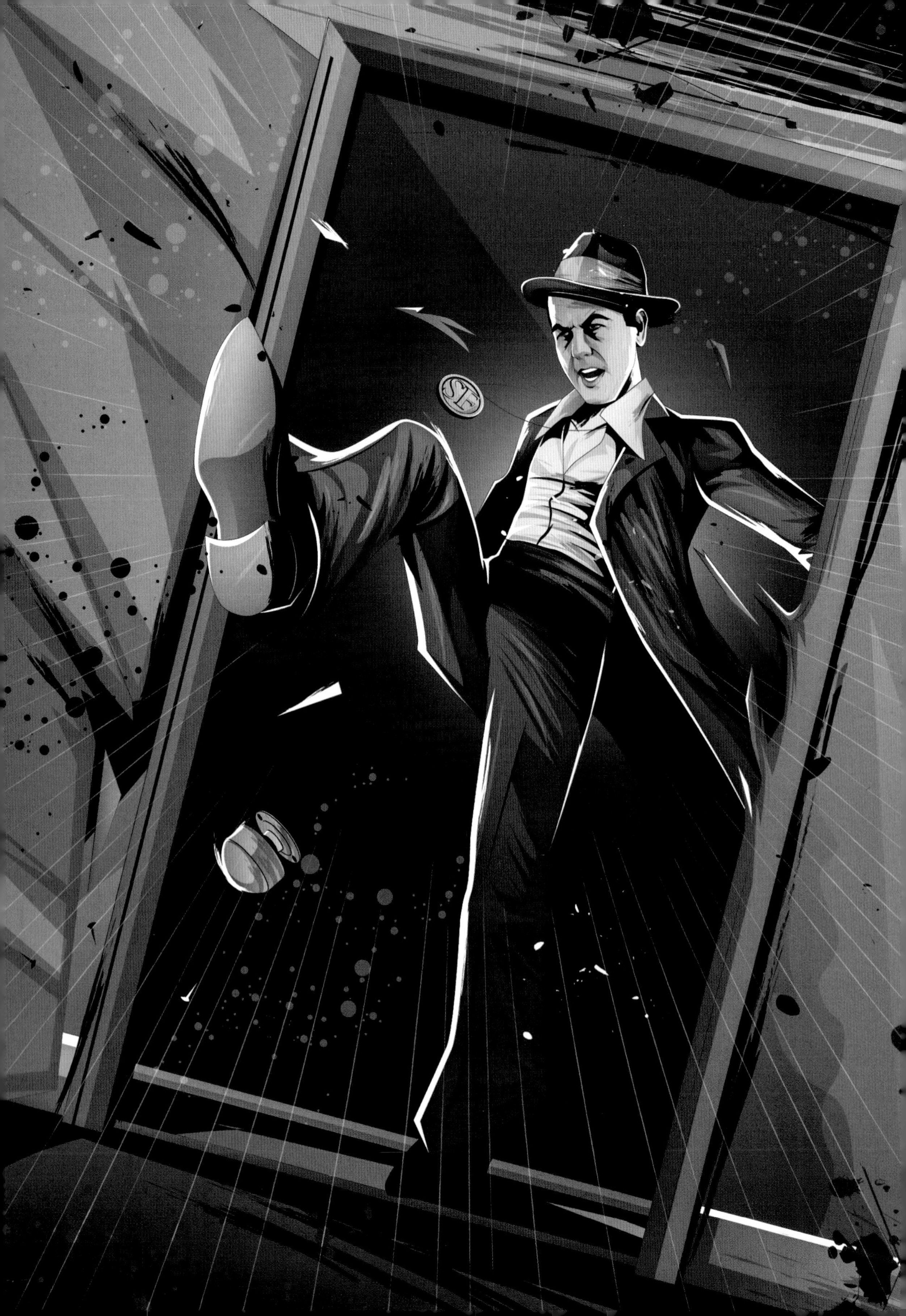

LOVE SHACK

INGREDIENTS

1	Egg white
2 DASHES	Dale DeGroff's Pimento Bitters
0.75 OZ	Lemon juice
1 OZ	Sunflower Orgeat (page 272)
0.75 OZ	Half & half
0.5 OZ	Teeling Small Batch Irish Whiskey
1.5 OZ	Coriander-Infused Glenmorangie Original (page 256)
1.5 OZ	Soda water (not to be shaken with other ingredients)

TOOLS
Jiggers, shaker tins, fine strainer, Hawthorne strainer

METHOD
Dry shake, long shake with ice; add soda water to glass; fine strain and serve up without ice

GLASSWARE
Highball

GARNISH
Top with soda, orange oil (discard peel)

ORIGIN
Gregory Buda

57.

GREGORY'S INSPIRATION

AT THE TIME, I WAS VERY INTERESTED IN NUT AND SEED SYRUPS AND WAS PLAYING WITH ONES THAT WEREN'T COMMONLY USED IN DRINKS.

I settled on sunflower seeds and made them into a really tasty orgeat. From there, I based the cocktail around the flavor set of sunflower, coriander and orange.

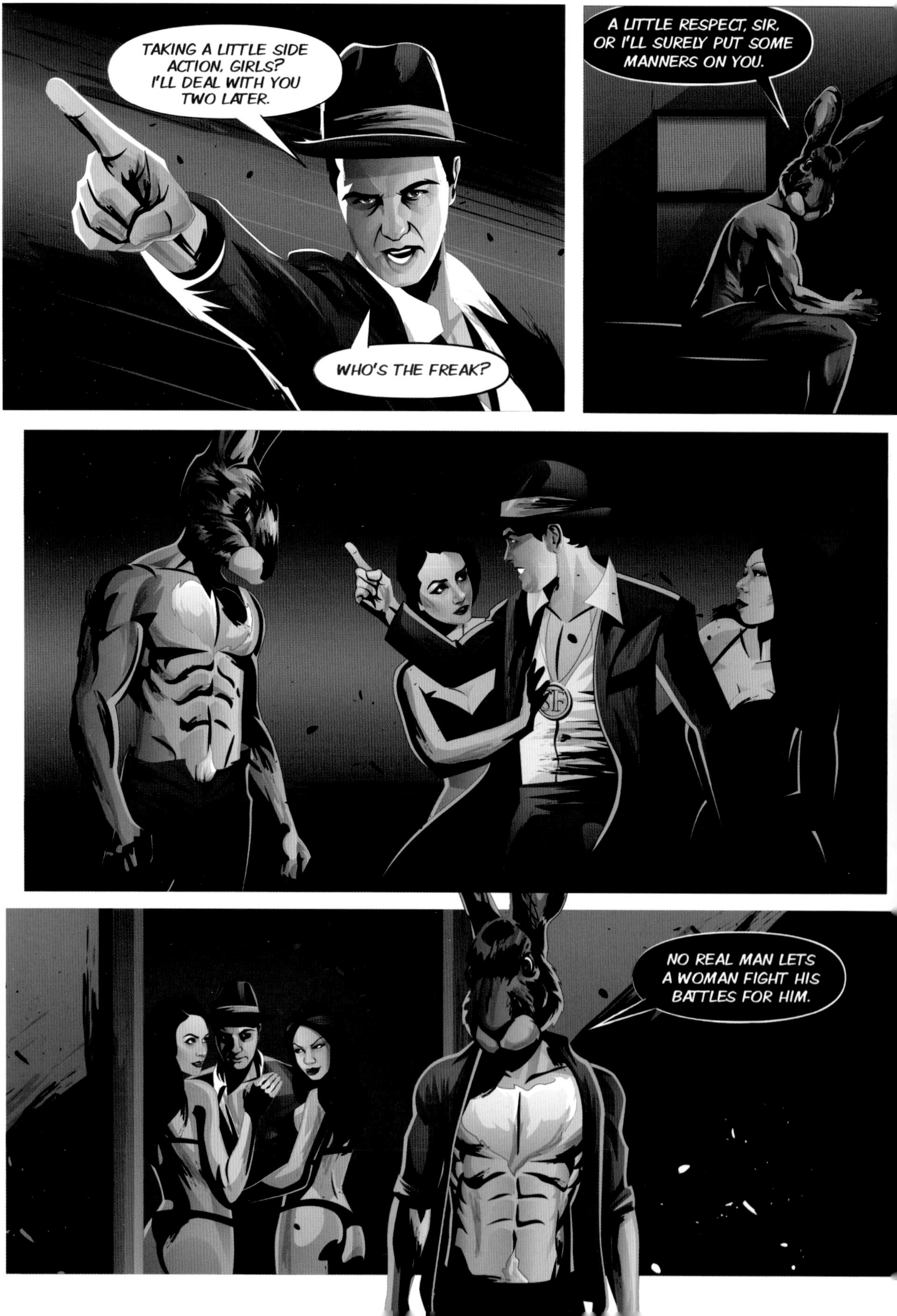
TAKING A LITTLE SIDE ACTION, GIRLS? I'LL DEAL WITH YOU TWO LATER.
WHO'S THE FREAK?
A LITTLE RESPECT, SIR, OR I'LL SURELY PUT SOME MANNERS ON YOU.
NO REAL MAN LETS A WOMAN FIGHT HIS BATTLES FOR HIM.

BIRTHDAY SUIT

INGREDIENTS

2	Lemon coins
	Absinthe to aromatize glass (not to be mixed in drink)
2 DASHES	House Cardamon Bitters (page 261)
2 DASHES	Chamomile Tincture (page 254)
1 TSP	Cane Syrup (page 254)
0.75 OZ	Cocchi Americano
1.5 OZ	Tullamore D.E.W. 12 Year Irish Whiskey

TOOLS
Jiggers, mixing glass, barspoon, julep strainer, atomizer
METHOD
Build drink, express lemon oils and drop lemon coins into mixing glass; stir with ice; aromatize old fashioned glass with absinthe; strain with julep strainer and serve up without ice
GLASSWARE
Small Old Fashioned
ORIGIN
Jillian Vose

59.

JILLIAN'S INSPIRATION

AN IRISH WHISKEY WHITE SAZERAC.

Chamomile, lemon oil and bitters brighten the components of Tullamore D.E.W.; Cocchi Americano provides length and complexity. The cane syrup adds balance and mouthfeel.

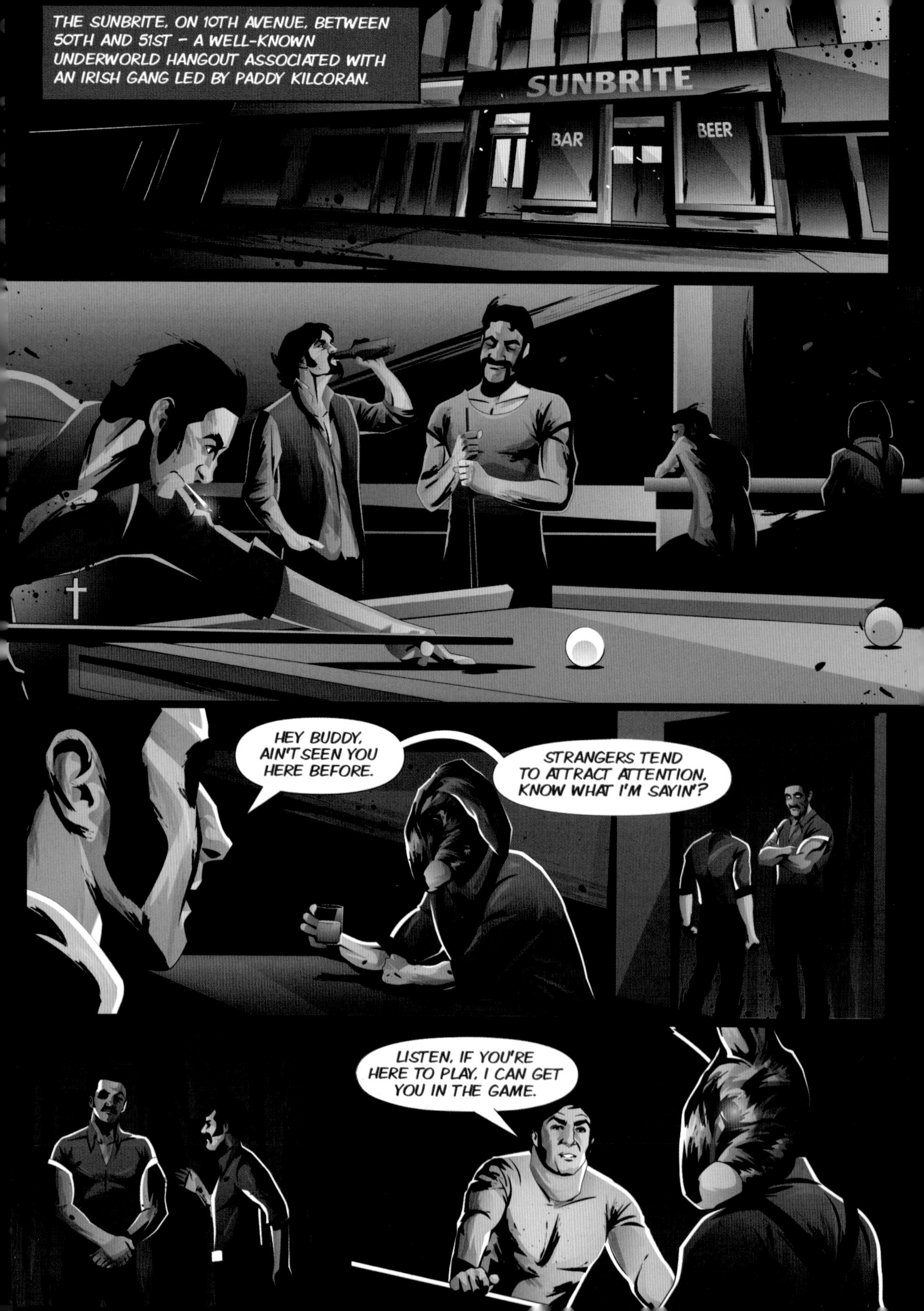
THE SUNBRITE, ON 10TH AVENUE, BETWEEN 50TH AND 51ST - A WELL-KNOWN UNDERWORLD HANGOUT ASSOCIATED WITH AN IRISH GANG LED BY PADDY KILCORAN.
SUNBRITE
BAR
BEER
HEY BUDDY, AIN'T SEEN YOU HERE BEFORE.
STRANGERS TEND TO ATTRACT ATTENTION, KNOW WHAT I'M SAYIN'?
LISTEN, IF YOU'RE HERE TO PLAY, I CAN GET YOU IN THE GAME.

BIG WIG

INGREDIENTS

2 DASHES	Angostura Bitters
0.75 OZ	Lime juice
0.25 OZ	Cane Syrup (page 254)
0.5 OZ	Fennel Syrup (page 258)
0.5 OZ	Cinnamon Bark Syrup (page 255)
0.5 OZ	Bulleit Rye Whiskey
1.5 OZ	Ardbeg Ten Years Old Scotch
2	Fresh curry leaves

TOOLS

Jiggers, shaker tins, fine strainer,
Hawthorne strainer

METHOD

Build drink in tin and add curry
leaves (do not muddle); shake
with ice; serve up without ice

GLASSWARE

Sour glass

ORIGIN

Jillian Vose

JILLIAN'S INSPIRATION

I WANTED TO CREATE A SMOKE-BOMB SCOTCH SOUR WITH UMAMI AND SPICE NOTES.

It proved something of a challenge, but the result is complex, sophisticated – and delicious.

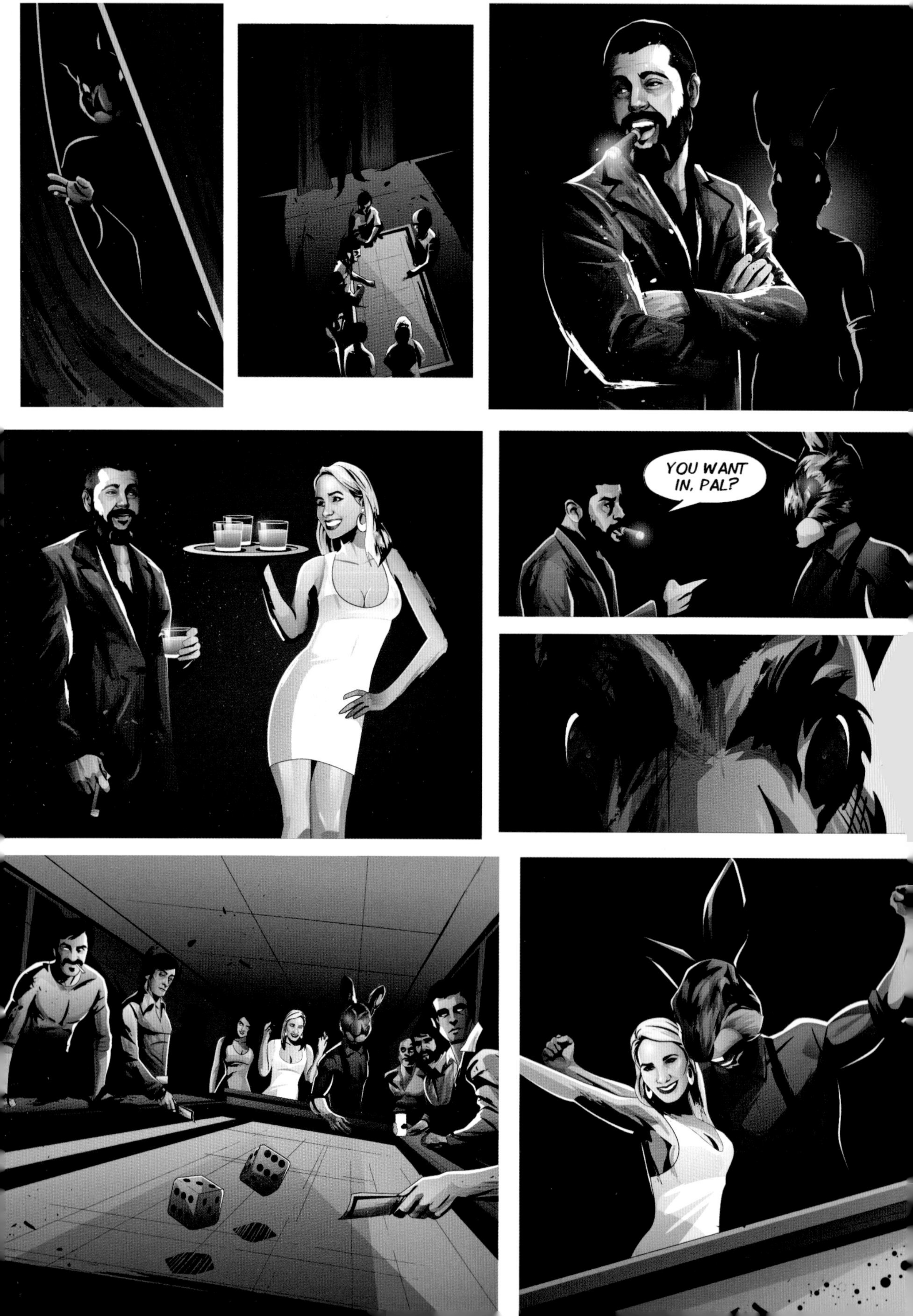
YOU WANT IN, PAL?

DEVIL WOMAN

INGREDIENTS

4 DASHES	Smoked Black Pepper Tincture (page 271)
0.75 OZ	Lime juice
0.25 OZ	Beet Syrup (page 252)
0.5 OZ	Coffee-Pecan Syrup (page 256)
0.5 OZ	Blackberry Shrub (page 252)
0.5 OZ	Manzanilla sherry
0.5 OZ	Teeling Single Grain Irish Whiskey
1.5 OZ	Famous Grouse Smoky Black Blended Scotch

TOOLS
Jiggers, shaker tins, fine strainer, Hawthorne strainer, ice pick

METHOD
Shake with ice; fine strain; serve with cracked ice

GLASSWARE
Highball

ORIGIN
Gregory Buda

RESURRECTION

DEVIL WOMAN

63.

GREGORY'S INSPIRATION

THIS DRINK CAME TO ME IN A DREAM, IN WHICH I WAS ALONE IN THE PARLOR MAKING AN INCREDIBLE COCKTAIL.

The cocktail was made with black pepper, blackberry and Black Grouse Scotch. I remember naming it the Black Black Black Grouse. When I got in to work, I made the drink and it got onto the menu. The original name didn't.

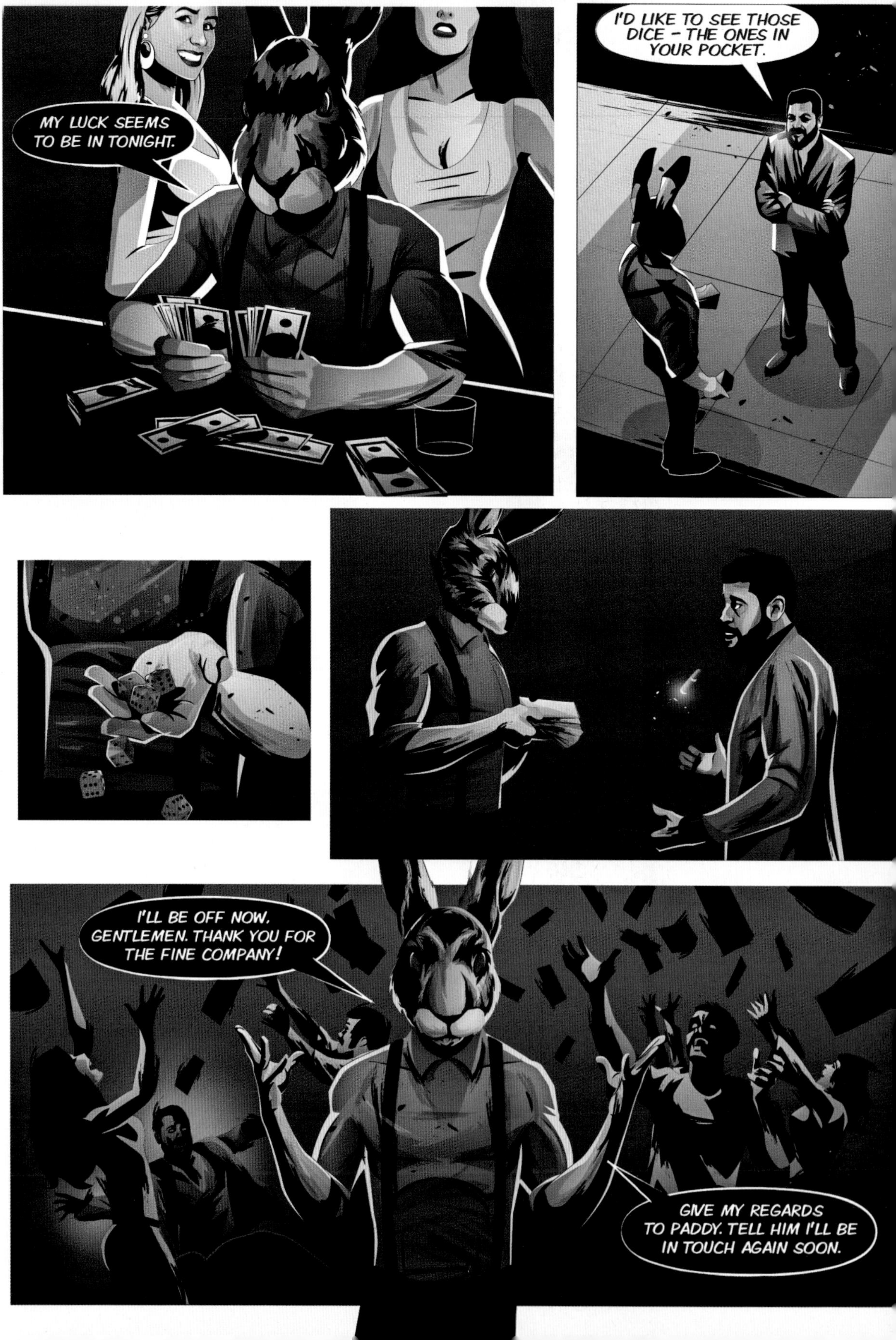

MY LUCK SEEMS TO BE IN TONIGHT.
I'D LIKE TO SEE THOSE DICE – THE ONES IN YOUR POCKET.
I'LL BE OFF NOW, GENTLEMEN. THANK YOU FOR THE FINE COMPANY!
GIVE MY REGARDS TO PADDY. TELL HIM I'LL BE IN TOUCH AGAIN SOON.

HUMBLE PIE

INGREDIENTS

2 DASHES	Vieux Pontarlier Absinthe
1 DASH	Bitter Truth Decanter Bitters
0.5 TSP	Cinnamon Bark Syrup (page 255)
1 TSP	Nutmeg Syrup (page 264)
0.5 OZ	Amaro Nardini
0.5 OZ	Rémy Martin 1738 Cognac
0.5 OZ	Laird's Bonded Applejack
1.5 OZ	Dickel Rye Whisky

TOOLS
Jiggers, mixing glass, ½ teaspoon, teaspoon, barspoon, julep strainer, ice pick

METHOD
Stir with ice; strain with julep strainer and serve over large block of ice

GLASSWARE
Old Fashioned

GARNISH
Lemon and orange oil (discard peels)

ORIGIN
Jillian Vose

65.

JILLIAN'S INSPIRATION

DICKEL RYE IS A PRETTY UNIQUE RYE, FILTERED LIKE THEIR TENNESSEE WHISKEY.

Here, I've used a split base of four spirits and then several different bitters and sweeteners.

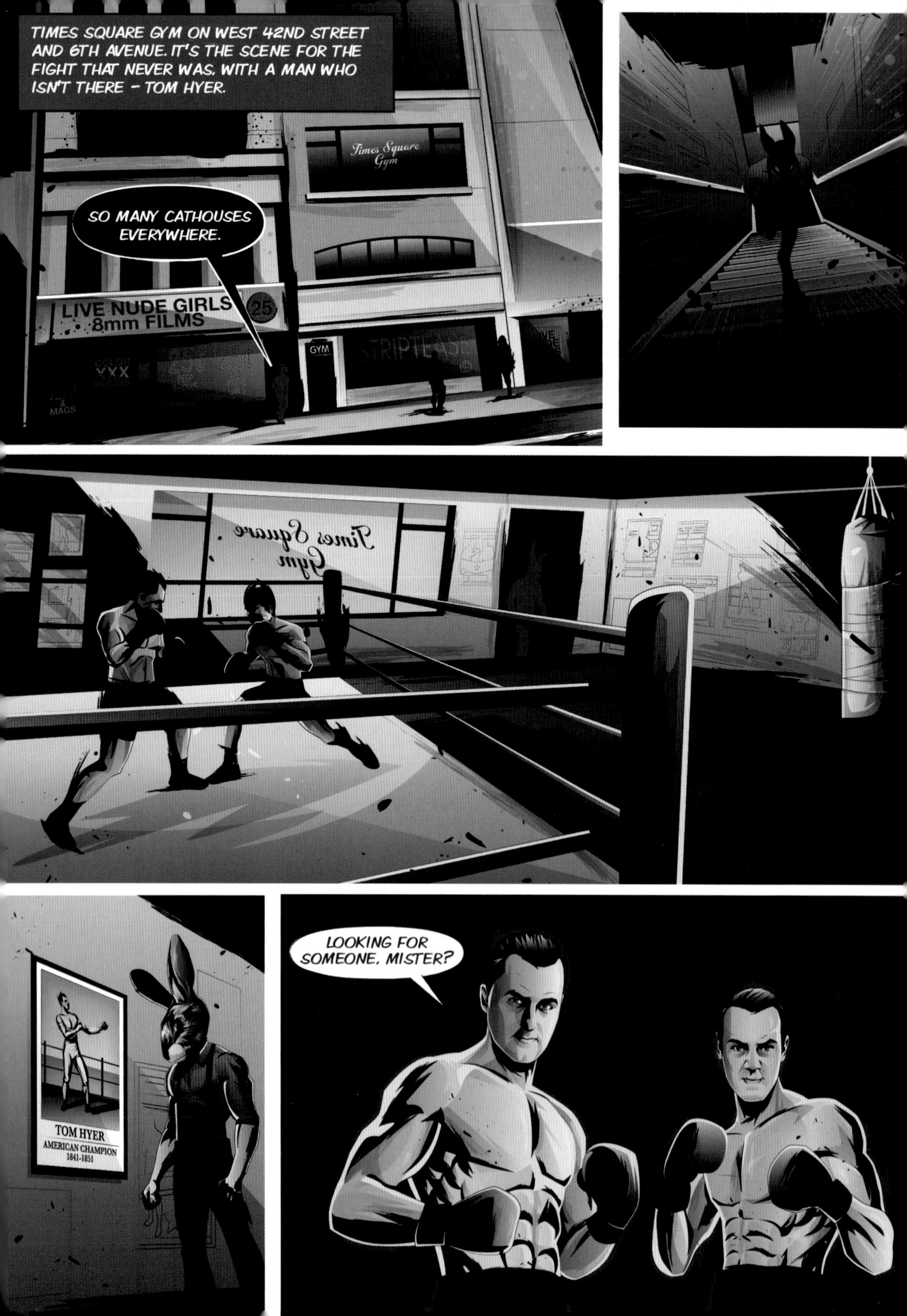
TIMES SQUARE GYM ON WEST 42ND STREET AND 6TH AVENUE. IT'S THE SCENE FOR THE FIGHT THAT NEVER WAS, WITH A MAN WHO ISN'T THERE – TOM HYER.
Times Square Gym
SO MANY CATHOUSES EVERYWHERE.
LIVE NUDE GIRLS
25
8mm FILMS
GYM
STRIPTEASE
Times Square Gym
TOM HYER
AMERICAN CHAMPION
1841-1851
LOOKING FOR SOMEONE, MISTER?

STRIPTEASE

INGREDIENTS

0.5 TSP	Cane Syrup (page 254)
0.5 OZ	Yellow Chartreuse
0.5 OZ	Becherovka
0.5 OZ	Noilly Prat Ambré Vermouth
0.5 OZ	Novo Fogo Aged Cachaça
1.5 OZ	Bacardi 8 Años Rum

TOOLS

Jiggers, mixing glass, barspoon, ½ teaspoon, julep strainer

METHOD

Stir with ice; strain with julep strainer and serve up without ice

GLASSWARE

Nick & Nora

ORIGIN

Jillian Vose

JILLIAN'S INSPIRATION

THINK BOOZY CINNAMON CHRISTMAS COOKIES FOR THIS ONE.

The rum is split with the cachaça for a bit of funk and extra layers. Becherovka is a Czech herbal liqueur with a strong cinnamon note that's pretty cool.

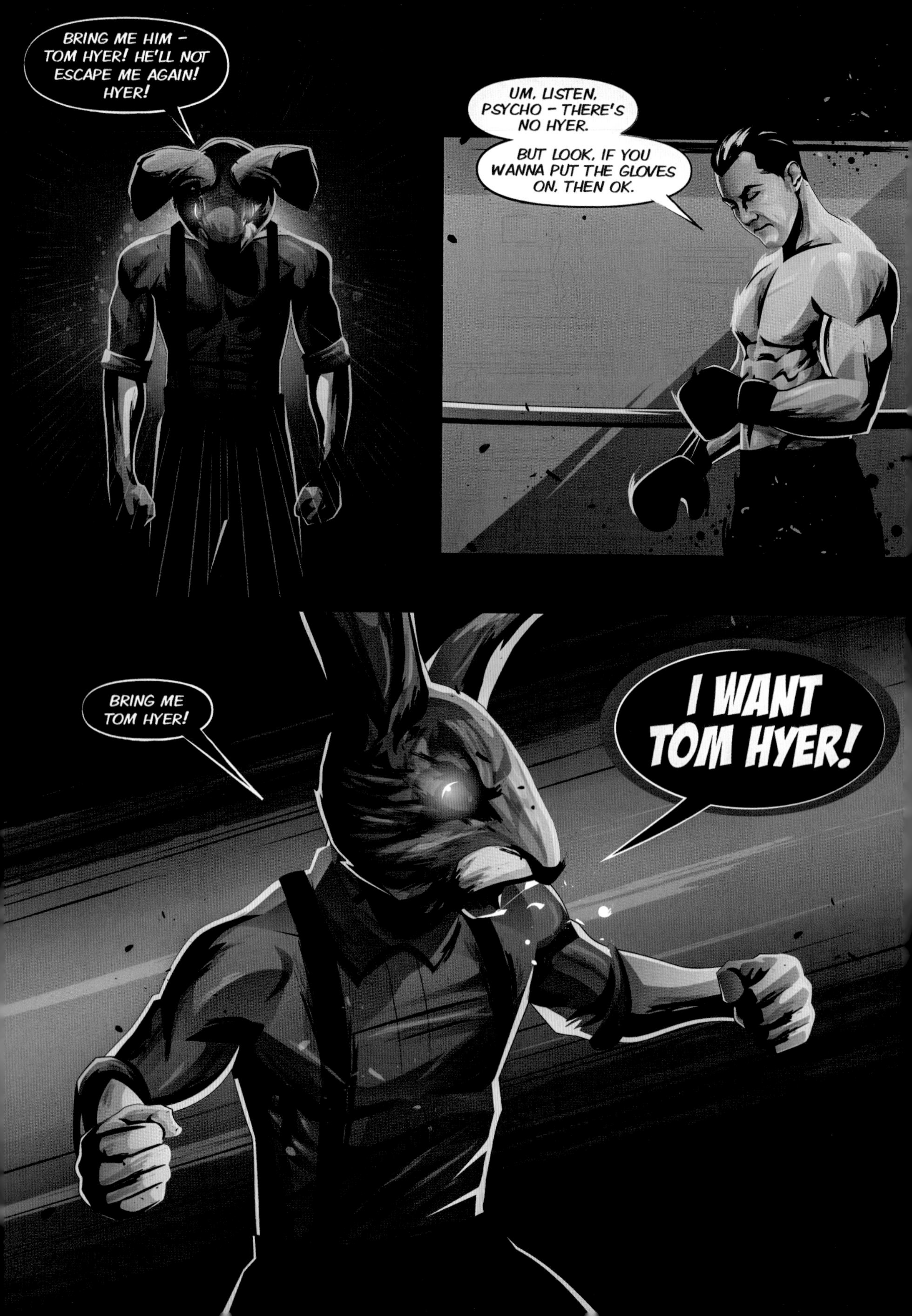
BRING ME HIM - TOM HYER! HE'LL NOT ESCAPE ME AGAIN! HYER!
UM, LISTEN, PSYCHO - THERE'S NO HYER.
BUT LOOK, IF YOU WANNA PUT THE GLOVES ON, THEN OK.
BRING ME TOM HYER!
I WANT TOM HYER!

DOWN AND OUT

INGREDIENTS

1 DASH	Bittermens Xocolatl Mole Bitters
0.25 OZ	Earl Grey Tea Cane Syrup (page 257)
0.25 OZ	Amaro CioCiaro
0.25 OZ	Green Chartreuse
1 OZ	Barbadillo Amontillado Sherry
1 OZ	Laphroaig 10 Year Scotch

TOOLS
Jiggers, mixing glass, barspoon, julep strainer, ice pick

METHOD
Stir with ice; strain with julep strainer and serve over large block of ice

GLASSWARE
Old Fashioned

GARNISH
Orange oil (discard peel)

ORIGIN
Jesse Vida

JESSE'S INSPIRATION

THIS DRINK STARTED WITH A CHALLENGE —

Balancing the aggressive flavors of peat with a heavy scotch base and formatting that into an approachable Old Fashioned variation. The profile that inspired the drink was lapsang-smoked black tea.

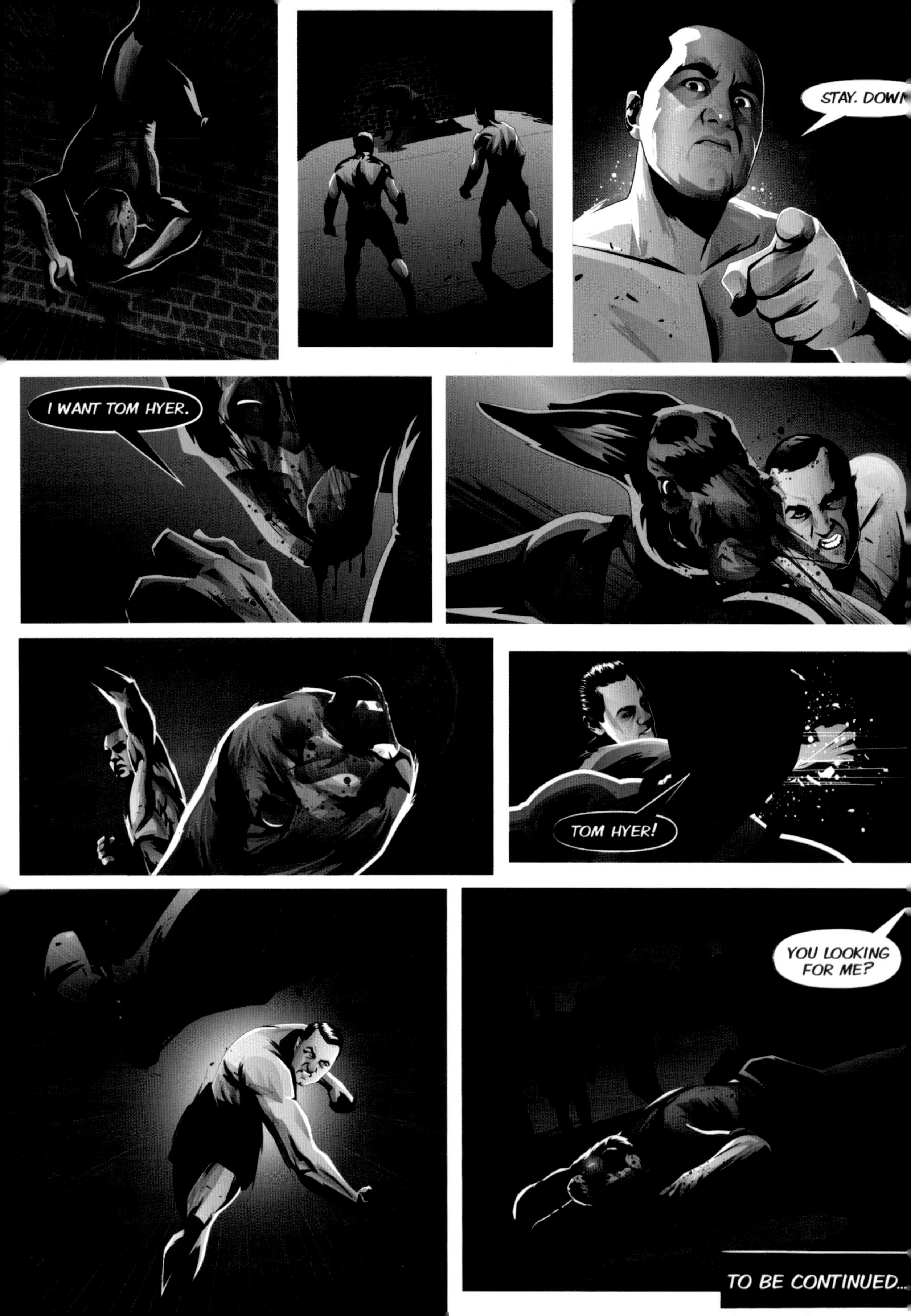
STAY. DOWN
I WANT TOM HYER.
TOM HYER!
YOU LOOKING FOR ME?
TO BE CONTINUED...

DREAM TICKET

INGREDIENTS

1	Whole egg
1 DASH	Angostura Bitters
0.5 OZ	Maple syrup (grade B)
0.75 OZ	Giffard Banane du Brésil
1 OZ	Tawny port wine
1 OZ	Bushmills Black Bush Irish Whiskey
0.75 OZ	High West Silver Oat Whiskey

TOOLS
Jiggers, shaker tins, fine strainer, Hawthorne strainer, nutmeg grater

METHOD
Dry shake; shake with ice; fine strain and serve up without ice

GLASSWARE
Georgian Irish coffee glass

GARNISH
Nutmeg

ORIGIN
Long Thai

71.

LONG'S INSPIRATION

A BREAKFAST COCKTAIL IN THE STYLE OF A FLIP . . .

The unaged oat whiskey and malt whiskey represent the oatmeal, the port, the berry, and so on. A whole egg made it more like a dessert drink than a breakfast drink, but the combo works beautifully.

THE MORE IT CHANGES,
THE MORE IT STAYS THE SAME.

A great city is on its knees, brought low by neglect, corruption, crime, decay. For the revenant spirit of John Morrissey, it's familiar territory.

Yet some things are new: The gangs have different accents. Drugs are bringing more havoc and making more money than the bottle ever did.

Loyalties are not written in blood. But this bad bunny knows how to make things work, how to gain influence — by twisting arms, by cracking skulls if need be.

WHATEVER IT TAKES,
AS IT ALWAYS HAS.

BETRAYAL

MIXED
DRINKS LIST | VOL
4 | ISSUE
2/6 |

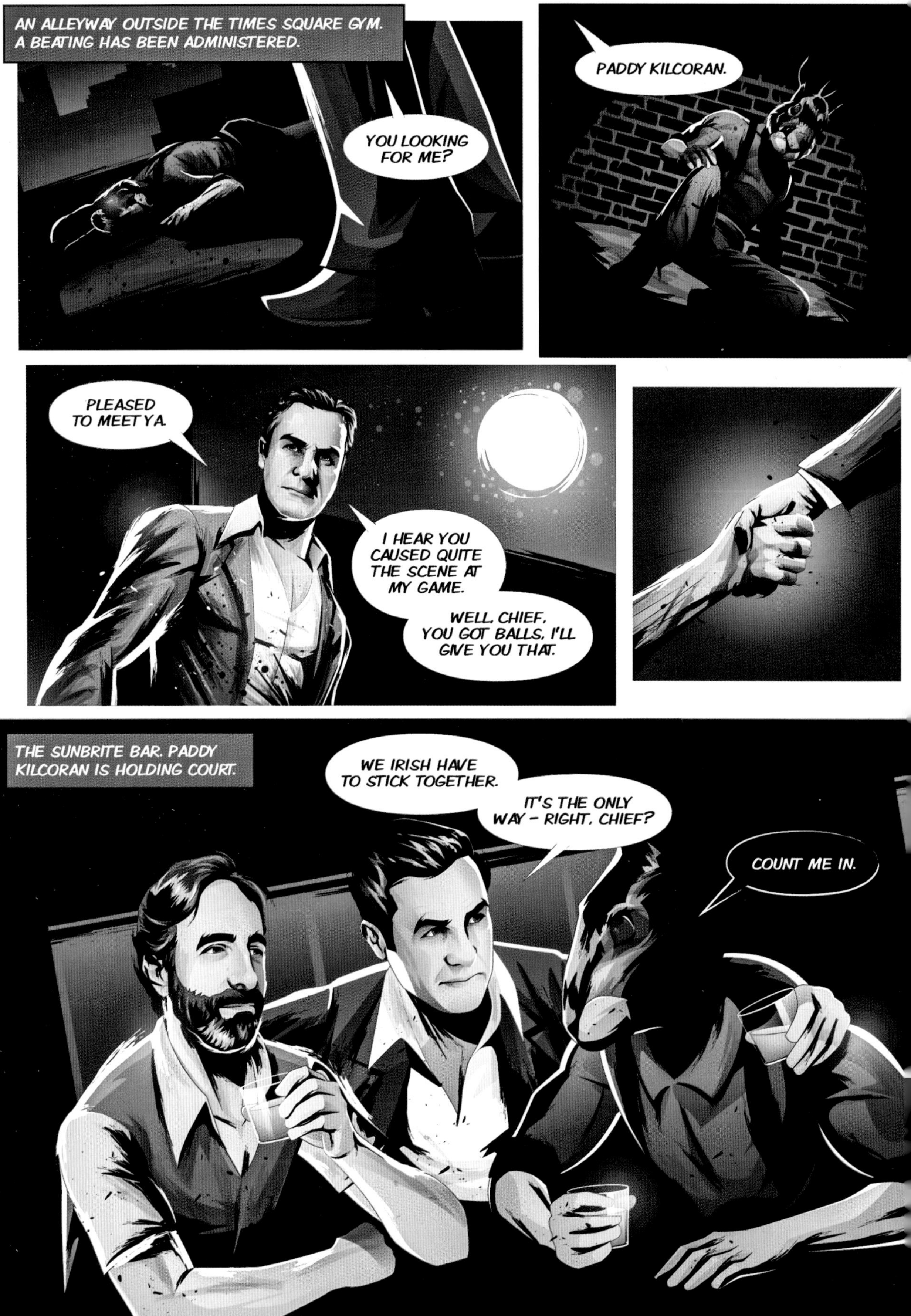
AN ALLEYWAY OUTSIDE THE TIMES SQUARE GYM. A BEATING HAS BEEN ADMINISTERED.
YOU LOOKING FOR ME?
PADDY KILCORAN.
PLEASED TO MEET YA.
I HEAR YOU CAUSED QUITE THE SCENE AT MY GAME.
WELL, CHIEF, YOU GOT BALLS, I'LL GIVE YOU THAT.
THE SUNBRITE BAR. PADDY KILCORAN IS HOLDING COURT.
WE IRISH HAVE TO STICK TOGETHER.
IT'S THE ONLY WAY - RIGHT, CHIEF?
COUNT ME IN.

KISSIN' COUSIN

INGREDIENTS

3 DASHES	Mace Tincture (page 263)
3 DASHES	Dandelion bitters
0.25 OZ	Salers Aperitif
0.5 OZ	Lemon juice
0.75 OZ	Lemon Sherbet (page 262)
0.25 OZ	Macadamia Orgeat (page 263)
1 OZ	Plantation Pineapple Rum
1.5 OZ	Barbadillo Fino Sherry

TOOLS
Jiggers, shaker tins
METHOD
Whip shake with 15 pieces of pebble ice until ice has melted; serve with pebble ice
GLASSWARE
Nog glass
GARNISH
Blueberries, ground mace
ORIGIN
Gregory Buda

GREGORY'S INSPIRATION

I'M THE SHERRY FANATIC AROUND HERE AND WAS INTERESTED IN PUTTING A FEW LOWER-PROOF ABV COCKTAILS ON THE LIST.

This is a clean, bright sherry cobbler with a hint of spice and gentian, lavishly garnished with blueberries and mace powder.

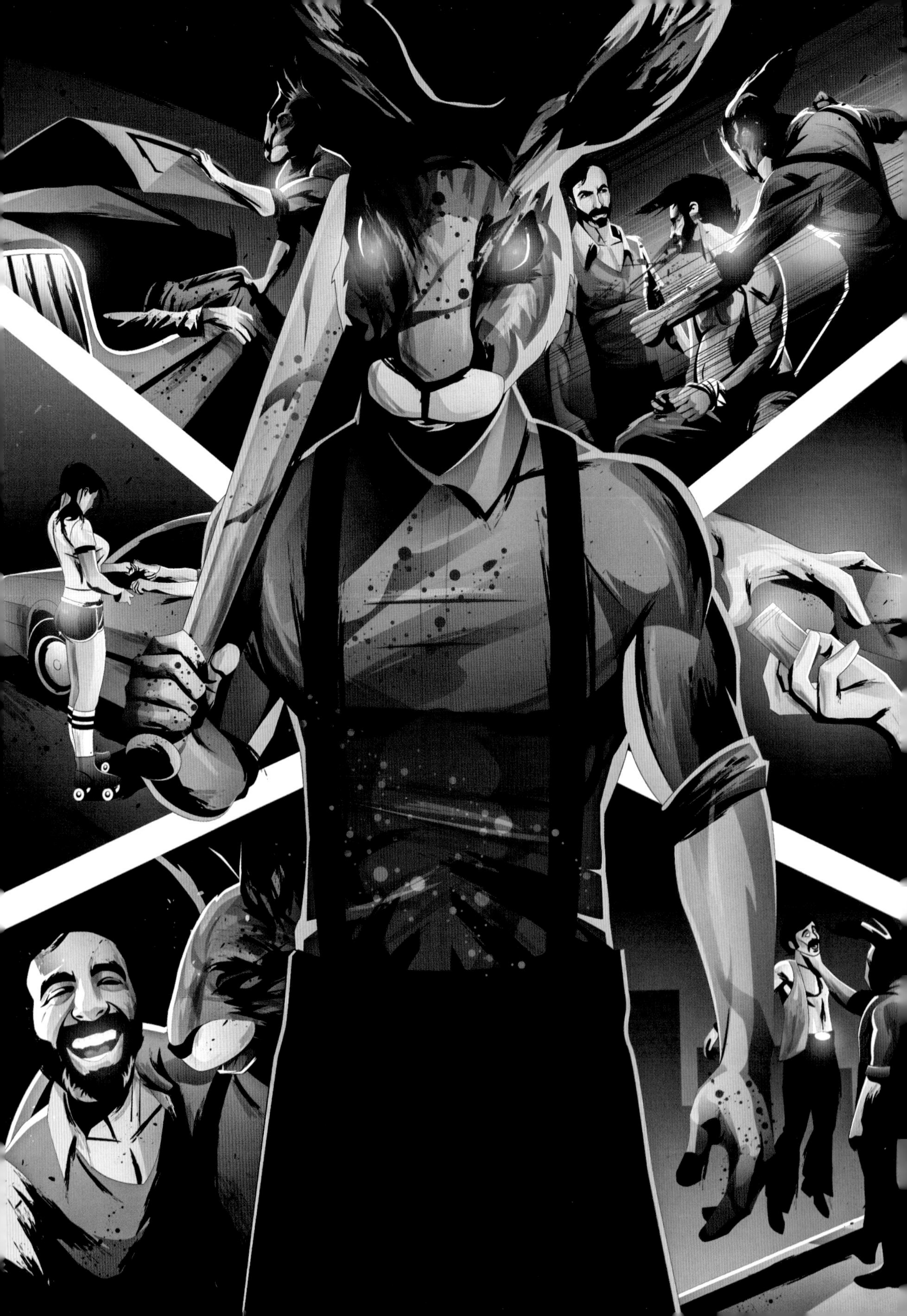

PAPA SMURF

INGREDIENTS

1 OZ	Champagne (not to be shaken with other ingredients)
1 DASH	Bittermens Boston Bittahs
1 DASH	Vieux Pontarlier Absinthe
0.75 OZ	Lemon juice
0.25 OZ	Cucumber juice
0.5 OZ	Celery Seed Syrup (page 254)
0.5 OZ	Fennel Syrup (page 258)
0.5 OZ	Dolin Blanc Vermouth
1.5 OZ	Fords Gin

TOOLS
Jiggers, shaker tins, fine strainer, Hawthorne strainer

METHOD
Add Champagne to the glass; shake drink with ice; fine strain into glass with Champagne and serve up without ice

GLASSWARE
Champagne flute

ORIGIN
Madeleine Solo Rapp

MADELEINE'S INSPIRATION

I WANTED TO MAKE A BRIGHT AND VEGETAL CHAMPAGNE COCKTAIL.

Celery and cucumber work really well together, and pairing that with a London Dry–style gin worked out great.

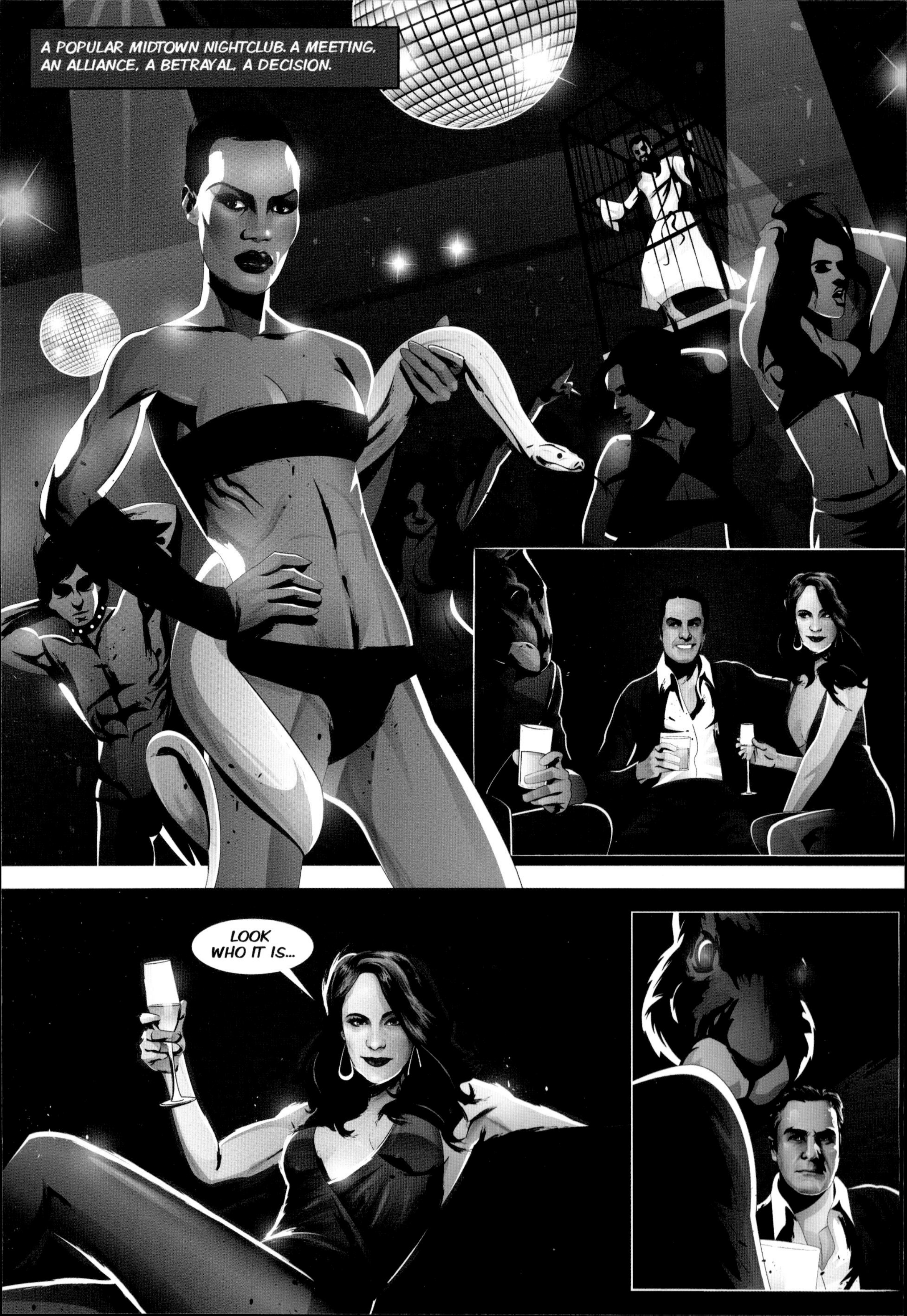
A POPULAR MIDTOWN NIGHTCLUB. A MEETING, AN ALLIANCE, A BETRAYAL, A DECISION.
LOOK WHO IT IS...

SPARK PLUG

INGREDIENTS

1 DASH	Lemongrass Tincture (page 262)
0.75 OZ	Lemon juice
0.5 OZ	Granny Smith Apple Juice (page 259)
0.25 OZ	Vanilla Syrup (page 275)
0.5 OZ	Passion Fruit Syrup (page 266)
1.5 OZ	Botanist Gin

TOOLS
Jiggers, shaker tins, fine strainer, Hawthorne strainer

METHOD
Shake with ice; fine strain and serve up without ice

GLASSWARE
Sour glass

GARNISH
Lemon oil (discard peel)

ORIGIN
Jillian Vose

JILLIAN'S INSPIRATION

A REAL CROWD-PLEASER, SPARK PLUG LOOKS SIMPLER THAN IT IS.

The flavor pairings of passion fruit, vanilla, lemon and green apple all intertwine at some point. The delicacy of the Botanist doesn't overpower the modifiers and lets the gin shine. Lemongrass adds a touch of brightness and dryness.

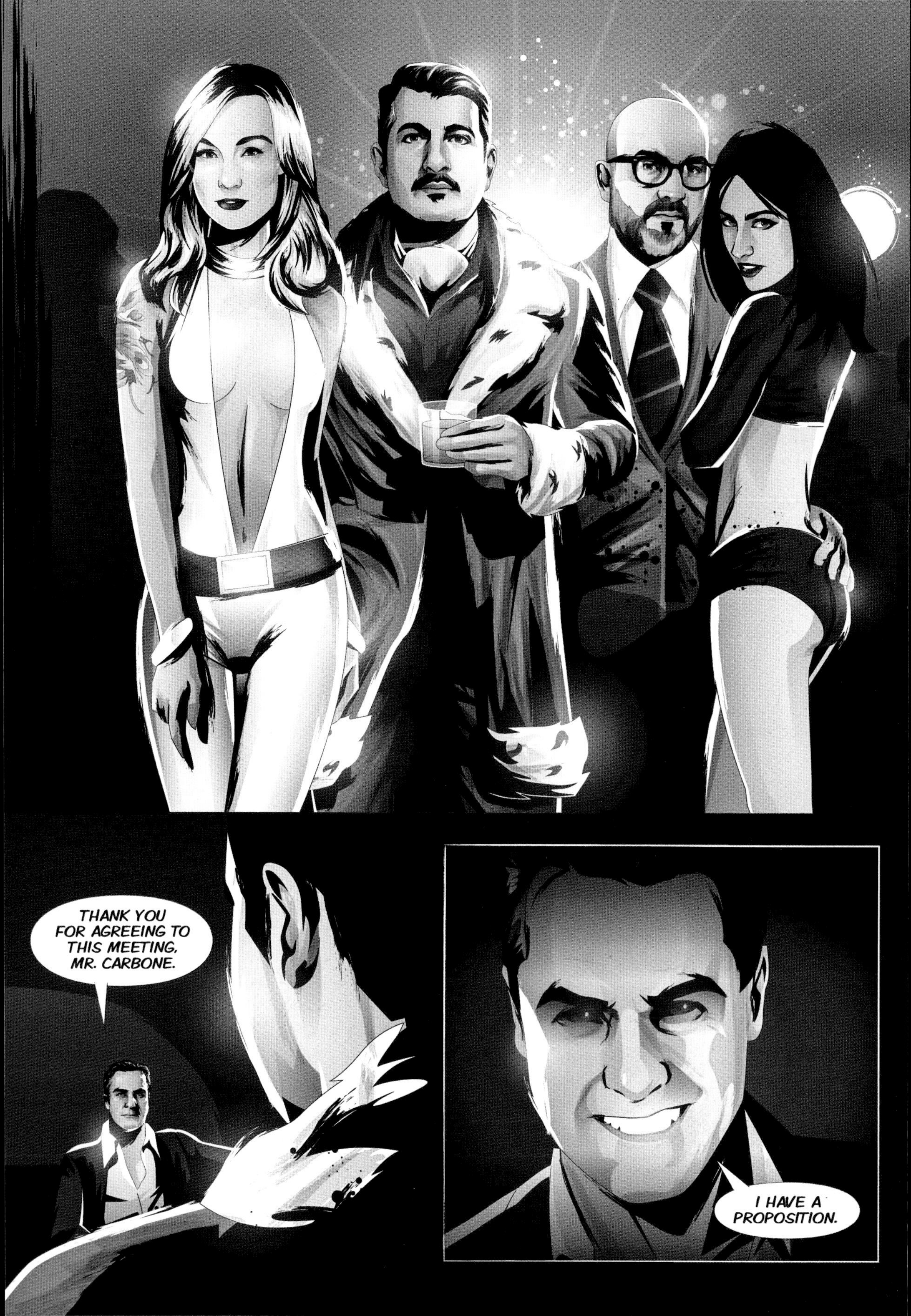
THANK YOU FOR AGREEING TO THIS MEETING, MR. CARBONE.
I HAVE A PROPOSITION.

BRUTE FORCE

INGREDIENTS

2 DASHES	Vieux Pontarlier Absinthe
0.75 OZ	Lime juice
0.5 OZ	Orgeat (page 265)
0.5 OZ	Merlet Crème de Poire Liqueur
0.25 OZ	Wray & Nephew White Overproof Rum
1.5 OZ	Green Tea–Infused Tapatio Blanco Tequila (page 260)

TOOLS
Jiggers, shaker tins, fine strainer, Hawthorne strainer, ice pick, nutmeg grater

METHOD
Shake with ice; fine strain and serve over large block of ice

GLASSWARE
Old Fashioned

GARNISH
Nutmeg

ORIGIN
Jillian Vose

JILLIAN'S INSPIRATION

A MARGARITA-STYLE DRINK, SWEETENED WITH ORGEAT INSTEAD OF AGAVE FOR MORE LAYERS.

It still needed something to make it more special. To add to the greenness, green tea was suggested, then the magic funky rum bump made it all come together.

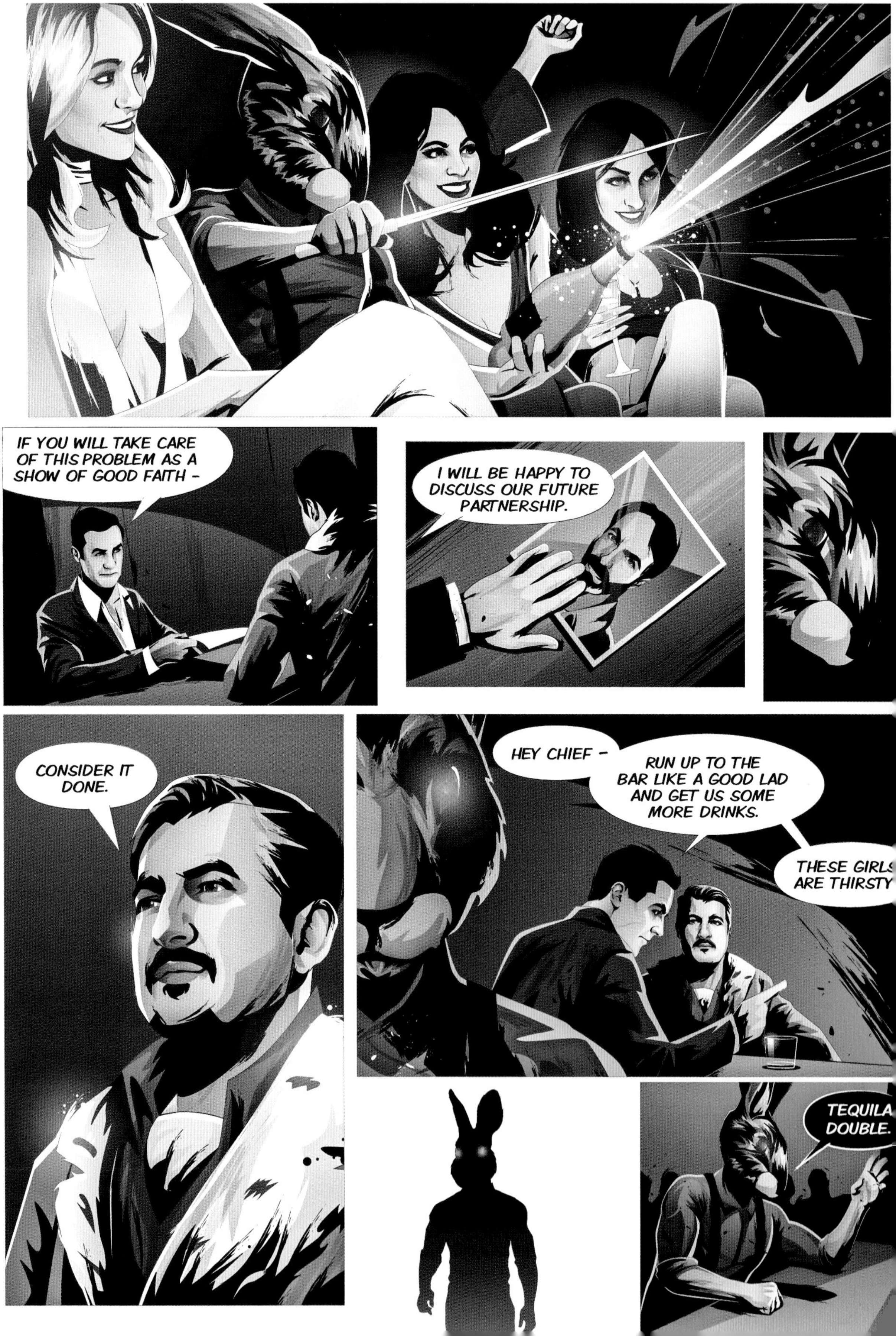
IF YOU WILL TAKE CARE OF THIS PROBLEM AS A SHOW OF GOOD FAITH -
I WILL BE HAPPY TO DISCUSS OUR FUTURE PARTNERSHIP.
CONSIDER IT DONE.
HEY CHIEF -
RUN UP TO THE BAR LIKE A GOOD LAD AND GET US SOME MORE DRINKS.
THESE GIRLS ARE THIRSTY
TEQUILA. DOUBLE.

GANGSTA'S PARADISE

INGREDIENTS

2 DASHES	Applewood Smoked Salt Solution (page 250)
3 DASHES	Dale DeGroff's Pimento Bitters
0.75 OZ	Lemon juice
0.75 OZ	Caramel Cane Syrup (page 254)
0.5 OZ	Lemorton Pinneau de Normandie
1.5 OZ	Montreuil Calvados Selection

TOOLS
Jiggers, shaker tins, fine strainer, Hawthorne strainer

METHOD
Shake with ice; fine strain and serve up without ice

GLASSWARE
Sour glass

ORIGIN
Jillian Vose

JILLIAN'S INSPIRATION

AN ATTEMPT TO RECREATE SALTED CARAMEL POPCORN.

Montreuil Calvados Selection always reminded me of buttered popcorn, so I started there. Pommeau's funky fermented apple quality brings a quirkiness, and applewood salt lends a smoky note. Pimento bitters enhance this and balance the caramel sweetness.

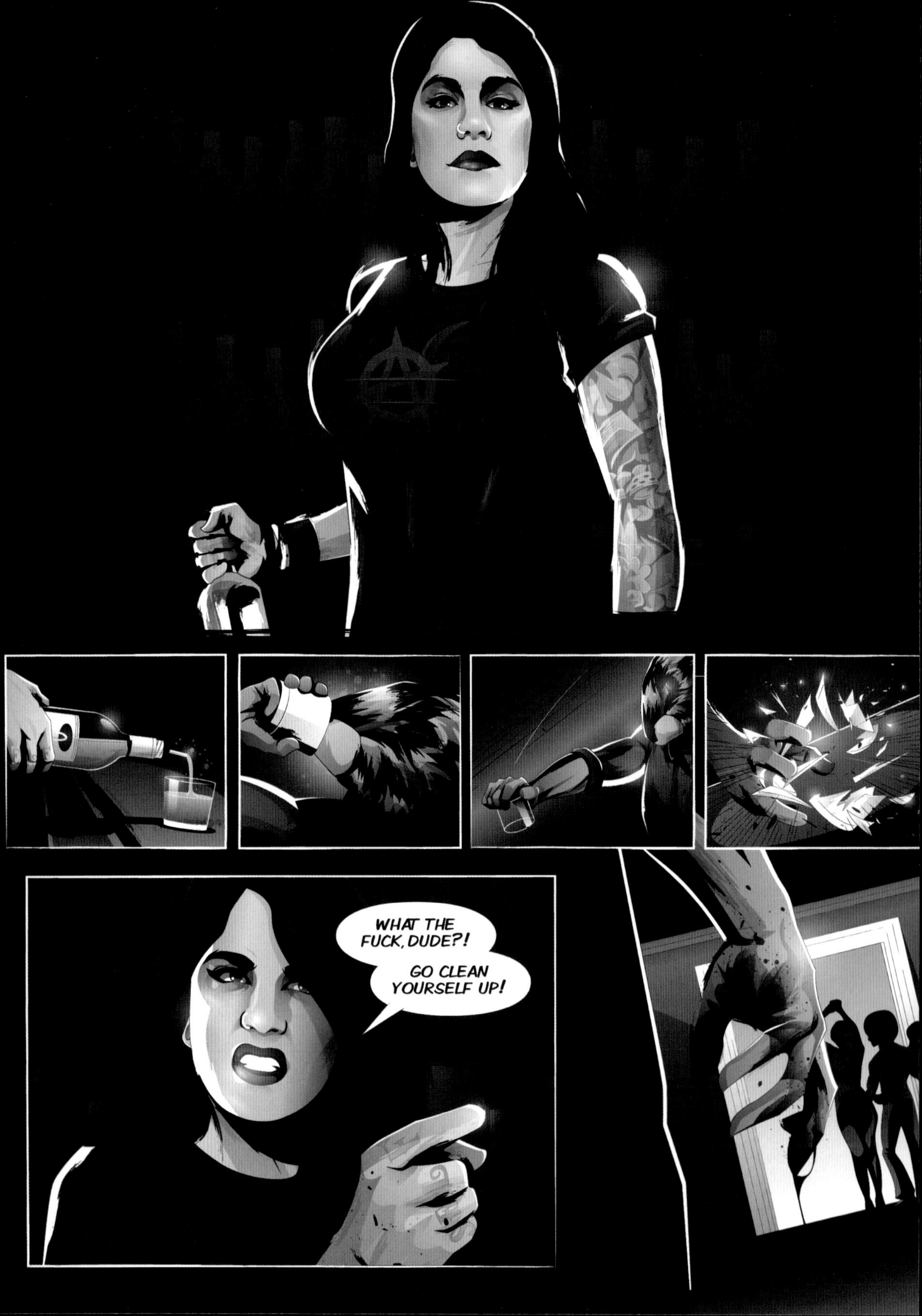
WHAT THE FUCK, DUDE?!
GO CLEAN YOURSELF UP!

RESURRECTION MAN

INGREDIENTS

1 DASH	Dandelion bitters
1 TSP	Merlet Crème De Pêche
1 TSP	Giffard Crème de Cacao (white)
1 TSP	Vanilla Syrup (page 275)
0.5 OZ	Barbadillo Manzanilla Sherry
1 OZ	Noilly Prat Dry Vermouth
1.5 OZ	Copper & King's Unaged Apple Brandy

TOOLS
Jiggers, mixing glass, barspoon, teaspoon, julep strainer

METHOD
Stir with ice; strain with julep strainer and serve up without ice

GLASSWARE
Nick & Nora

GARNISH
Lemon oil (discard peel)

ORIGIN
Jillian Vose

85.

JILLIAN'S INSPIRATION

THIS GOT DREAMED UP AFTER FALLING IN LOVE WITH A NEW SPIRIT I'D DISCOVERED – AN UNAGED APPLE DISTILLATE.

It was fresh, bright and minerally fragrant. I immediately thought of a martini – and it developed into this.

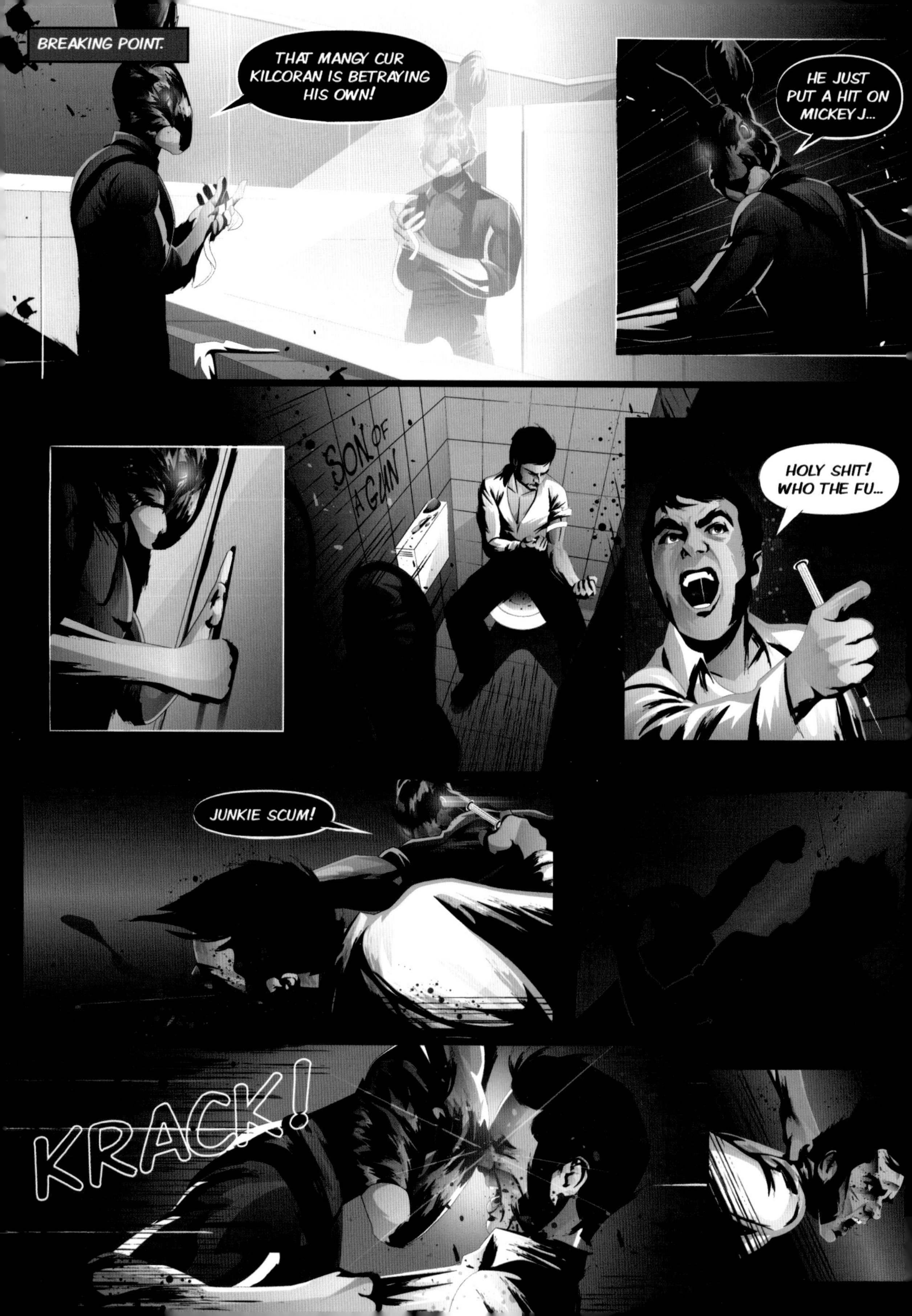
BREAKING POINT.
THAT MANGY CUR KILCORAN IS BETRAYING HIS OWN!
HE JUST PUT A HIT ON MICKEY J...
SON OF A GUN
HOLY SHIT! WHO THE FU...
JUNKIE SCUM!
KRACK!

KING OF CLUBS

INGREDIENTS

2	Sage leaves
1 BAR SPN	Kumquat preserves
0.5 OZ	Lemon juice
0.75 OZ	Granny Smith Apple Juice (page 259)
0.5 OZ	Honey Syrup (page 260)
0.25 OZ	Strega
2 OZ	Powers Gold Irish Whiskey

TOOLS
Jiggers, barspoon, shaker tins, Hawthorne strainer, fine strainer, ice pick

METHOD
Build drink in tin and add sage leaves (do not muddle); shake with ice; fine strain and serve with ice nugget

GLASSWARE
Coupette

ORIGIN
Jillian Vose

87.

JILLIAN'S INSPIRATION

THIS IS INSPIRED BY A DRINK I'D DONE IN THE PAST, BUT WHICH I FELT I COULD IMPROVE.

I switched out the original sweetener, changed the flavor of preserves from marmalade to kumquat and added a small amount of Strega for depth and some anise to complement the sage.

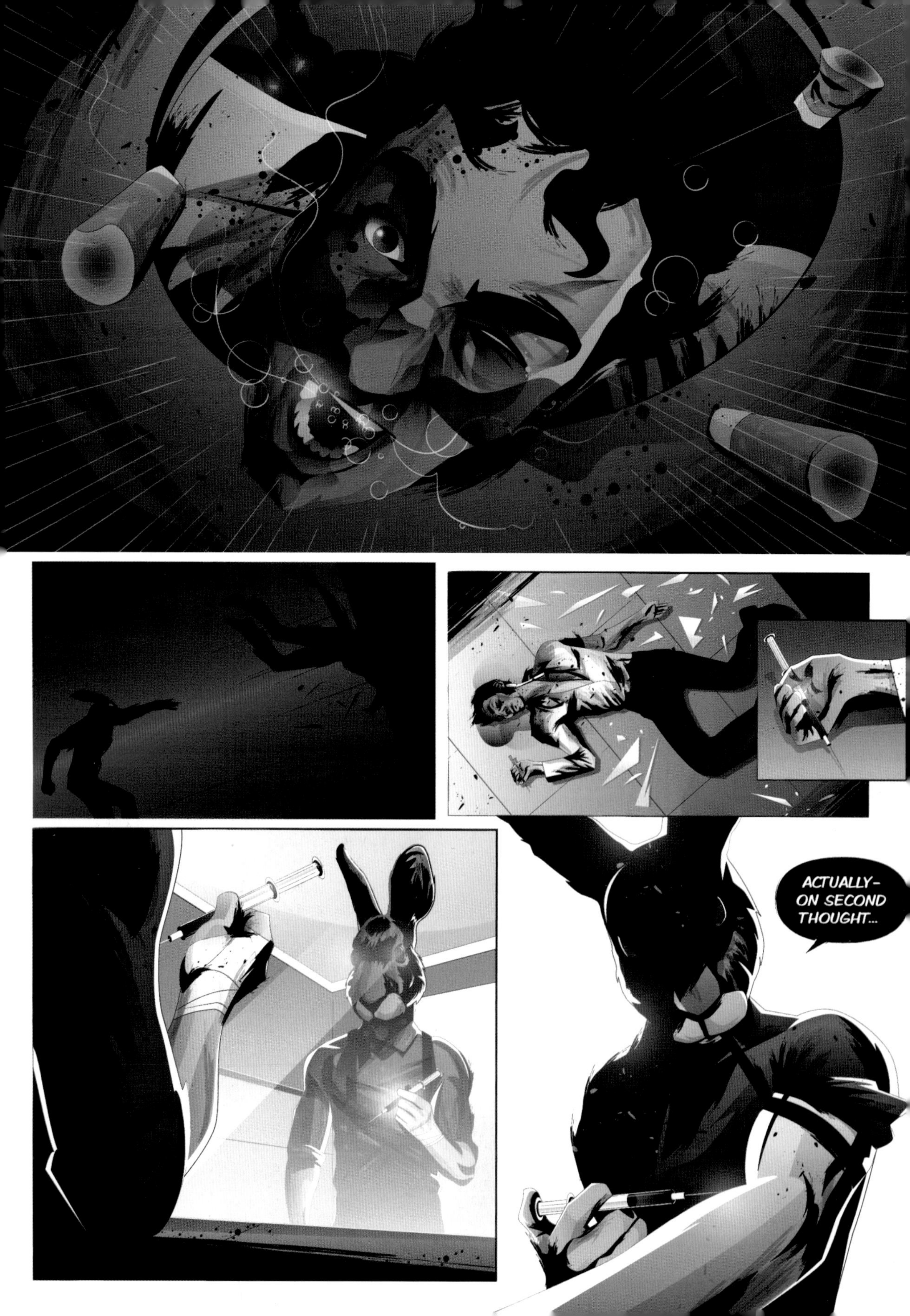
ACTUALLY-
ON SECOND
THOUGHT...

MAFIOSO

INGREDIENTS

2 DASHES	Bittermens Hellfire Habanero Shrub
1 TSP	Fennel Syrup (page 258)
0.25 OZ	Aperol
0.5 OZ	Fusion Verjus Blanc
0.25 OZ	Giffard Abricot Brandy
0.5 OZ	Alvear Pale Cream Sherry
1 OZ	Tequila Cabeza

TOOLS

Jiggers, mixing glass, barspoon, teaspoon, julep strainer

METHOD

Stir with ice; strain with julep strainer and serve up without ice

GLASSWARE

Nick & Nora

GARNISH

Lemon oil (discard peel)

ORIGIN

Jesse Vida

BETRAYAL

89.

MAFIOSO

JESSE'S INSPIRATION

THE IDEA HERE WAS A SLIGHTLY SPICY, STIRRED AGAVE COCKTAIL.

It's common to see these flavors in a citrus-forward, shaken drink but not so much in this format. With a habanero shrub to spice it, I based the rest of the flavors around that.

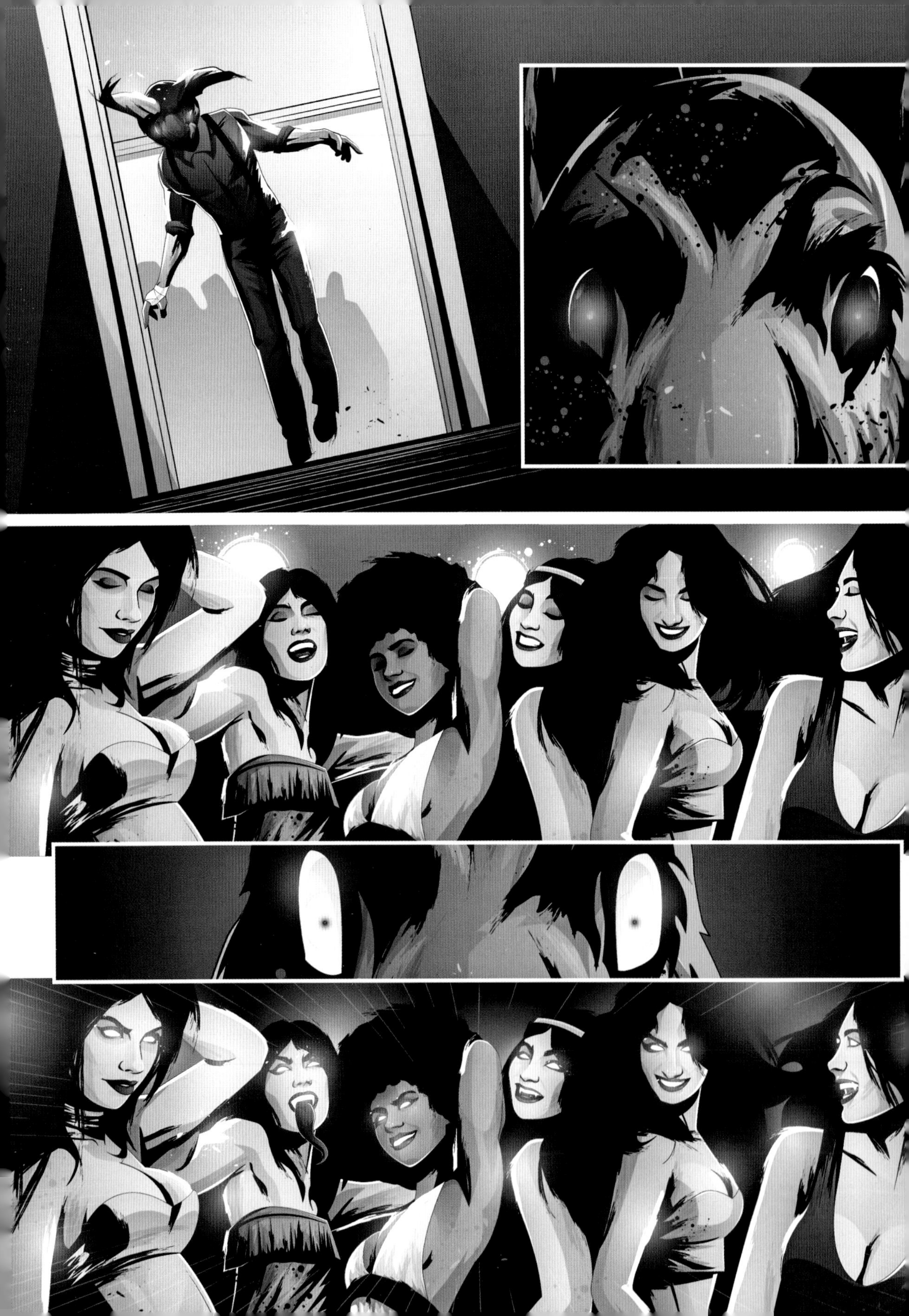

CHASING THE DRAGON

INGREDIENTS

1 DASH	Bitter Truth Aromatic Bitters
1 TSP	Cinnamon Bark Syrup (page 255)
0.75 OZ	Lemon juice
0.5 OZ	Grapefruit juice
0.5 OZ	Poppy Seed Syrup (page 268)
0.5 OZ	Orgeat (page 265)
1 OZ	Scarlet Ibis Rum
1 OZ	Eagle Rare 10 Year Bourbon

TOOLS

Jiggers, teaspoon, shaker tins, fine strainer, Hawthorne strainer, ice pick, nutmeg grater

METHOD

Shake with ice; fine strain and serve with ice nugget

GLASSWARE

Punch glass

GARNISH

Nutmeg

ORIGIN

Jillian Vose

JILLIAN'S INSPIRATION

A BOURBON SOUR VARIATION, THIS JUST SCREAMS FALL.

Warmly spiced and refreshing with poppy seed giving the drink its edge.

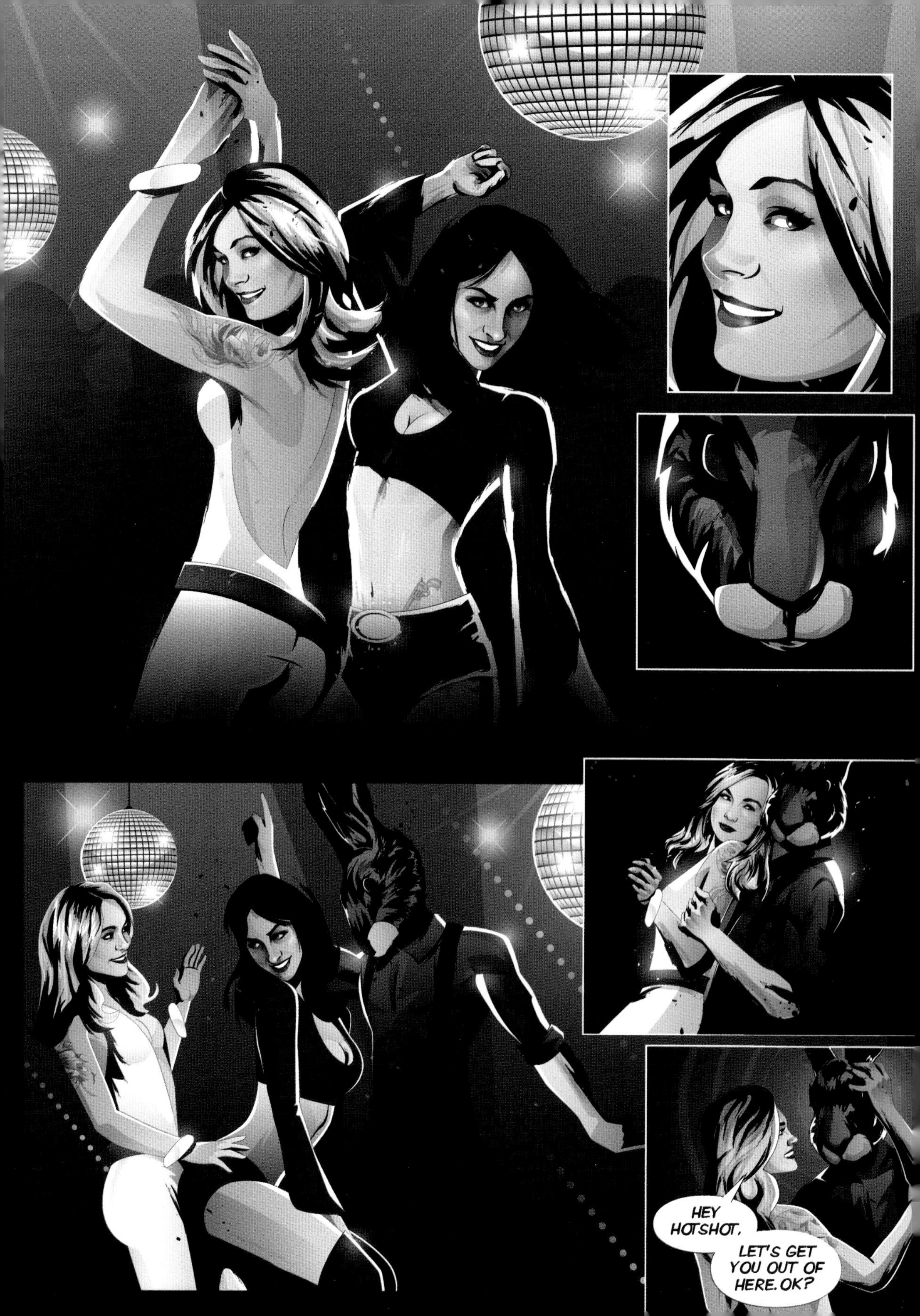
HEY HOTSHOT,
LET'S GET YOU OUT OF HERE. OK?

HONG KONG PHOOEY

INGREDIENTS

3 DASHES	Bay Leaf Tincture (page 252)
1 DASH	Vieux Pontarlier Absinthe
0.5 OZ	Lemon juice
0.5 OZ	Grapefruit juice
0.25 OZ	Pistachio Orgeat (page 267)
0.75 OZ	Avocado Cane Syrup (page 251)
0.75 OZ	Half & half
0.5 OZ	Krogstad Gamle Aquavit
0.5 OZ	Banks 5 Island Blend Rum
1 OZ	Avocado-Infused Caña Brava Rum (page 251)

TOOLS
Jiggers, shaker tins, fine strainer, Hawthorne strainer

METHOD
Short shake with ice; fine strain and serve with pebble ice

GLASSWARE
Nog glass

GARNISH
Nutmeg

ORIGIN
Jessica Friedman

BETRAYAL

93.

HONG KONG PHOOEY

JESSICA'S INSPIRATION

I BASED THIS DRINK AROUND AVOCADO.

Since avocado is such a delicate flavor, I incorporated it in the drink in two ways – a fat wash and a rich cane syrup. Once I figured out how to get the avocado flavor right, the drink came together naturally.

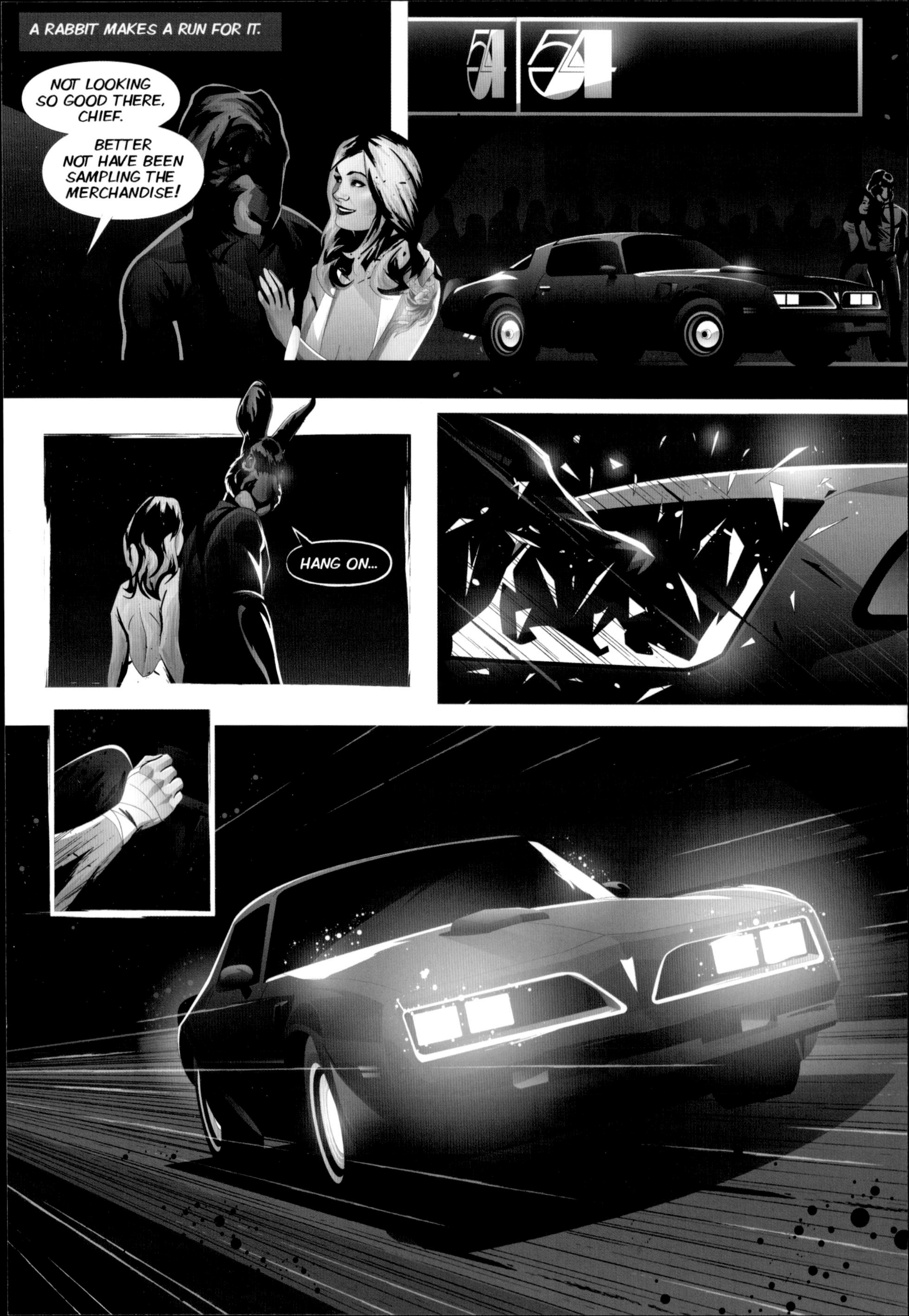
A RABBIT MAKES A RUN FOR IT.
NOT LOOKING SO GOOD THERE, CHIEF.
BETTER NOT HAVE BEEN SAMPLING THE MERCHANDISE!
54
HANG ON...

BENGALI MENACE

INGREDIENTS

3 DASHES	Vieux Pontarlier Absinthe
0.5 TSP	Cane Syrup (page 254)
0.5 OZ	Suze Saveur d'Autrefois
0.75 OZ	American Fruits Aged Apple Liqueur
0.75 OZ	Cocchi Americano
1 OZ	Glenfiddich 12 Year Scotch

TOOLS

Jiggers, mixing glass, ½ teaspoon, barspoon, julep strainer, ice pick

METHOD

Stir with ice; strain with julep strainer and serve over large block of ice

GLASSWARE

Old Fashioned

GARNISH

Lemon oil (discard peel)

ORIGIN

Jillian Vose

95.

JILLIAN'S INSPIRATION

I WANTED TO DO A SCOTCH-BASED WHITE NEGRONI VARIATION.

I really love the green apple and other bright fruit notes of Glenfiddich, which led me to modifiers of an apple liqueur made in upstate New York and absinthe, while keeping the classic Suze and Cocchi of a white negroni.

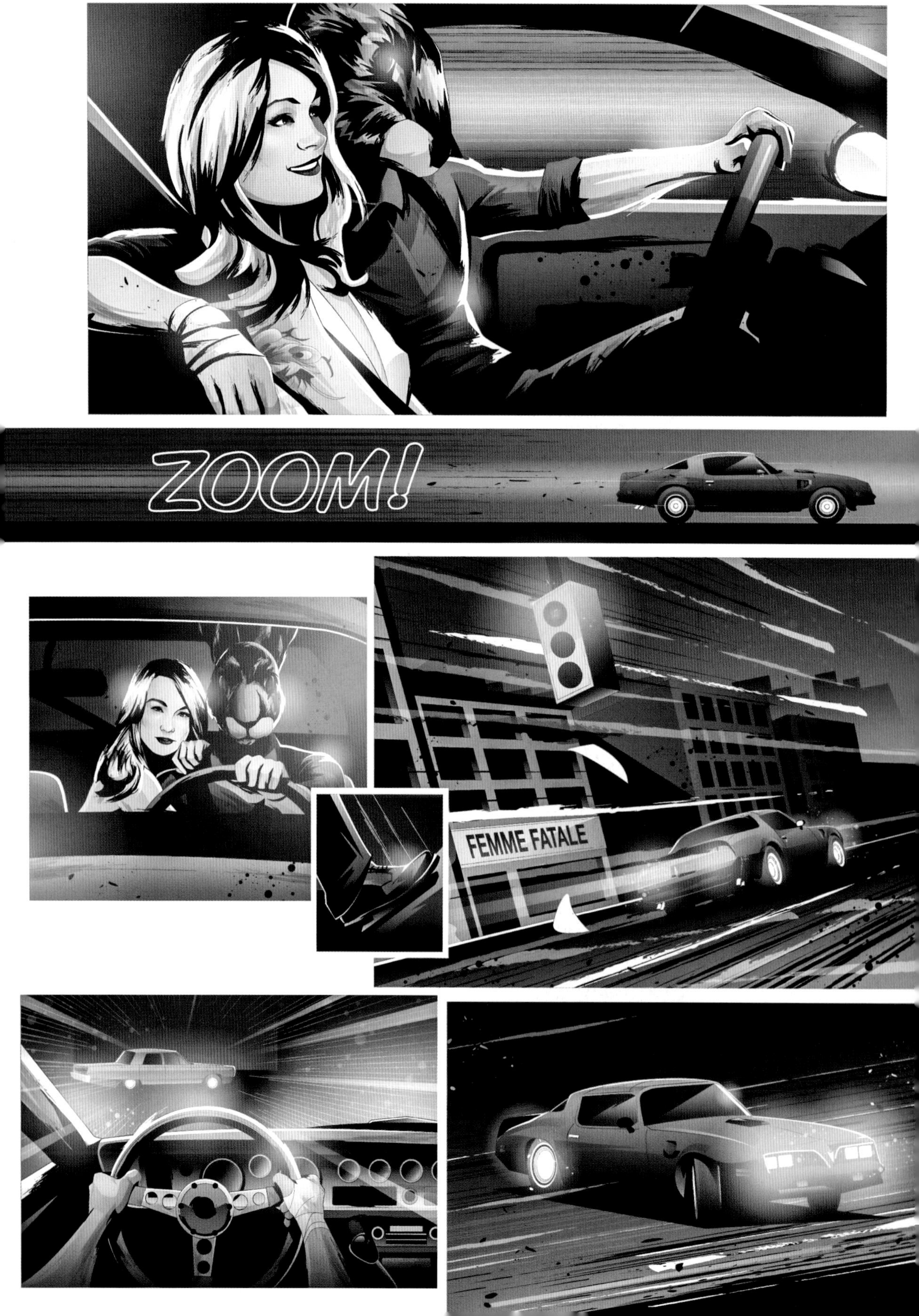
ZOOM!
FEMME FATALE

30 SECONDS 'TIL TAKEOFF

INGREDIENTS

1.5 OZ	Goose Island Matilda Belgian Ale
1 DASH	House Orange Bitters (page 261)
0.75 OZ	Lemon juice
0.75 OZ	Lemon Sherbet (page 262)
0.75 OZ	Giffard Banane du Brésil
0.5 OZ	Martini & Rossi Bianco Vermouth
0.5 OZ	Coriander-Infused Glenmorangie Original (page 256)
1.5 OZ	Black Dirt Apple Jack

TOOLS

Jiggers, shaker tins, fine strainer, Hawthorne strainer, ice pick, nutmeg grater

METHOD

Add ale to mustache cup; shake with ice; fine strain and serve with ice nugget

GLASSWARE

Mustache cup

GARNISH

Nutmeg

ORIGIN

Long Thai

97.

LONG'S INSPIRATION

I WANTED AN APPROACHABLE YET COMPLEX COCKTAIL WHERE THE STAR WAS BEER.

Belgian-style beers have a bright fruit, cloves, anise and herb-like quality. Bananas and apples go along with the baking spice quality of the beer, while coriander and Martini & Rossi emphasize the herbaceous side of the ale.

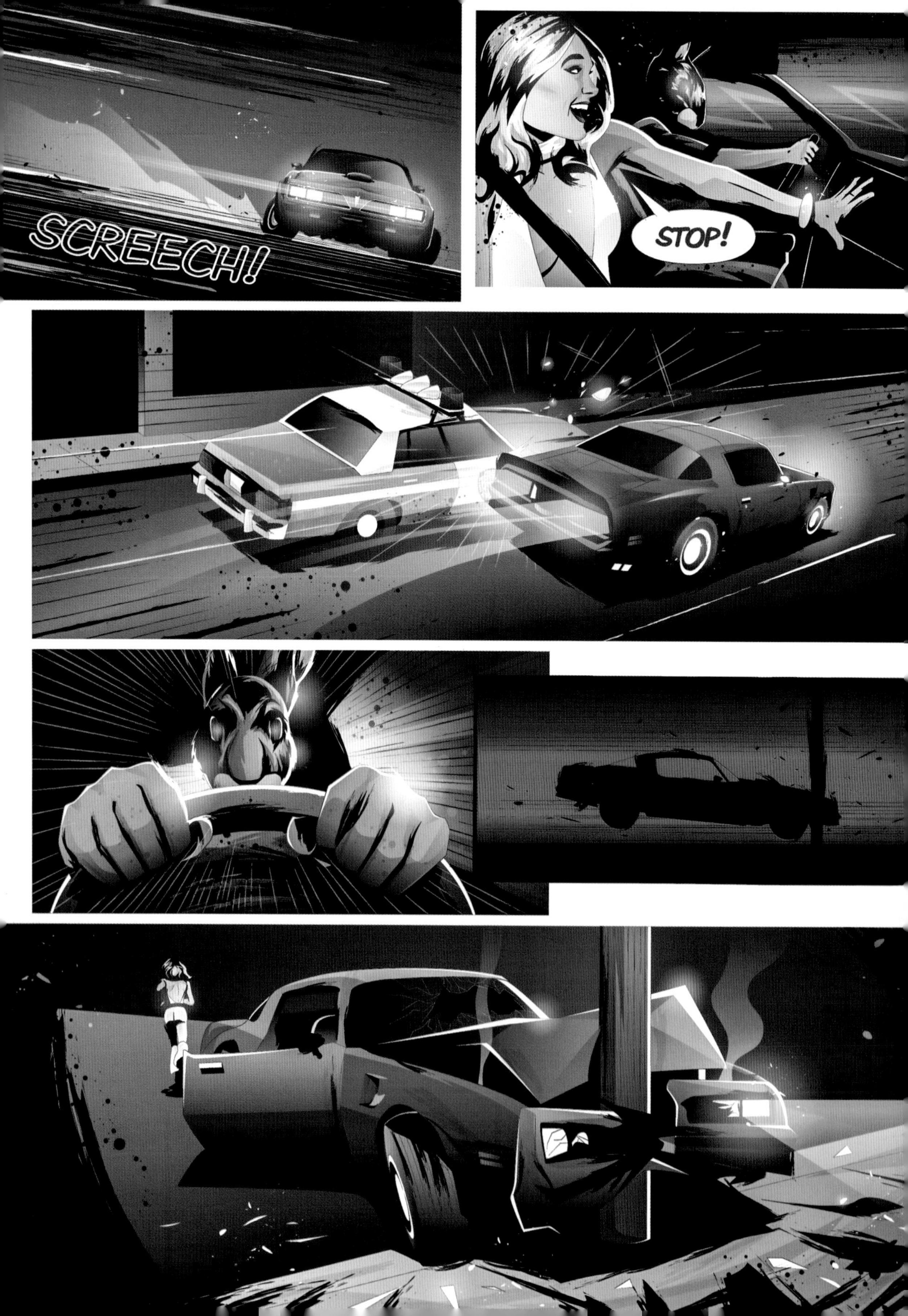
SCREECH!
STOP!

GUARDIAN ANGEL

INGREDIENTS

2	Cherry tomatoes
3 DASHES	Chipotle Tincture (page 255)
0.75 OZ	Lemon juice
0.5 OZ	Sumac Syrup (page 272)
0.25 OZ	Sapins liqueur
1 OZ	Extra Virgin Olive Oil–Washed Del Maguey Vida Mezcal (page 258)
1 OZ	Mellow Corn Whiskey

TOOLS

Jiggers, muddler, shaker tins, fine strainer, Hawthorne strainer, ice pick

METHOD

Muddle tomatoes; build drink; shake with ice; fine strain and serve with ice nugget

GLASSWARE

Coupette

ORIGIN

Long Thai

LONG'S INSPIRATION

OLIVE OIL–WASHED MEZCAL WAS THE STARTING POINT; THE OTHER INGREDIENTS WERE ADDED TO ACCENTUATE THAT.

The corn whiskey downplays the smokiness of the mezcal, and the chipotle adds dark, vegetal, spicy aromatics. Sumac's tart floral aromatics were paired with the tomato. The result is smoky and spicy yet light and refreshing.

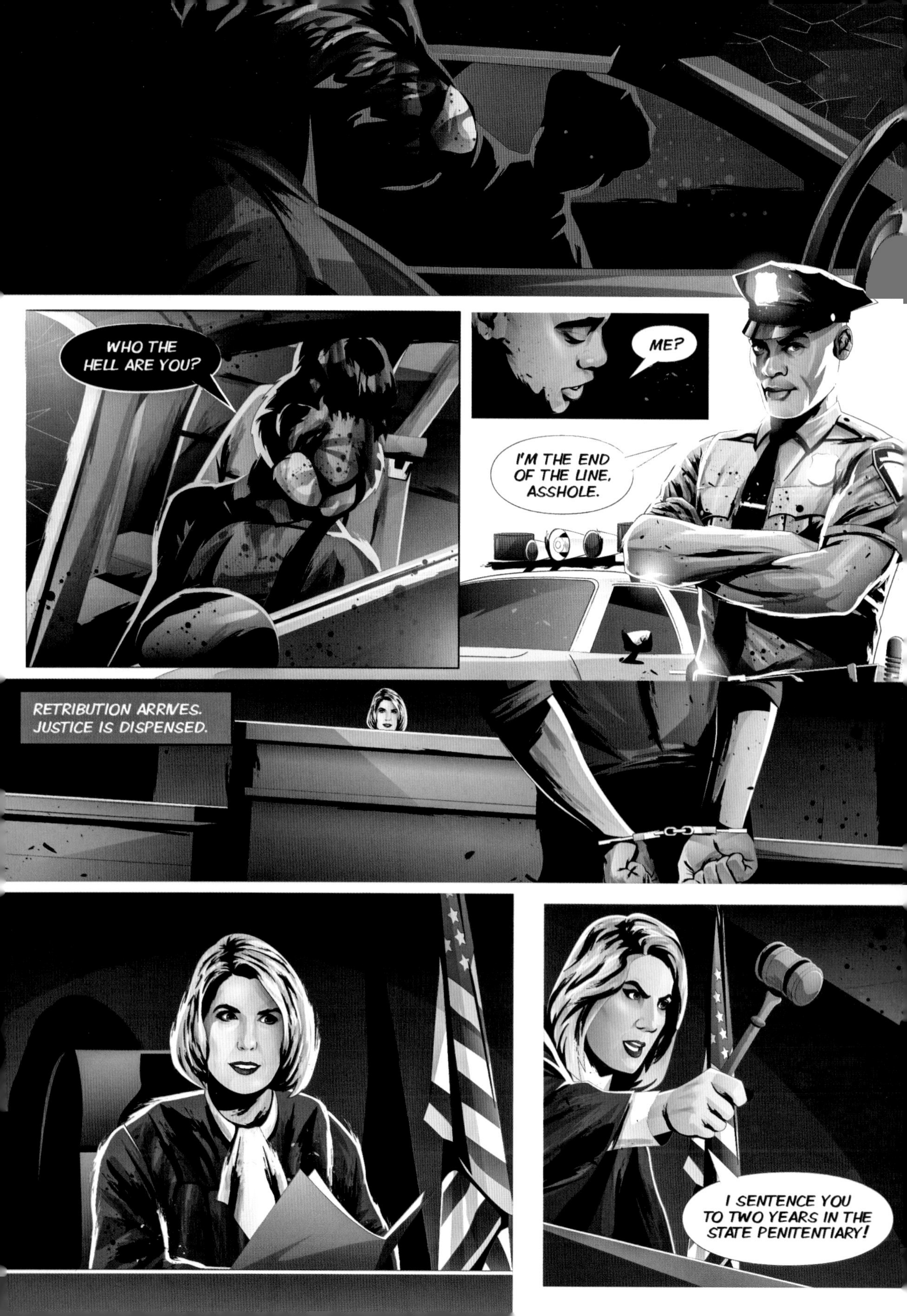
WHO THE HELL ARE YOU?
ME?
I'M THE END OF THE LINE, ASSHOLE.
RETRIBUTION ARRIVES. JUSTICE IS DISPENSED.
I SENTENCE YOU TO TWO YEARS IN THE STATE PENITENTIARY!

FIFTH GEAR

INGREDIENTS

1 DASH	Saline Solution (page 270)
1 DASH	Vieux Pontarlier Absinthe
0.5 TSP	Giffard Banane du Brésil
0.25 OZ	Giffard Crème de Cacao (white)
0.5 OZ	Blandy's 5 Year Malmsey Madeira
1 OZ	Amaro Montenegro
1 OZ	Powers John's Lane Irish Whiskey

TOOLS

Jiggers, mixing glass, ½ teaspoon, barspoon, julep strainer, ice pick

METHOD

Stir with ice; strain with julep strainer and serve over large block of ice

GLASSWARE

Old Fashioned

GARNISH

Orange oil (discard peel)

ORIGIN

Jesse Vida

BETRAYAL

101.

FIFTH GEAR

JESSE'S INSPIRATION

THIS IS ONE OF MY ALL-TIME FAVORITE CREATIONS.

A very rich and decadent Old Fashioned variation, splitting base with my preferred amaro and pot still Irish whiskey. This cocktail represents a meeting of my own style with the layering and balancing techniques I've acquired at The Dead Rabbit.

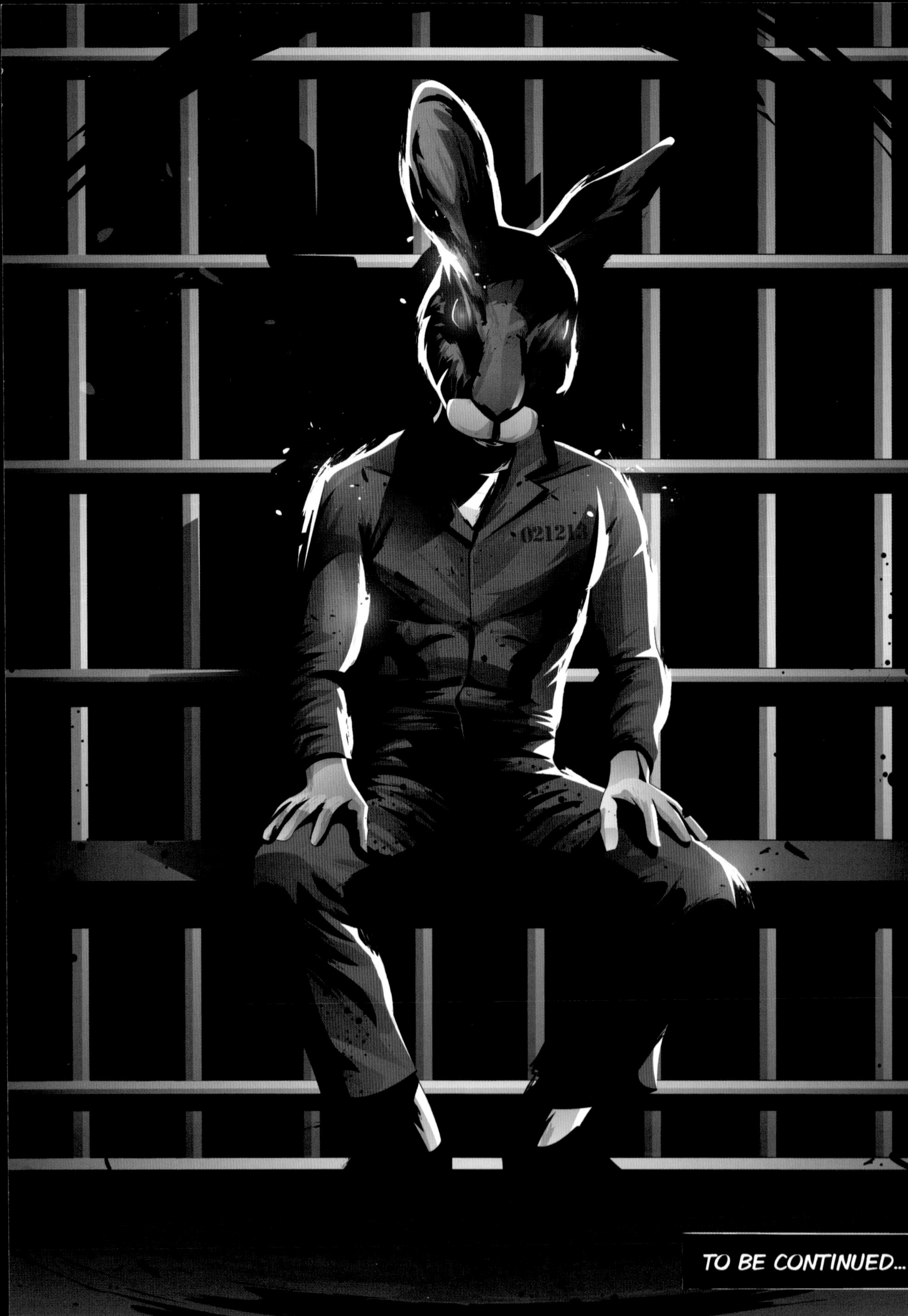
021213
TO BE CONTINUED...

RUSH JOB

INGREDIENTS

0.5 TSP	Amaro Sibilla
0.75 OZ	Lime juice
0.75 OZ	Pistachio Orgeat (page 267)
0.75 OZ	Rice milk
2 OZ	Suntory Toki Japanese Whisky
1	Fresh kaffir lime leaf
1	Fresh basil leaf

TOOLS

Jiggers, ½ teaspoon, shaker tins, fine strainer, Hawthorne strainer, ice pick

METHOD

Build drink in tin; add herbs (do not muddle); shake with ice; fine strain and serve with ice nugget

GLASSWARE

Punch cup

ORIGIN

Gregory Buda

GREGORY'S INSPIRATION

A FRIEND CHALLENGED ME TO COME UP WITH A DRINK USING AN HERB CALLED LIME BASIL.

I couldn't track down a reliable supply of lime basil, but I found that fresh basil and kaffir lime leaves mimicked it quite closely. I wanted to pursue an Asian theme for this cocktail and ended up with a delicate Japanese Whisky Sour variation, with rice milk standing in for an egg white.

REPUTATION DOESN'T COUNT FOR MUCH

WHEN YOU ARRIVE ON THE CELLBLOCK.

You start at the bottom rung and what you get you earn.
BECAUSE LIFE HERE IS HARD. BRUTAL.

You need to find out quickly where you fit in,
because in here, the tribe is all that matters.

For John Morrissey, the reborn spirit of the Dead Rabbits
adrift in a strange world, that realization is sweetly familiar.
A world so tightly organized is a world in which the fault
lines are clear to see.

**THEY'RE WHERE THE EARTHQUAKE WILL
HAPPEN.**

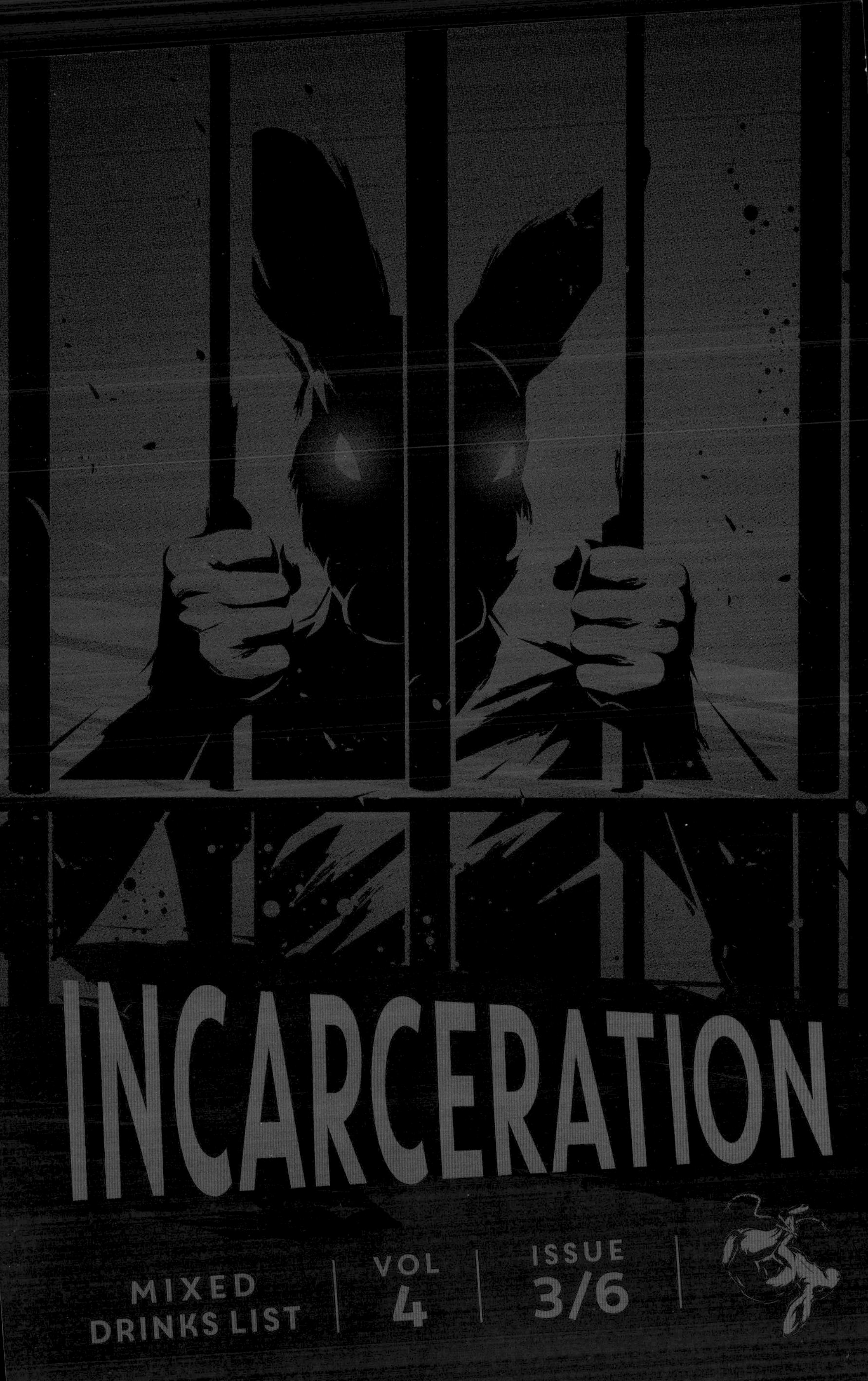
INCARCERATION
MIXED DRINKS LIST
VOL 4
ISSUE 3/6

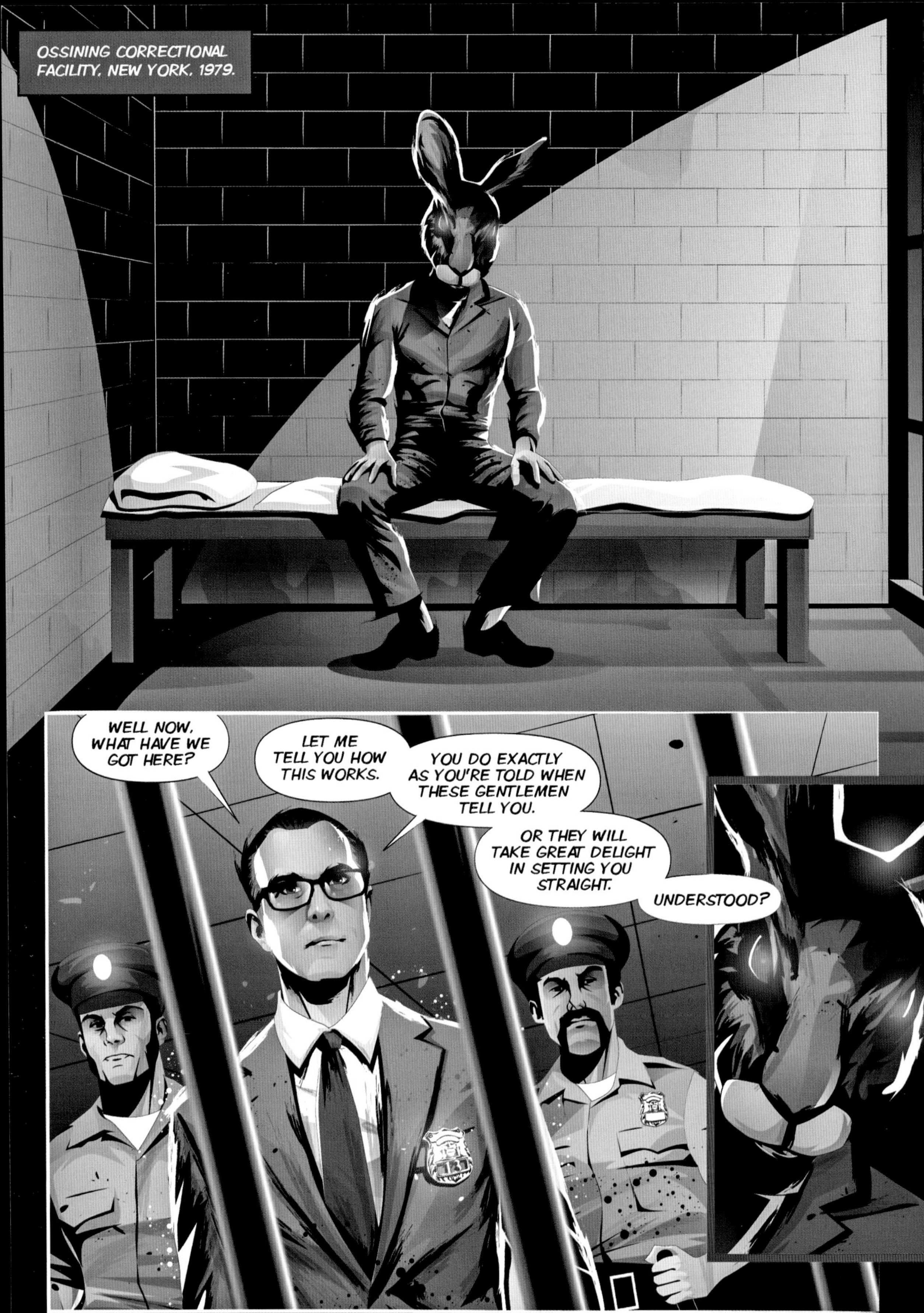
OSSINING CORRECTIONAL FACILITY, NEW YORK, 1979.
WELL NOW, WHAT HAVE WE GOT HERE?
LET ME TELL YOU HOW THIS WORKS.
YOU DO EXACTLY AS YOU'RE TOLD WHEN THESE GENTLEMEN TELL YOU.
OR THEY WILL TAKE GREAT DELIGHT IN SETTING YOU STRAIGHT.
UNDERSTOOD?

BIG WHEEL

INGREDIENTS

2 DASHES	Kaffir Lime Leaf Tincture (page 262)
0.5 TSP	Cinnamon Bark Syrup (page 255)
0.5 TSP	Pür•likör Williams Pear
1 OZ	Barbadillo Manzanilla Sherry
1 OZ	Noilly Prat Dry Vermouth
1.25 OZ	Perry's Tot Navy Strength Gin

TOOLS
Jiggers, mixing glass, ½ teaspoon, barspoon, julep strainer
METHOD
Stir with ice; strain with julep strainer and serve up without ice
GLASSWARE
Nick & Nora
GARNISH
Lime oil (discard peel)
ORIGIN
Gregory Buda

107.

GREGORY'S INSPIRATION

I WANTED TO BASE A MARTINI VARIATION AROUND THE CINNAMON AND CITRUS BOTANICAL MAKEUP OF PERRY'S TOT NAVY STRENGTH GIN.

I use a relatively small pour of the gin and balance it with heavy doses of sherry and dry vermouth. A little cinnamon bark syrup and kaffir lime to accentuate the flavors in the gin, and voilà!

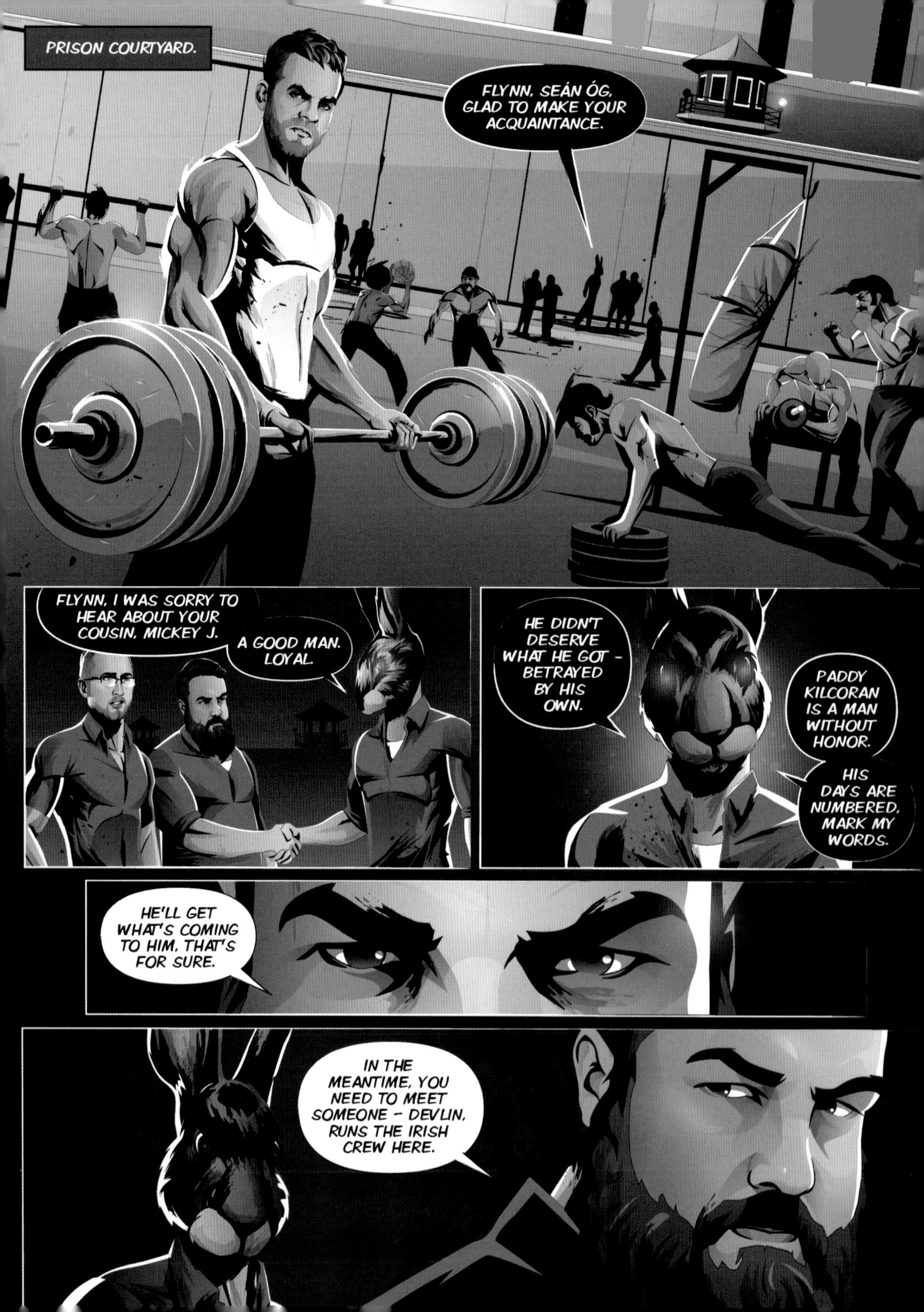
PRISON COURTYARD.
FLYNN, SEÁN ÓG, GLAD TO MAKE YOUR ACQUAINTANCE.
FLYNN, I WAS SORRY TO HEAR ABOUT YOUR COUSIN, MICKEY J.
A GOOD MAN. LOYAL.
HE DIDN'T DESERVE WHAT HE GOT - BETRAYED BY HIS OWN.
PADDY KILCORAN IS A MAN WITHOUT HONOR.
HIS DAYS ARE NUMBERED, MARK MY WORDS.
HE'LL GET WHAT'S COMING TO HIM, THAT'S FOR SURE.
IN THE MEANTIME, YOU NEED TO MEET SOMEONE - DEVLIN, RUNS THE IRISH CREW HERE.

SHOW-OFF

INGREDIENTS

1 OZ	Champagne (not to be shaken with other ingredients)
0.5 OZ	Salers Apertif
0.75 OZ	Lemon juice
0.5 OZ	Kiwi juice
0.25 OZ	Vanilla Syrup (page 275)
0.5 OZ	Macadamia Orgeat (page 263)
0.5 OZ	Massanez Green Apple Liqueur
1.5 OZ	Pellehaut Armagnac Blanche

TOOLS
Jiggers, shaker tins, fine strainer, Hawthorne strainer
METHOD
Add Champagne to the glass; shake drink with ice; fine strain into glass with Champagne; serve up without ice
GLASSWARE
Champagne flute
ORIGIN
Jillian Vose

109.

JILLIAN'S INSPIRATION

THIS DRINK WAS BASED AROUND THE MASSANEZ LIQUEUR.

I already had my flavor combinations for green apple that worked well in the past, but I wanted to incorporate new flavors. These were the kiwi and gentian. It worked really well – fresh, fruity and balanced.

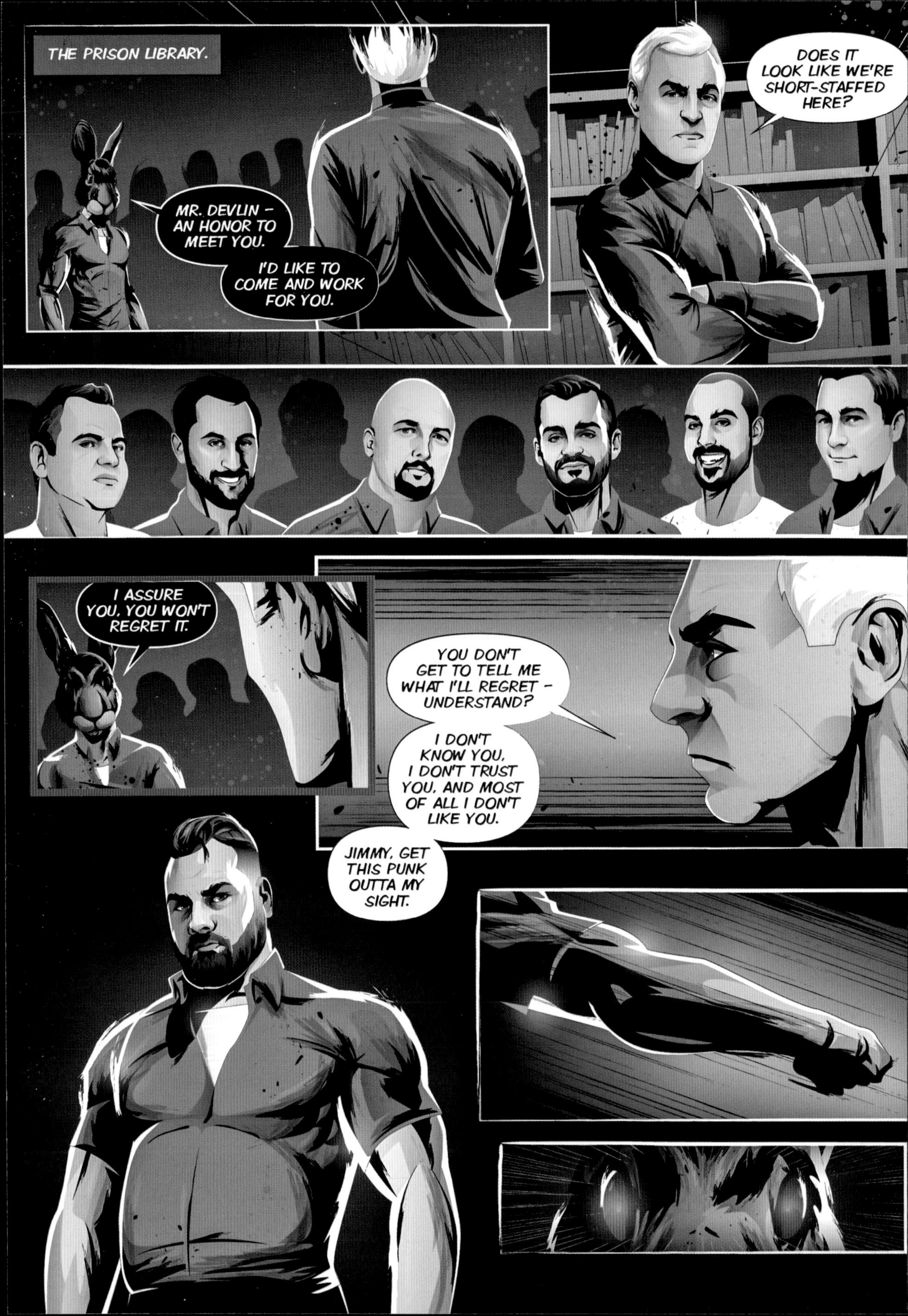
THE PRISON LIBRARY.
MR. DEVLIN - AN HONOR TO MEET YOU.
I'D LIKE TO COME AND WORK FOR YOU.
DOES IT LOOK LIKE WE'RE SHORT-STAFFED HERE?
I ASSURE YOU, YOU WON'T REGRET IT.
YOU DON'T GET TO TELL ME WHAT I'LL REGRET - UNDERSTAND?
I DON'T KNOW YOU, I DON'T TRUST YOU, AND MOST OF ALL I DON'T LIKE YOU.
JIMMY, GET THIS PUNK OUTTA MY SIGHT.

FUN LOVIN' CRIMINAL

INGREDIENTS

1 DASH	House Cardamom Bitters (page 261)
2 DASHES	Bittermens Hopped Grapefruit Bitters
0.5 OZ	Combier Crème de Pamplemousse Rose Liqueur
1 OZ	Lillet Rosé
0.5 OZ	Clear Creek Apple Brandy
1 OZ	Fortaleza Blanco Tequila

TOOLS
Jiggers, mixing glass, barspoon, julep strainer

METHOD
Stir with ice; strain with julep strainer and serve up without ice

GLASSWARE
Nick & Nora

GARNISH
Lemon oil (discard peel)

ORIGIN
Long Thai

111.

LONG'S INSPIRATION

I WANTED A MARTINI-STYLE STIRRED AGAVE COCKTAIL IN A SIESTA FORM (I.E., CAMPARI, LIME, GRAPEFRUIT AND TEQUILA).

Grapefruit and apples is a great pairing, hence the apple brandy and Pamplemousse Rose. The Lillet helps bind the ingredients together, and the grapefruit bitters bring out the tequila's earthy, vegetal notes.

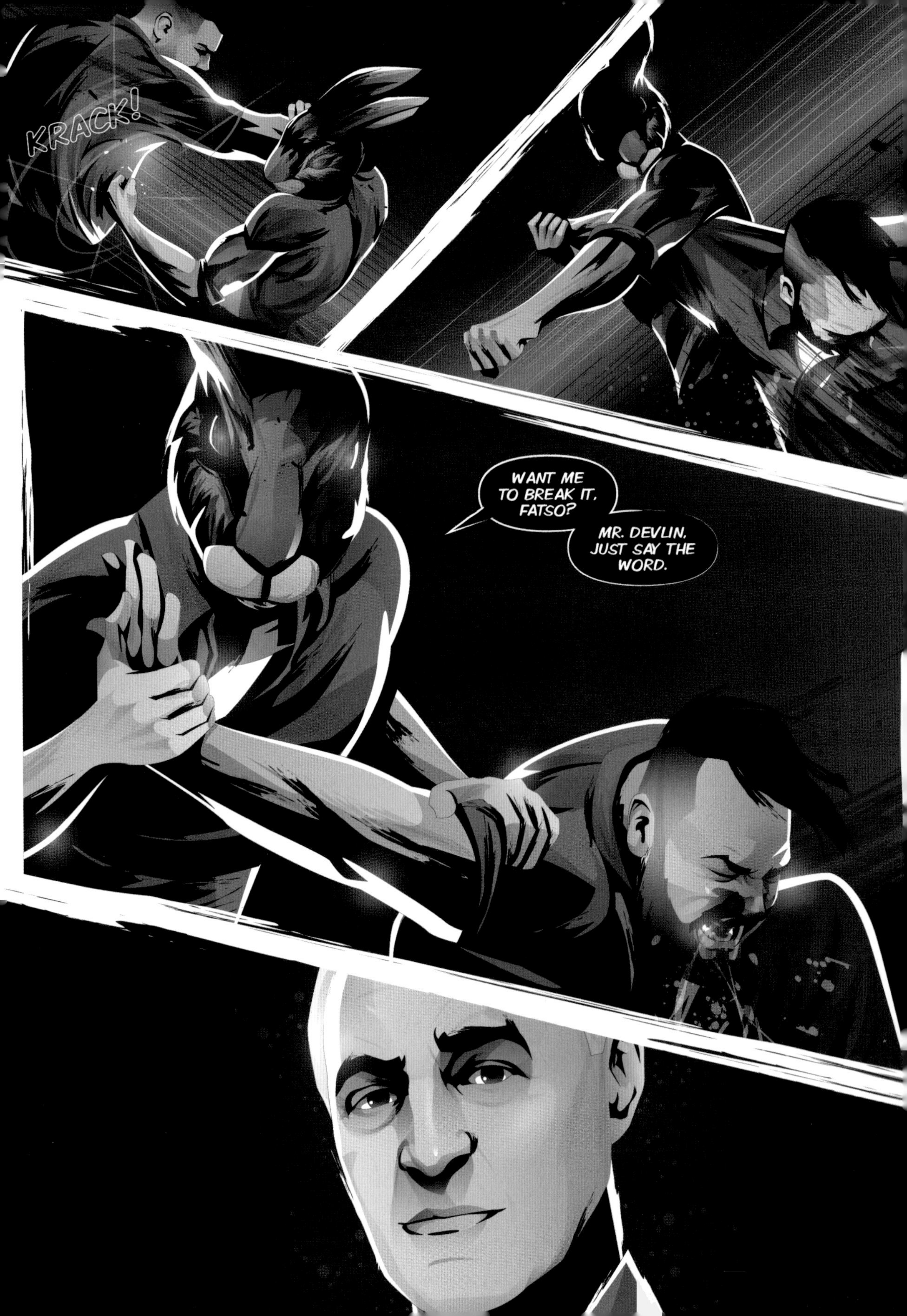
KRACK!
WANT ME TO BREAK IT, FATSO?
MR. DEVLIN, JUST SAY THE WORD.

SUCKER PUNCH

INGREDIENTS

1 DASH	Bittermens Hopped Grapefruit Bitters
0.75 OZ	Lemon juice
0.25 OZ	Raspberry Syrup (page 269)
0.75 OZ	Tomato Syrup (page 274)
0.25 OZ	Barbadillo Manzanilla Sherry
0.5 OZ	Lillet Rosé Vermouth
0.5 OZ	Boomsma Oude Genever
1.5 OZ	123 Organic Uno Blanco Tequila

TOOLS

Jiggers, shaker tins, fine strainer, Hawthorne strainer, ice pick

METHOD

Shake with ice; fine strain and serve with ice nugget

GLASSWARE

Coupette

ORIGIN

Madeleine Solo Rapp

MADELEINE'S INSPIRATION

DID I SAY I REALLY LOVE AGAVE? WELL, HERE I WANTED TO PLAY WITH TOMATO.

I tried it with raspberry and it turned out great. The saltiness from the manzanilla really brought the flavors together. The genever added some depth and fat to the drink, and paired well with the tequila.

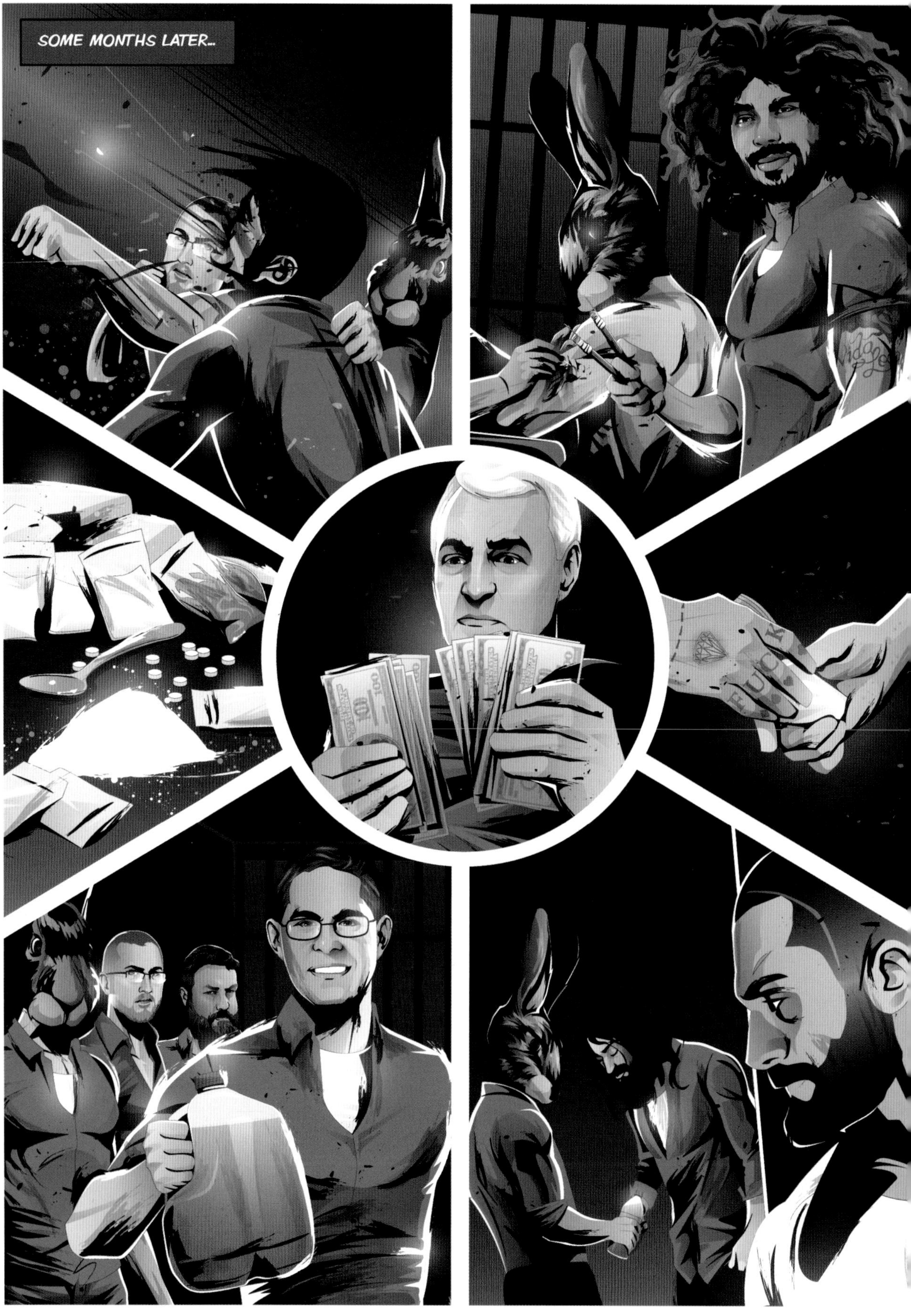
SOME MONTHS LATER...
FUCK

LOAN SHARK

INGREDIENTS

2 DASHES	Tansy Tincture (page 273)
1 DASH	Vieux Pontarlier Absinthe
0.75 OZ	Lime juice
0.5 OZ	Granny Smith Apple Juice (page 259)
0.25 OZ	Vanilla Syrup (page 275)
0.5 OZ	Wasabi Syrup (page 276)
0.5 OZ	Dolin Blanc Vermouth
0.25 OZ	Wray & Nephew White Overproof Rum
1.5 OZ	Citadelle Gin

TOOLS
Jiggers, shaker tins, fine strainer, Hawthorne strainer, ice pick

METHOD
Shake with ice; fine strain and serve with ice nugget

GLASSWARE
Punch glass

ORIGIN
Jillian Vose

JILLIAN'S INSPIRATION

THIS DRINK WAS INSPIRED BY THE GREEN COLOR OF WASABI.

This made me think of lime and green apple, and then spiraled into absinthe and tansy. With such a green list of ingredients, it only seemed fitting to use gin. It needed some length and more depth, so the Dolin Blanc did the trick.

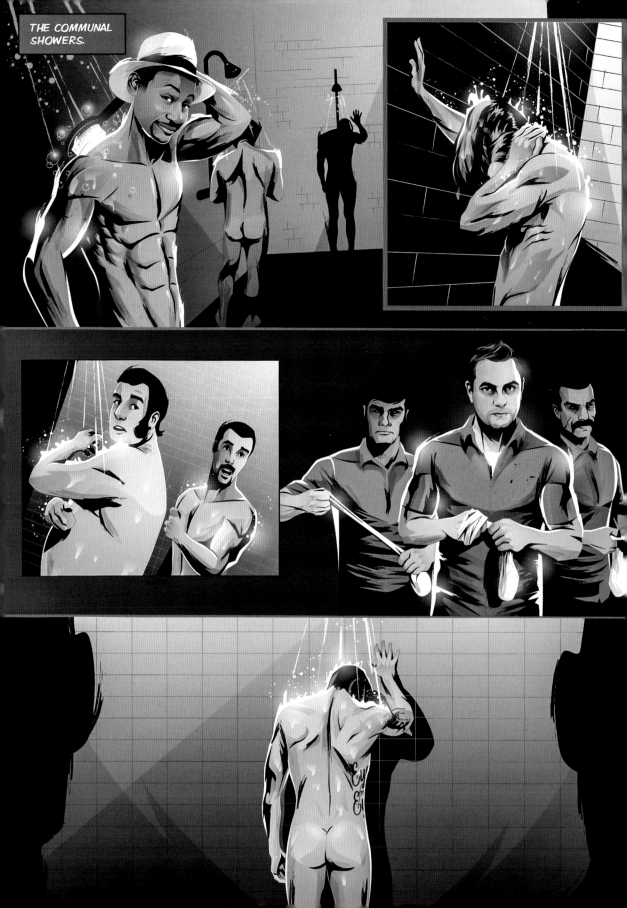

THE COMMUNAL
SHOWERS.

TRUE BLUE

INGREDIENTS

2 DASHES	Peychaud's Bitters
1 TSP	Ginger Syrup (page 259)
0.75 OZ	Lemon juice
0.75 OZ	White Miso Syrup (page 276)
0.25 OZ	Barbadillo Pedro Ximenez Sherry
0.5 OZ	Guinness Draught
0.5 OZ	Clear Creek Apple Brandy
1.5 OZ	Tullamore D.E.W. 12 Year Irish Whiskey

TOOLS
Jiggers, teaspoon, shaker tins, fine strainer, Hawthorne strainer, ice pick, nutmeg grater

METHOD
Shake with ice; fine strain and serve with ice nugget

GLASSWARE
Coupette

GARNISH
Nutmeg

ORIGIN
Harrison Ginsberg

INCARCERATION

117.

TRUE BLUE

HARRISON'S INSPIRATION

I WANTED TO LAYER UMAMI FLAVORS TO MAKE A HARMONIOUS REFRESHING WHISKEY COCKTAIL.

Slightly sweet and salty, this cocktail really explodes on your palate. Apple, ginger and miso complemented the Irish whiskey. The Guinness lends a great texture: frothy, rich, salty and pleasantly refreshing. Savory at its finest.

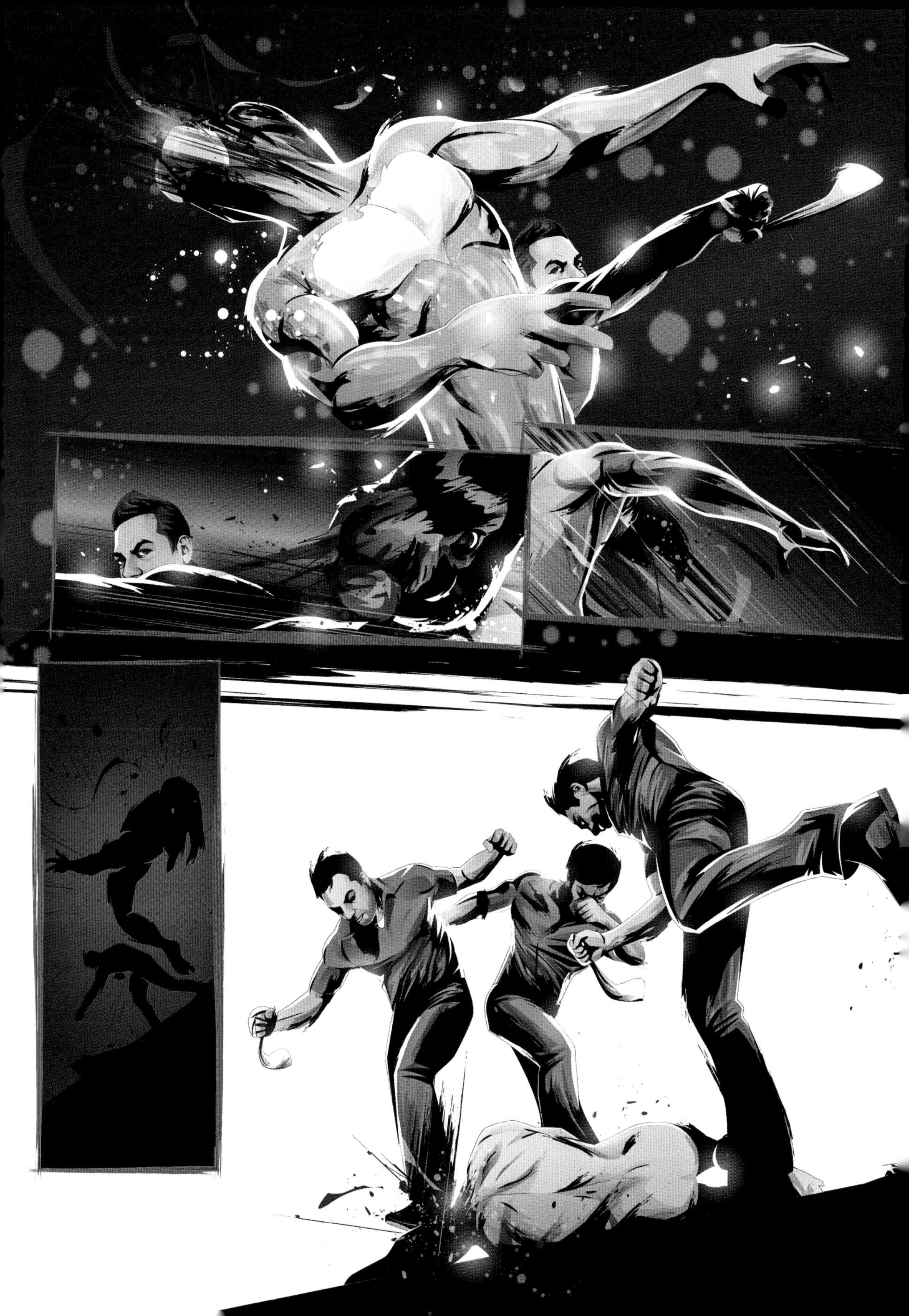

MAELSTROM

INGREDIENTS

1 TSP	Cinnamon Bark Syrup (page 255)
1 TSP	Pür•likör Williams Pear
0.5 OZ	Amero Apertif
0.25 OZ	Combier Crème de Pamplemousse Rose Liqueur
0.75 OZ	Barbadillo Amontillado Sherry
1 OZ	Templeton Rye Whiskey

TOOLS

Jiggers, mixing glass, barspoon, teaspoon, julep strainer

METHOD

Stir with ice; strain with julep strainer; serve up without ice

GLASSWARE

Nick & Nora

GARNISH

Lemon oil (discard peel)

ORIGIN

Alan McGillivray

119.

ALAN'S INSPIRATION

A BIT MORE THAN A COIN'S THROW FROM A BOULEVARDIER, BUT IT'S IN THERE SOMEWHERE.

With summer in mind and a classic to work from, I replaced each part of the classic with a cousin of the original for a light-bodied and slightly floral sipper. For depth, I paired each component with a complementing flavor: pamplemousse with amero, cinnamon with amontillado and pear with rye.

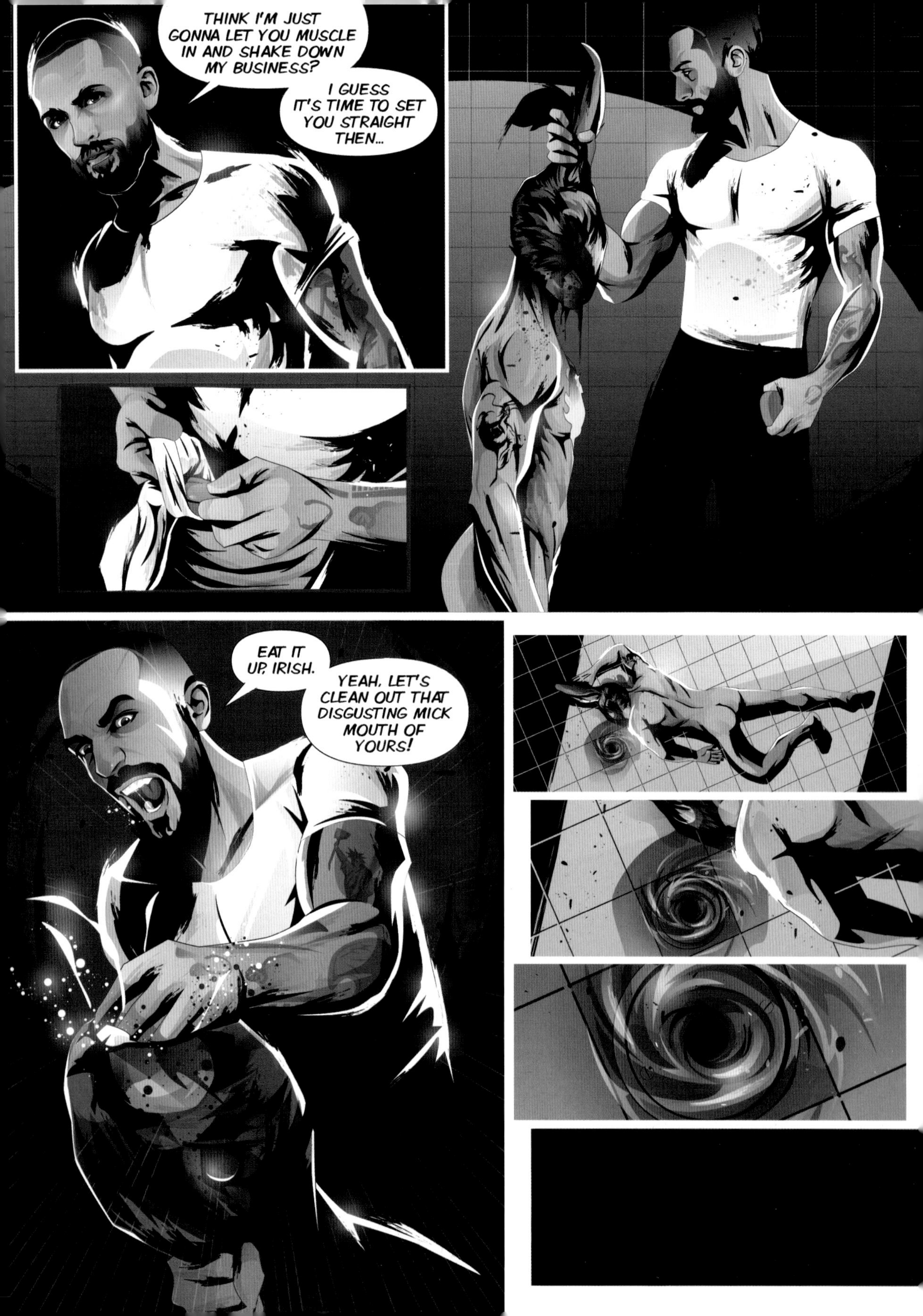
THINK I'M JUST GONNA LET YOU MUSCLE IN AND SHAKE DOWN MY BUSINESS?
I GUESS IT'S TIME TO SET YOU STRAIGHT THEN...
EAT IT UP, IRISH.
YEAH, LET'S CLEAN OUT THAT DISGUSTING MICK MOUTH OF YOURS!

SWITCHBLADE

INGREDIENTS

2 DASHES	Bittercube Blackstrap Bitters
0.25 OZ	Banana Syrup (page 251)
0.5 OZ	Pierre Ferrand Pineau des Charentes
1 OZ	Noilly Prat Dry Vermouth
1.5 OZ	Coconut-Infused Pisco (page 255)

TOOLS

Jiggers, mixing glass, spoon, julep strainer

METHOD

Stir with ice; strain with julep strainer and serve up without ice

GLASSWARE

Nick & Nora

ORIGIN

Jillian Vose

JILLIAN'S INSPIRATION

I WANTED TO DO A 50/50 MARTINI VARIATION; ALSO, I'D NEVER REALLY DONE A COCONUT DRINK WITHOUT COCO LÓPEZ.

I did an infusion, and the pisco worked really nicely. It was elegant and subtle so it could be used in a stirred drink. I built the drink by adding other tropical components and the dry vermouth and Pineau des Charentes for length.

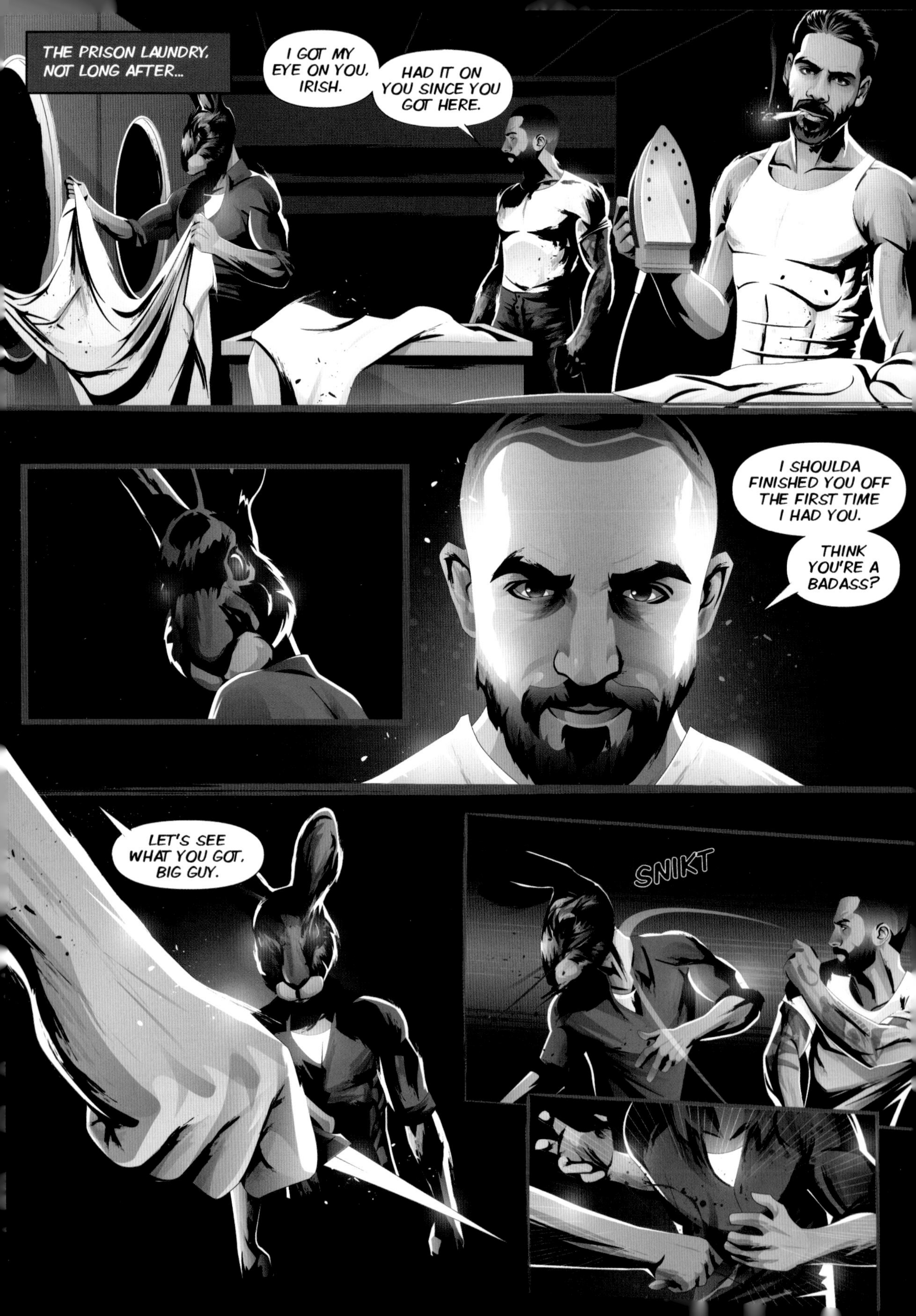
THE PRISON LAUNDRY, NOT LONG AFTER...
I GOT MY EYE ON YOU, IRISH.
HAD IT ON YOU SINCE YOU GOT HERE.
I SHOULDA FINISHED YOU OFF THE FIRST TIME I HAD YOU.
THINK YOU'RE A BADASS?
LET'S SEE WHAT YOU GOT, BIG GUY.
SNIKT

CUT AND DRY

INGREDIENTS

5 DASHES	Scrappy's Firewater Habanero Tincture
0.75 OZ	Lime juice
0.25 OZ	Sumac Syrup (page 272)
0.5 OZ	Passion Berry Syrup (page 266)
0.5 OZ	Royal Combier Liqueur
2 OZ	Plantation 3 Stars Rum

TOOLS
Jiggers, shaker tins, fine strainer, Hawthorne strainer, nutmeg grater

METHOD
Shake with ice; fine strain and serve up without ice

GLASSWARE
Sour glass

GARNISH
Nutmeg

ORIGIN
Jillian Vose

JILLIAN'S INSPIRATION

THIS IS A FRESH AND SPICY DRINK OUR GUESTS CONSTANTLY ASK FOR.

The first time I smelled passion berry my brain almost exploded. It was like passion fruit, with a really cool herbal quality. The tangy passion berry and sumac, contrasted with spicy habanero in a dry daiquiri format, work delightfully.

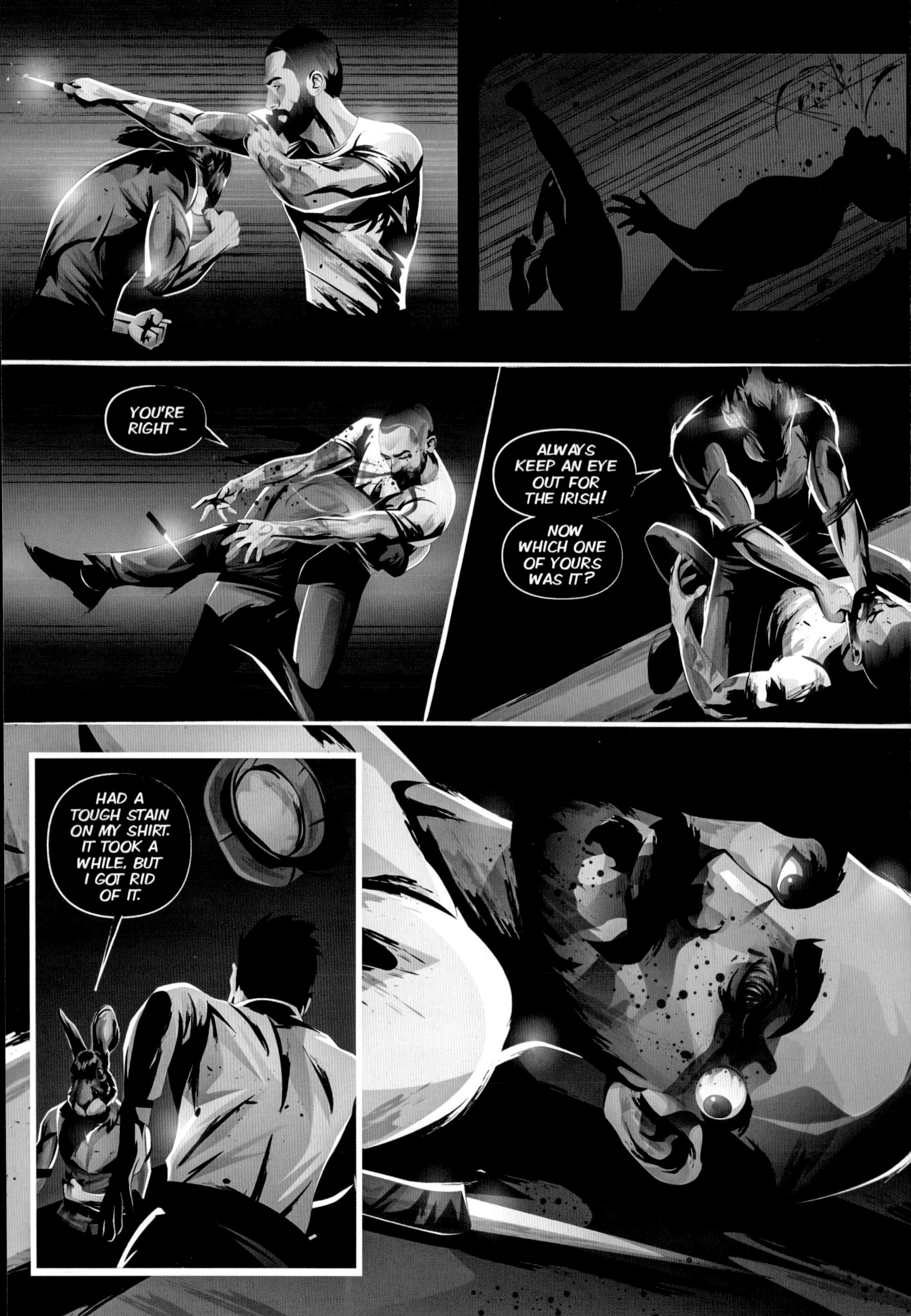

YOU'RE RIGHT -
ALWAYS KEEP AN EYE OUT FOR THE IRISH!
NOW WHICH ONE OF YOURS WAS IT?
HAD A TOUGH STAIN ON MY SHIRT. IT TOOK A WHILE, BUT I GOT RID OF IT.

SHADOWBOXER

INGREDIENTS

1 DASH	House Orange Bitters (page 261)
0.75 OZ	Lemon juice
0.5 OZ	Carrot juice
0.5 OZ	Orange Sherbet (page 265)
0.5 OZ	Paprika Syrup (page 266)
0.75 OZ	Barbadillo Oloroso Sherry
0.75 OZ	Novo Fogo Tanager Cachaça
1 OZ	Chief Gowanus New Netherland Gin

TOOLS
Jiggers, shaker tins, fine strainer, Hawthorne strainer, nutmeg grater, ice pick

METHOD
Shake with ice; fine strain and serve with ice nugget

GLASSWARE
Punch glass

GARNISH
Nutmeg

ORIGIN
Jillian Vose

125.

JILLIAN'S INSPIRATION

THIS DRINK WAS INSPIRED BY THE CHIEF GOWANUS NEW NETHERLAND GIN.

It's a unique spirit with a rye base flavored with juniper and hops. I introduced the paprika and carrot to match the gin's savory quality. The other components are the balancing act for the bases to shine.

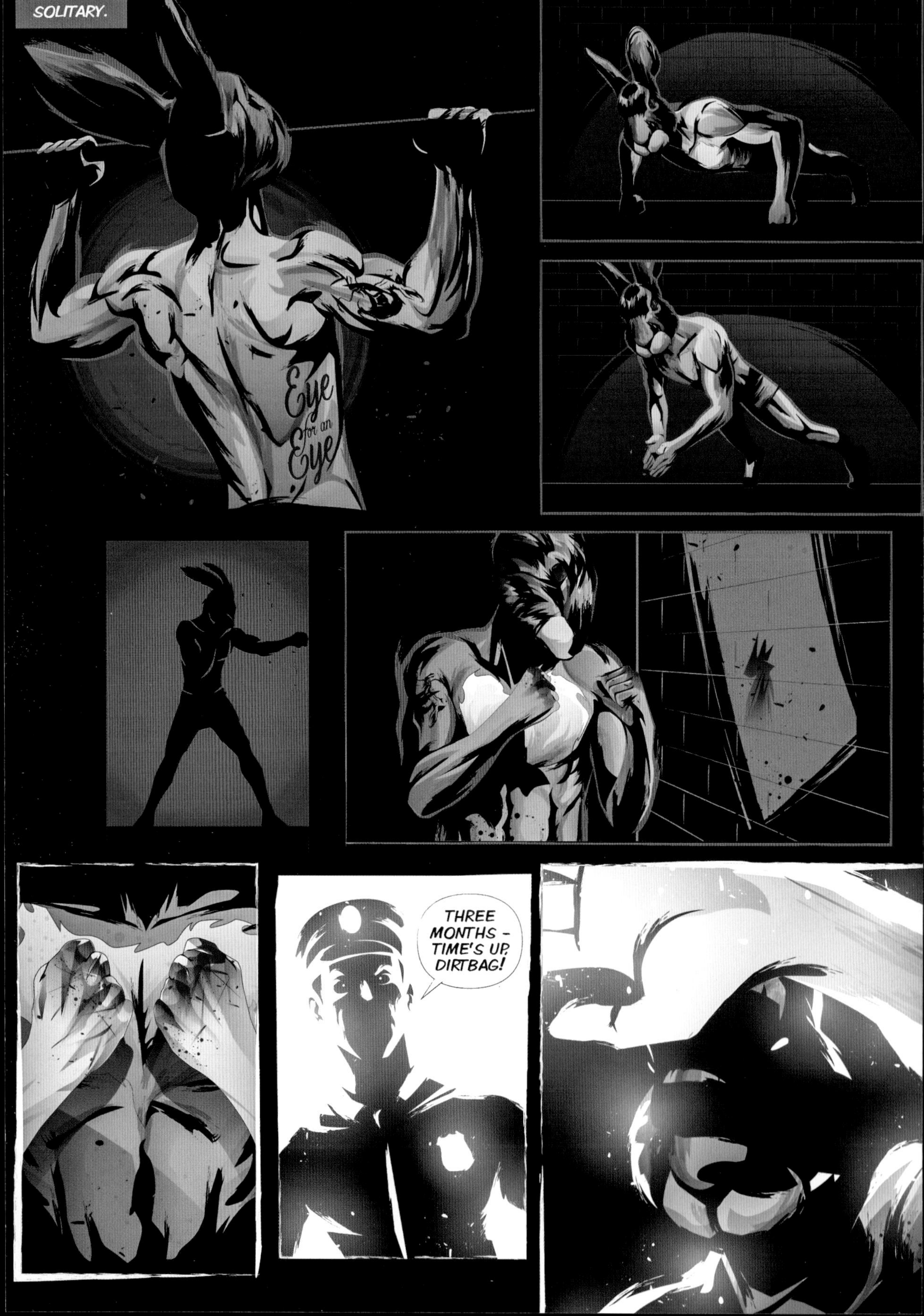
SOLITARY.
Eye for an Eye
THREE MONTHS - TIME'S UP, DIRTBAG!

GOODY TWO-SHOES

INGREDIENTS

1 TSP	Pomegranate Syrup (page 267)
0.25 OZ	Amaro Averna
0.5 OZ	Noilly Prat Ambré Vermouth
0.5 OZ	Ancho Chili–Infused Sweet Vermouth (page 250)
0.25 OZ	Del Maguey Mezcal Vida
1.5 OZ	Pumpkin Seed–Washed Powers Gold Irish Whiskey (page 268)

TOOLS
Jiggers, mixing glass, barspoon, julep strainer

METHOD
Stir with ice; strain with julep strainer and serve up without ice

GLASSWARE
Nick & Nora

GARNISH
Orange oil (discard peel)

ORIGIN
Harrison Ginsberg

127.

HARRISON'S INSPIRATION

I WANTED TO TAKE THE QUINTESSENTIAL MEXICAN FALL FLAVORS AND PUT THEM INTO A MANHATTAN-STYLE COCKTAIL.

Chilis, calabaza (pumpkin), herbs and dark fruits. Herbaceous amaro and vermouth, combined with ancho chilis, pomegranate and a touch of mezcal made for a great base. The infused whiskey ties it together and adds a nutty backbone.

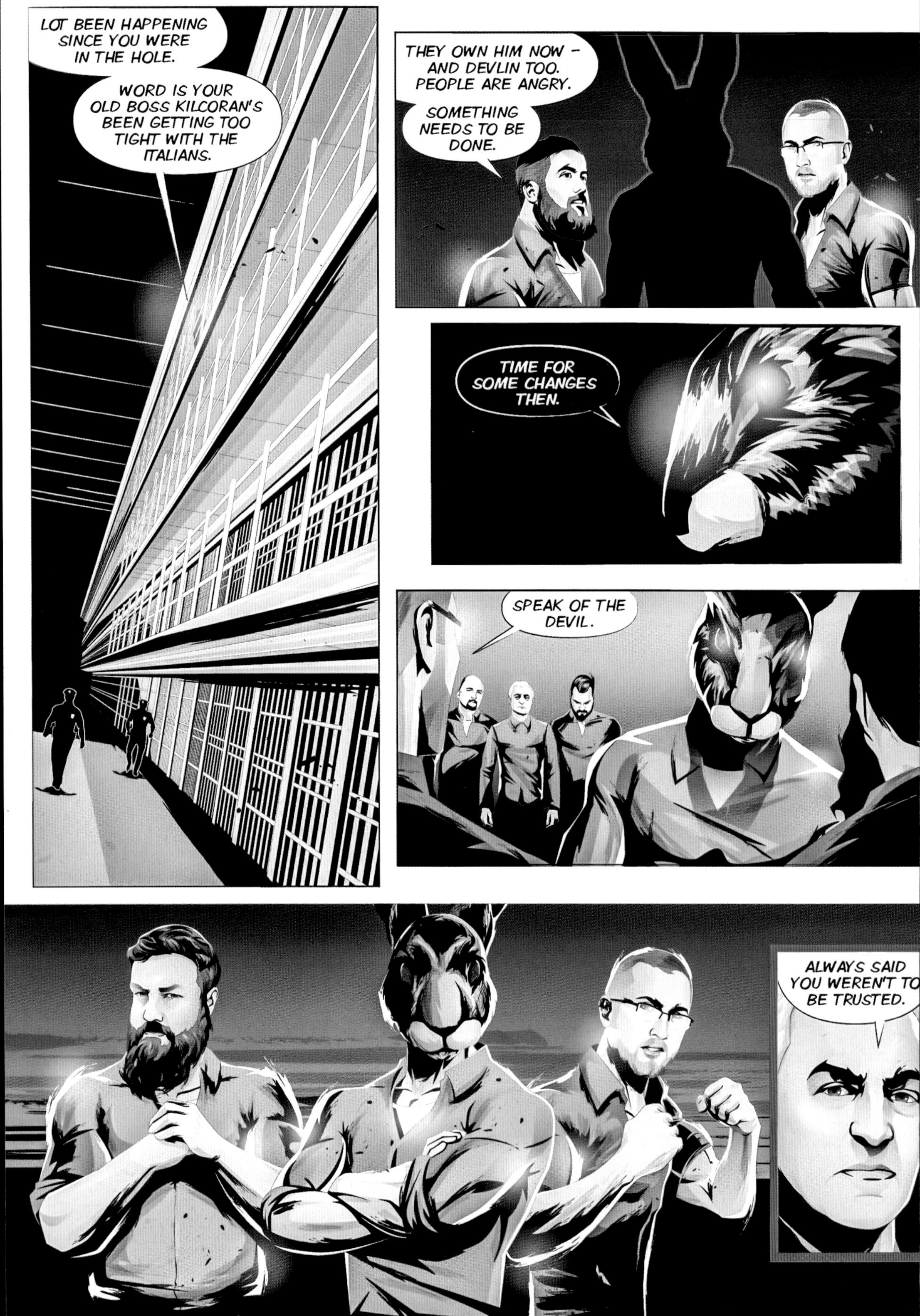
LOT BEEN HAPPENING SINCE YOU WERE IN THE HOLE.
WORD IS YOUR OLD BOSS KILCORAN'S BEEN GETTING TOO TIGHT WITH THE ITALIANS.
THEY OWN HIM NOW – AND DEVLIN TOO. PEOPLE ARE ANGRY.
SOMETHING NEEDS TO BE DONE.
TIME FOR SOME CHANGES THEN.
SPEAK OF THE DEVIL.
ALWAYS SAID YOU WEREN'T TO BE TRUSTED.

RIOT ACT

INGREDIENTS

2 DASHES	Saline Solution (page 270)
1 DASH	Bitter Truth Aromatic Bitters
0.5 OZ	Nonino Amaro
0.5 OZ	Genmaicha Tea Syrup (page 259)
1 OZ	Torres 15 Year Spanish Brandy
1 OZ	Grilled Pineapple–Infused Bols Genever

TOOLS
Jiggers, mixing glass, barspoon, julep strainer, ice pick

METHOD
Stir with ice; strain with julep strainer and serve over large block of ice

GLASSWARE
Old Fashioned

GARNISH
Lemon oil (discard peel)

ORIGIN
Jillian Vose

JILLIAN'S INSPIRATION

THE GRILLED PINEAPPLE– INFUSED BOLS GENEVER WE HAVE MAKES FOR A RICH, TROPICAL AND MALTY COMBINATION.

Brown rice syrup matched the flavor profile but gave an unappealing, cloudy presentation. Genmaicha tea is a brown-rice green tea with brown rice kernels that seemed to do the trick. We steeped it and made a syrup. I'm fond of split bases for extra layers, and aged Spanish brandy balances the genever, giving beautiful dark fruit notes.

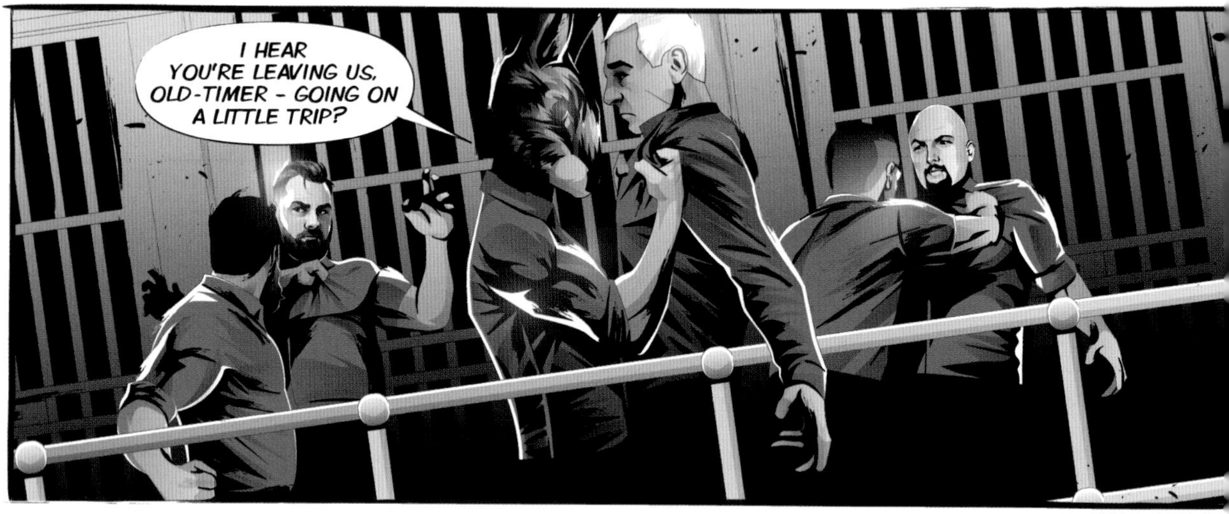
I HEAR YOU'RE LEAVING US, OLD-TIMER - GOING ON A LITTLE TRIP?

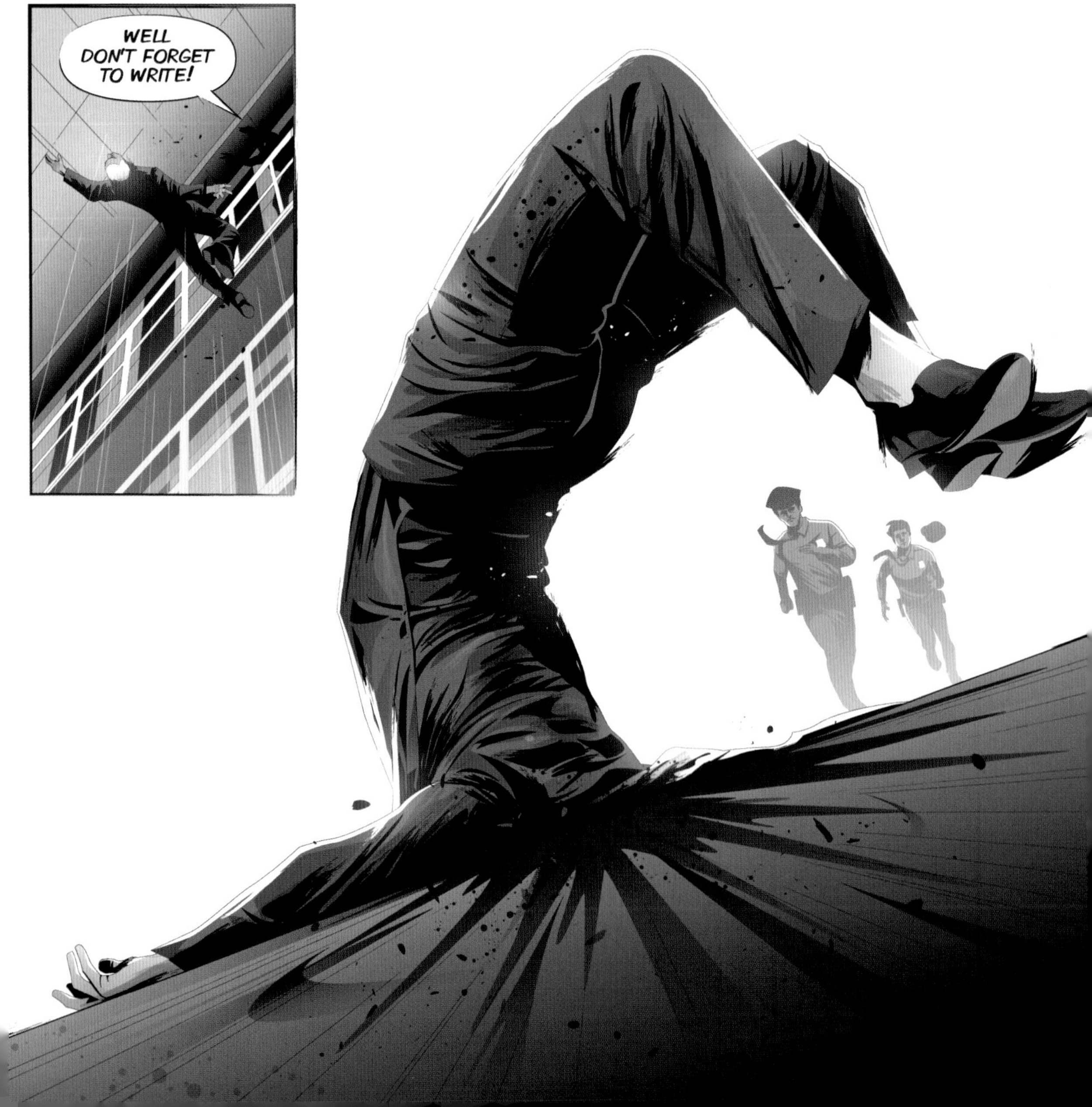
WELL DON'T FORGET TO WRITE!

HUSH MONEY

INGREDIENTS

1 DASH	Bitter Truth Aromatic Bitters
1 TSP	Pecan Orgeat (page 267)
0.5 OZ	Campari
0.5 OZ	Pür•likör Spiced Blood Orange
0.5 OZ	Cocchi Vermouth di Torino
1.5 OZ	Chase Smoked Vodka

TOOLS
Jiggers, mixing glass, barspoon, teaspoon, julep strainer

METHOD
Stir with ice; strain with julep strainer and serve up without ice

GLASSWARE
Nick & Nora

GARNISH
Lemon oil (discard peel)

ORIGIN
Jillian Vose

131.

JILLIAN'S INSPIRATION

WHEN WE DO VODKA DRINKS, WE REALLY TRY TO INCORPORATE INGREDIENTS AND STYLES OF DRINKS THAT YOU WOULDN'T NORMALLY ASSOCIATE WITH THE SPIRIT.

I thought that Chase made a really great smoked vodka and immediately after trying it, a negroni variation popped into my mind . . .

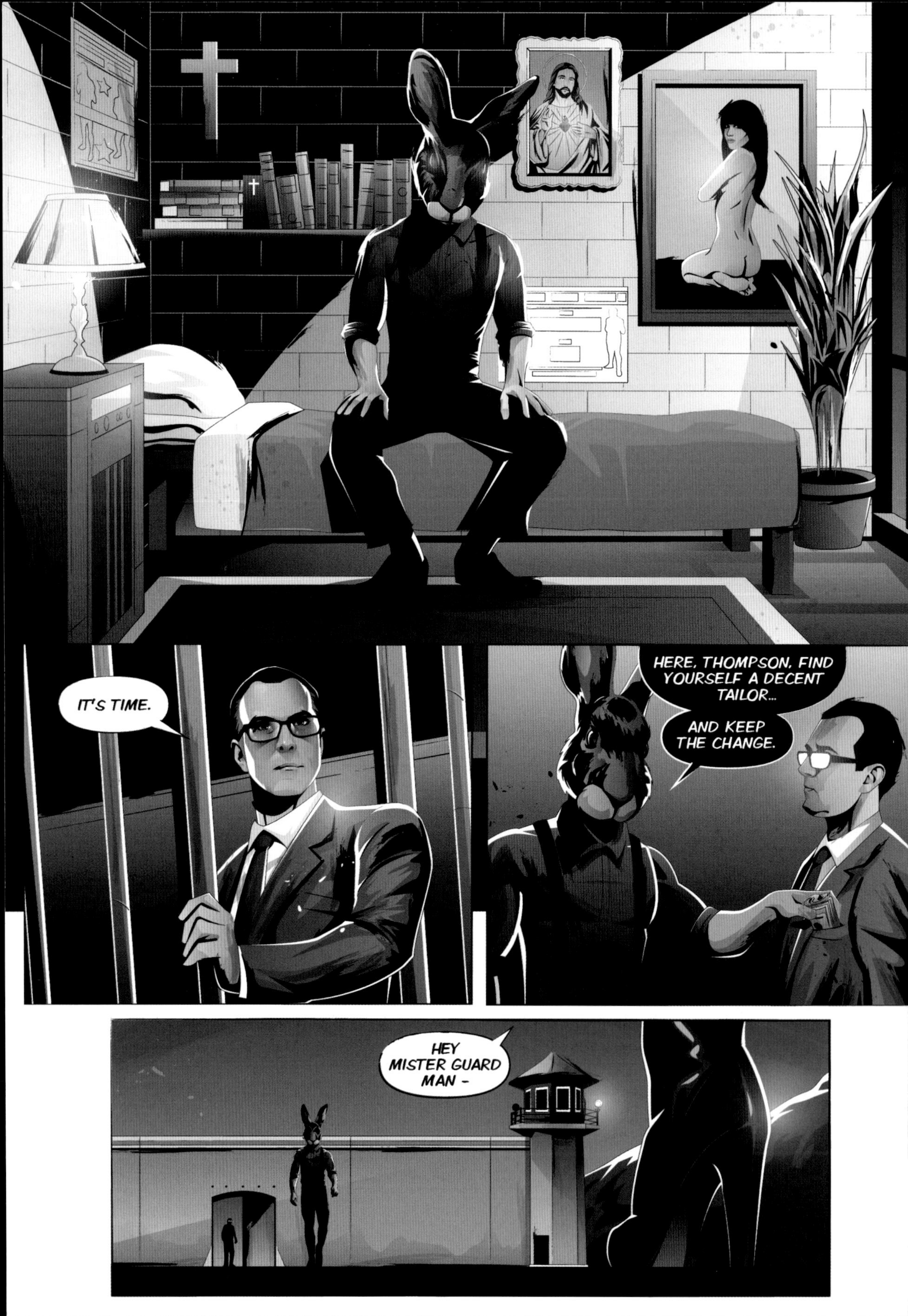
IT'S TIME.
HERE, THOMPSON, FIND YOURSELF A DECENT TAILOR...
AND KEEP THE CHANGE.
HEY MISTER GUARD MAN -

HOLY SMOKE

INGREDIENTS

1 TSP	Matcha Green Tea Coco López (page 264)
1 DASH	Bitter Truth Decanter Bitters
0.5 OZ	Lime juice
0.5 OZ	Pineapple juice
0.5 OZ	Half & half
0.25 OZ	Vanilla Syrup (page 275)
0.5 OZ	Tonka Bean Cane Syrup (page 274)
0.5 OZ	Pierre Ferrand Dry Curaçao
0.25 OZ	Plantation OFTD Rum
0.5 OZ	Ardbeg 10 Years Old Scotch
1 OZ	Glenmorangie Original Scotch
1	Curry leaf

TOOLS
Jiggers, teaspoon, shaker tins, fine strainer, Hawthorne strainer, nutmeg grater

METHOD
Build drink in tin; add curry leaf (do not muddle); whip shake with ice; fine strain and serve over pebble ice

GLASSWARE
Highball

GARNISH
Nutmeg

ORIGIN
Jillian Vose

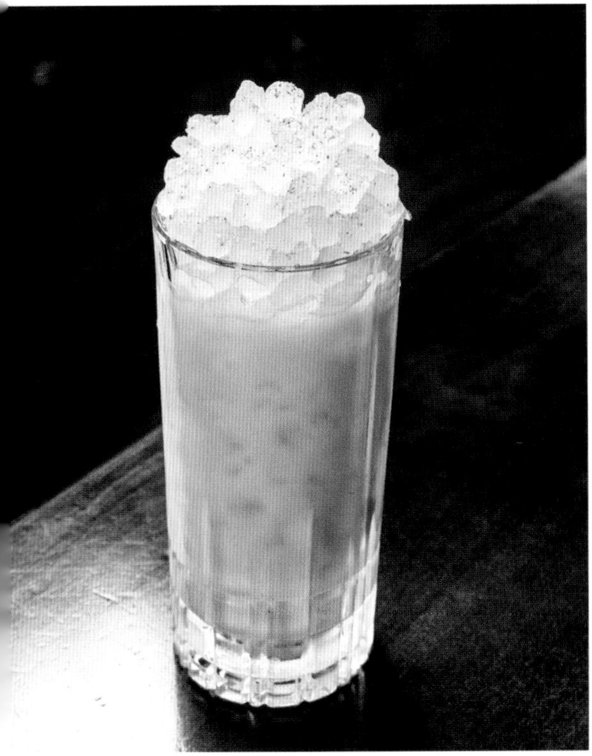

JILLIAN'S INSPIRATION

THIS DRINK WAS INSPIRED BY A TIKI DRINK I DID A LONG TIME AGO USING BOWMORE – A SMOKY SINGLE MALT SCOTCH.

The original turned out surprisingly tasty, and I've since made several variations. I knew that curry leaf, coconut and peat all work together, so I started there. Pineapple was added to fatten it up, but also to give it a tropical note. I added a touch of half & half to complement the Coco López and vanilla for sweetness. Then, a balance of heavily peated scotch, a milder and fruitier single malt scotch and a high-proof rum – because, well we're talking tiki, right?

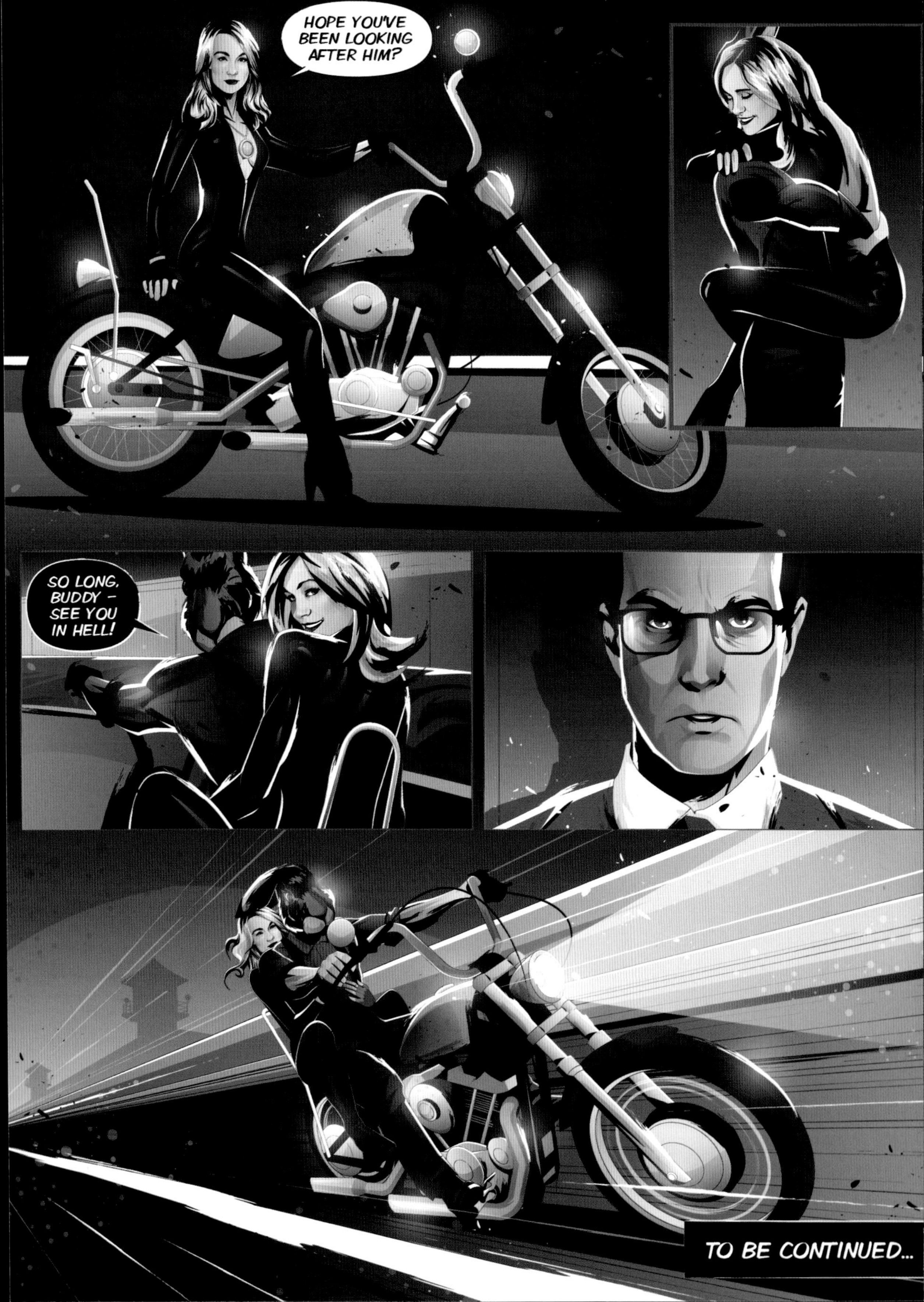
HOPE YOU'VE BEEN LOOKING AFTER HIM?
SO LONG, BUDDY - SEE YOU IN HELL!
TO BE CONTINUED...

HUNKY DORY

INGREDIENTS

1	Whole egg
1 DASH	Angostura Bitters
0.25 OZ	Lemon juice
0.5 OZ	Cane Syrup (page 254)
0.25 OZ	Walnut Orgeat (page 275)
0.25 OZ	Barley Orgeat (page 251)
0.25 OZ	Smith & Cross Jamaican Rum
0.25 OZ	Amaro Nardini
0.25 OZ	Clear Creek Apple Brandy
0.5 OZ	Half & half
0.75 OZ	Laird's Straight Apple Brandy
0.75 OZ	Powers Signature Release Irish Whiskey

TOOLS

Jiggers, shaker tins, fine strainer, Hawthorne strainer, nutmeg grater, ice pick

METHOD

Dry shake; shake with ice; fine strain and serve with chunk of ice

GLASSWARE

Nog glass

GARNISH

Nutmeg

ORIGIN

Nick Rolin

135.

NICK'S INSPIRATION

I BEGAN WITH THE CLASSIC FALL COMBINATION OF WALNUTS AND APPLES.

However, the tannin in walnuts makes it a difficult, astringent ingredient. Three ingredients allowed me to turn the corner: barley, Jamaican rum and raw egg yolk. A little acidity from lemon and some spice from amaro filled out the flavor profile.

(And, yes, we batch some of these ingredients for service.)

ADVERSITY AND HARDSHIP CAN SHAPE YOU OR BREAK YOU.

THEY PUT CHARACTER TO THE TEST
AND MAKE YOU QUESTION ALL
THAT YOU HAVE KNOWN.
WHAT ARE YOU TRULY MADE OF?
WHAT ARE YOU CAPABLE OF?

For John Morrissey, the raging spirit of the
Dead Rabbits at large in a world that is not his own,
there is no question. His is a resolve tempered, like
steel, in the white heat of fury.

AND NOW THINGS ARE
ABOUT TO BURN.

NEW YORK U.S.A.

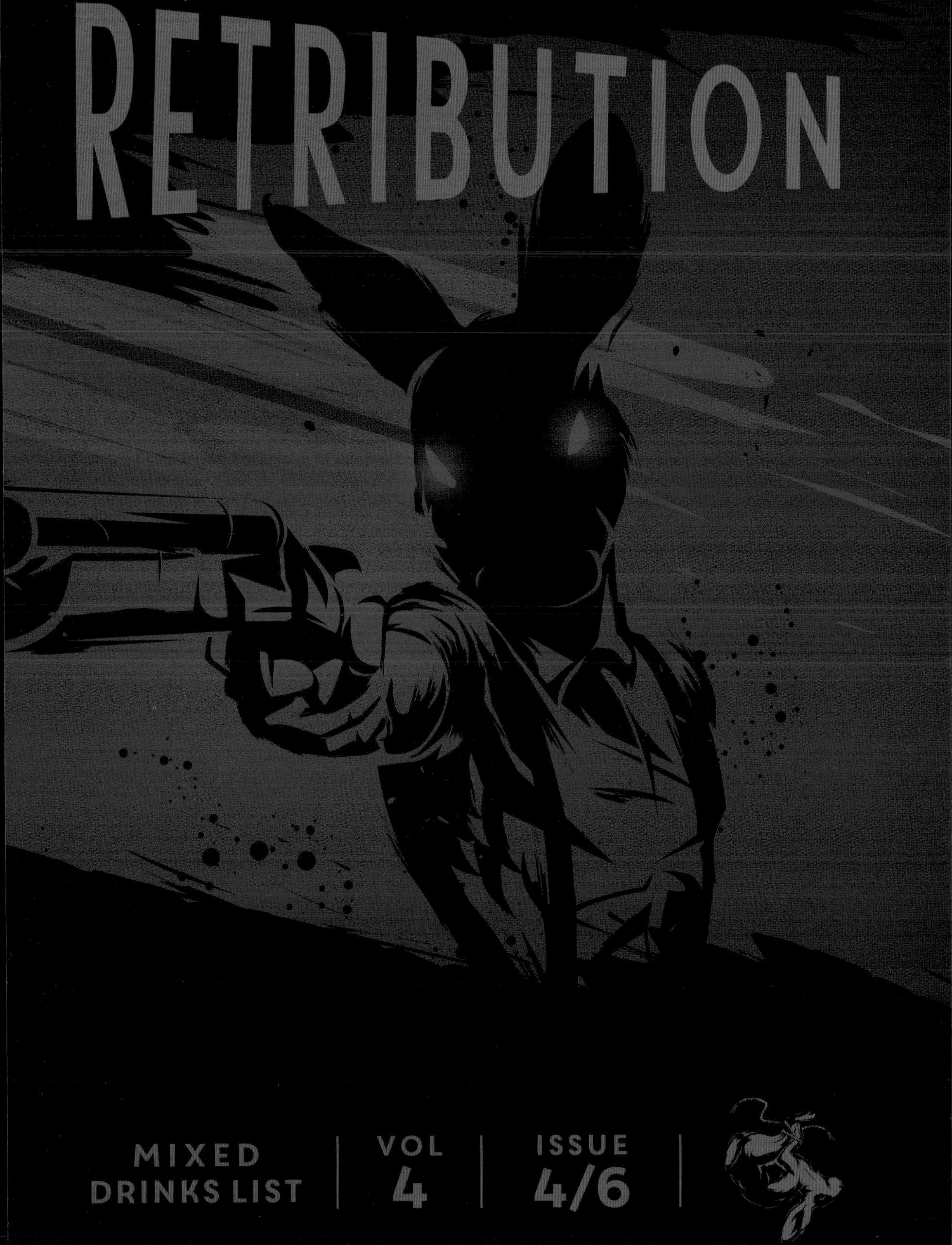
RETRIBUTION
MIXED DRINKS LIST
VOL 4
ISSUE 4/6

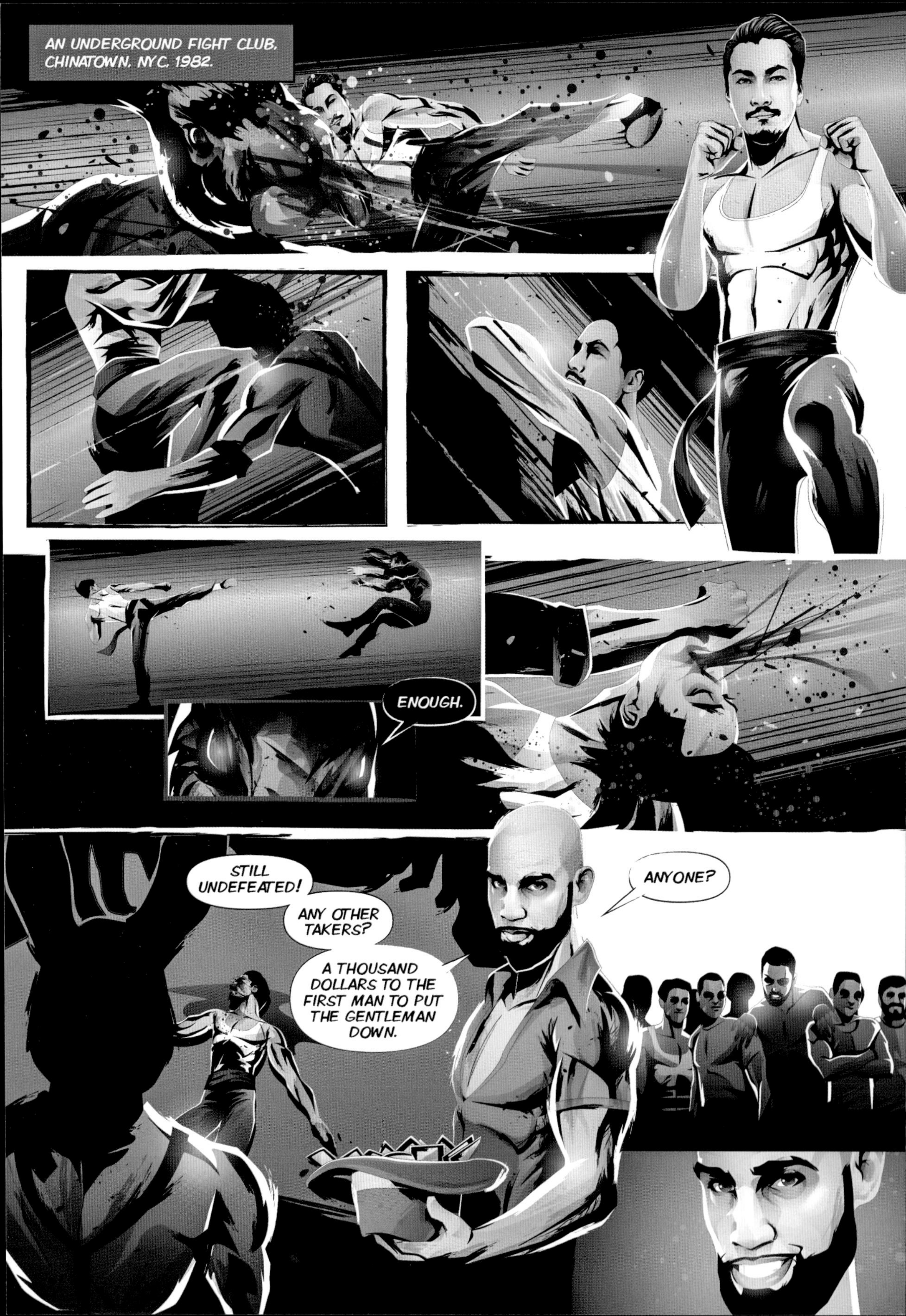
AN UNDERGROUND FIGHT CLUB. CHINATOWN, NYC. 1982.
ENOUGH.
STILL UNDEFEATED!
ANY OTHER TAKERS?
A THOUSAND DOLLARS TO THE FIRST MAN TO PUT THE GENTLEMAN DOWN.
ANYONE?

GODZILLA

INGREDIENTS

1 DASH	Peychaud's Bitters
1 TSP	Cinnamon Bark Syrup (page 255)
1 OZ	Lillet Rosé
0.5 OZ	Clear Creek Reserve 8 Year Apple Brandy
1.5 OZ	Italicus Rosolio
0.5 OZ	Soda water
1.5 OZ	Champagne (not to be shaken with other ingredients)

TOOLS

Jiggers, teaspoon, shaker tins, ice pick

METHOD

Whip shake with 15 pieces of pebble ice until ice is melted; add soda water and Champagne to tin; pour into highball glass filled with cracked ice

GLASSWARE

Highball

GARNISH

Grapefruit oils (discard peel)

ORIGIN

Jillian Vose

139.

JILLIAN'S INSPIRATION

ITALICUS WAS DEVELOPED BY OUR FRIEND GIUSEPPE GALLO, AND AS IT HAPPENED, HE WAS TO BE FEATURED IN THIS PARTICULAR COMIC.

So I wanted to come up with a drink that would be placed in the scene where he appeared. The Rosolio called out for a a refreshing spritz rather than a complex tiki-style drink. It then became a matter of matching the bergamot and floral elements with other subtle flavors including cinnamon and apple. Champagne and soda were a must – and voilà!

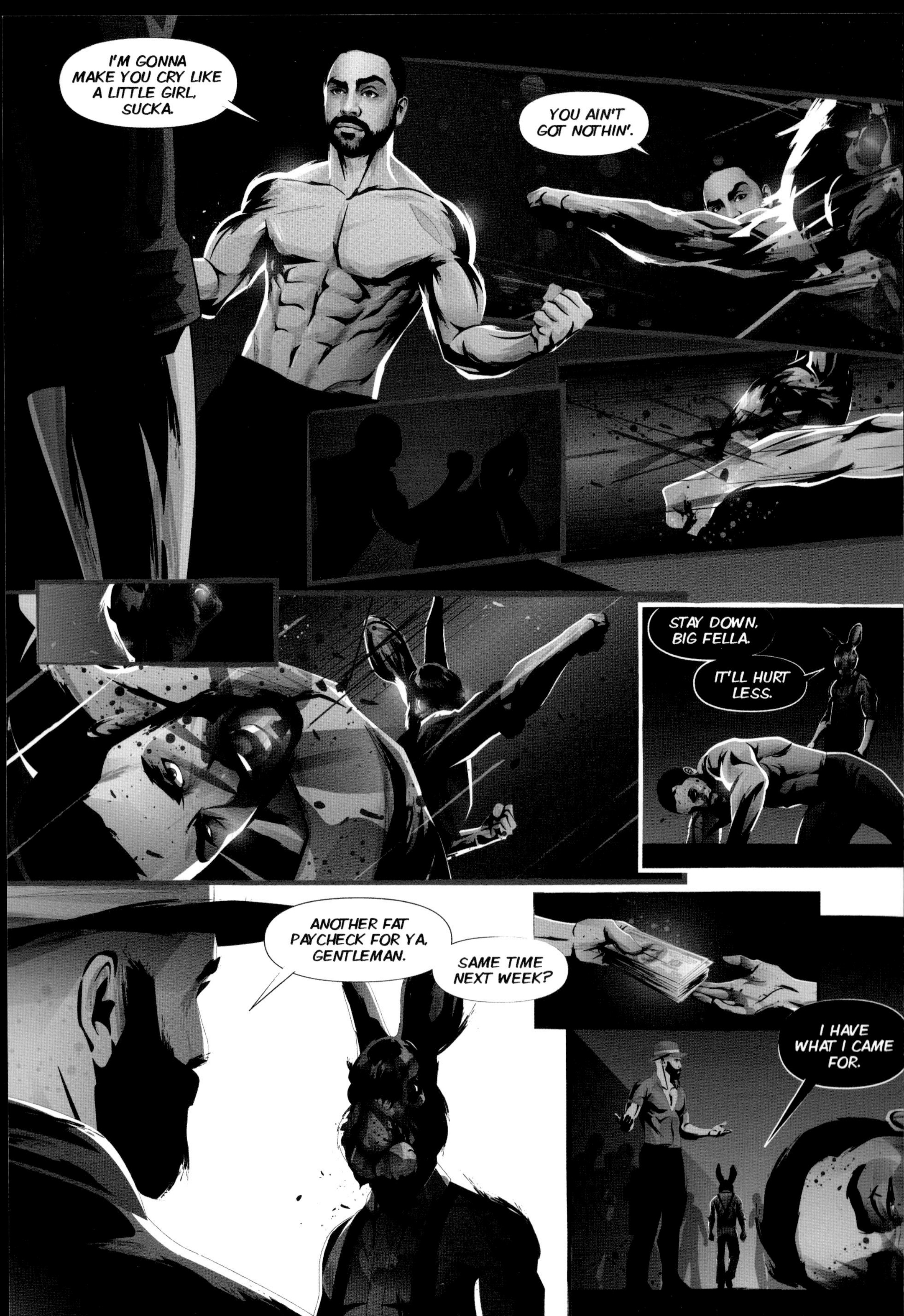
I'M GONNA MAKE YOU CRY LIKE A LITTLE GIRL, SUCKA.
YOU AIN'T GOT NOTHIN'.
STAY DOWN, BIG FELLA.
IT'LL HURT LESS.
ANOTHER FAT PAYCHECK FOR YA, GENTLEMAN.
SAME TIME NEXT WEEK?
I HAVE WHAT I CAME FOR.

DARK HORSE

INGREDIENTS

1 DASH	Dale DeGroff's Pimento Bitters
0.75 OZ	Lemon juice
0.25 OZ	Nutmeg Syrup (page 264)
0.5 OZ	Banana Syrup (page 251)
0.5 OZ	Green Spot Irish Whiskey
1 OZ	Alvear Pale Cream Sherry
1.5 OZ	Barbadillo Amontillado Sherry

TOOLS

Jiggers, shaker tins, fine strainer, Hawthorne strainer, nutmeg grater

METHOD

Shake with ice; fine strain and serve up without ice

GLASSWARE

Sour glass

GARNISH

Nutmeg

ORIGIN

Gregory Buda

GREGORY'S INSPIRATION

THIS COCKTAIL IS A DELICATE, LOW-PROOF SOUR WITH AMONTILLADO SHERRY AS THE BASE.

I've always loved the combination of banana and amontillado, so it was a natural pairing. The Green Spot Irish Whiskey provides just enough punch and body to balance the drink, with the nutmeg and allspice added for complexity.

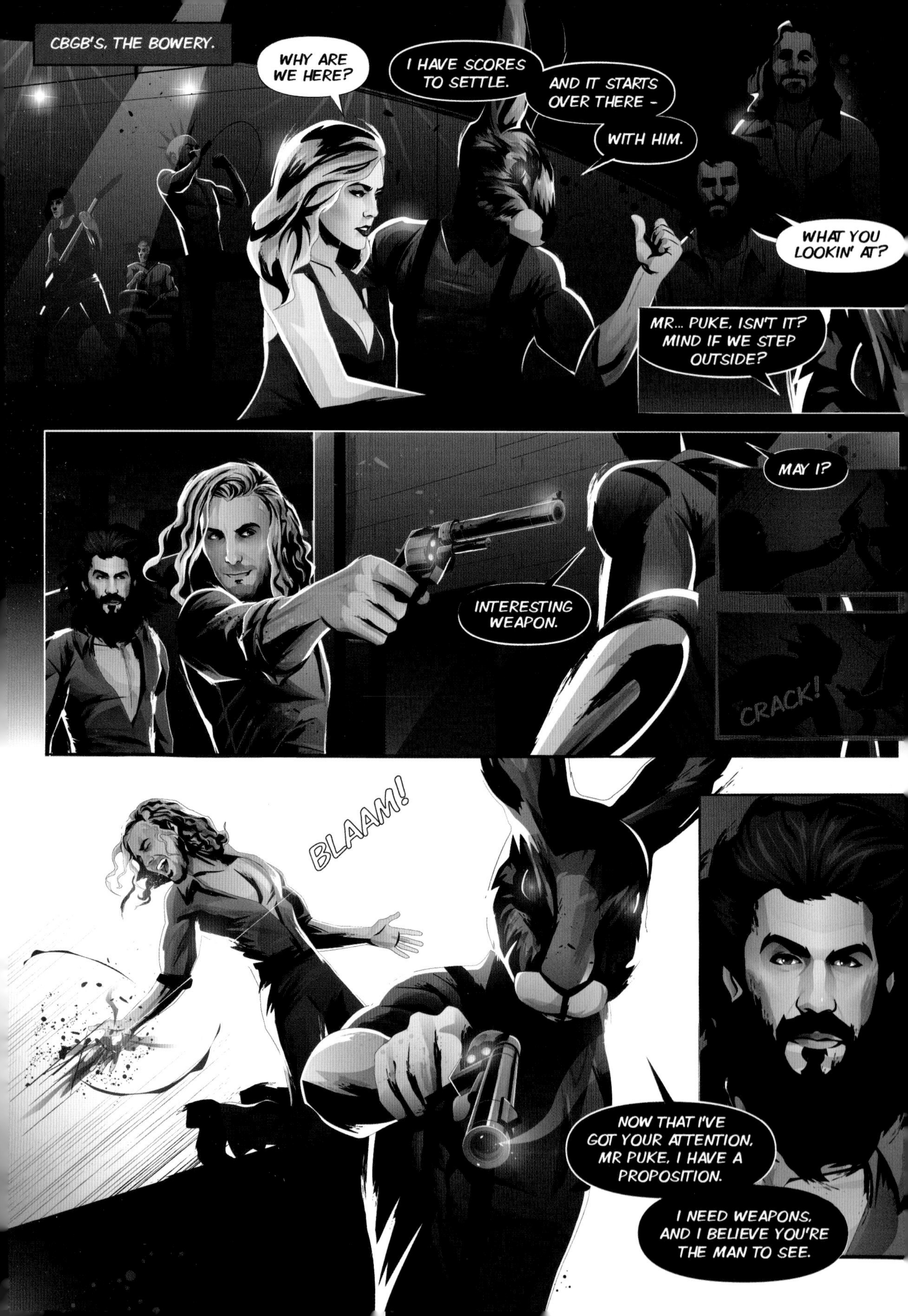
CBGB'S, THE BOWERY.
WHY ARE WE HERE?
I HAVE SCORES TO SETTLE.
AND IT STARTS OVER THERE -
WITH HIM.
WHAT YOU LOOKIN' AT?
MR... PUKE, ISN'T IT? MIND IF WE STEP OUTSIDE?
MAY I?
INTERESTING WEAPON.
CRACK!
BLAAM!
NOW THAT I'VE GOT YOUR ATTENTION, MR PUKE, I HAVE A PROPOSITION.
I NEED WEAPONS, AND I BELIEVE YOU'RE THE MAN TO SEE.

HAT TRICK

INGREDIENTS

1 DASH	Bittermens Boston Bittahs
1 DASH	Peychaud's Bitters
1 OZ	Lime juice
0.25 OZ	Giffard Banane du Brésil
0.25 OZ	Blume Marillen Apricot Eau-de-Vie
0.75 OZ	Passion Fruit Syrup (page 266)
1.5 OZ	Banks 5 Island Blend Rum

TOOLS
Jiggers, shaker tins, fine strainer, Hawthorne strainer

METHOD
Shake with ice; fine strain and serve up without ice

GLASSWARE
Sour glass

ORIGIN
Jillian Vose

JILLIAN'S INSPIRATION

THIS FITS THE MENU'S DAIQUIRI BOX.

The twist is tangy passion fruit with apricot and banana as background notes. I based the drink off Banks rum and around Stilo Pimentel, who works with Banks and was to be featured in the menu. It was easy to make a delightful daiquiri drink with fun and bright ingredients to match his relaxed demeanor.

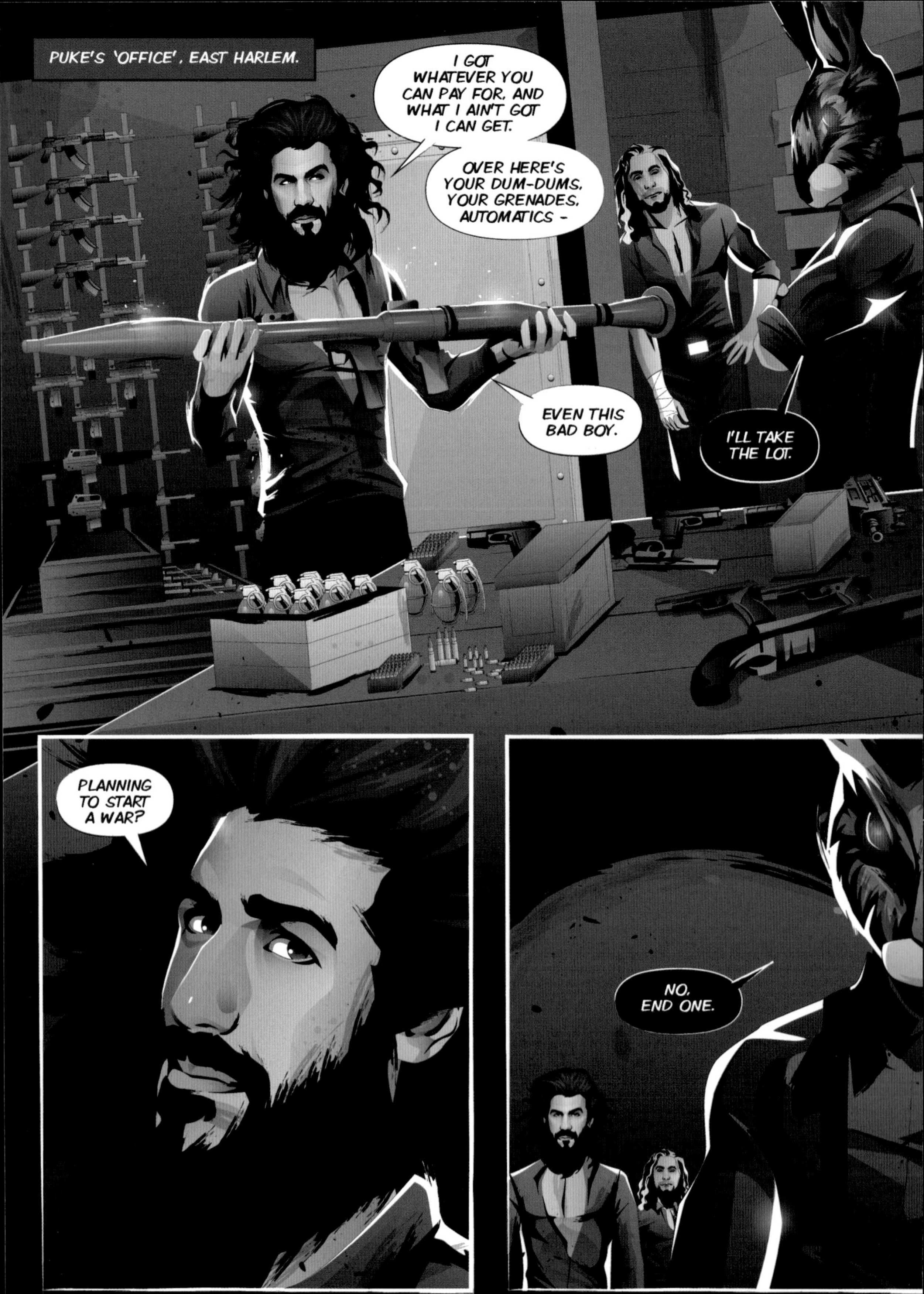
PUKE'S 'OFFICE', EAST HARLEM.
I GOT WHATEVER YOU CAN PAY FOR, AND WHAT I AIN'T GOT I CAN GET.
OVER HERE'S YOUR DUM-DUMS, YOUR GRENADES, AUTOMATICS -
EVEN THIS BAD BOY.
I'LL TAKE THE LOT.
PLANNING TO START A WAR?
NO, END ONE.

TALL POPPY

INGREDIENTS

1 DASH	Bittermens Orchard Street Celery Shrub
0.75 OZ	Lime juice
0.25 OZ	Ginger Syrup (page 259)
0.5 OZ	Wasabi Syrup (page 276)
0.5 OZ	Sage-Infused Dolin Blanc Vermouth (page 269)
0.5 OZ	Barbadillo Oloroso Sherry
2 OZ	Suntory Toki Japanese Whisky
1 OZ	Soda water (not to be shaken with other ingredients)

TOOLS
Jiggers, shaker tins, ice pick, nutmeg grater

METHOD
Whip shake with 15 pieces of pebble ice until ice is melted; add soda water to tin; pour into highball glass filled with cracked ice

GLASSWARE
Highball

GARNISH
Nutmeg

ORIGIN
Long Thai

145.

LONG'S INSPIRATION

THE CHALLENGE WAS TO CREATE A LIGHT, REFRESHING HIGHBALL WITH JAPANESE WHISKY AND JAPANESE INFLUENCED INGREDIENTS.

A cocktail to be paired with traditional sushi, hence the ginger and wasabi. The sherry provides the savory umami backbone, and Suntory Toki delivers light, slightly sweet, fruit and citrus notes. The soda water enhances the refreshing aspect of the highball.

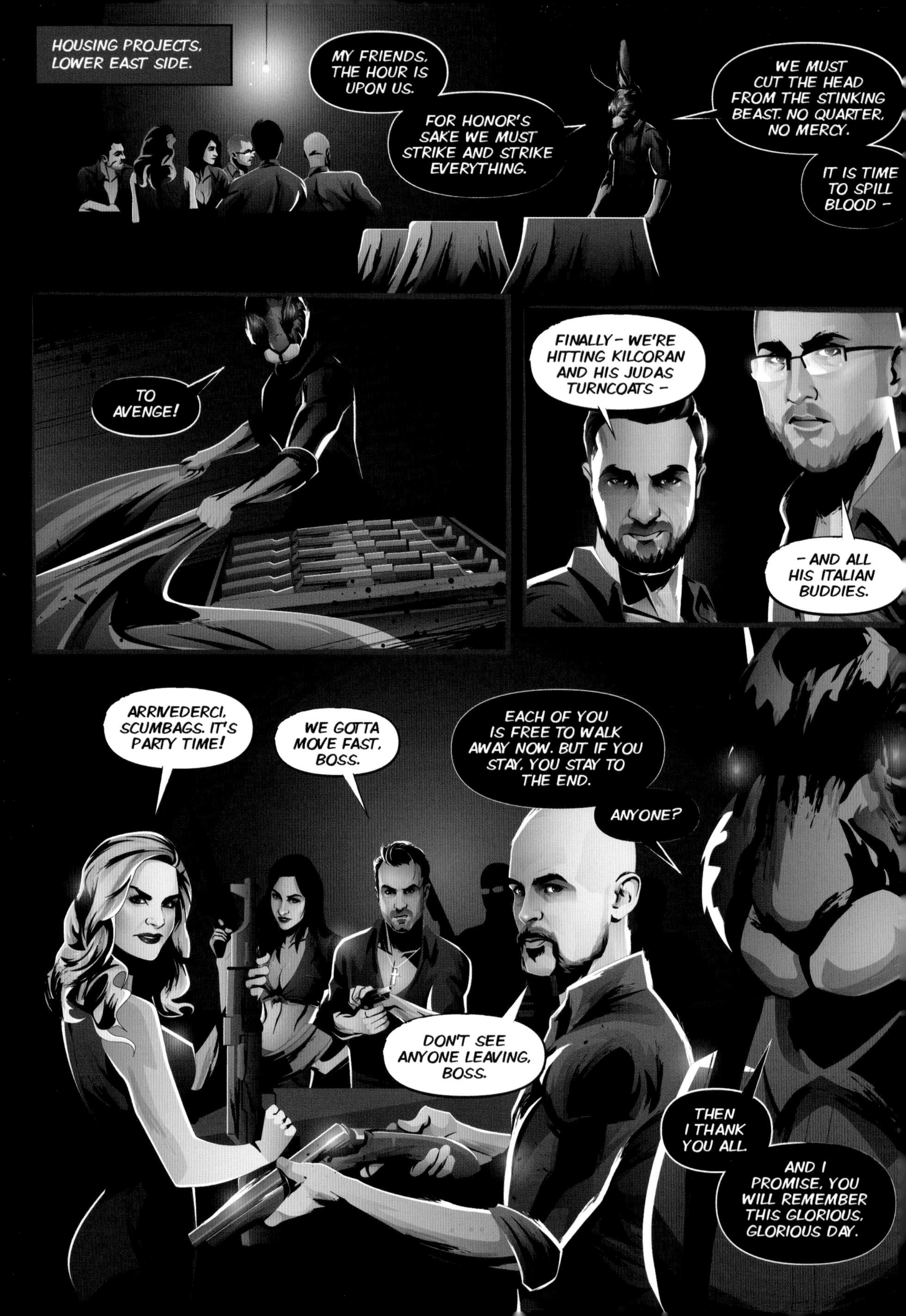
HOUSING PROJECTS, LOWER EAST SIDE.
MY FRIENDS, THE HOUR IS UPON US.
FOR HONOR'S SAKE WE MUST STRIKE AND STRIKE EVERYTHING.
WE MUST CUT THE HEAD FROM THE STINKING BEAST. NO QUARTER, NO MERCY.
IT IS TIME TO SPILL BLOOD -
TO AVENGE!
FINALLY - WE'RE HITTING KILCORAN AND HIS JUDAS TURNCOATS -
- AND ALL HIS ITALIAN BUDDIES.
ARRIVEDERCI, SCUMBAGS. IT'S PARTY TIME!
WE GOTTA MOVE FAST, BOSS.
EACH OF YOU IS FREE TO WALK AWAY NOW. BUT IF YOU STAY, YOU STAY TO THE END.
ANYONE?
DON'T SEE ANYONE LEAVING, BOSS.
THEN I THANK YOU ALL.
AND I PROMISE, YOU WILL REMEMBER THIS GLORIOUS, GLORIOUS DAY.

PUNK ROCKER

INGREDIENTS

1 OZ	Lemon juice
0.25 OZ	Pineapple juice
0.5 OZ	Fennel Syrup (page 258)
0.25 OZ	Macadamia Orgeat (page 263)
0.5 OZ	Dolin Génépy des Alpes
0.5 OZ	Altos Reposado Tequila
1.5 OZ	Grilled Pineapple–Infused Bols Genever (page 260)

TOOLS
Jiggers, shaker tins, fine strainers, Hawthorne strainer, ice pick, nutmeg grater

METHOD
Shake with ice; fine strain and serve with ice nugget

GLASSWARE
Coupette

GARNISH
Nutmeg

ORIGIN
Madeleine Solo Rapp

MADELEINE'S INSPIRATION

OUR GRILLED PINEAPPLE– INFUSED GENEVER IS AMAZING AND I WANTED TO MAKE A BRIGHT AND SLIGHTLY FUNKY DRINK.

Pairing it with reposed tequila turned out really well and the génépy gave it more complexity and herbaceous notes.

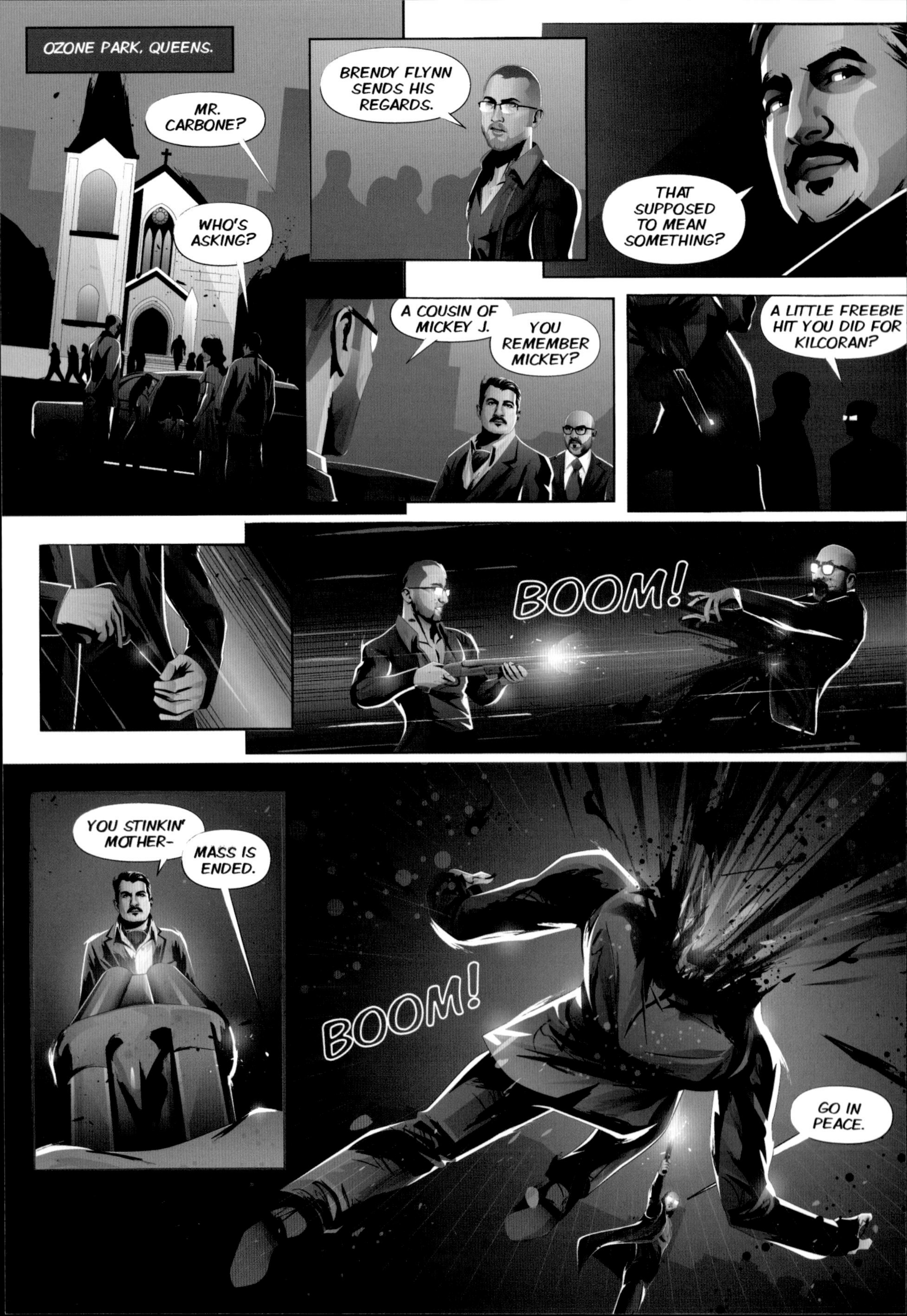
OZONE PARK, QUEENS.
MR. CARBONE?
WHO'S ASKING?
BRENDY FLYNN SENDS HIS REGARDS.
THAT SUPPOSED TO MEAN SOMETHING?
A COUSIN OF MICKEY J.
YOU REMEMBER MICKEY?
A LITTLE FREEBIE HIT YOU DID FOR KILCORAN?
BOOM!
YOU STINKIN' MOTHER-
MASS IS ENDED.
BOOM!
GO IN PEACE.

SMART ALEC

INGREDIENTS

1 DASH	Bittermens Orchard Street Celery Shrub
0.5 TSP	Cinnamon Bark Syrup (page 255)
0.5 OZ	Fusion Verjus Blanc
0.25 OZ	Barbadillo Manzanilla Sherry
0.5 OZ	Pierre Ferrand Pineau des Charentes
0.5 OZ	Linie Aquavit
1.5 OZ	Montreuil Calvados Selection

TOOLS

Jiggers, mixing glass, barspoon, ½ teaspoon, julep strainer

METHOD

Stir with ice; strain with julep strainer and serve up without ice

GLASSWARE

Nick & Nora

GARNISH

Lemon oil (discard peel)

ORIGIN

Jessica Friedman

JESSICA'S INSPIRATION

I LOVE CALVADOS, BUT HAD NEVER MADE A DRINK USING THE STUFF.

The savory elements of aquavit and celery gave it a unique character, while verjus and Pineau des Charentes supported the calvados and gave the drink length.

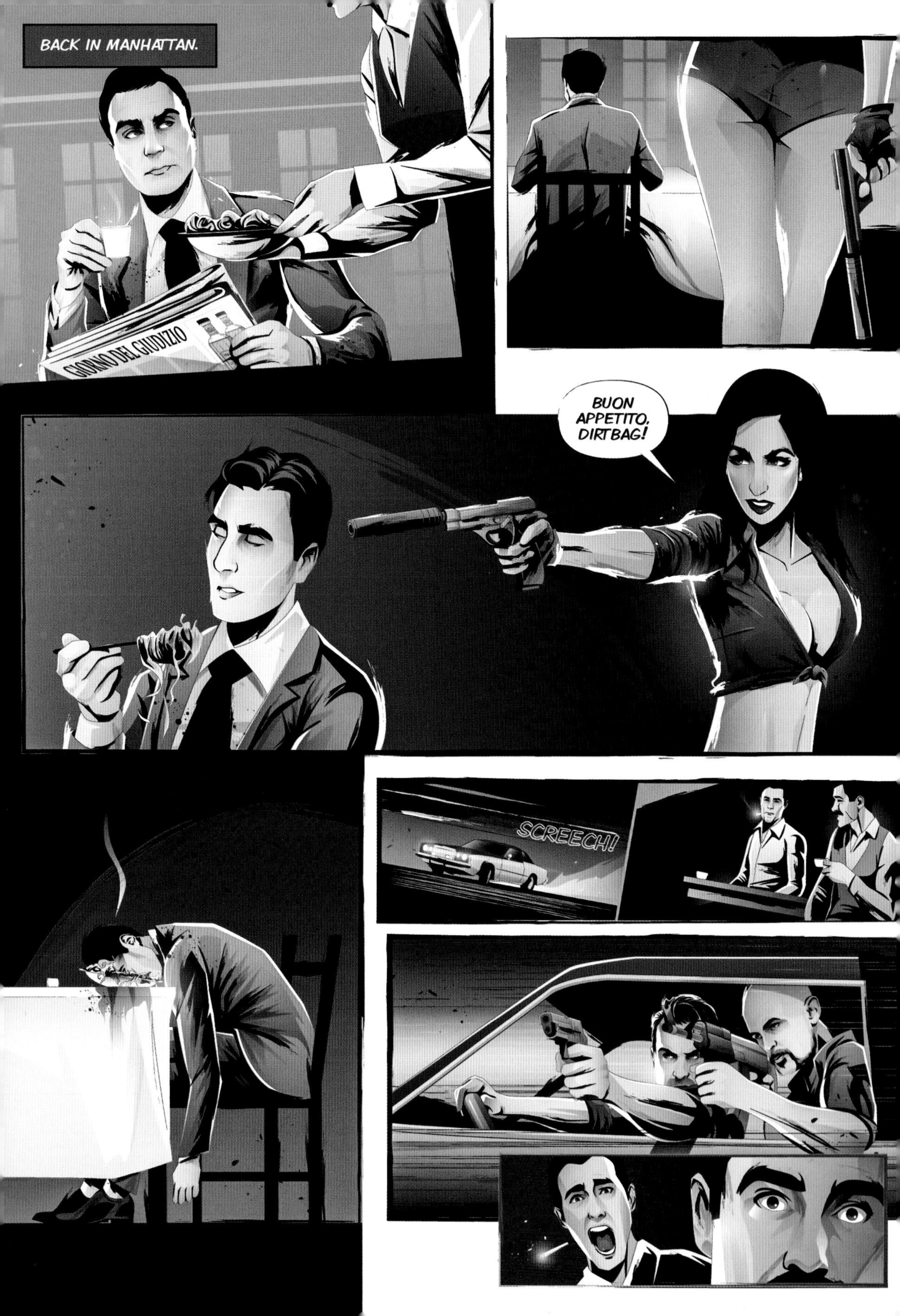

BACK IN MANHATTAN.
GIORNO DEL GIUDIZIO
BUON APPETITO, DIRTBAG!
SCREECH!

WHEELER-DEALER

INGREDIENTS

1 DASH	Black Cardamom Tincture (page 253)
0.5 OZ	Lemon juice
0.5 OZ	Granny Smith Apple Juice (page 259)
0.25 OZ	Ginger Syrup (page 259)
0.5 OZ	Pistachio Orgeat (page 267)
0.5 OZ	Del Maguey Mezcal Vida
1.5 OZ	Redbreast 12 Year Irish Whiskey

TOOLS

Jiggers, shaker tins, fine strainer, Hawthorne strainer, ice pick, nutmeg grater

METHOD

Shake with ice; fine strain and serve with ice nugget

GLASSWARE

Coupette

GARNISH

Nutmeg

ORIGIN

Becca Pesce

BECCA'S INSPIRATION

WHEELER-DEALER STARTED OUT AS AN INSIDE JOKE FOR MY OLD WORK HUSBAND.

I used as many of his favorite ingredients that complemented each other as possible. This was my first cocktail to make the menu at Dead Rabbit, and it is inspired by the person who encouraged me to pursue my dreams in this industry. This is my ode to a friendship.

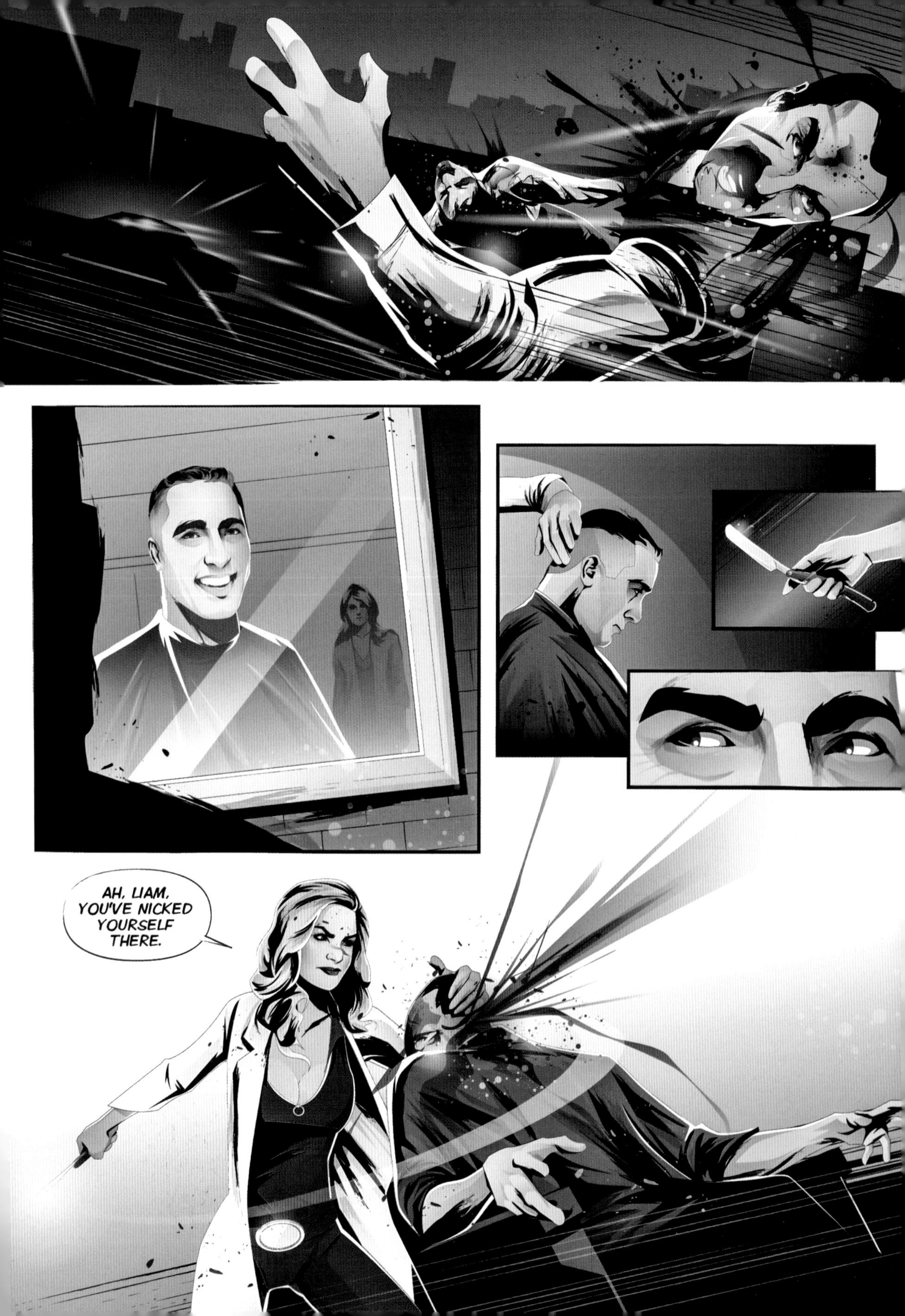
AH, LIAM, YOU'VE NICKED YOURSELF THERE.

EARLY BIRD

INGREDIENTS

1	Egg white
0.75 OZ	Lemon juice
0.25 OZ	Cinnamon Bark Syrup (page 255)
0.5 OZ	Fig Syrup (page 258)
0.5 OZ	Pür•likör Williams Pear
0.5 OZ	Barbadillo Oloroso Sherry
2 OZ	Botanist Gin

TOOLS
Jiggers, shaker tins, fine strainer, Hawthorne strainer

METHOD
Dry shake; shake with ice; fine strain and serve up without ice

GLASSWARE
Punch glass

GARNISH
Lemon oil (discard peel)

ORIGIN
Jillian Vose

153.

JILLIAN'S INSPIRATION

HERE WE ARE WITH YET ANOTHER TAKE ON EIDOLON, ITSELF A RIFF ON THE ARMY & NAVY COCKTAIL.

For the fall and winter months, I wanted to embrace those flavors. I first thought to use Oloroso rather than a Manzanilla, fino or pale cream sherry as I wanted to incorporate dried fruit notes rather than bright fruit ones. Cinnamon for fall is obvious but necessary to bring the fig and pear together just right. The rest of the template is kept the same.
Damn, son.

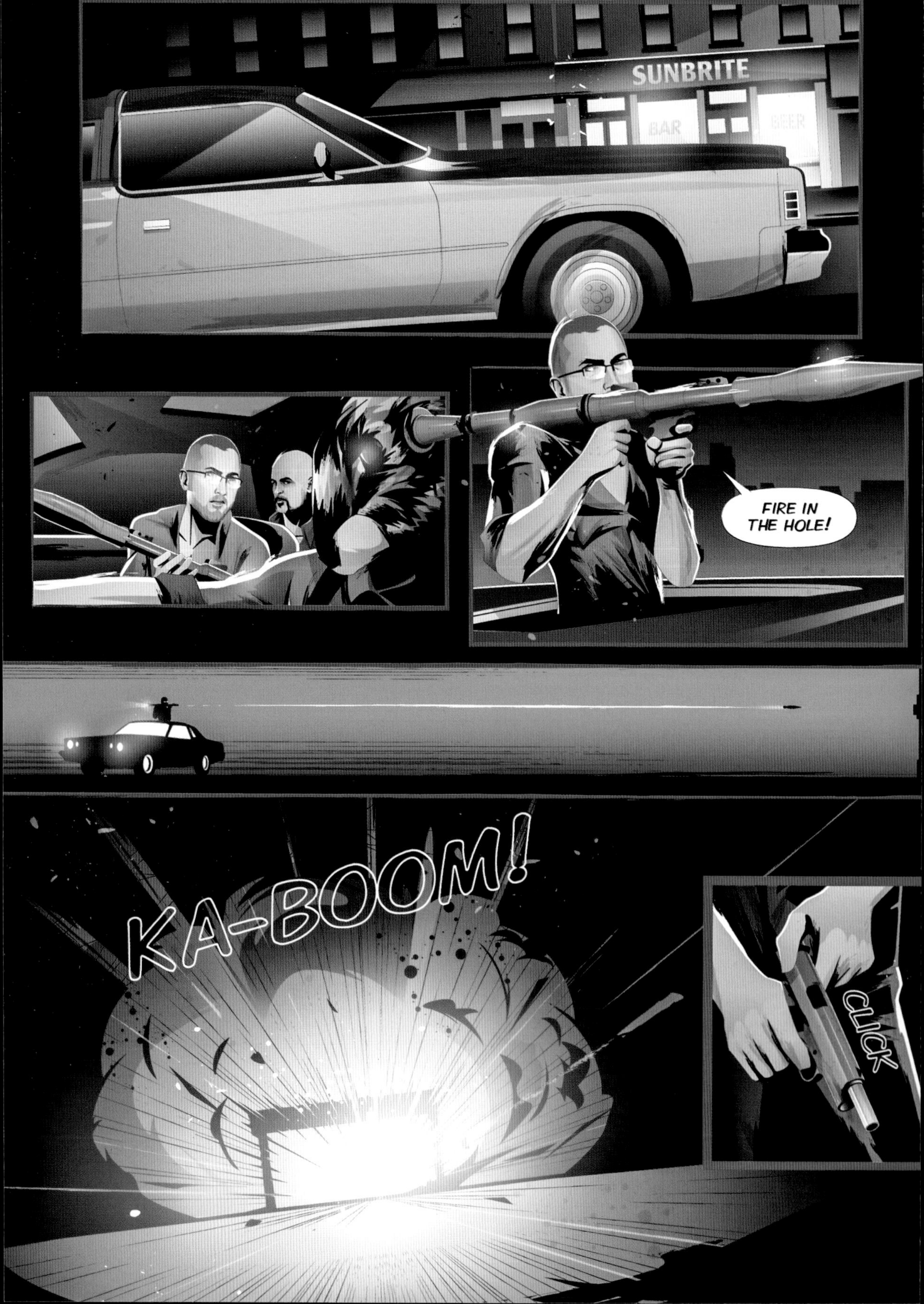
SUNBRITE
BAR
BEER
FIRE IN THE HOLE!
KA-BOOM!
CLICK

SHOOT FROM THE HIP

INGREDIENTS

1 DASH	Celery bitters
1 DASH	Cilantro Tincture (page 255)
0.5 OZ	Amaro Nonino
0.75 OZ	Lemon juice
0.25 OZ	Caramel Cane Syrup (page 254)
0.5 OZ	Spiced Pear Syrup (page 271)
1.5 OZ	Tullamore D.E.W. 12 Year Irish Whiskey

TOOLS
Jiggers, shaker tins, fine strainer, Hawthorne strainer, ice pick, nutmeg grater

METHOD
Shake with ice; fine strain and serve over cracked ice

GLASSWARE
Julep glass

GARNISH
Nutmeg

ORIGIN
Jillian Vose

155.

JILLIAN'S INSPIRATION

THIS DRINK WAS CREATED TO MEET A NEED ON THIS MENU FOR A PARTICULAR TYPE OF IRISH WHISKEY.

I knew I wanted to use the Tullamore 12 Year in a drink, so I started there with a focus on fall flavors. I made a spiced pear syrup, which turned out great. That alone had enough character for a simple sour cocktail, but you know us: Why stop there? Going through pear pairings, celery and cilantro (coriander) came up. Now I just needed a lengthener and a touch more character. Nonino worked wonderfully with the spiced pear, and caramel gave it all the bump of sweetness to balance out the drink. Job done.

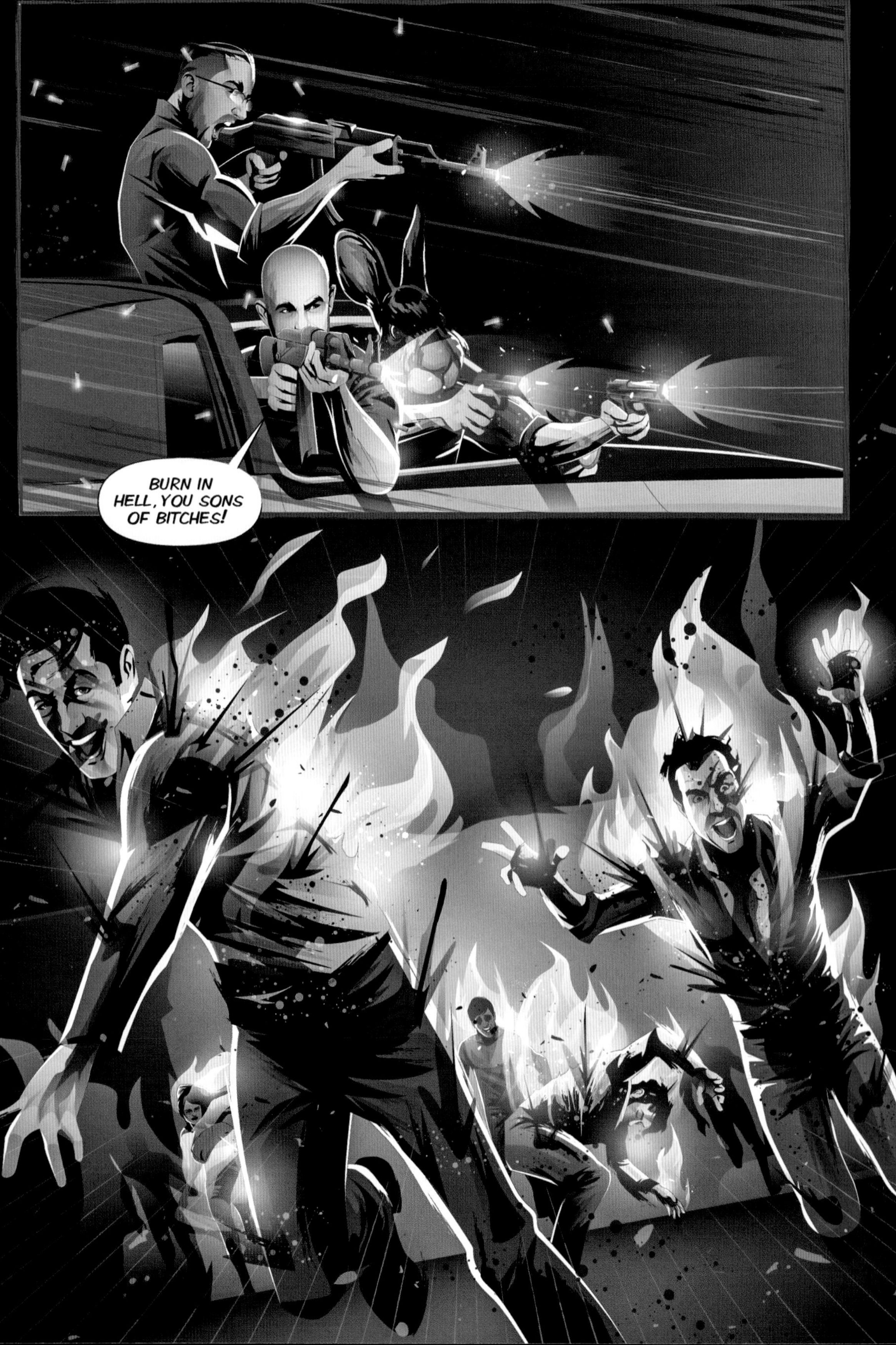
BURN IN HELL, YOU SONS OF BITCHES!

BLINK OF AN EYE

INGREDIENTS

1 DASH	Vieux Pontarlier Absinthe
0.5 OZ	Massenez Green Apple Liqueur
0.75 OZ	Dolin Blanc Vermouth
0.5 OZ	Barbancourt White Rhum
1 OZ	El Silencio Mezcal

TOOLS

Jiggers, mixing glass, barspoon, julep strainer

METHOD

Stir with ice; strain with julep strainer and serve up without ice

GLASSWARE

Nick & Nora

GARNISH

Lemon oil (discard peel)

ORIGIN

Jillian Vose

JILLIAN'S INSPIRATION

I DECIDED TO MAKE A MARTINI-STYLE DRINK FOR THOSE WHO WANTED SOMETHING BOOZY AND SMOKY.

The drink is quite approachable if you like mezcal. Dolin Blanc lengthened out the green apple for fruit and the absinthe for an herbal note.

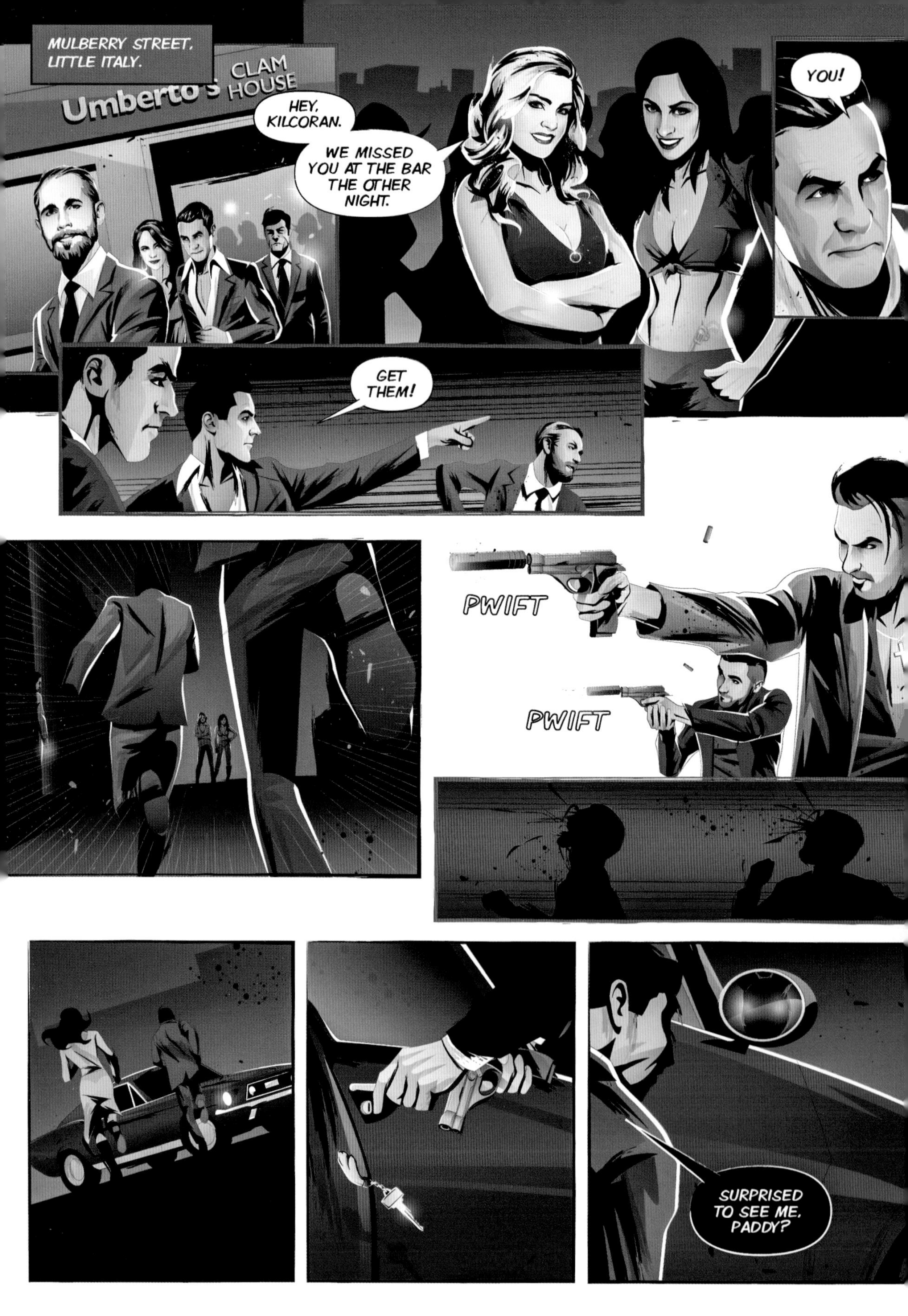
MULBERRY STREET, LITTLE ITALY.
Umberto's CLAM HOUSE
HEY, KILCORAN.
WE MISSED YOU AT THE BAR THE OTHER NIGHT.
YOU!
GET THEM!
PWIFT
PWIFT
SURPRISED TO SEE ME, PADDY?

DEAD RINGER

INGREDIENTS

1 DASH	Turmeric Citrus (page 274)
1 DASH	Chipotle Tincture (page 255)
1 TSP	Sumac Syrup (page 272)
0.25 OZ	Yellow Chartreuse
0.75 OZ	Cocchi Americano
0.5 OZ	Plantation Pineapple Rum
1.5 OZ	Bushmills 10 Year Irish Whiskey

TOOLS

Jiggers, mixing glass, teaspoon, barspoon, julep strainer, ice pick, nutmeg grater

METHOD

Stir with ice; strain with julep strainer and serve over large block of ice

GLASSWARE

Old Fashioned

GARNISH

Lemon oil (discard peel)

ORIGIN

Jillian Vose

RETRIBUTION

159.

DEAD RINGER

JILLIAN'S INSPIRATION

THERE IS ALWAYS A PLACE FOR A LIGHTER-STYLE OLD FASHIONED.

Irish whiskey pairs well with tropical flavors, so the Plantation worked well. To complement this, I chose tumeric and chipotle. The honey notes of Yellow Chartreuse as another modifier and the lengthening agent of the Cocchi Americano worked well to balance the drink. Sumac gives a tangy citrusy note.

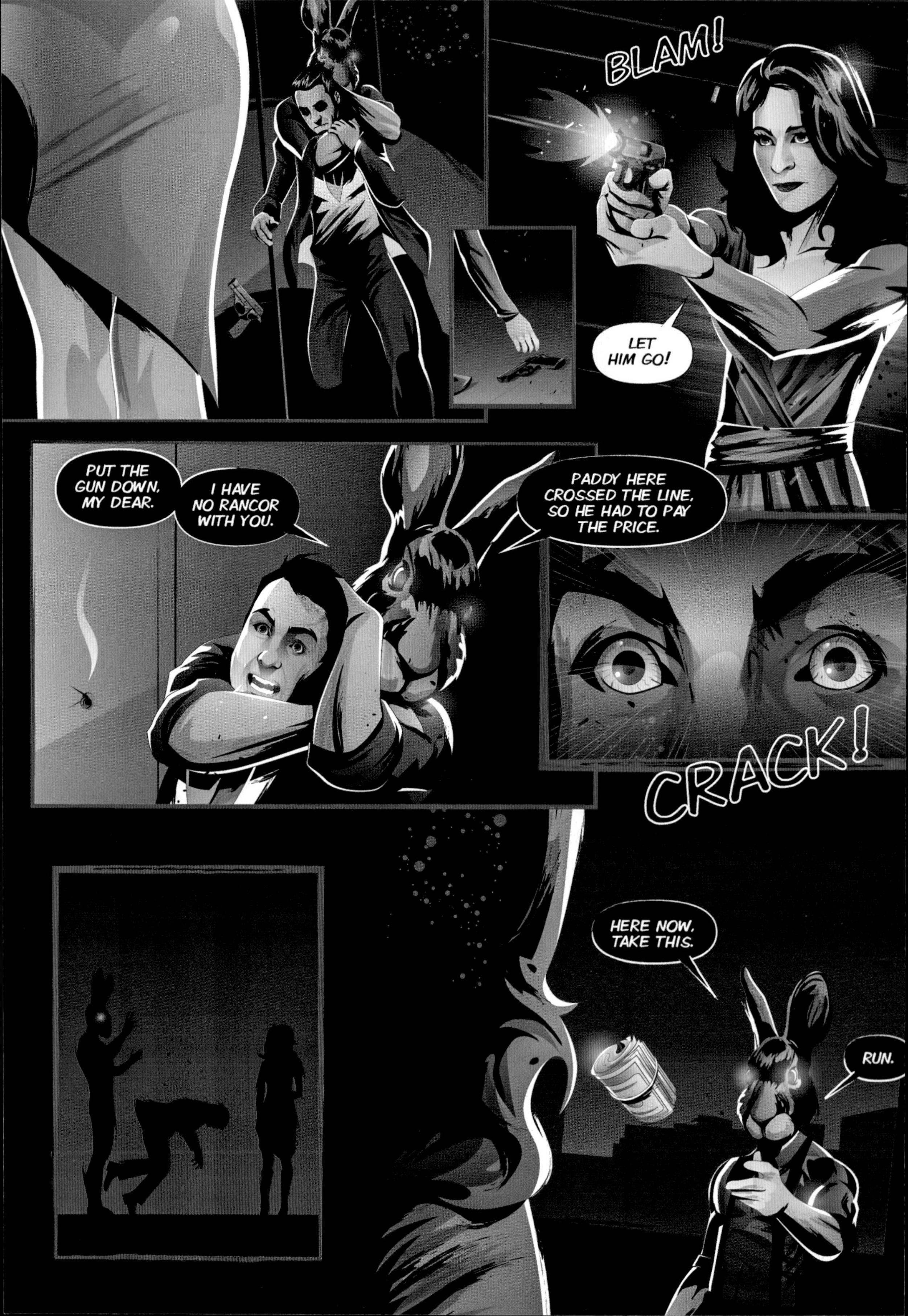
BLAM!
LET HIM GO!
PUT THE GUN DOWN, MY DEAR.
I HAVE NO RANCOR WITH YOU.
PADDY HERE CROSSED THE LINE, SO HE HAD TO PAY THE PRICE.
CRACK!
HERE NOW, TAKE THIS.
RUN.

LOOSE CANNON

INGREDIENTS

1 DASH	Bittered Sling Clingstone Peach Bitters
1 TSP	Coco López
0.75 OZ	Lime juice
0.5 OZ	Carrot juice
0.25 OZ	Paprika Syrup (page 266)
0.5 OZ	Fennel Syrup (page 258)
0.25 OZ	Half & half
0.5 OZ	Del Maguey Mezcal Vida
1.5 OZ	123 Uno Organic Blanco Tequila
2	Curry leaves

TOOLS
Jiggers, teaspoon, shaker tins, fine strainer, Hawthorne strainer, nutmeg grater

METHOD
Build drink in tin; add curry leaves (do not muddle); whip shake with cube ice; fine strain and serve over pebble ice

GLASSWARE
Old Fashioned

GARNISH
Nutmeg

ORIGIN
Jessica Friedman

RETRIBUTION

161.

LOOSE CANNON

JESSICA'S INSPIRATION

THIS ONE STARTED WITH FOOD – CURRY, TO BE PRECISE.

Once I had the sweet carrot and aromatic curry together, I thought of previous Indian dishes I'd had and the distinctive flavors they used. This is the result.

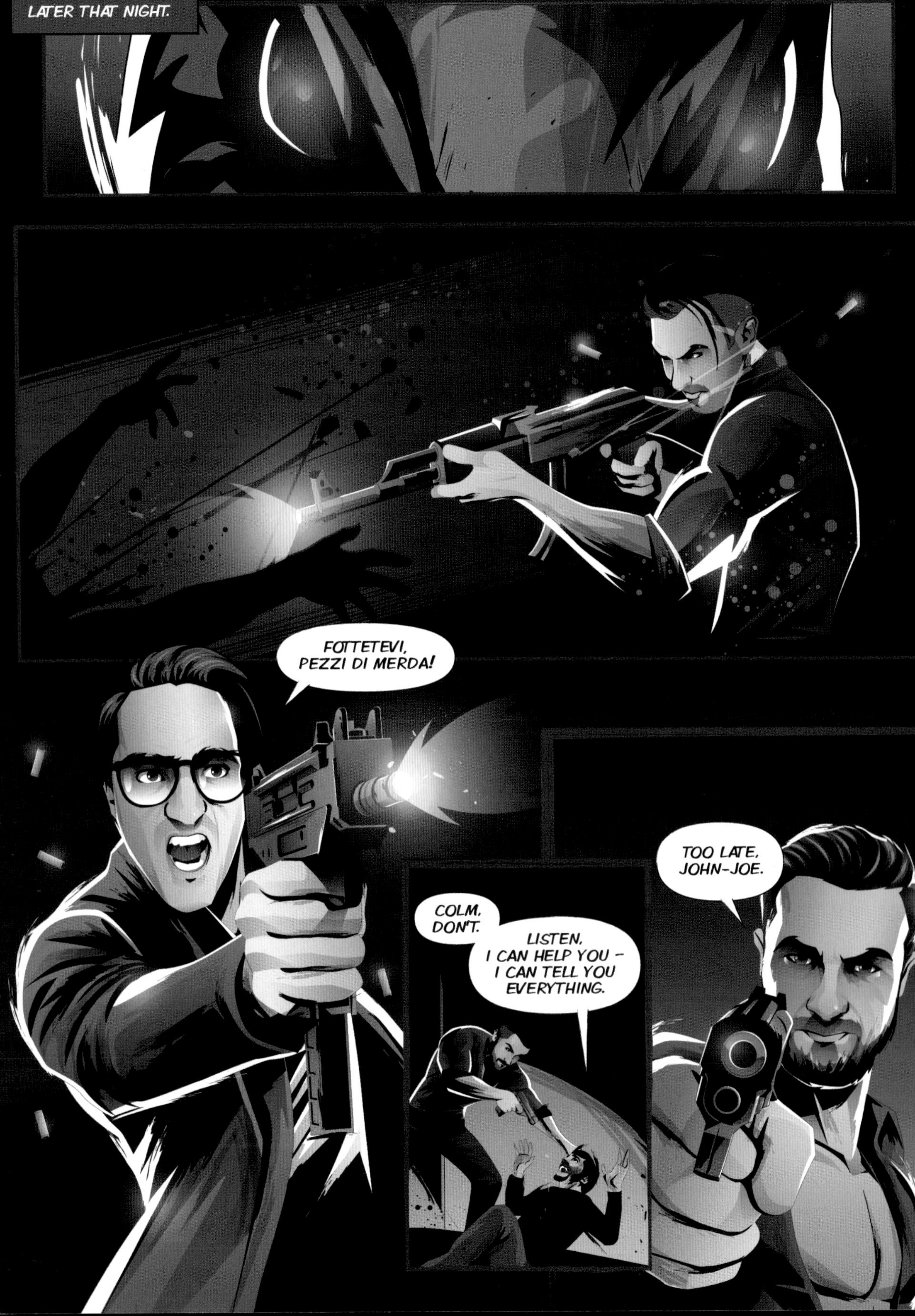
LATER THAT NIGHT.
FOTTETEVI, PEZZI DI MERDA!
TOO LATE, JOHN-JOE.
COLM, DON'T.
LISTEN, I CAN HELP YOU - I CAN TELL YOU EVERYTHING.

KILL DEVIL

INGREDIENTS

1 DASH	Angostura Bitters
0.75 OZ	Lime juice
0.5 OZ	Pineapple juice
1 OZ	Togarashi Syrup (page 273)
0.5 OZ	Barbadillo Oloroso Sherry
0.5 OZ	Banks 7 Golden Age Blend Rum
1.5 OZ	Mount Gay Black Barrel Rum

TOOLS
Jiggers, shaker tins, fine strainer, Hawthorne strainer, ice pick, nutmeg grater

METHOD
Shake with ice; fine strain and serve with ice nugget

GLASSWARE
Punch glass

GARNISH
Nutmeg

ORIGIN
Jillian Vose

RETRIBUTION

163.

KILL DEVIL

JILLIAN'S INSPIRATION

I USED TO WORK AT A RESTAURANT THAT USED TOGARASHI A LOT IN THEIR DISHES, AND IT INSPIRED ME TO USE IT IN COCKTAILS.

We often get requests for spicy drinks, so I decided to start out with a daiquiri and let the sweetener be the togarashi syrup. It went from there and developed with sherry, a blend of rums and bitters.

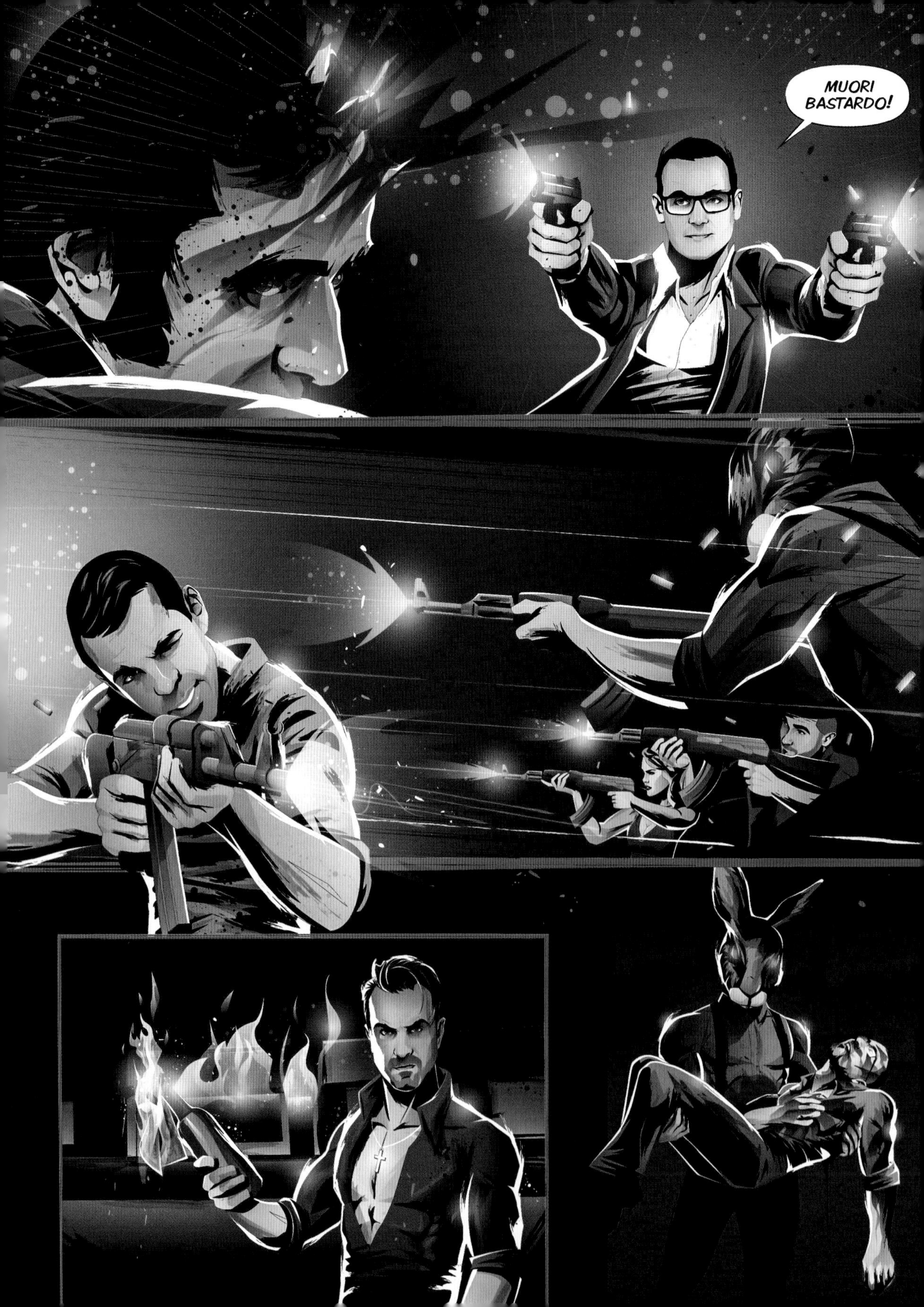
MUORI BASTARDO!

MONEY TO BURN

INGREDIENTS

0.5 OZ	Lime juice
0.25 OZ	Pineapple juice
0.25 OZ	Vanilla Syrup (page 275)
0.75 OZ	Horchata Syrup (page 261)
0.25 OZ	Avuá Amburana Cachaça
0.5 OZ	Torres 15 Year Spanish Brandy
1.5 OZ	Basil Hayden's Bourbon

TOOLS

Jiggers, shaker tins, fine strainer, Hawthorne strainer, ice pick, nutmeg grater

METHOD

Shake with ice; fine strain and serve with ice nugget

GLASSWARE

Punch cup

GARNISH

Nutmeg

ORIGIN

Nick Rolin

165.

NICK'S INSPIRATION

THIS COCKTAIL WAS INSPIRED BY HORCHATA – THE RICH MEXICAN BEVERAGE MADE FROM RICE, ALMONDS AND SUGAR.

I wanted something that echoed that dense texture but with more elegance. I made an horchata syrup and tried to pair it with a combination of bourbon and tequila, but it was never balanced. The answer turned out to be a blend of bourbon, Spanish brandy and cachaça. The final drink borders on the richness of a dessert cocktail, but the lime and pineapple juice create enough acidic balance to keep it refreshing.

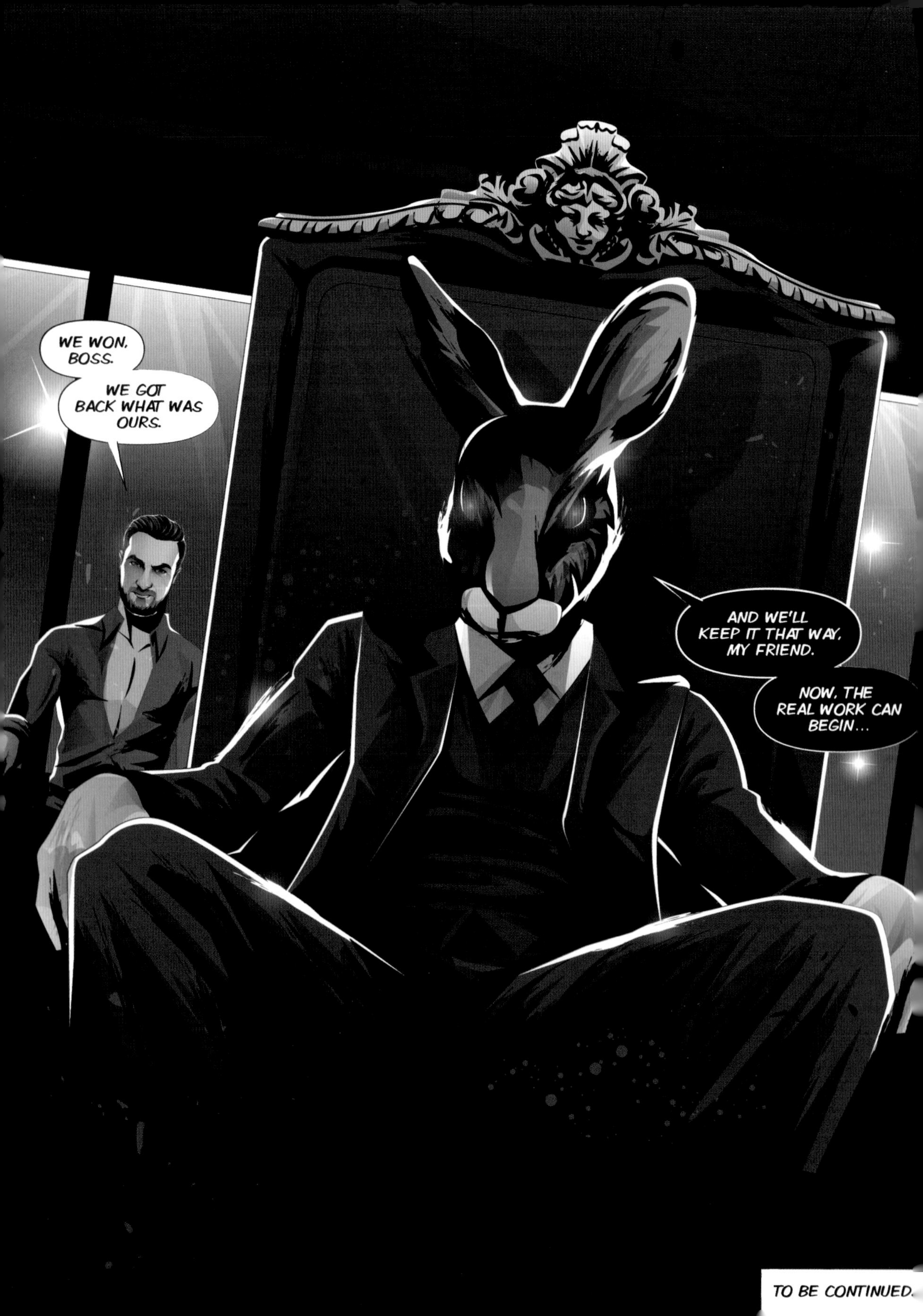
WE WON, BOSS.
WE GOT BACK WHAT WAS OURS.
AND WE'LL KEEP IT THAT WAY, MY FRIEND.
NOW, THE REAL WORK CAN BEGIN...
TO BE CONTINUED.

BILLION DOLLAR MAN

INGREDIENTS

1 OZ	Heavy cream
1 DASH	Smoked Black Pepper Tincture (page 271)
2 DASHES	Pumpkin Tincture (page 268)
0.25 OZ	Orgeat (page 265)
0.5 OZ	Buckwheat Orgeat (page 253)
0.75 OZ	Novo Fogo Tanager Cachaça
0.75 OZ	Laird's Bonded Applejack
1.5 OZ	Piping-hot water

TOOLS
Jiggers, kettle, nutmeg grater

METHOD
Whip cold heavy cream until it thickens enough to float on top of the drink and is still pourable. (We suggest using cream that is 35 to 38% milk fat.) Build drink in a warm glass; add water and float cream.

GLASSWARE
Georgian Irish coffee glass

GARNISH
Nutmeg

ORIGIN
Jillian Vose

RETRIBUTION

167.

BILLION DOLLAR MAN

JILLIAN'S INSPIRATION

FOR WINTER WE ALWAYS LIKE TO HAVE ANOTHER HOT DRINK OPTION IN ADDITION TO OUR DELECTABLE IRISH COFFEE.

This has some warming fall spice with sweet apple: perfect for a cold day.

IT'S SAID THAT EVIL HAS
TWO FACES: ONE HIDDEN
IN DARKNESS, THE OTHER
TURNED TOWARDS
THE LIGHT.

BY NATURE, WE FEAR WHAT WE CANNOT SEE.
BUT SOMETIMES THE GREATER WICKEDNESS
IS HIDING IN PLAIN SIGHT. IT SMILES AND
SHAKES YOUR HAND, BUT BEHIND THE SMILE,
THE EYES ARE LIFELESS.

Now that he has secured his empire, The Rabbit is ready to make
his biggest move – into politics, a world where friends are kept
close and enemies even closer.

A WORLD WITH ITS FACE HALF IN LIGHT,
HALF IN DARKEST SHADOW.

NEW YORK, U.S.A.

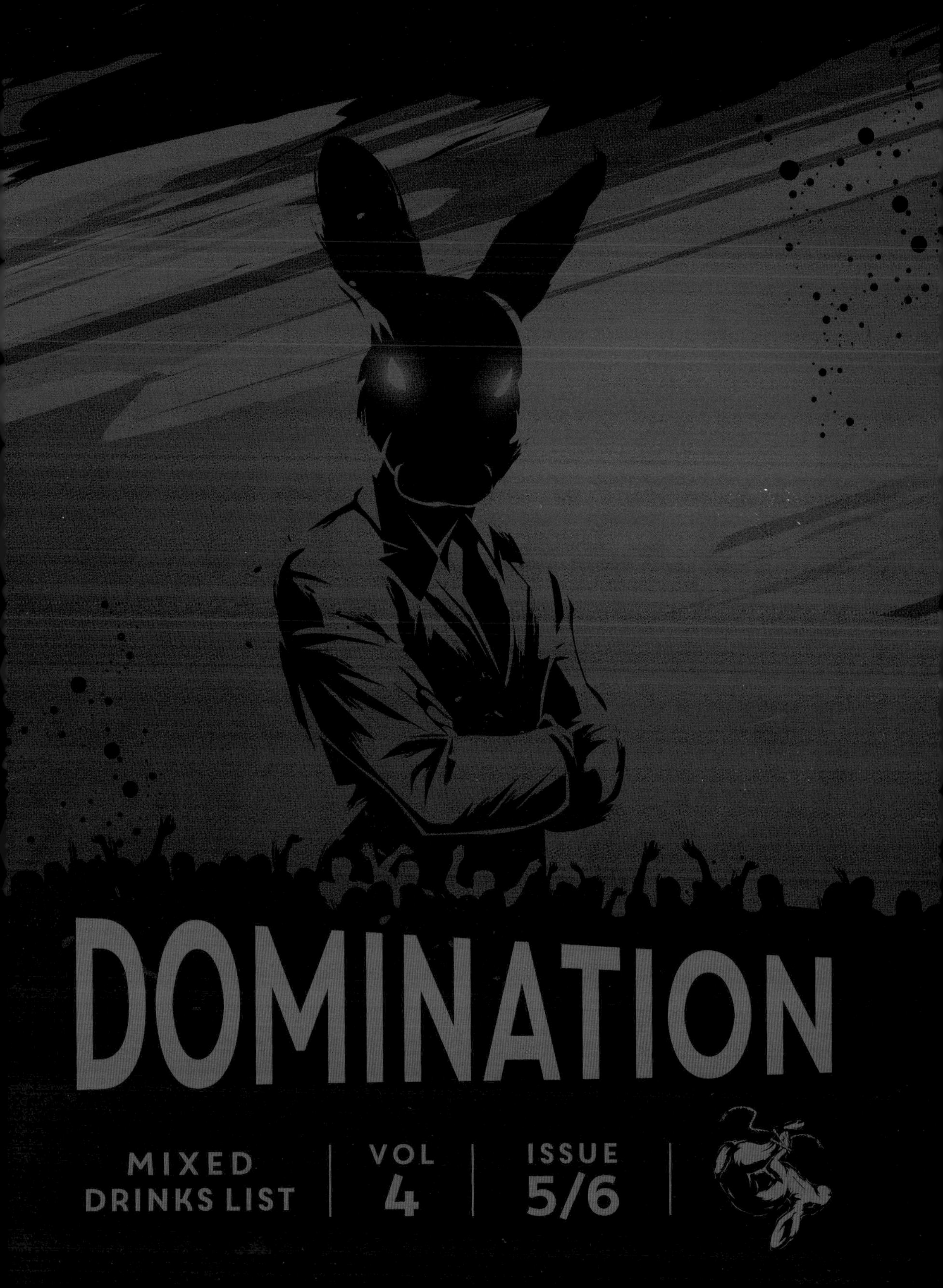
DOMINATION
MIXED DRINKS LIST
VOL 4
ISSUE 5/6

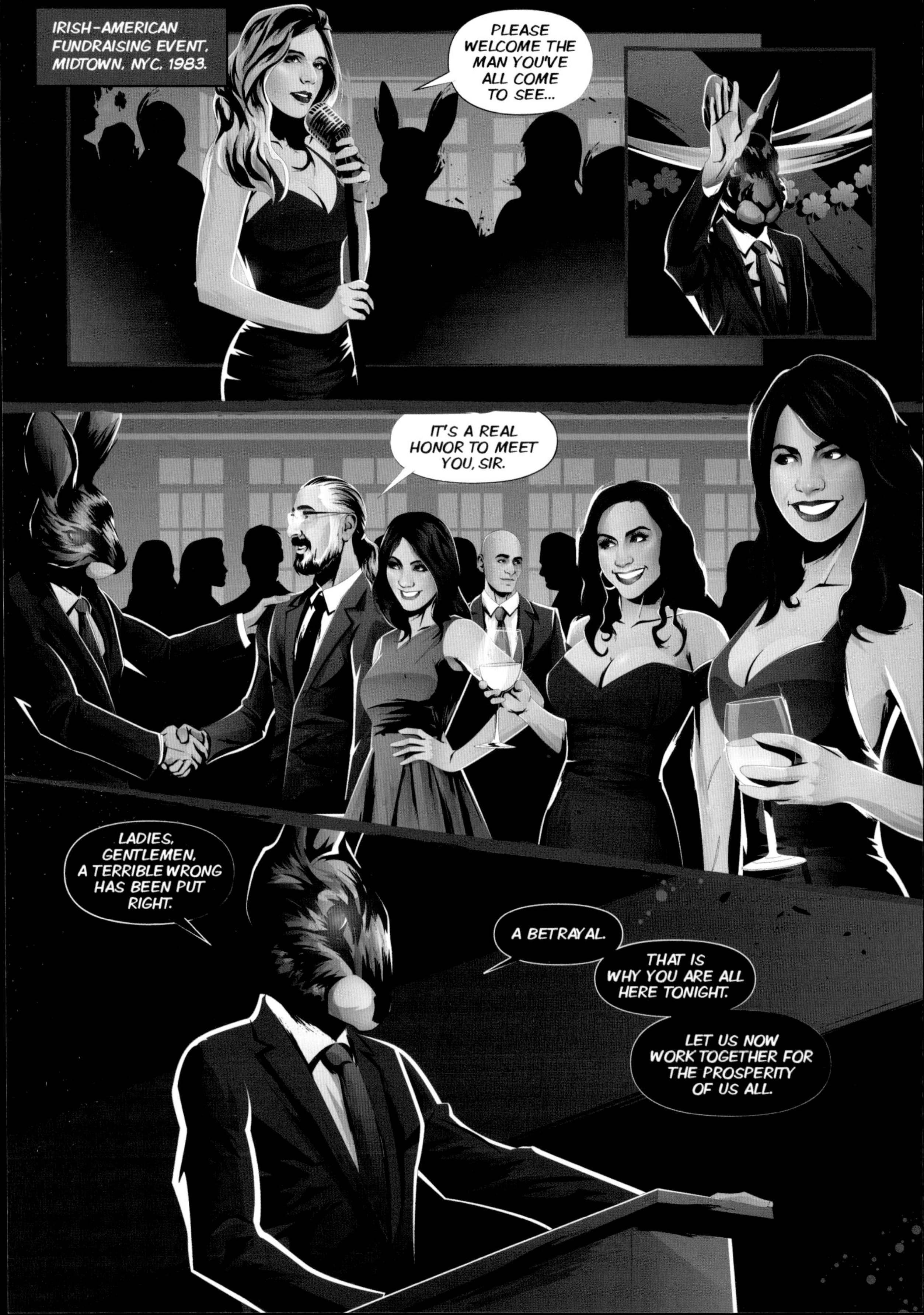
IRISH-AMERICAN FUNDRAISING EVENT, MIDTOWN, NYC, 1983.
PLEASE WELCOME THE MAN YOU'VE ALL COME TO SEE...
IT'S A REAL HONOR TO MEET YOU, SIR.
LADIES, GENTLEMEN, A TERRIBLE WRONG HAS BEEN PUT RIGHT.
A BETRAYAL.
THAT IS WHY YOU ARE ALL HERE TONIGHT.
LET US NOW WORK TOGETHER FOR THE PROSPERITY OF US ALL.

TALK OF THE DEVIL

INGREDIENTS

1.5 OZ	Champagne (not to be shaken with other ingredients)
0.75 OZ	Lemon juice
0.5 OZ	Honeydew
0.75 OZ	Mint Syrup (page 264)
0.5 OZ	Martini & Rossi Bianco Vermouth
1 OZ	Perry's Tot Navy Strength Gin
1 OZ	Apostoles Gin

TOOLS
Jiggers, shaker tins, fine strainer, Hawthorne strainer

METHOD
Add Champagne to glass; shake drink with ice; fine strain into glass with Champagne and serve up without ice

GLASSWARE
Champagne flute

ORIGIN
Long Thai

DOMINATION

171.

TALK OF THE DEVIL

LONG'S INSPIRATION

ON A HOT SUMMER DAY, SOMETHING SPARKLY AND REFRESHING IS DEFINITELY IN ORDER.

Let's start with honeydew and add mint – a killer combo. Apostoles is a unique gin from Argentina with flavors of yerba mate, eucalyptus, pink grapefruit and peppermint. Martini & Rossi Bianco gives a boost of refreshing green herbs and botanicals. Perry's Tot Gin lends extra oomph with its Navy Strength Proof (57% ABV). Finally, top off with Champagne. Now, if only The Dead Rabbit had a rooftop bar . . .

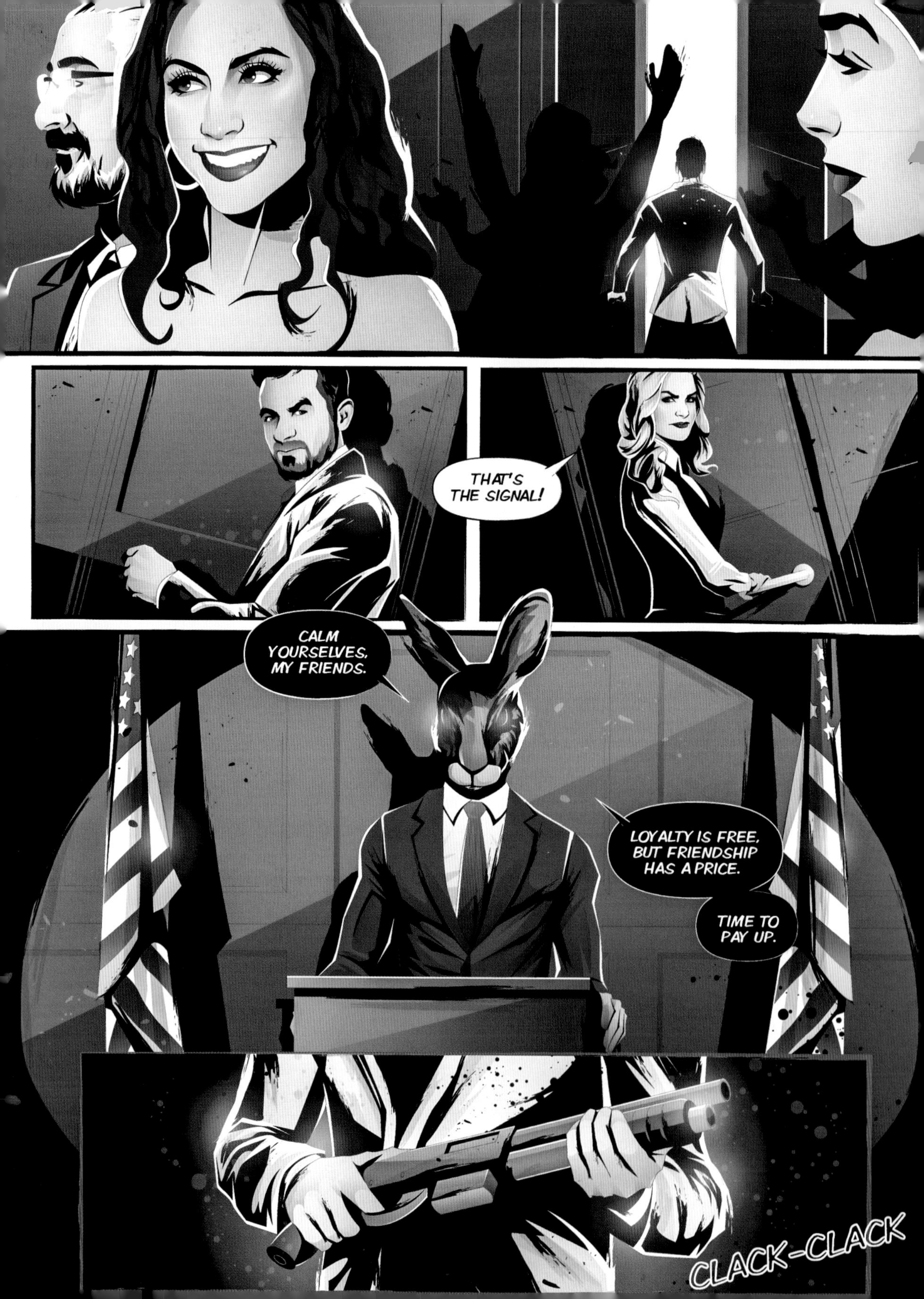
THAT'S THE SIGNAL!
CALM YOURSELVES, MY FRIENDS.
LOYALTY IS FREE, BUT FRIENDSHIP HAS A PRICE.
TIME TO PAY UP.
CLACK-CLACK

ACE OF SPADES

INGREDIENTS

1 DASH	Saline Solution (page 270)
1 DASH	Silver Needle Tincture (page 270)
0.75 OZ	Lime juice
0.5 OZ	Cucumber juice
0.5 OZ	Tarragon Syrup (page 273)
0.25 OZ	Viura Rioja Pear Syrup (page 275)
0.5 OZ	Pineau des Charentes
0.25 OZ	Blume Marillen Apricot Eau-de-Vie
0.25 OZ	Sotol Por Siempre
1.5 OZ	Casa Magdalena Ron Blanco Rum

TOOLS
Jiggers, shaker tins, fine strainer, Hawthorne strainer, ice pick

METHOD
Shake with ice; fine strain and serve with ice nugget

GLASSWARE
Coupette

ORIGIN
Jillian Vose

DOMINATION

173.

ACE OF SPADES

JILLIAN'S INSPIRATION

THIS IS ANOTHER ONE OF THOSE DRINKS INSPIRED BY SPRING.

I know it seems a bit busy, but it just worked out that way – like a daiquiri with a lot of other interesting stuff in it. When we have drinks with a lot of elements in them, we batch up a portion of the ingredients for easy execution during service. In this case, we'll make a mix of equal parts pear syrup, apricot eau-de-vie and Sotol and pour 0.75 ounce of the mix instead of 0.25 ounce of all three separately. So you'll still have your drink in just a few minutes.

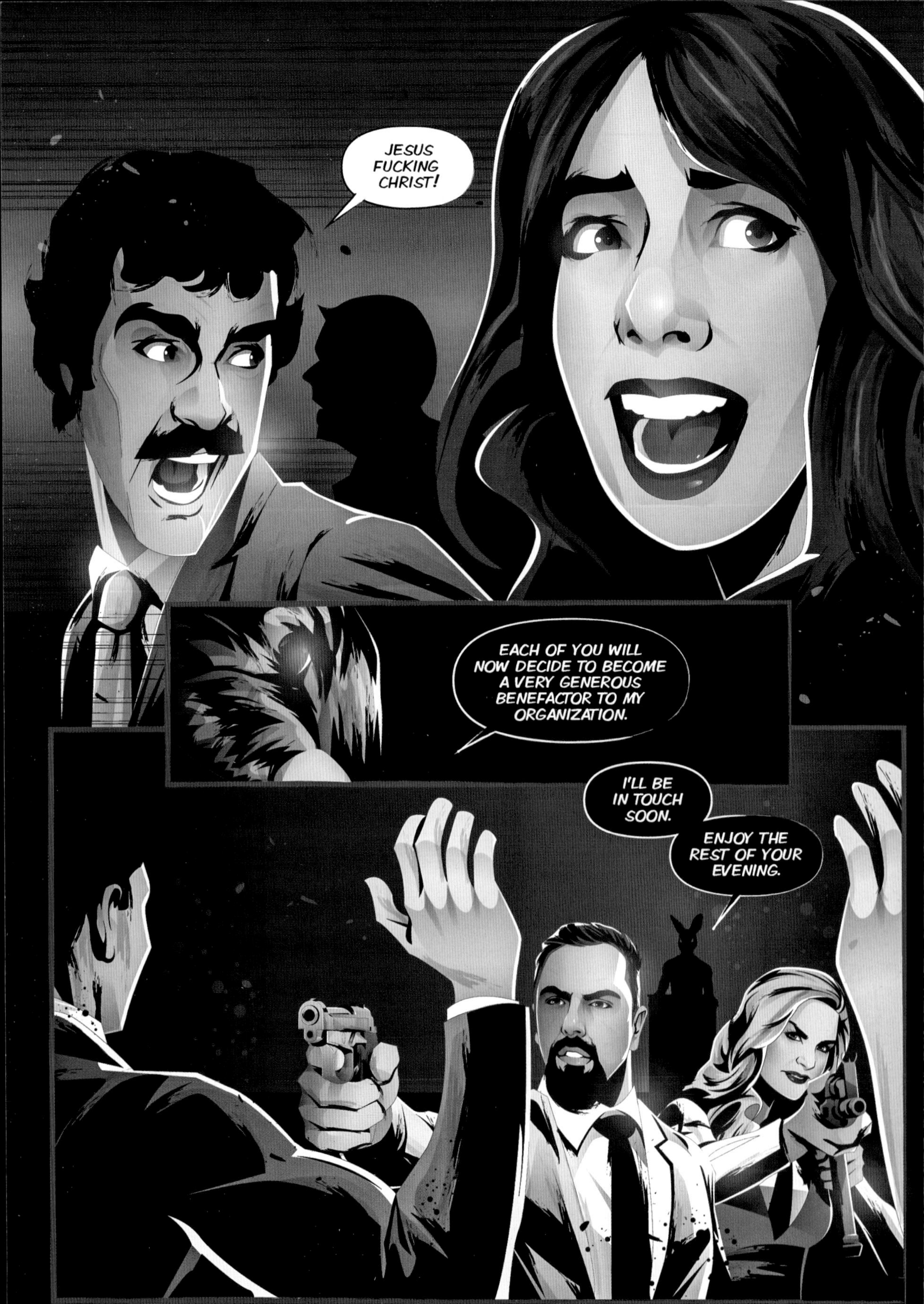
JESUS FUCKING CHRIST!
EACH OF YOU WILL NOW DECIDE TO BECOME A VERY GENEROUS BENEFACTOR TO MY ORGANIZATION.
I'LL BE IN TOUCH SOON.
ENJOY THE REST OF YOUR EVENING.

YOURS TRULY

INGREDIENTS

3 DASHES	Smoked Black Pepper Tincture (page 271)
1 DASH	Saline Solution (page 270)
0.5 TSP	Macadamia Orgeat (page 263)
1 TSP	Strawberry Syrup (page 271)
0.25 OZ	Combier Crème de Pamplemousse Rose Liqueur
0.75 OZ	Noilly Prat Dry Vermouth
1 OZ	High West Silver Oat Whiskey
1 OZ	Barr Hill Vodka

TOOLS

Jiggers, mixing glass, ½ teaspoon, teaspoon, barspoon, ice pick, julep strainer

METHOD

Stir with ice; strain with julep strainer and serve over large block of ice

GLASSWARE

Old Fashioned

GARNISH

Grapefruit twist (discard peel)

ORIGIN

Jillian Vose

DOMINATION

175.

YOURS TRULY

JILLIAN'S INSPIRATION

THE UNLIKELY VODKA DRINK STRIKES AGAIN. THIS TIME WITH ANOTHER SPIRIT YOU WON'T TYPICALLY FIND ME USING, WHITE WHISKEY.

However, I find High West Silver Oat works well in cocktails and has some interesting notes of banana, flowers, strawberry and grapefruit. The whiskey was a bit much for a full base so I split it with Barr Hill Vodka, which is distilled from raw honey. The honey comes through, and the texture of it is rich yet clean. The drink does read a bit sweet, but adding the dry vermouth and black peppercorn fixed that.

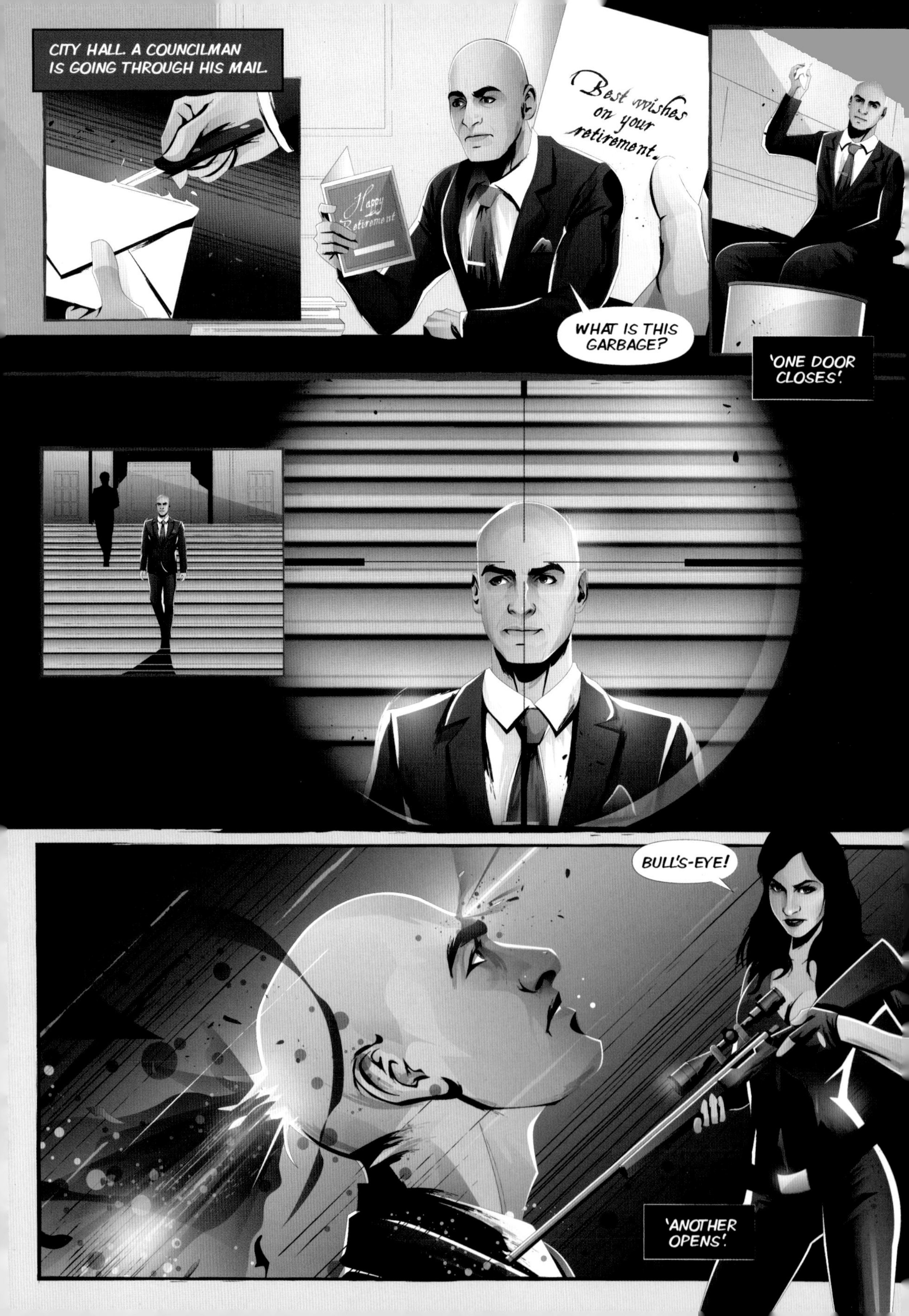
CITY HALL. A COUNCILMAN IS GOING THROUGH HIS MAIL.
Happy Retirement
Best wishes on your retirement.
WHAT IS THIS GARBAGE?
'ONE DOOR CLOSES'.
BULL'S-EYE!
'ANOTHER OPENS'.

ONE-HIT WONDER

INGREDIENTS

1	Egg white
0.75 OZ	Lemon juice
0.25 OZ	Vanilla Syrup (page 275)
0.5 OZ	Rhubarb Syrup (page 269)
0.5 OZ	Giffard Lichi-Li Liqueur
0.75 OZ	Barbadillo Manzanilla Sherry
2 OZ	Barbancourt White Rhum

TOOLS

Jiggers, shaker tins, fine strainer, Hawthorne strainer

METHOD

Dry shake; shake with ice; fine strain and serve up without ice

GLASSWARE

Punch glass

GARNISH

Lemon oil (discard peel)

ORIGIN

Jillian Vose

DOMINATION

177.

ONE-HIT WONDER

JILLIAN'S INSPIRATION

YES, I DID IT AGAIN — ANOTHER RIFF ON EIDOLON...

As we're looking at spring and summer, I went for lighter and bright fruit flavors. The idea came to me when I finally found a lychee liqueur I liked. The gin simply didn't work this time with the floral components of the drink, so I tried the slightly funky Barbancourt Haitian rum. I also went for a lighter and creamier style sherry as it complemented the rhubarb, lychee and vanilla better.

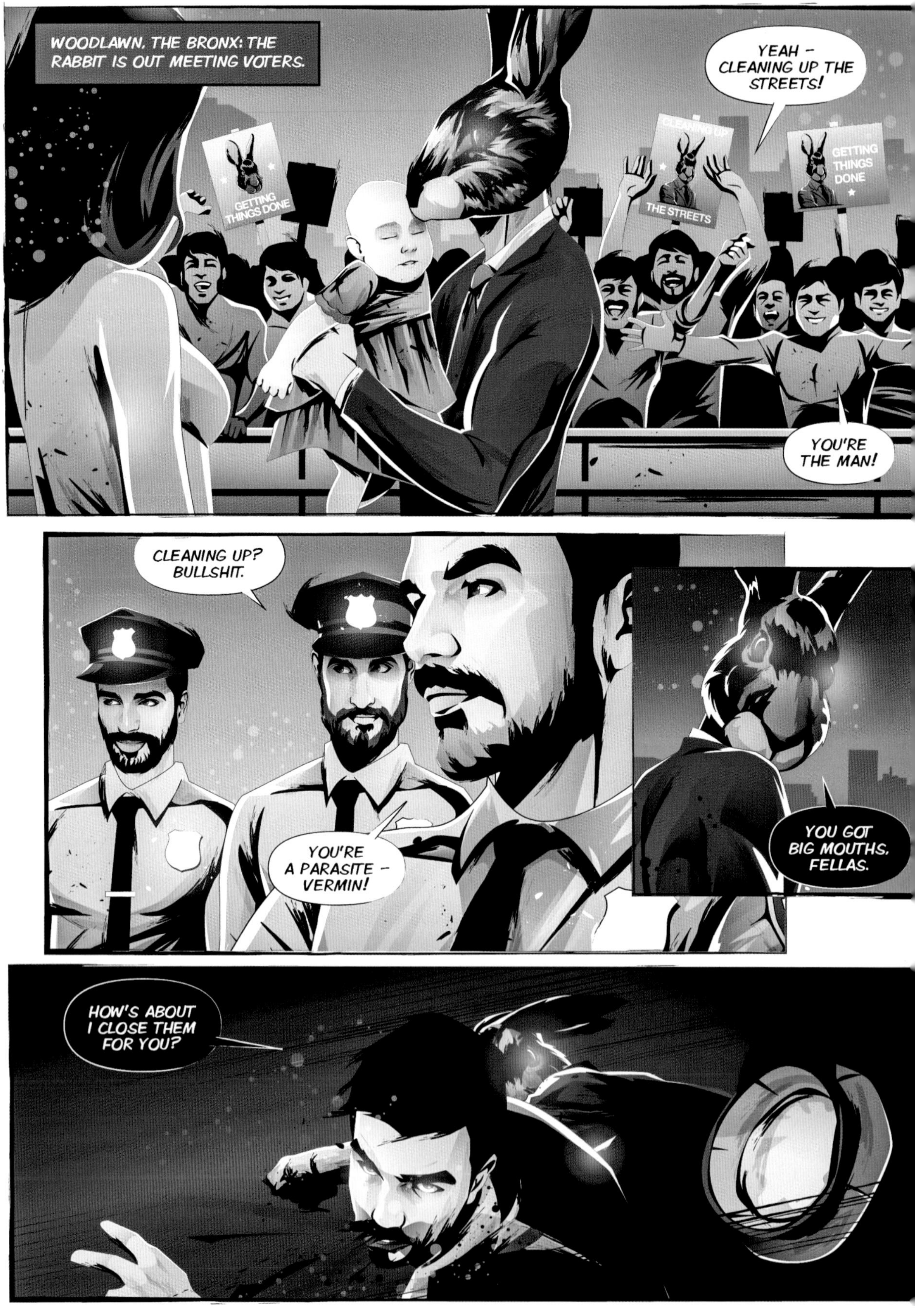
WOODLAWN, THE BRONX: THE RABBIT IS OUT MEETING VOTERS.
GETTING THINGS DONE
CLEANING UP THE STREETS
GETTING THINGS DONE
YEAH - CLEANING UP THE STREETS!
YOU'RE THE MAN!
CLEANING UP? BULLSHIT.
YOU'RE A PARASITE - VERMIN!
YOU GOT BIG MOUTHS, FELLAS.
HOW'S ABOUT I CLOSE THEM FOR YOU?

BABY FACE

INGREDIENTS

2 DASHES	Bittered Sling Clingstone Peach Bitters
1 OZ	Lime juice
0.25 OZ	Guava Syrup (page 260)
0.75 OZ	Togarashi Syrup (page 273)
0.25 OZ	Boukman Botanical Rhum
2 OZ	Oro de Lidia Reposado Tequila

TOOLS
Jiggers, shaker tins, fine strainer, Hawthorne strainer, nutmeg grater
METHOD
Shake with ice; fine strain and serve up without ice
GLASSWARE
Sour glass
GARNISH
Nutmeg
ORIGIN
Jessica Friedman

DOMINATION

179.

BABY FACE

JESSICA'S INSPIRATION

I NEEDED TO MAKE A TEQUILA COCKTAIL FOR MY BOXING DEBUT.

I was looking for something that would be tropical and refreshing – and who doesn't like a bit of spice with their margarita? Exactly.

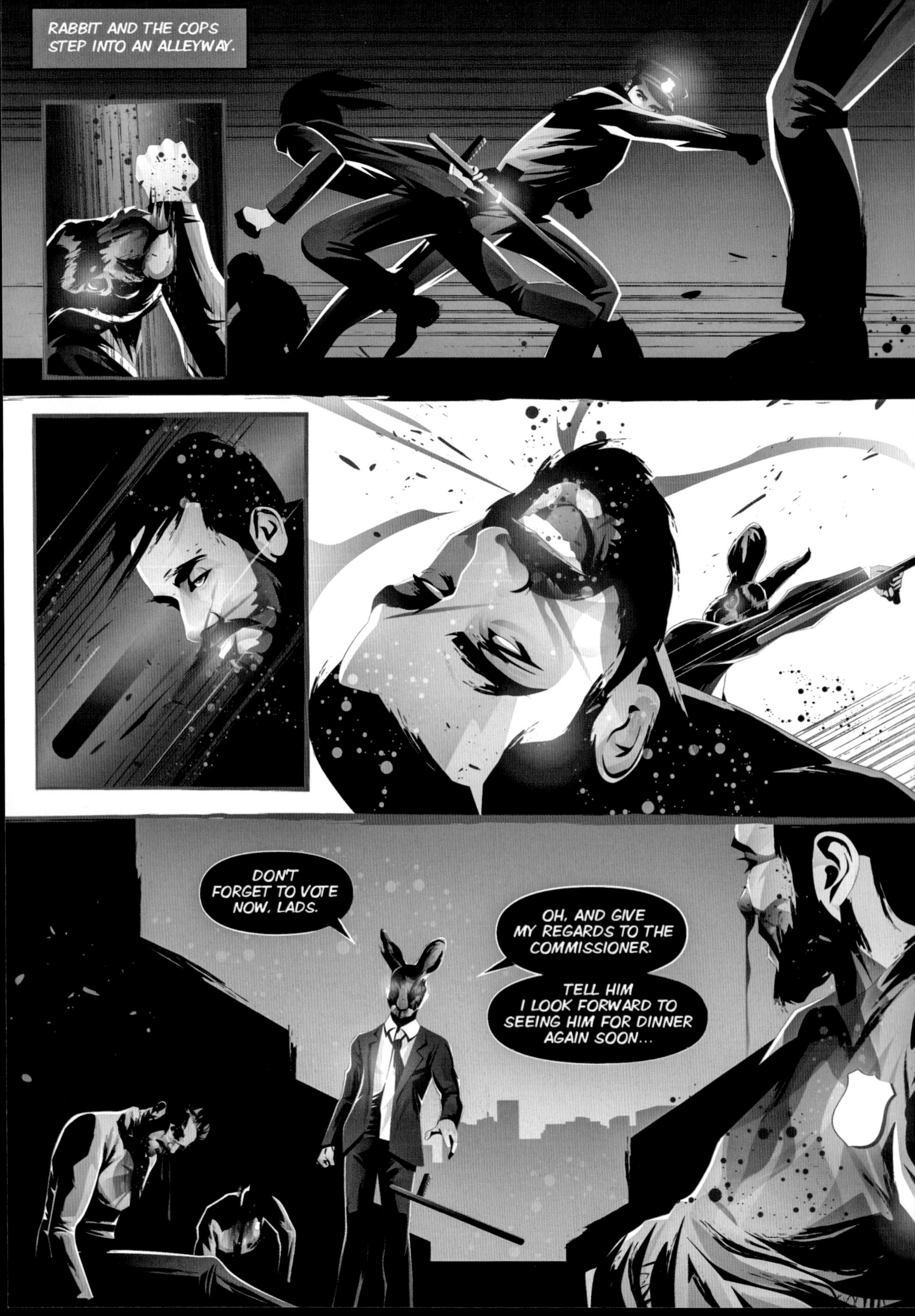
RABBIT AND THE COPS STEP INTO AN ALLEYWAY.
DON'T FORGET TO VOTE NOW, LADS.
OH, AND GIVE MY REGARDS TO THE COMMISSIONER.
TELL HIM I LOOK FORWARD TO SEEING HIM FOR DINNER AGAIN SOON...

CITIZEN KANE

INGREDIENTS

1 DASH	Bittermens Orchard Street Celery Shrub
0.25 OZ	John D. Taylor's Velvet Falernum Liqueur
0.75 OZ	Dolin Blanc Vermouth
0.25 OZ	Rhum J.M. Agricole
1.5 OZ	Sugar Snap Pea–Infused El Tesoro Platinum Tequila (page 272)

TOOLS
Jiggers, mixing glass, barspoon, julep strainer

METHOD
Stir with ice; strain with julep strainer; serve up without ice

GLASSWARE
Nick & Nora

GARNISH
Lemon oil; discard

ORIGIN
Jillian Vose

181.

JILLIAN'S INSPIRATION

WE ALWAYS HAVE A FRESH-STYLE MARTINI ON THE MENU, AND I WANTED TO MAKE SURE WE DID THAT THIS TIME AS WELL.

Also, I'd been missing our sugar snap pea tequila. Ryan made the infusion and I plugged it into that 50/50 template with falernum and celery bitters to match the snap peas. It was a bit rich and a touch flat. I bumped it up with rum. A good agricole or high-proof Wray & Nephew usually does the trick – especially in tequila-based cocktails. QED.

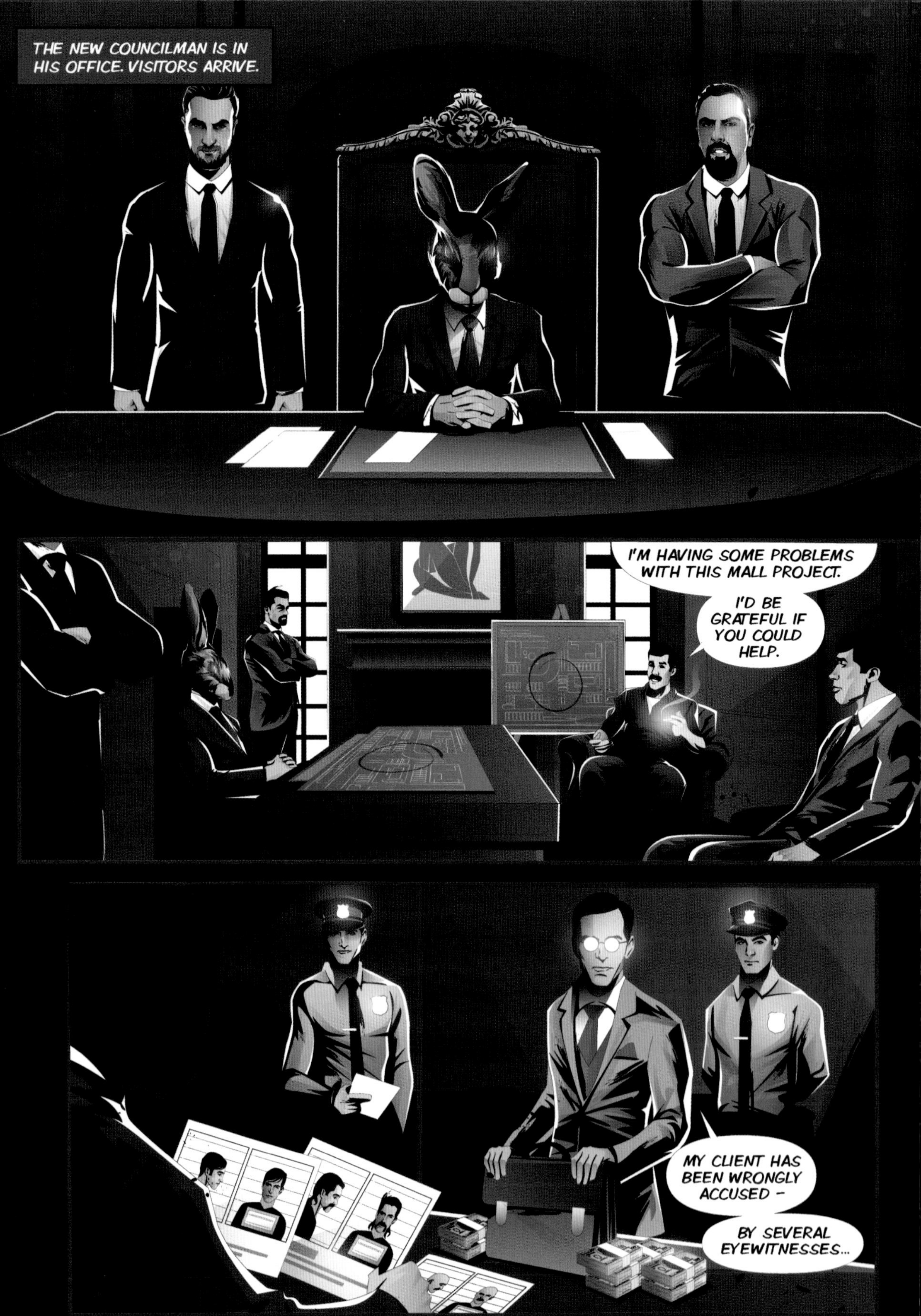
THE NEW COUNCILMAN IS IN HIS OFFICE. VISITORS ARRIVE.
I'M HAVING SOME PROBLEMS WITH THIS MALL PROJECT.
I'D BE GRATEFUL IF YOU COULD HELP.
MY CLIENT HAS BEEN WRONGLY ACCUSED -
BY SEVERAL EYEWITNESSES...

CONTROL FREAK

INGREDIENTS

1.5 OZ	Bell's Two Hearted IPA (not to be shaken with other ingredients)
2 DASHES	White Peony Tea Tincture (page 276)
0.75 OZ	Lemon juice
0.5 OZ	Lemon Sherbet (page 262)
0.5 OZ	Passion Fruit Syrup (page 266)
0.5 OZ	Combier Crème de Pamplemousse Rose Liqueur
0.5 OZ	Siembra Valles Blanco Tequila
1.5 OZ	Mango-Infused Pisco (page 263)

TOOLS
Jiggers, shaker tins, fine strainer, Hawthorne strainer, ice pick, nutmeg grater

METHOD
Add ale to mustache cup; shake drink with ice; fine strain into cup with ale and serve with ice nugget

GLASSWARE
Mustache cup

GARNISH
Nutmeg

ORIGIN
Long Thai

DOMINATION

183.

CONTROL FREAK

LONG'S INSPIRATION

I WANTED A BEER COCKTAIL WITH MASS APPEAL, BUT ALSO WITH THE COMPLEXITIES OF AN AMAZING COCKTAIL.

All ingredients were based on the flavor profile of the Bell's Two Hearted IPA – a malt-forward beer bursting with grapefruit and pine flavors and aroma. The tequila and white peony tea heighten the pine element, with a touch of herbaceous notes. Bright, tropical, citrusy, herbaceous: What's not to love? Beer for the win!

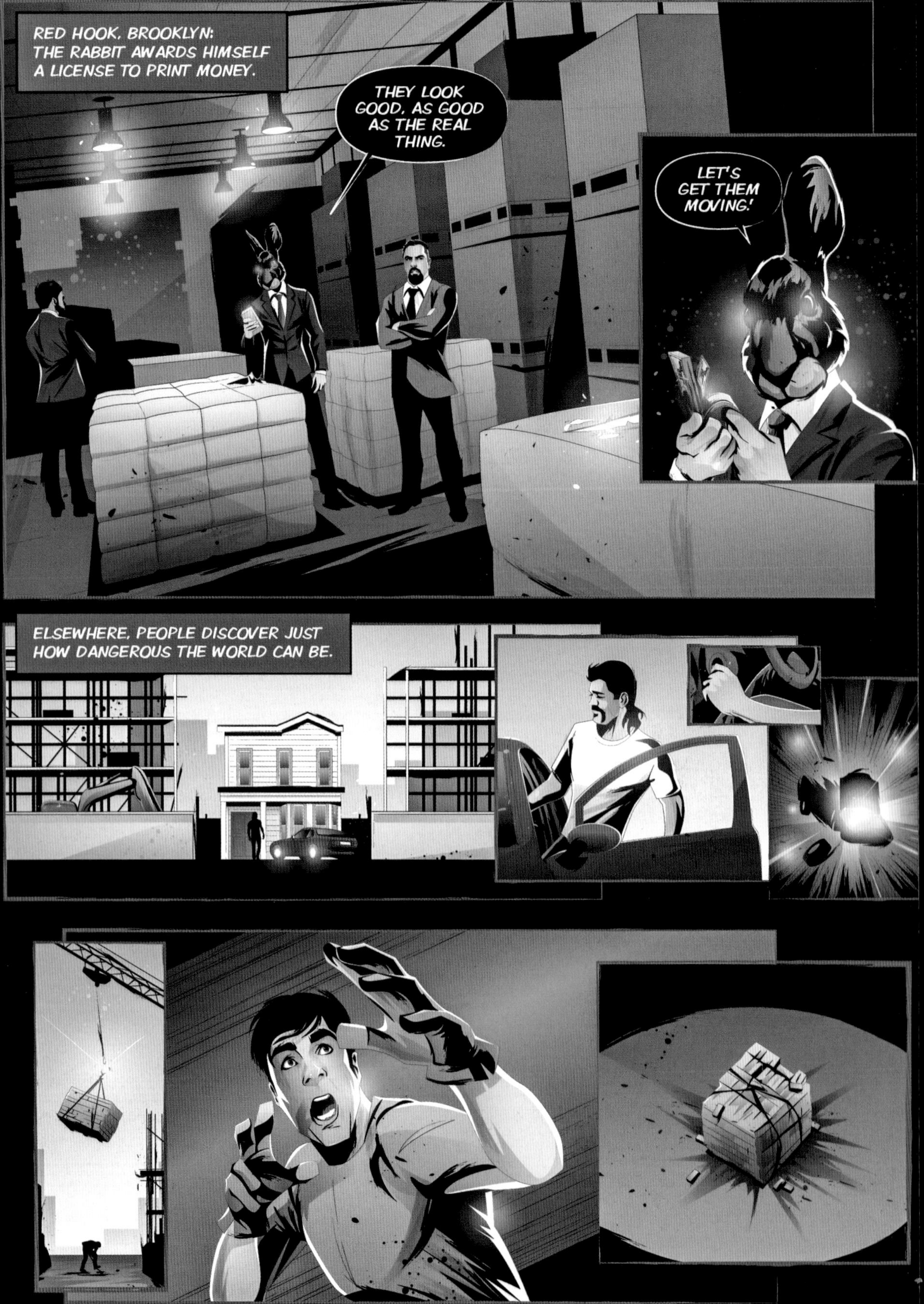
RED HOOK, BROOKLYN: THE RABBIT AWARDS HIMSELF A LICENSE TO PRINT MONEY.
THEY LOOK GOOD, AS GOOD AS THE REAL THING.
LET'S GET THEM MOVING!
ELSEWHERE, PEOPLE DISCOVER JUST HOW DANGEROUS THE WORLD CAN BE.

BANG OUT OF ORDER

INGREDIENTS

1 DASH	Bitter Truth Decanter Bitters
1 DASH	Bittermens 'Elemakule Tiki Bitters
0.75 OZ	Lemon juice
0.25 OZ	Fennel Syrup (page 258)
0.25 OZ	Beet Syrup (page 252)
0.5 OZ	Blackberry Syrup (page 252)
0.5 OZ	Lillet Rosé
2 OZ	Dead Rabbit Irish Whiskey

TOOLS
Jiggers, shaker tins, fine strainer, Hawthorne strainer

METHOD
Shake with ice; fine strain and serve up without ice

GLASSWARE
Sour glass

ORIGIN
Jillian Vose

JILLIAN'S INSPIRATION

I CHOSE OUR DEAD RABBIT IRISH WHISKEY FOR ITS HIGHER PROOF AND VIRGIN AMERICAN OAK FINISH.

It's really versatile in mixed drinks, especially shaken ones, as it doesn't get lost in the mix. I started with a simple sour of the syrups, lemon and whiskey. After tasting it, I picked two bitters that complemented the syrups well. The tiki brought a spicy, tropical high note and the decanter bound everything together. The sour was better but too sweet and too short. Sherry didn't seem like it would be acceptable, sweet vermouth too muddy, dry vermouth would clash, Bonal too bitter . . . Ooh, I know – Lillet Rosé. Perfecto!

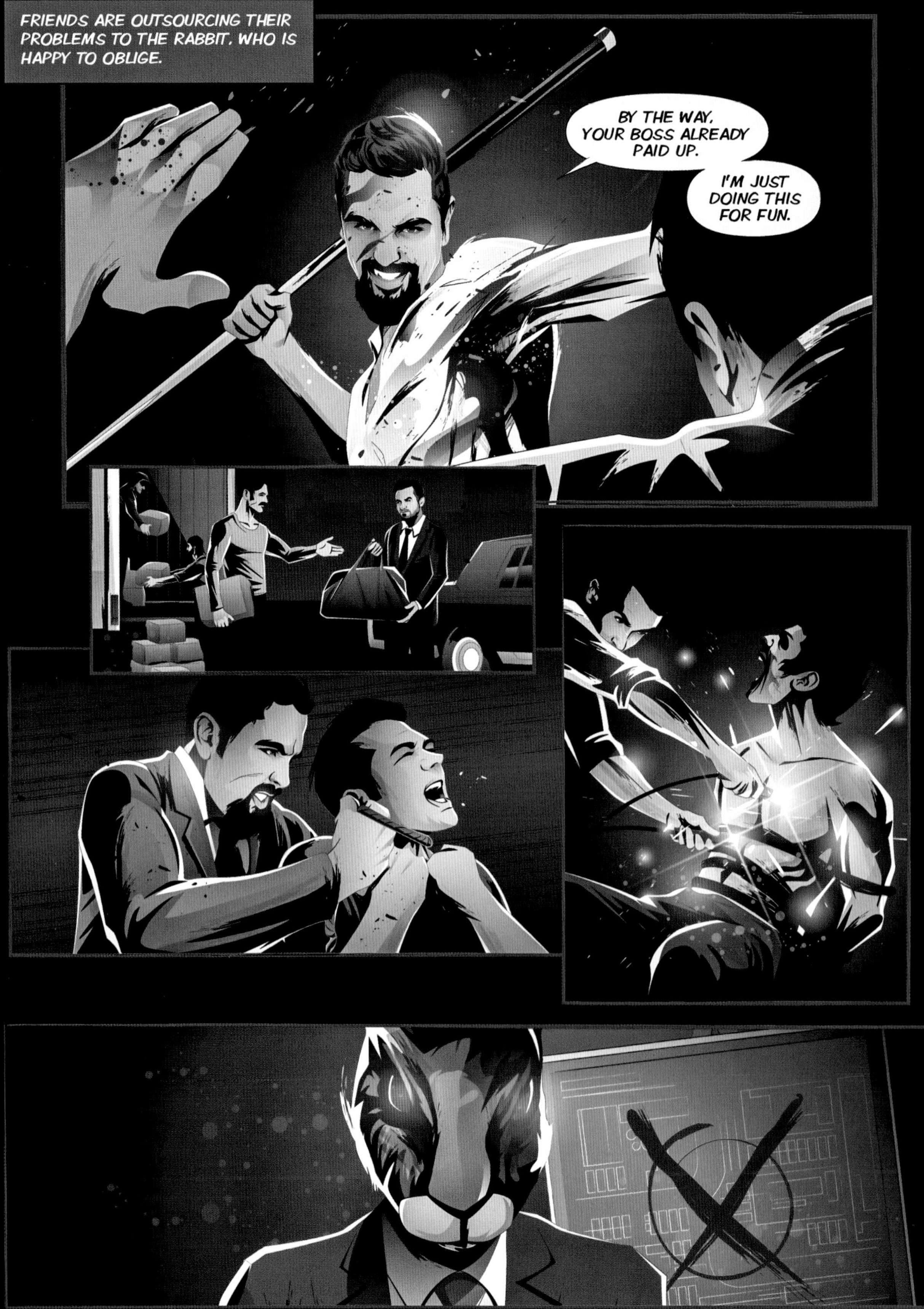
FRIENDS ARE OUTSOURCING THEIR PROBLEMS TO THE RABBIT, WHO IS HAPPY TO OBLIGE.
BY THE WAY, YOUR BOSS ALREADY PAID UP.
I'M JUST DOING THIS FOR FUN.

INDIAN ROPE TRICK

INGREDIENTS

1 DASH	Bitter Truth Aromatic Bitters
1 TSP	Nick Biz (equal parts Bonal and Vanilla Syrup, page 275)
1 TSP	Giffard Caribbean Pineapple Liqueur
1 OZ	Ancho Chili–Infused Sweet Vermouth (page 250)
0.5 OZ	Old Duff Genever
1 OZ	Glorious Gin: Oaked

TOOLS
Mixing glass, teaspoon, barspoon, julep strainer

METHOD
Stir with ice; strain with julep strainer and serve up without ice

GLASSWARE
Nick & Nora

GARNISH
Lemon oil (discard peel)

ORIGIN
Jillian Vose

DOMINATION

187.

INDIAN ROPE TRICK

JILLIAN'S INSPIRATION

IT'D BEEN SOME TIME SINCE I DID A MARTINEZ VARIATION.

I thought of it after tasting a new product, Glorious Gin, plus Phil Duff's new genever was on the market finally. It all came together with the martinez template. I'm not a huge fan of maraschino, so I opted for a different modifier with a split of Bonal and vanilla. Ancho chili sweet vermouth gave it a unique character, and the pineapple liqueur was the last tweak to take it to Dead Rabbit standards.

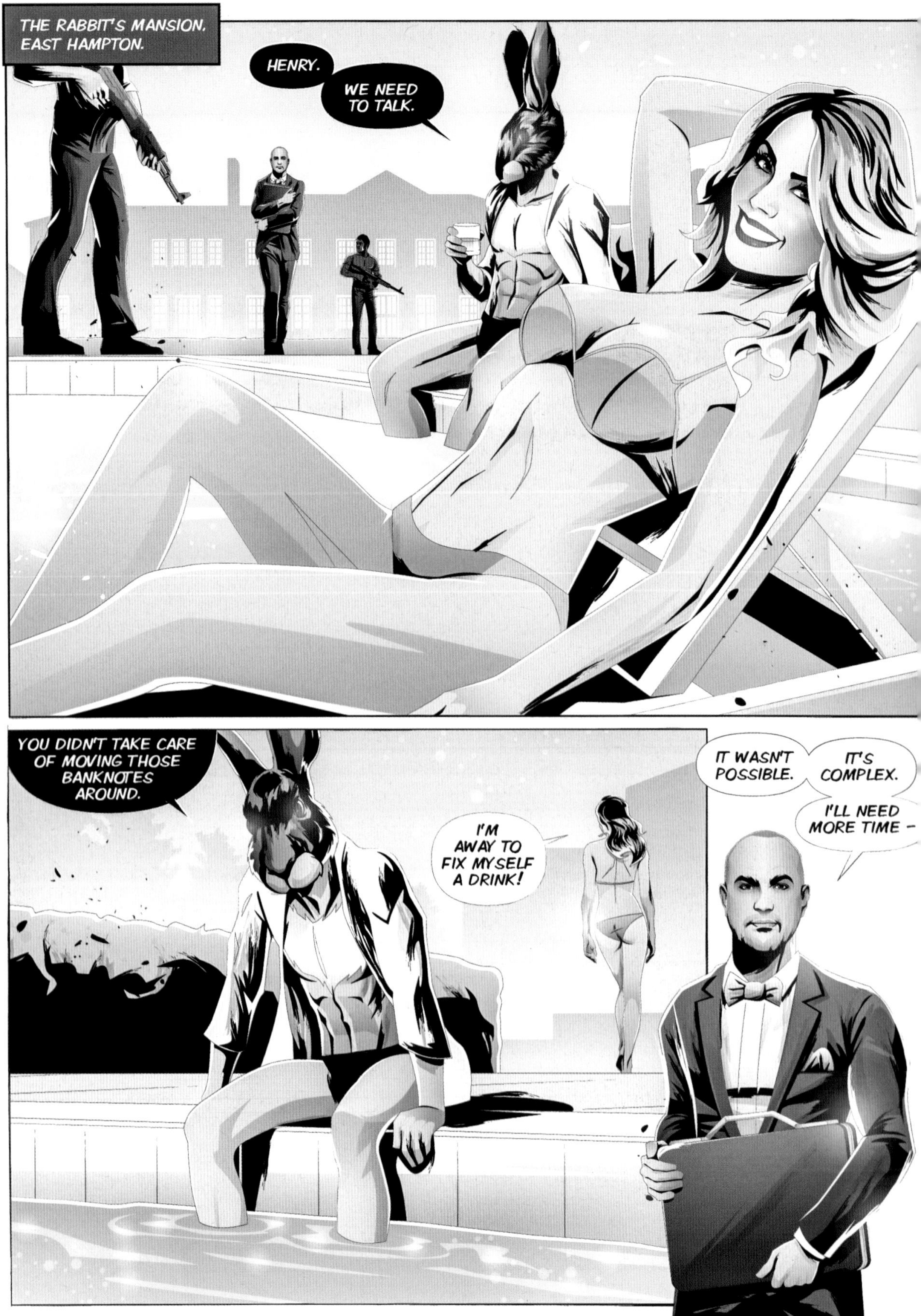
THE RABBIT'S MANSION. EAST HAMPTON.
HENRY.
WE NEED TO TALK.
YOU DIDN'T TAKE CARE OF MOVING THOSE BANKNOTES AROUND.
I'M AWAY TO FIX MYSELF A DRINK!
IT WASN'T POSSIBLE.
IT'S COMPLEX.
I'LL NEED MORE TIME –

SUNNY-SIDE UP

INGREDIENTS

1 DASH	Bittermens Xocolatl Mole Bitters
1 DASH	Angostura Bitters
0.25 OZ	Giffard Banane du Brésil
0.25 OZ	Pierre Ferrand Dry Curaçao
1 OZ	Cocchi Vermouth di Torino
1.5 OZ	Tullamore D.E.W. Caribbean Rum Cask Finish Irish Whiskey

TOOLS

Jiggers, mixing glass, barspoon, julep strainer

METHOD

Stir with ice; strain with julep strainer and serve up without ice

GLASSWARE

Nick & Nora

ORIGIN

Jillian Vose

DOMINATION

189.

SUNNY-SIDE UP

I WAS LUCKY ENOUGH TO TRY THIS NEW TULLAMORE D.E.W. EXPRESSION BEFORE IT HIT THE MARKET.

The rum cask finish lends it some beautiful tropical notes, which I enhanced with the banana liqueur. This is a Manhattan variation: nothing too crazy, but it reads really well and so is quite approachable – the complexity of the whiskey itself does all the talking.

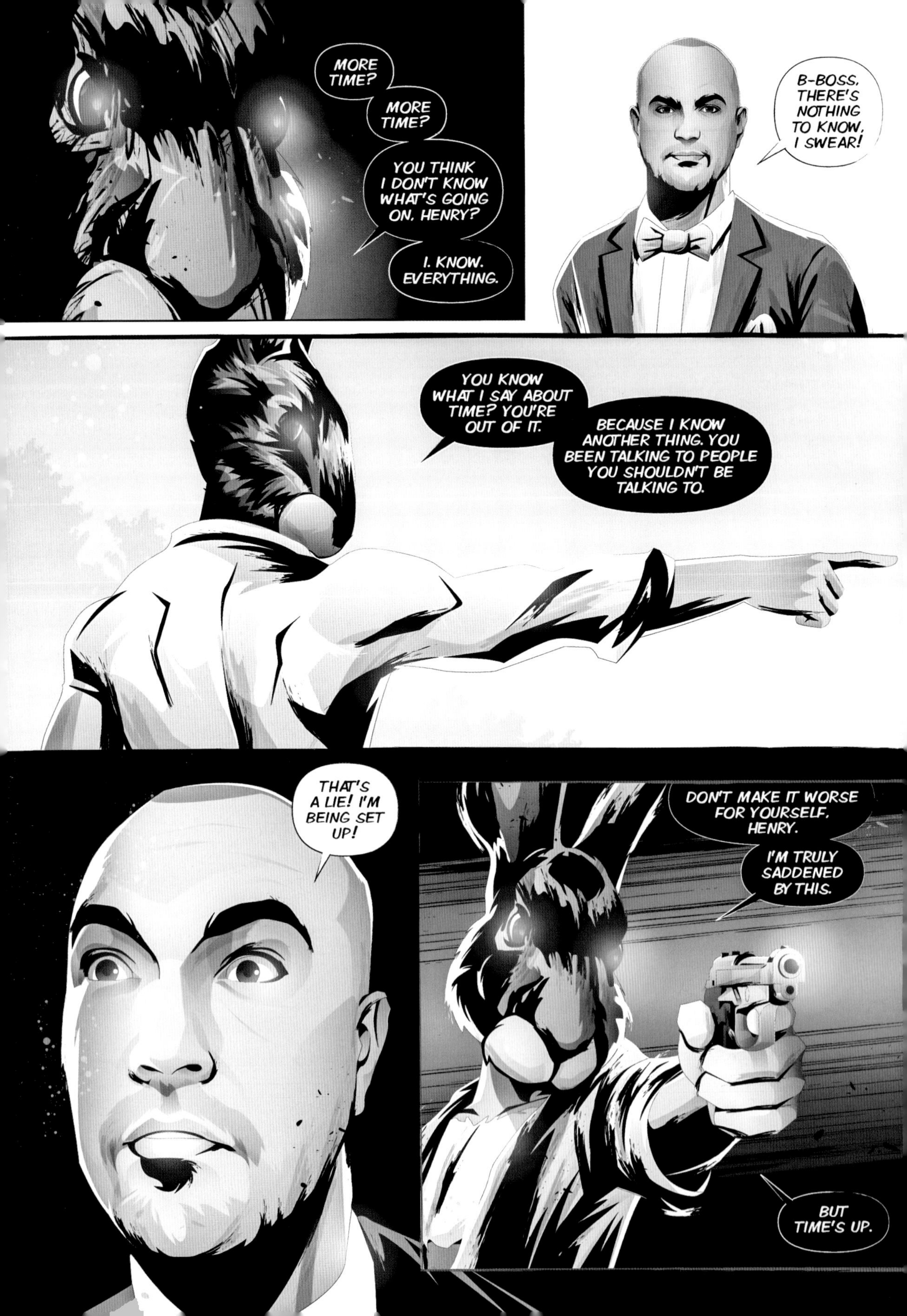
MORE TIME?
MORE TIME?
YOU THINK I DON'T KNOW WHAT'S GOING ON, HENRY?
I. KNOW. EVERYTHING.
B-BOSS, THERE'S NOTHING TO KNOW, I SWEAR!
YOU KNOW WHAT I SAY ABOUT TIME? YOU'RE OUT OF IT.
BECAUSE I KNOW ANOTHER THING. YOU BEEN TALKING TO PEOPLE YOU SHOULDN'T BE TALKING TO.
THAT'S A LIE! I'M BEING SET UP!
DON'T MAKE IT WORSE FOR YOURSELF, HENRY.
I'M TRULY SADDENED BY THIS.
BUT TIME'S UP.

BUSINESS BEFORE PLEASURE

INGREDIENTS

1	Egg white
1 BAR SPN	Mascarpone cheese
2 DASHES	Mace Tincture (page 263)
2 DASHES	Angostura Bitters
0.75 OZ	Lime juice
0.25 OZ	Tart Cherry Syrup (page 273)
0.75 OZ	Pistachio Orgeat (page 267)
0.25 OZ	Tempus Fugit Crème de Noyaux
1 OZ	Rémy Martin 1738 Cognac
1 OZ	Eagle Rare 10 Year Old Bourbon

TOOLS
Jiggers, barspoon, shaker tins, fine strainer, Hawthorne strainer

METHOD
Dry shake; shake with ice; fine strain and serve up without ice

GLASSWARE
Punch glass

GARNISH
Nutmeg

ORIGIN
Gregory Buda

GREGORY'S INSPIRATION

THE IDEA FOR THIS COCKTAIL CAME FROM A WONDERFUL DESSERT I HAD A LONG TIME AGO AT NOMAD, A RESTAURANT HERE IN NYC.

It was sort of a crumble made with pistachios, sour cherries and mascarpone cheese. That trio of flavors really stuck in my head. It took a while to figure out how to get them into a drink together. This rich whiskey sour variation was the answer.

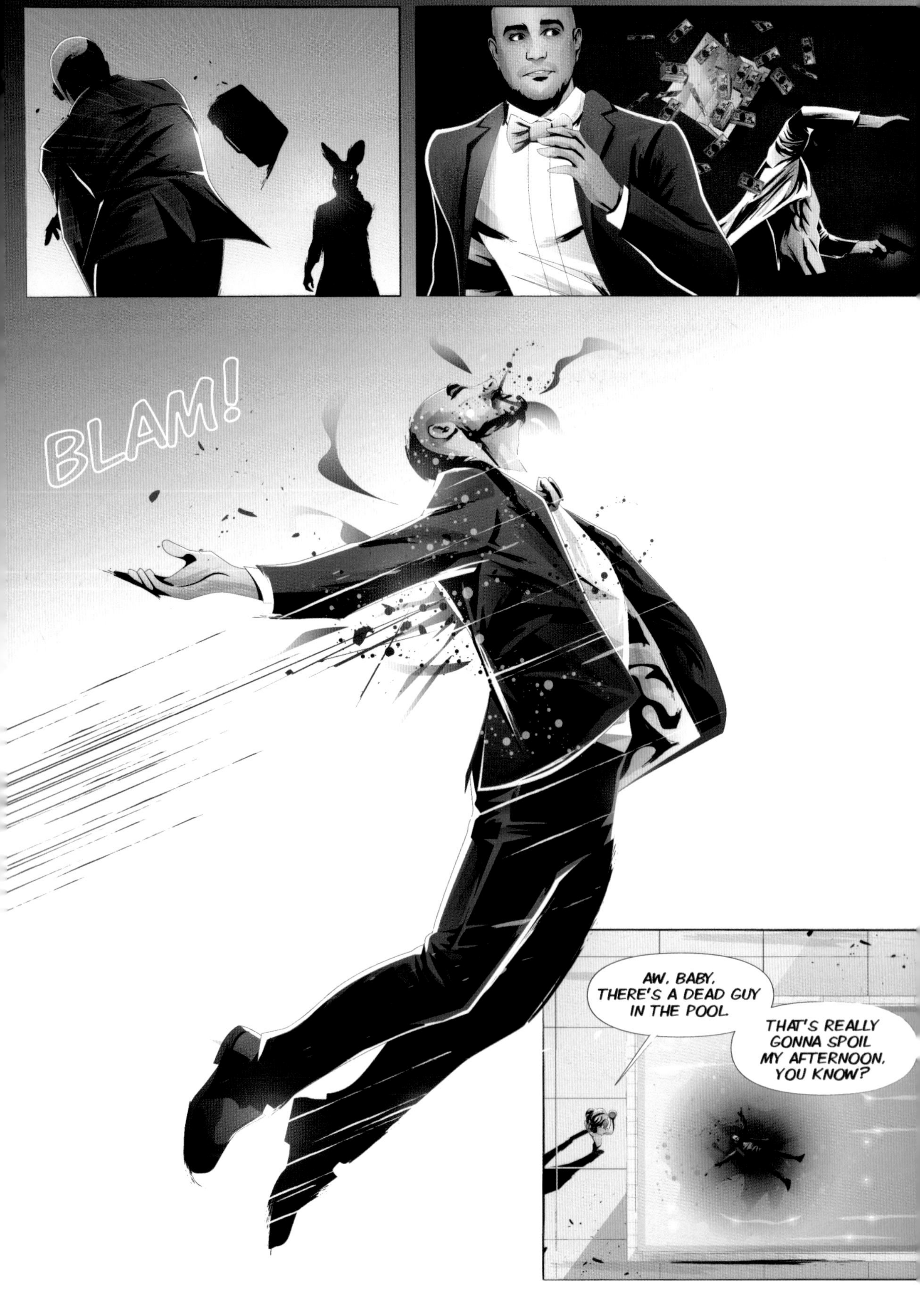
BLAM!
AW, BABY, THERE'S A DEAD GUY IN THE POOL.
THAT'S REALLY GONNA SPOIL MY AFTERNOON, YOU KNOW?

GUILT TRIP

INGREDIENTS

1 BAR SPN	Greek yogurt
1 DASH	House Orange Bitters (page 261)
4 DASHES	Za'atar Tincture (page 277)
1 TSP	Strega
0.75 OZ	Lemon juice
0.75 OZ	Sumac Syrup (page 272)
1.5 OZ	Teeling Single Grain Irish Whiskey

TOOLS

Jiggers, teaspoon, barspoon, shaker tins, fine strainer, Hawthorne strainer

METHOD

Shake with ice; fine strain and serve up without ice

GLASSWARE

Sour glass

GARNISH

Nutmeg

ORIGIN

Harrison Ginsberg

193.

HARRISON'S INSPIRATION

I WAS WATCHING AN ISRAELI DOCUMENTARY ON CUISINE — WHICH IS ESSENTIALLY A MISHMASH FROM ALL OVER THE MIDDLE EAST AND MEDITERRANEAN.

I wanted to impart these flavors into a cocktail. Starting with a base of the whiskey sour, I swapped Greek yogurt for egg white and added a little bit of za'atar, the Middle Eastern spice blend made from sesame seeds, dried oregano and parsley and some ground sumac. A little more sumac and a clean single grain Irish whiskey was the perfect match for this drink.

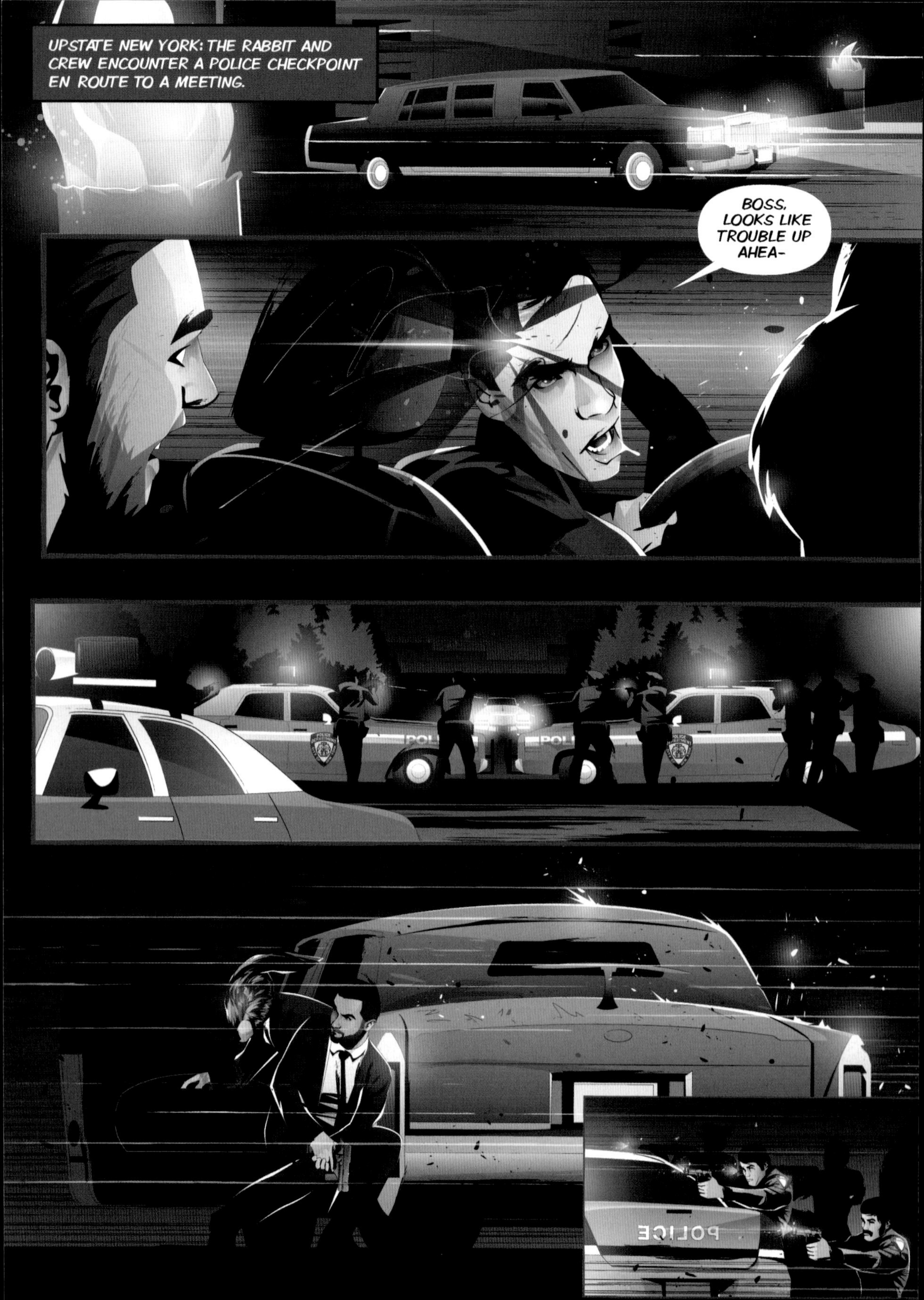
UPSTATE NEW YORK: THE RABBIT AND CREW ENCOUNTER A POLICE CHECKPOINT EN ROUTE TO A MEETING.
BOSS, LOOKS LIKE TROUBLE UP AHEA-
POLICE
POLICE
POLICE

HOME RUN

INGREDIENTS

0.75 OZ	Lime juice
0.5 OZ	Pineapple juice
0.25 OZ	Cinnamon Bark Syrup (page 255)
0.75 OZ	Genmaicha Tea Syrup (page 259)
0.5 OZ	Amaro Nonino
0.5 OZ	Montreuil Calvados Selection
1 OZ	Highland Park Magnus Scotch

TOOLS
Jiggers, shaker tins, fine strainer, Hawthorne strainer, nutmeg grater

METHOD
Shake with ice; fine strain and serve up without ice

GLASSWARE
Sour glass

GARNISH
Nutmeg

ORIGIN
Jillian Vose

DOMINATION

195.

HOME RUN

JILLIAN'S INSPIRATION

WE WERE LOW ON SCOTCH COCKTAILS, SO THAT WAS MY STARTING POINT.

When I'm basing a drink off a particular spirit, I do a thorough tasting, writing down all the aromas I can get. I'll use these notes to base the flavor pairing for modifiers. I thought that our genmaicha syrup would pair well with the scotch, and I knew pineapple was a great match to the brown rice as well. I then split Highland Park with calvados. Amaro Nonino is a softer style of amaro, so I picked that to add layers and complexity. Cinnamon was a nice accent to the drink.

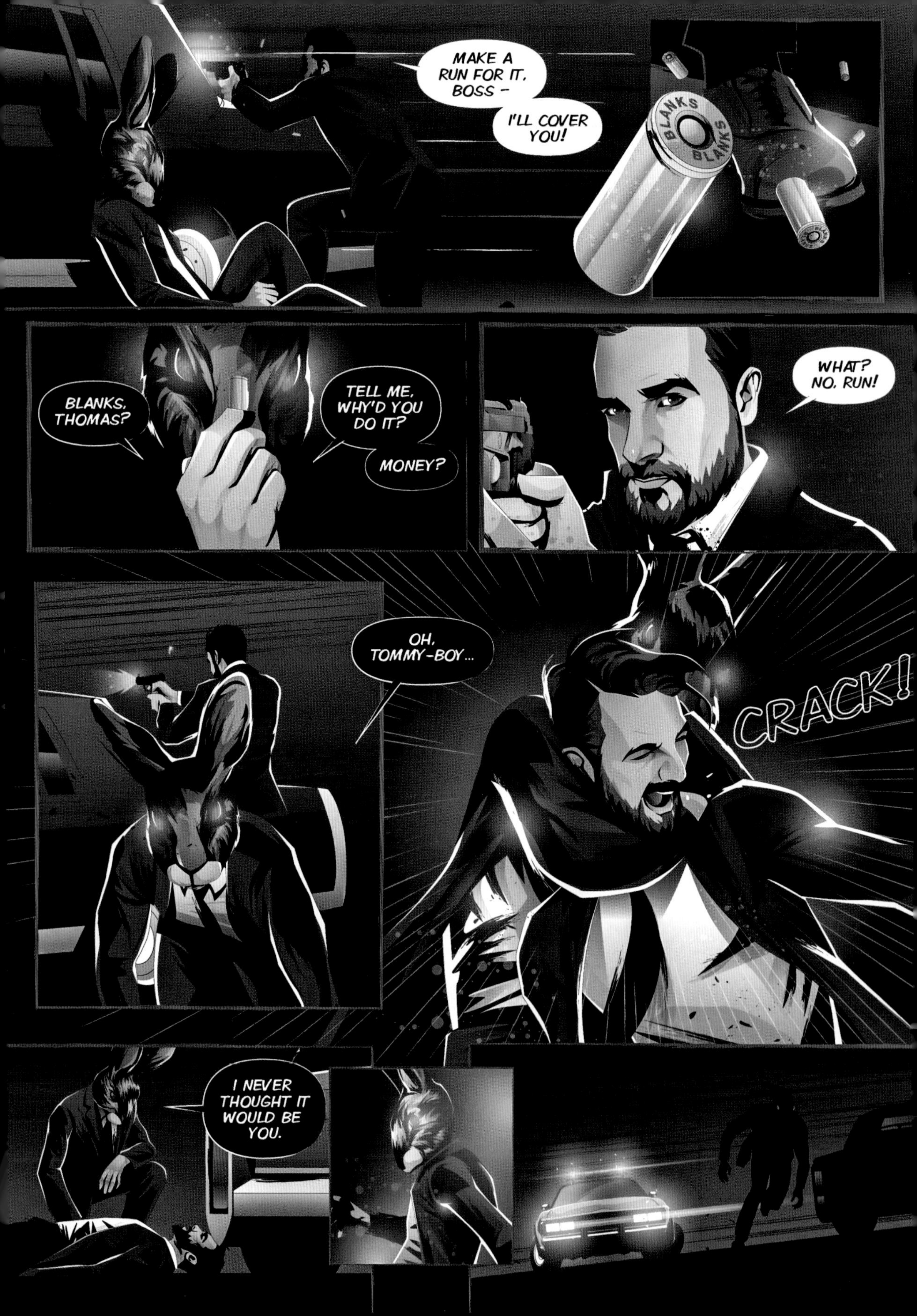
MAKE A RUN FOR IT, BOSS -
I'LL COVER YOU!
BLANKS
BLANKS, THOMAS?
TELL ME, WHY'D YOU DO IT?
MONEY?
WHAT? NO, RUN!
OH, TOMMY-BOY...
CRACK!
I NEVER THOUGHT IT WOULD BE YOU.

MAGIC BULLET

INGREDIENTS

0.5 TSP	Demerara Syrup (page 257)
0.5 TSP	Galliano Ristretto
0.5 OZ	Raspberry-Infused Bruto Americano (page 269)
0.25 OZ	Giffard Crème de Cacao (white)
0.5 OZ	Cocchi Rosa
0.5 OZ	Barbadillo Oloroso Sherry
0.75 OZ	Torres 15 Year Spanish Brandy
0.75 OZ	Scarlet Ibis Rum

TOOLS
Jiggers, mixing glass, ½ teaspoon, barspoon, julep strainer, ice pick

METHOD
Stir with ice; strain with julep strainer and serve over large block of ice

GLASSWARE
Old Fashioned

GARNISH
Orange oil (discard peel)

ORIGIN
Nick Rolin

NICK'S INSPIRATION

EVERY NOW AND THEN, A SPECIFIC PRODUCT WILL INSPIRE A COCKTAIL.

In this case, it was Bruto Americano – a bitter, fruit- and pine-forward aperitif. I thought it would pair well with raspberry and coffee. This turned out to be fairly difficult, and I went through many versions. In the end, I reduced the original amount of Bruto, but the end product is a herbal, dark riff on a negroni.

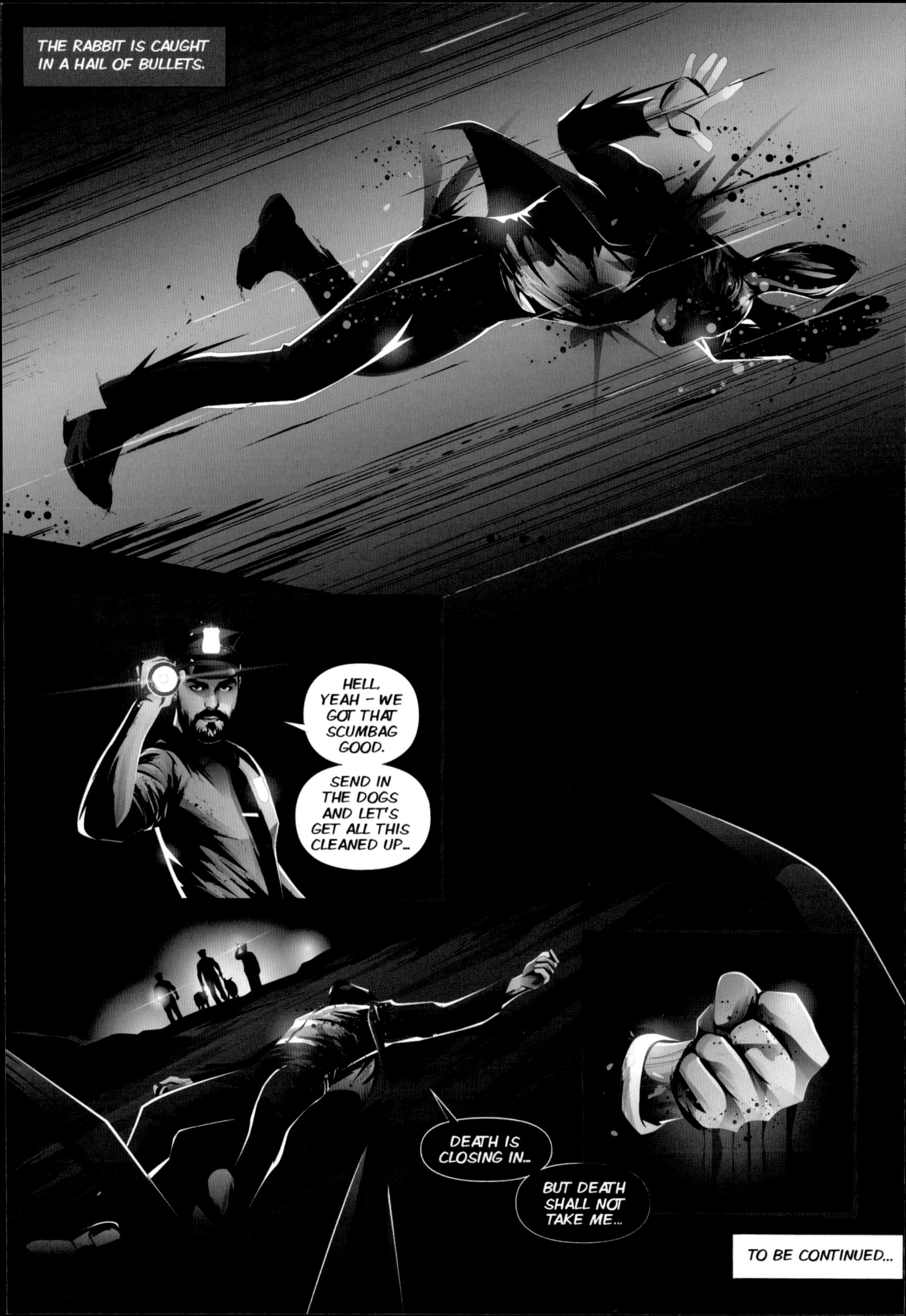
THE RABBIT IS CAUGHT IN A HAIL OF BULLETS.
HELL, YEAH - WE GOT THAT SCUMBAG GOOD.
SEND IN THE DOGS AND LET'S GET ALL THIS CLEANED UP...
DEATH IS CLOSING IN...
BUT DEATH SHALL NOT TAKE ME...
TO BE CONTINUED...

DEEP DOWN AND DIRTY

INGREDIENTS

1 DASH	Bitter Truth Aromatic Bitters
0.75 OZ	Lemon juice
0.5 OZ	Grapefruit juice
0.5 OZ	Poppy Seed Syrup (page 268)
0.25 OZ	Macadamia Orgeat (page 263)
0.25 OZ	Blueberry Cane Syrup (page 253)
1 OZ	Tariquet VS Classique Armagnac
1 OZ	Basil Hayden's Bourbon

TOOLS
Jiggers, shaker tins, fine strainer, Hawthorne strainer, ice pick, nutmeg grater

METHOD
Shake with ice; fine strain and serve with ice nugget

GLASSWARE
Punch glass

GARNISH
Nutmeg

ORIGIN
Jillian Vose

DOMINATION

199.

DEEP DOWN AND DIRTY

JILLIAN'S INSPIRATION

I WAS SEEKING INSPIRATION FOR THIS MENU AS I HAD A FEW SLOTS TO FILL, SO I STARTED FLIPPING THROUGH SOME OF MY OLDER DRINKS NOTEBOOKS.

I have a ton of them – some organized, some definitely not. I found some dumb ideas and some really great ones. I went back to a drink called Witchdoctor I did at Death & Co, and then another at The Dead Rabbit called Rag & Bone. I morphed them together to make this drink.

IT IS SAID THAT ONE LIFE
IS IN FACT MANY LIVES.
THAT WE EACH CONTAIN
MULTITUDES. THAT TIME
AND EVENTS SHAPE US,
TRANSFORM US DOWN
THE YEARS.

PERHAPS. BUT IT IS NOT TRUE OF ALL OF
US. THERE ARE THOSE WHO WALK AMONG
US WHO ARE UNTOUCHED BY TIME.

For they have been here before, and perhaps will be again.
Theirs is a different life-force, a darker light. Unbidden, it stirs
within them, calls to them in the night; and they heed the call.

Though he appears close to death, The Rabbit once again
hears that ancient siren voice. It says: Rise, rise up once more
against your enemies. Then leave this place behind.

WHERE TIME HAS NO DOMINION, EVERY
BEGINNING IS AN END. AND VICE VERSA.

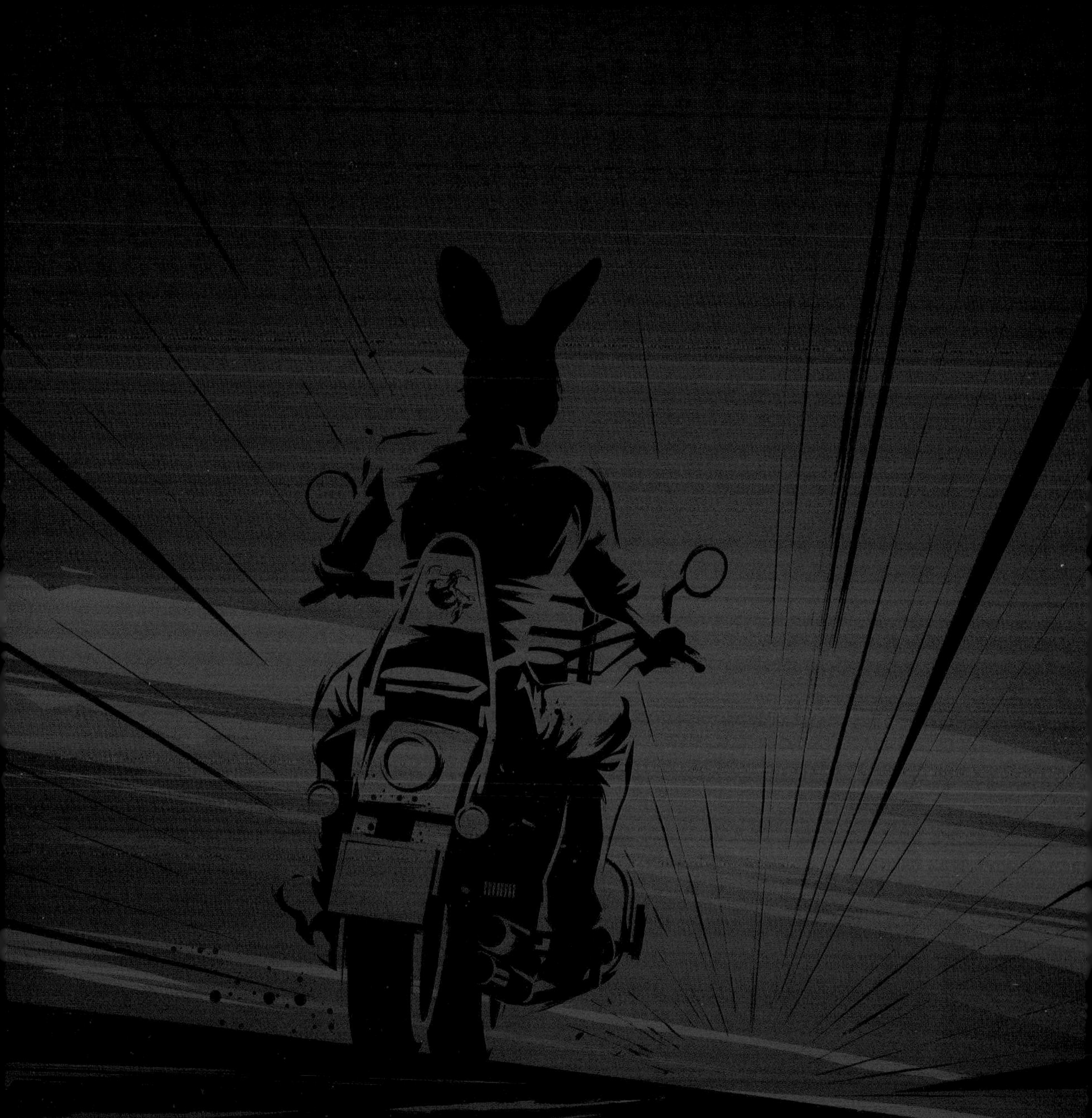

ENDGAME

MIXED DRINKS LIST | VOL 4 | ISSUE 6/6

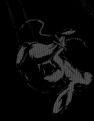

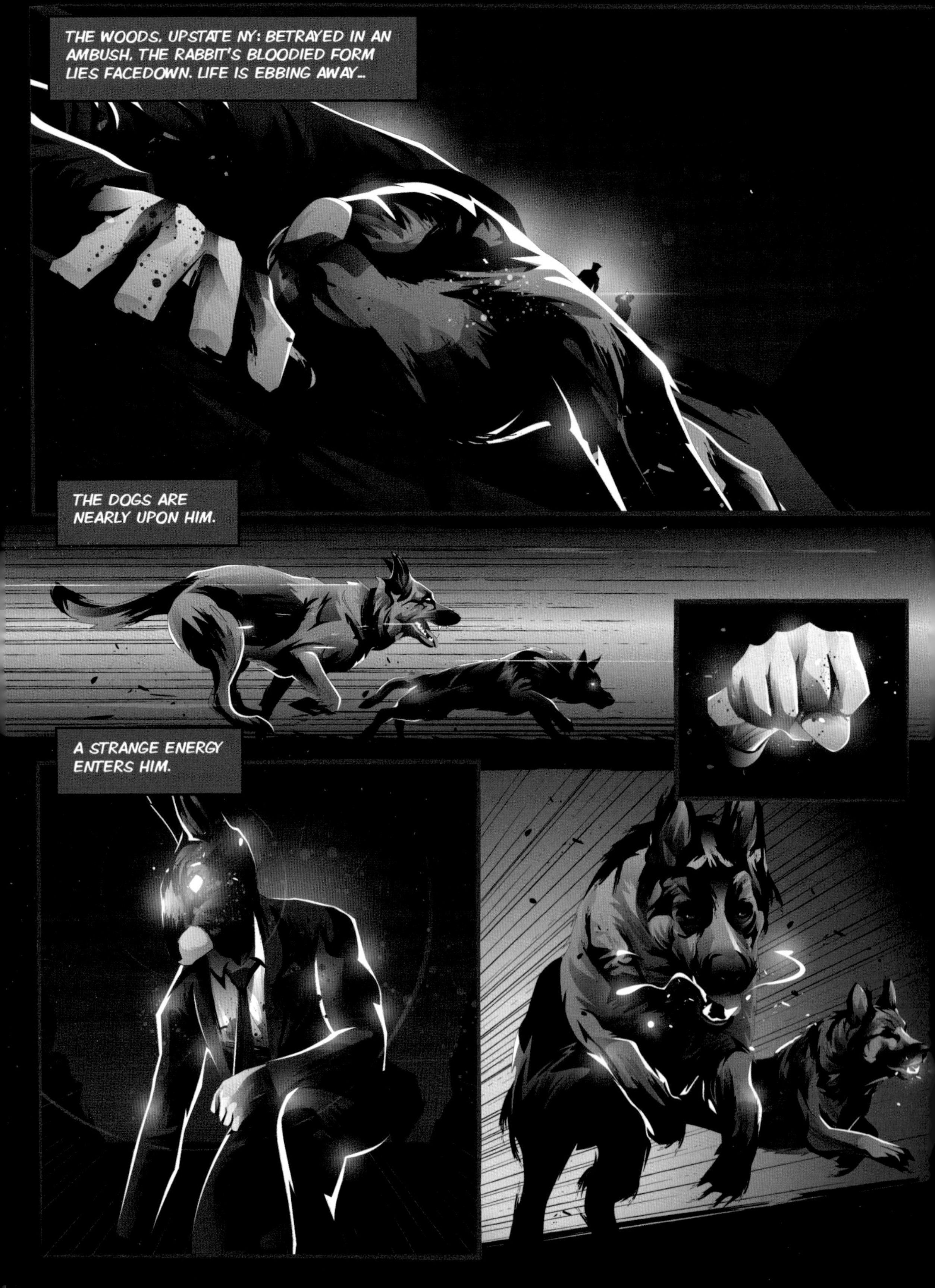
THE WOODS, UPSTATE NY: BETRAYED IN AN AMBUSH, THE RABBIT'S BLOODIED FORM LIES FACEDOWN. LIFE IS EBBING AWAY...
THE DOGS ARE NEARLY UPON HIM.
A STRANGE ENERGY ENTERS HIM.

POINT BLANK

INGREDIENTS

1 DASH	Bittermens Boston Bittahs
0.25 OZ	John D. Taylor's Velvet Falernum Liqueur
1.5 OZ	Dolin Blanc Vermouth
2 OZ	Honeydew and Cucumber–Infused Botanist Gin (page 261)

TOOLS

Jiggers, mixing glass, barspoon, julep strainer

METHOD

Stir with ice; strain with julep strainer and serve up without ice

GLASSWARE

Nick & Nora

GARNISH

Lemon oil (discard peel)

ORIGIN

Jillian Vose

203.

JILLIAN'S INSPIRATION

THIS IS A SUMMER MARTINI WITH RIPE MELON INFUSED INTO DELICATE BOTANIST GIN.

Cucumber adds herbaceous notes; the chamomile and citrus bitters and spiced falernum give depth. Dolin Blanc 'fattens' and sweetens the drink, lending balance and finish.

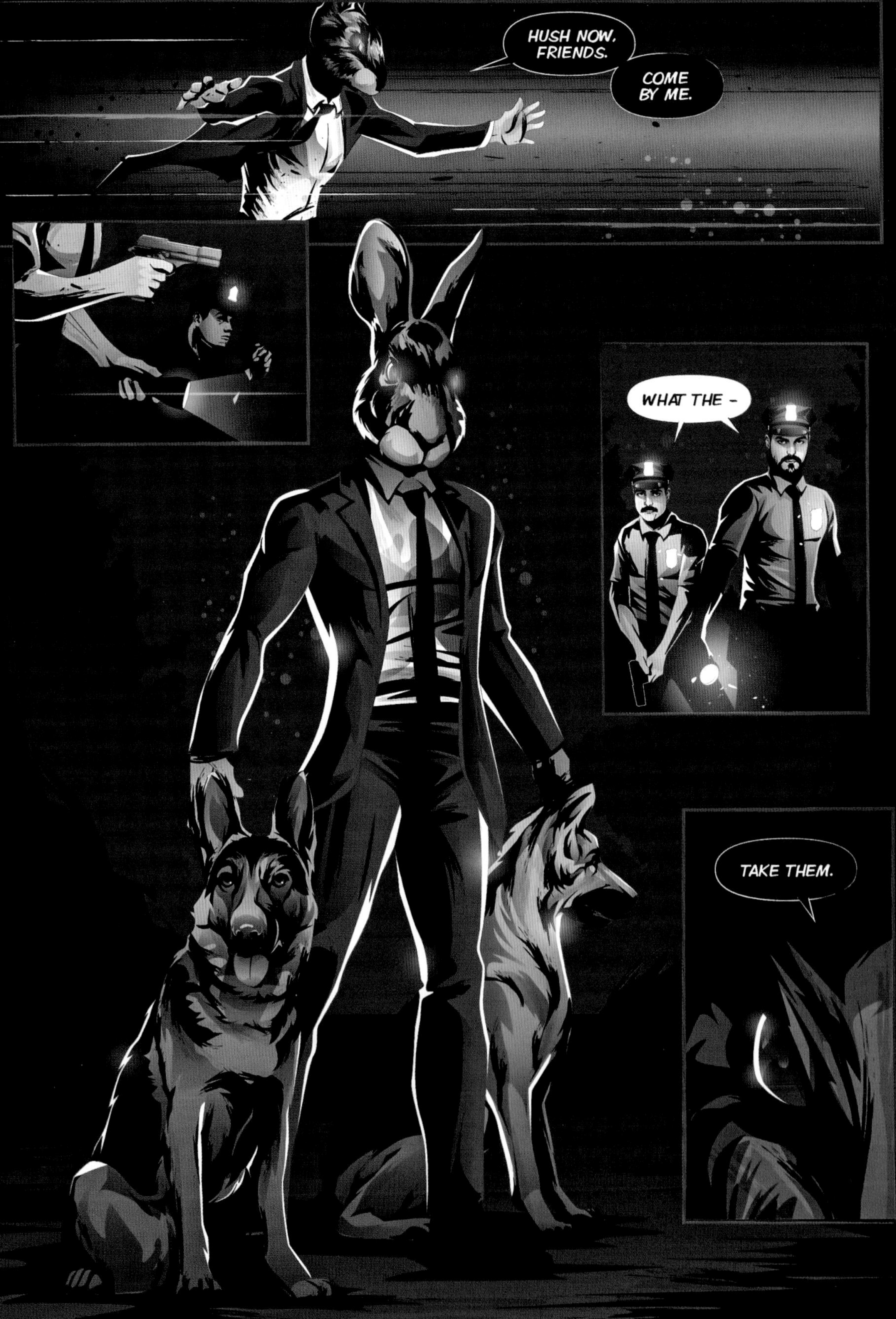
HUSH NOW, FRIENDS.
COME BY ME.
WHAT THE -
TAKE THEM.

TOTAL DIVA

INGREDIENTS

1 TBSP	Matcha Green Tea Coco López (page 264)
0.75 OZ	Lime juice
0.5 OZ	Orgeat (page 265)
0.25 OZ	Fennel Syrup (page 258)
0.25 OZ	Half & half
2 OZ	Citadelle Gin
1	Fresh kaffir lime leaf

TOOLS
Jiggers, tablespoon, shaker tins, fine strainer, Hawthorne strainer, nutmeg grater

METHOD
Build drink in tin; add kaffir lime leaf (do not muddle); whip shake with cube ice; fine strain and serve over pebble ice

GLASSWARE
Nog glass

GARNISH
Nutmeg

ORIGIN
Jillian Vose

JILLIAN'S INSPIRATION

THIS EVOLVED INTO A TIKI DRINK, WITH ANISE-GREEN TEA-COCONUT-ALMOND-LIME FLAVOR NOTES.

Gin was picked as a base to keep it on the refreshing side. Its piña colada–style required a cream quality for body, so a touch of half & half was added. Kaffir lime leaf was shaken in to cut through the richness, giving the drink a high note and a beautiful fragrance.

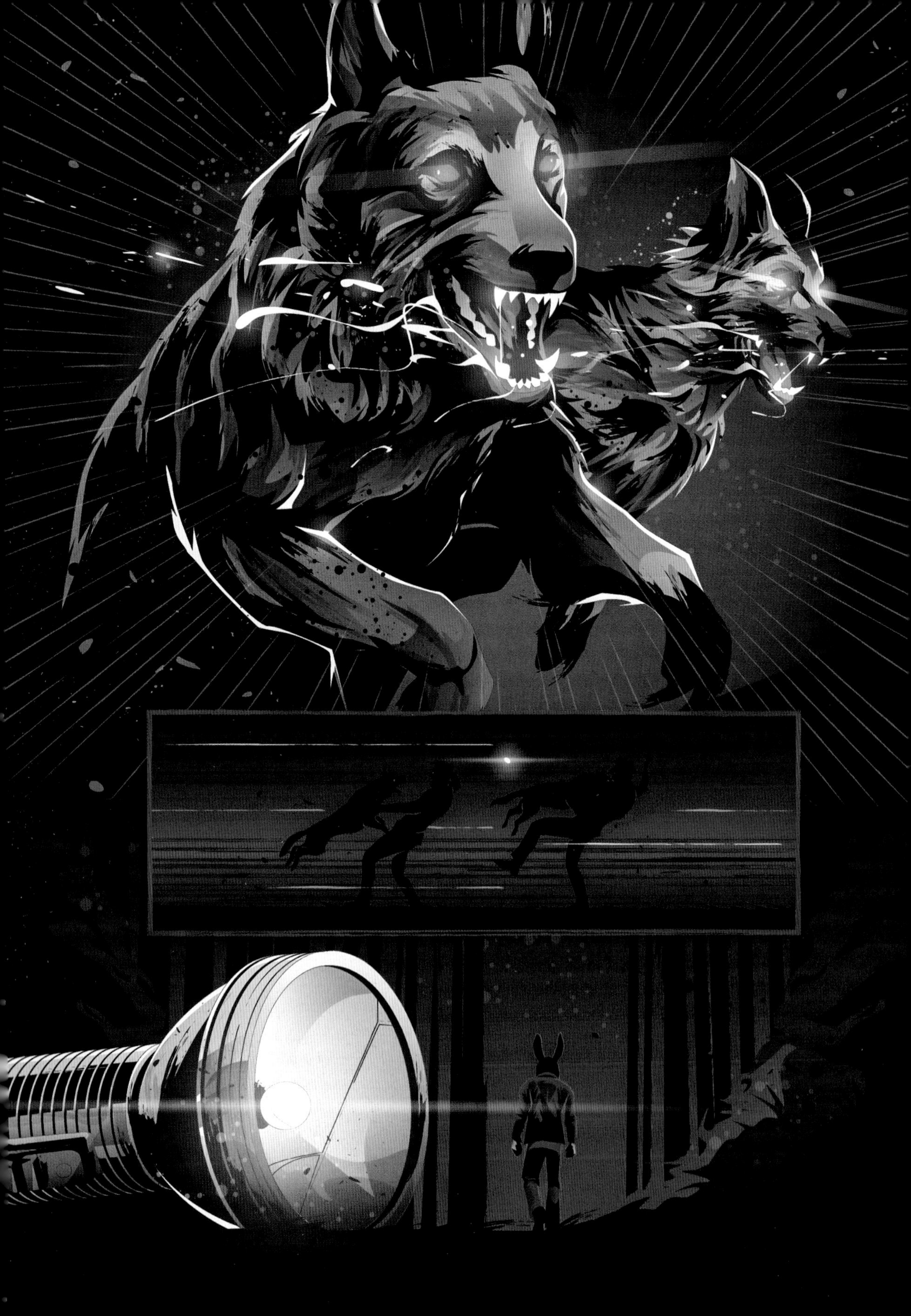

PSYCHO KILLER

INGREDIENTS

2 DASHES	Vieux Pontarlier Absinthe
0.75 OZ	Campari
0.5 OZ	Giffard Crème de Cacao (white)
0.5 OZ	Giffard Banane du Brésil
2 OZ	Redbreast 12 Year Irish Whiskey

TOOLS
Jiggers, mixing glass, barspoon, julep strainer
METHOD
Stir with ice; strain with julep strainer and serve up without ice
GLASSWARE
Nick & Nora
ORIGIN
Jillian Vose

207.

JILLIAN'S INSPIRATION

AN IRISH WHISKEY VARIATION ON A BOULEVARDIER.

Spruced up with banana and chocolate liqueurs to match the Christmas-cake qualities of the Redbreast . . .

A real favorite.

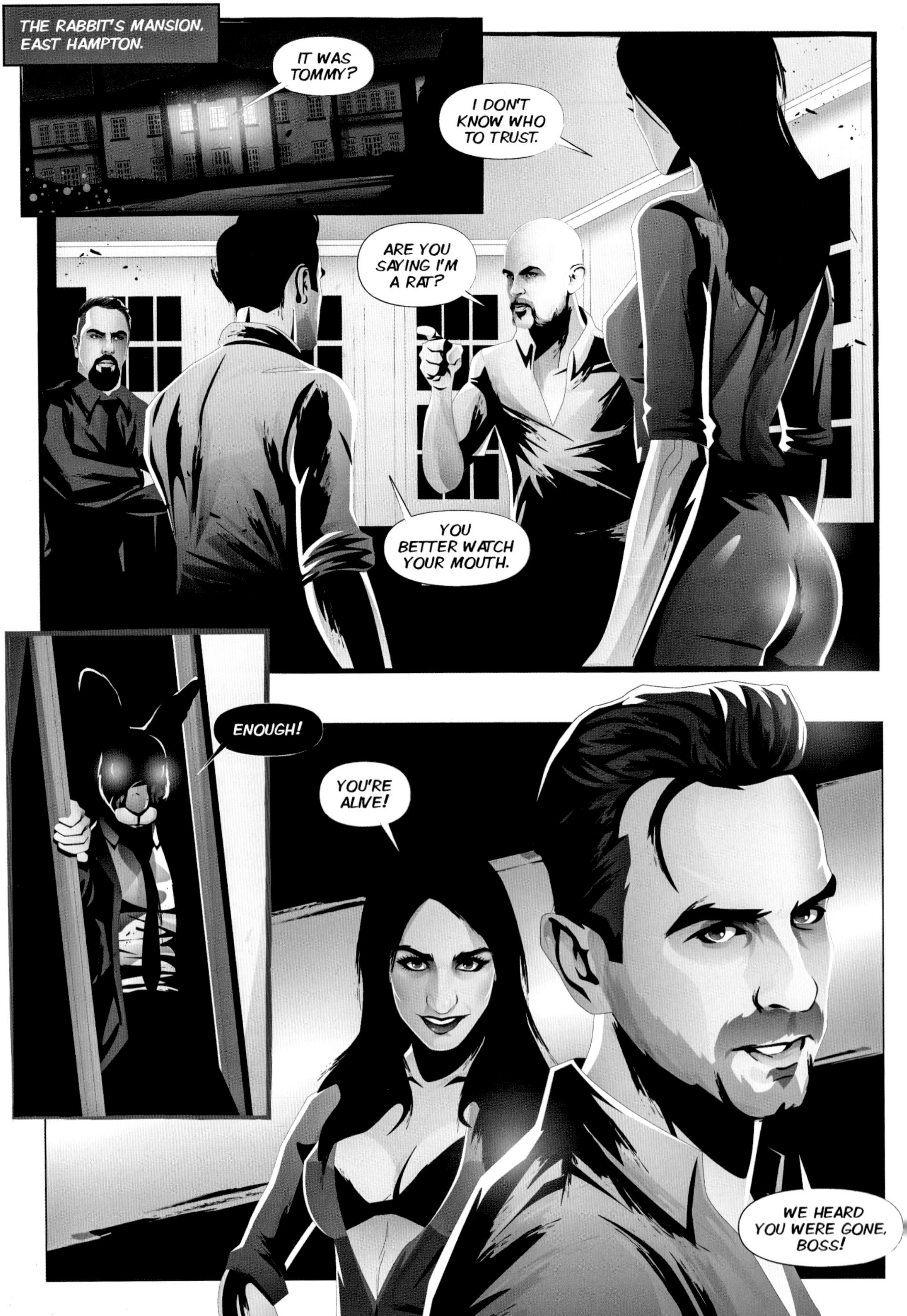
THE RABBIT'S MANSION, EAST HAMPTON.
IT WAS TOMMY?
I DON'T KNOW WHO TO TRUST.
ARE YOU SAYING I'M A RAT?
YOU BETTER WATCH YOUR MOUTH.
ENOUGH!
YOU'RE ALIVE!
WE HEARD YOU WERE GONE, BOSS!

FEMME FATALE

INGREDIENTS

1 TBSP	Lingonberry preserves
1 DASH	Peychaud's Bitters
0.75 OZ	Lemon juice
0.5 OZ	Cane Syrup (page 254)
0.5 OZ	Kronan Swedish Punsch Liqueur
0.5 OZ	Banks 5 Island Blend Rum
1 OZ	Brennivín Aquavit

TOOLS

Jiggers, tablespoon, shaker tins, fine strainer, Hawthorne strainer, ice pick

METHOD

Shake with ice; fine strain and serve with ice nugget

GLASSWARE

Punch glass

ORIGIN

Madeleine Solo Rapp

MADELEINE'S INSPIRATION

LINGONBERRIES ARE SOMETHING I HAVEN'T SEEN IN COCKTAILS IN THE U.S., THOUGH THEY'RE A FAMILIAR PART OF MY SCANDINAVIAN BACKGROUND.

I decided I wanted to incorporate them into a distinctively fall drink.

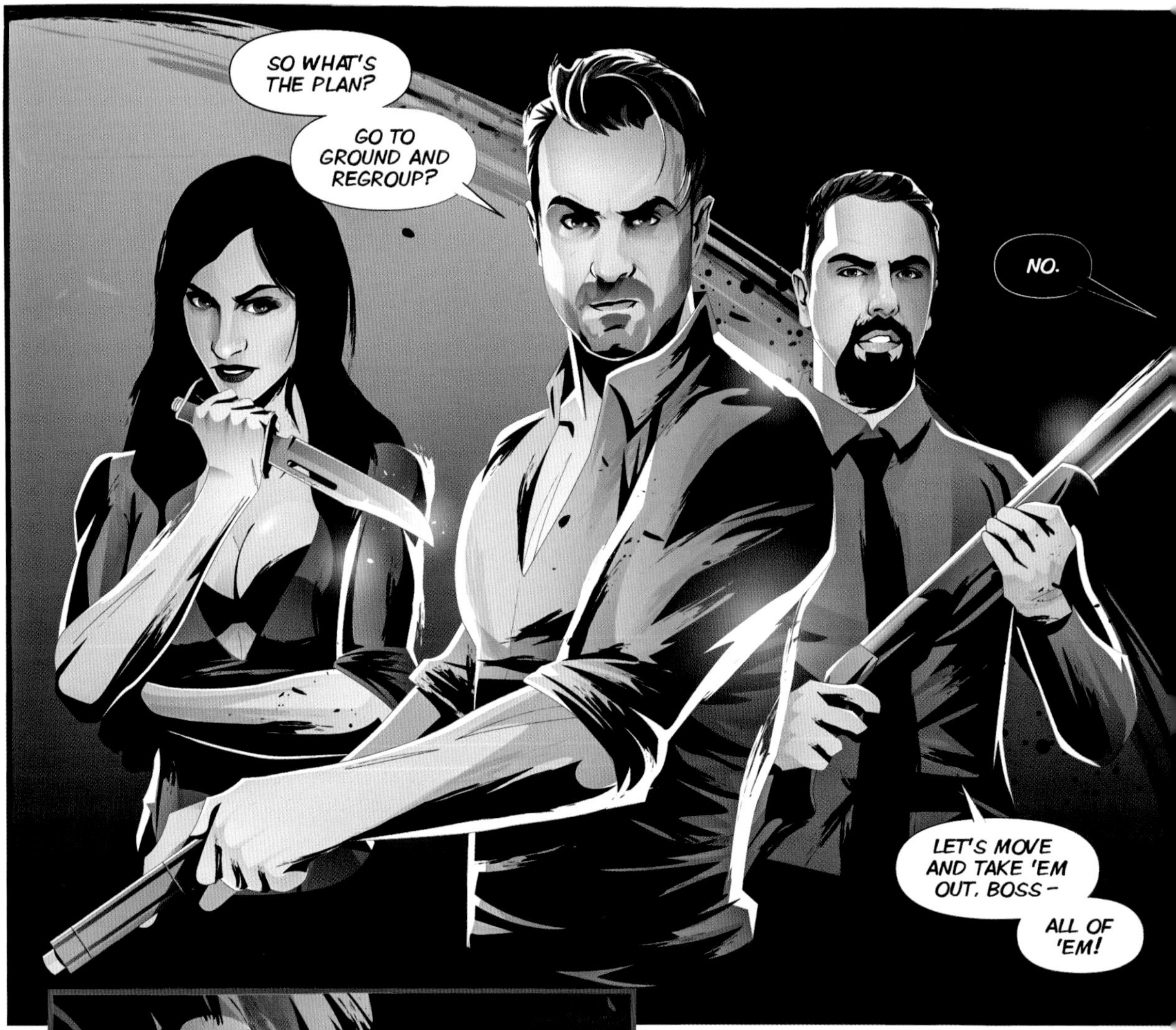
SO WHAT'S THE PLAN?
GO TO GROUND AND REGROUP?
NO.
LET'S MOVE AND TAKE 'EM OUT, BOSS -
ALL OF 'EM!

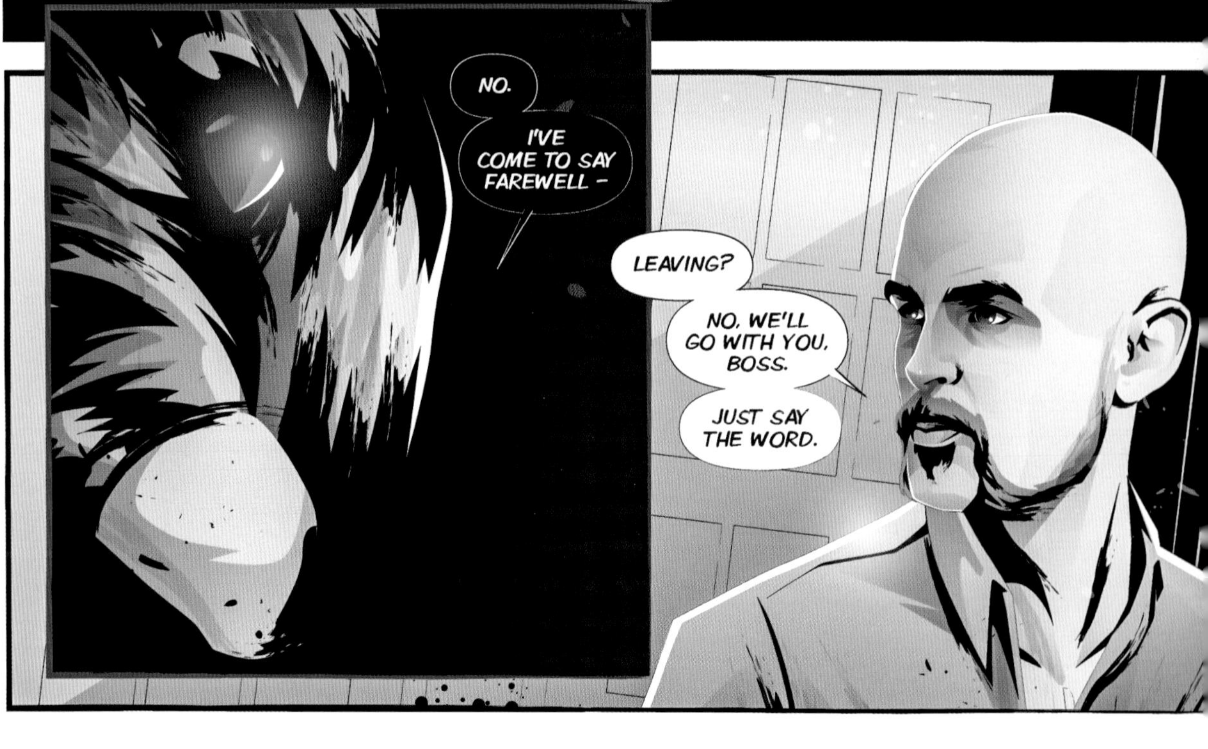
NO.
I'VE COME TO SAY FAREWELL -
LEAVING?
NO, WE'LL GO WITH YOU, BOSS.
JUST SAY THE WORD.

GOD IS A DJ

INGREDIENTS

2 DASHES	Dale DeGroff's Pimento Bitters
1 TSP	Cinnamon Bark Syrup (page 255)
0.75 OZ	Lemon juice
0.25 OZ	Maple syrup (grade B)
0.5 OZ	Banana Syrup (page 251)
0.5 OZ	Alvear Pale Cream Sherry
1.5 OZ	Sesame-Infused Powers Gold Irish Whiskey (page 270)

TOOLS

Jiggers, teaspoon, shaker tins, fine strainer, Hawthorne strainer, nutmeg grater

METHOD

Shake with ice; fine strain and serve up without ice

GLASSWARE

Sour glass

GARNISH

Nutmeg

ORIGIN

Jillian Vose

JILLIAN'S INSPIRATION

GOLD DIGGER WAS A STIRRED LIGHT MANHATTAN ON THE 3RD EDITION MENU AND A REAL FAVORITE.

To keep the drink alive and the sesame infusion we loved so much, I made a shaken version without the original's Cocchi Americano, but with maple syrup as an additional sweetener to balance out the lemon juice.

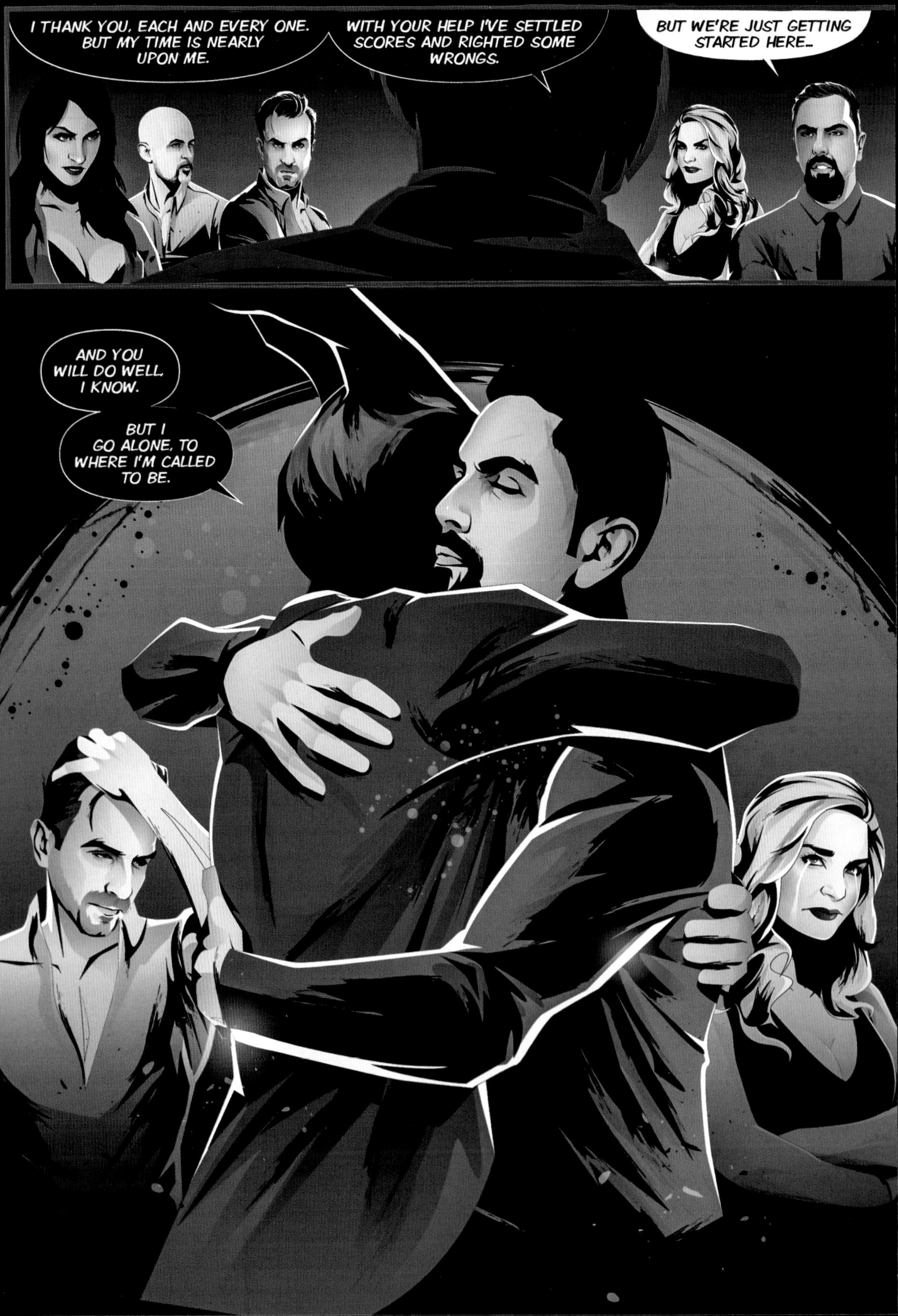
I THANK YOU, EACH AND EVERY ONE. BUT MY TIME IS NEARLY UPON ME.
WITH YOUR HELP I'VE SETTLED SCORES AND RIGHTED SOME WRONGS.
BUT WE'RE JUST GETTING STARTED HERE...
AND YOU WILL DO WELL, I KNOW.
BUT I GO ALONE, TO WHERE I'M CALLED TO BE.

BEAT THE DRAG

INGREDIENTS

2 DASHES	Bittermens Hopped Grapefruit Bitters
0.75 OZ	Amaro Nardini
0.25 OZ	Vanilla Syrup (page 275)
0.5 OZ	Jean-Luc Pasquet Marie-Framboise
0.5 OZ	Arbol Chili–Infused Old Forester
1.5 OZ	Rittenhouse Rye Whiskey

TOOLS
Jiggers, mixing glass, barspoon, julep strainer, ice pick

METHOD
Stir with ice; strain with julep strainer and serve up without ice

GLASSWARE
Nick & Nora

GARNISH
Orange oil (discard peel)

ORIGIN
Jillian Vose

213.

JILLIAN'S INSPIRATION

OUR GUESTS OFTEN WANT SOMETHING SPICY, SOMETHING AMERICAN WHISKEY AND SOMETHING BITTER.

This is an attempt to making sense of that, using flavor combinations I know work well: vanilla, amaro and raspberry. Add some heat and a spicy rye – and we're in business.

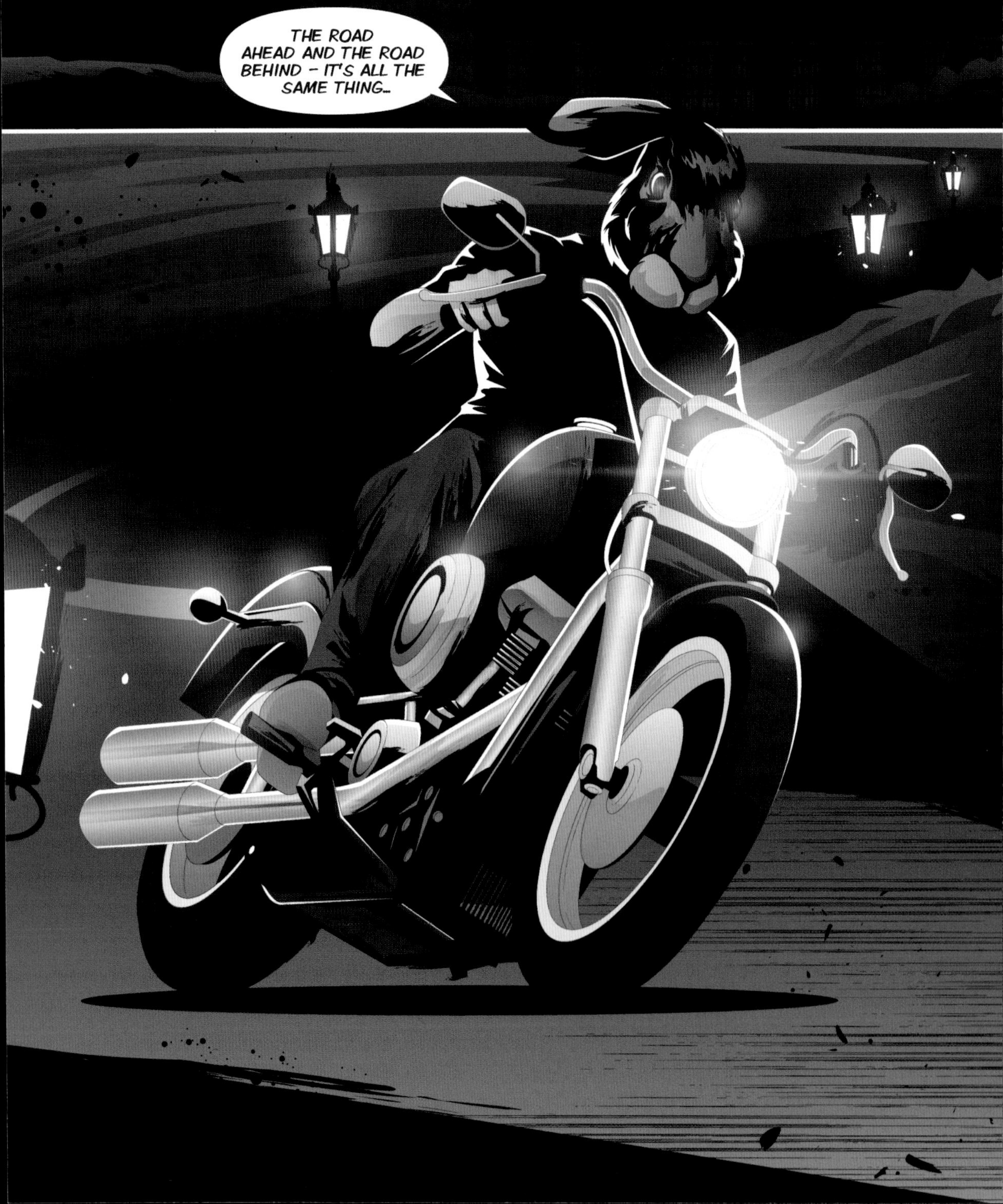
THE ROAD AHEAD AND THE ROAD BEHIND – IT'S ALL THE SAME THING...

BACHELOR PAD

INGREDIENTS

1	Egg white
0.75 OZ	Lemon juice
0.75 OZ	Poppy Seed Syrup (page 268)
0.5 OZ	Combier Crème de Pamplemousse Rose Liqueur
0.5 OZ	Alvear Pale Cream Sherry
2 OZ	Botanist Gin

TOOLS

Jiggers, shaker tins, fine strainer, Hawthorne strainer

METHOD

Dry shake; shake with ice; fine strain and serve up without ice

GLASSWARE

Punch glass

GARNISH

Lemon oil (discard peel)

ORIGIN

Jillian Vose

JILLIAN'S INSPIRATION

THIS DRINK WAS INSPIRED BY GREGORY'S EIDOLON.

It was such a hit, we needed to create something within the same realm for the new menu. I kept the template of his Army & Navy riff and changed out the sweetener and the liqueur. It worked out great.

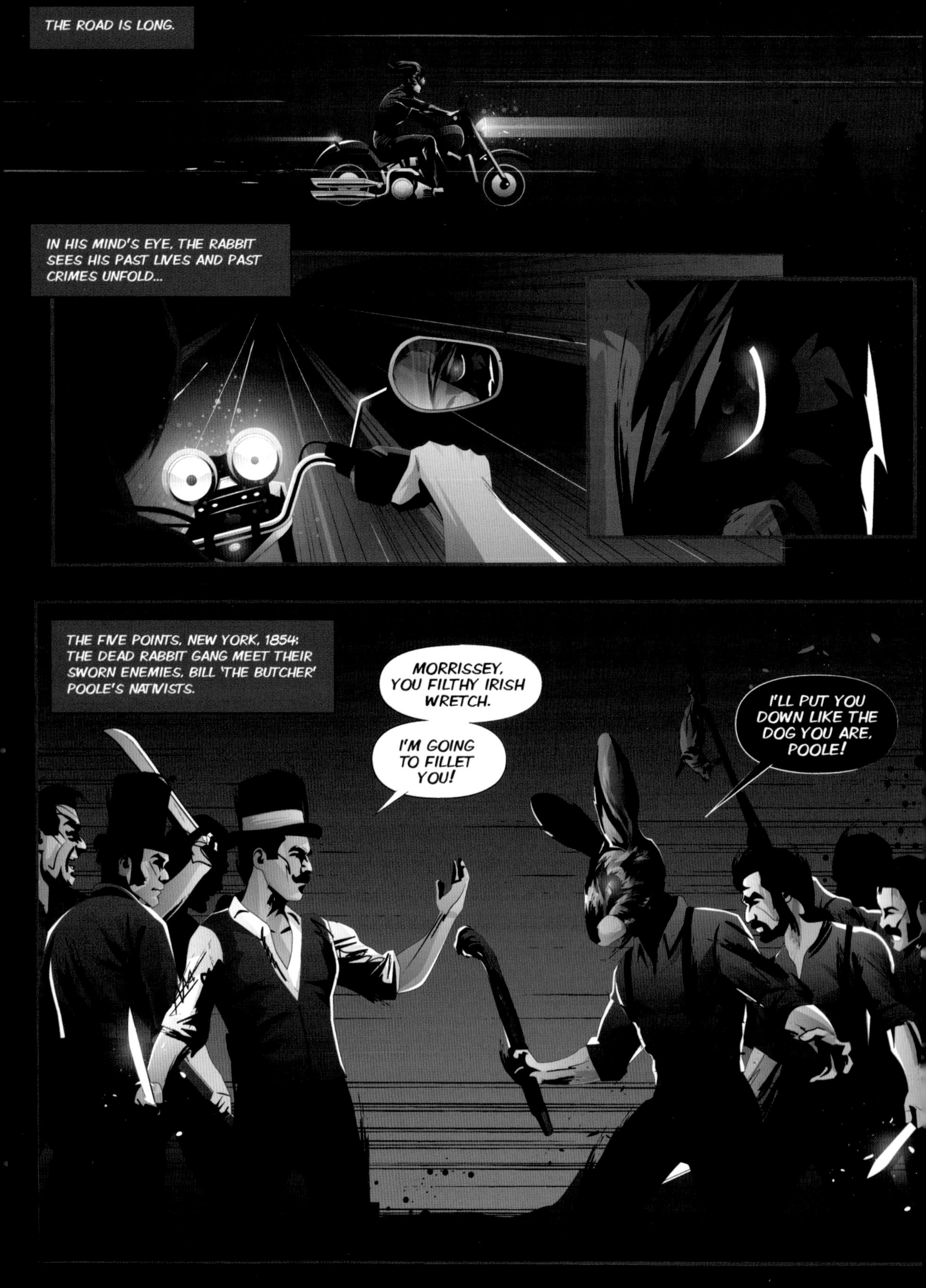
THE ROAD IS LONG.
IN HIS MIND'S EYE, THE RABBIT SEES HIS PAST LIVES AND PAST CRIMES UNFOLD...
THE FIVE POINTS, NEW YORK, 1854: THE DEAD RABBIT GANG MEET THEIR SWORN ENEMIES, BILL 'THE BUTCHER' POOLE'S NATIVISTS.
MORRISSEY, YOU FILTHY IRISH WRETCH.
I'M GOING TO FILLET YOU!
I'LL PUT YOU DOWN LIKE THE DOG YOU ARE, POOLE!

TOM, DICK AND HARRY

INGREDIENTS

2 DASHES	Bittermens Burlesque Bitters
0.75 OZ	Lime juice
0.5 OZ	Red bell pepper juice
0.25 OZ	Fennel Syrup (page 258)
0.25 OZ	Rhubarb Syrup (page 269)
0.5 OZ	Strawberry Syrup (page 271)
0.5 OZ	Waqar Pisco
1.5 OZ	Ketel One Vodka

TOOLS

Jiggers, shaker tins, fine strainer, Hawthorne strainer

METHOD

Shake with ice; fine strain and serve up without ice

GLASSWARE

Sour glass

ORIGIN

Jillian Vose

JILLIAN'S INSPIRATION

THIS WAS FLAVOR-DRIVEN, FOCUSED ON THE STRAWBERRY, RHUBARB AND HIBISCUS COMBINATION.

It seemed the perfect setting for a vodka drink. Adding the bell pepper and pisco perked it up and added a floral note. It was a great way to introduce pisco to the vodka drinker as well – which was a gateway to try new drinks.

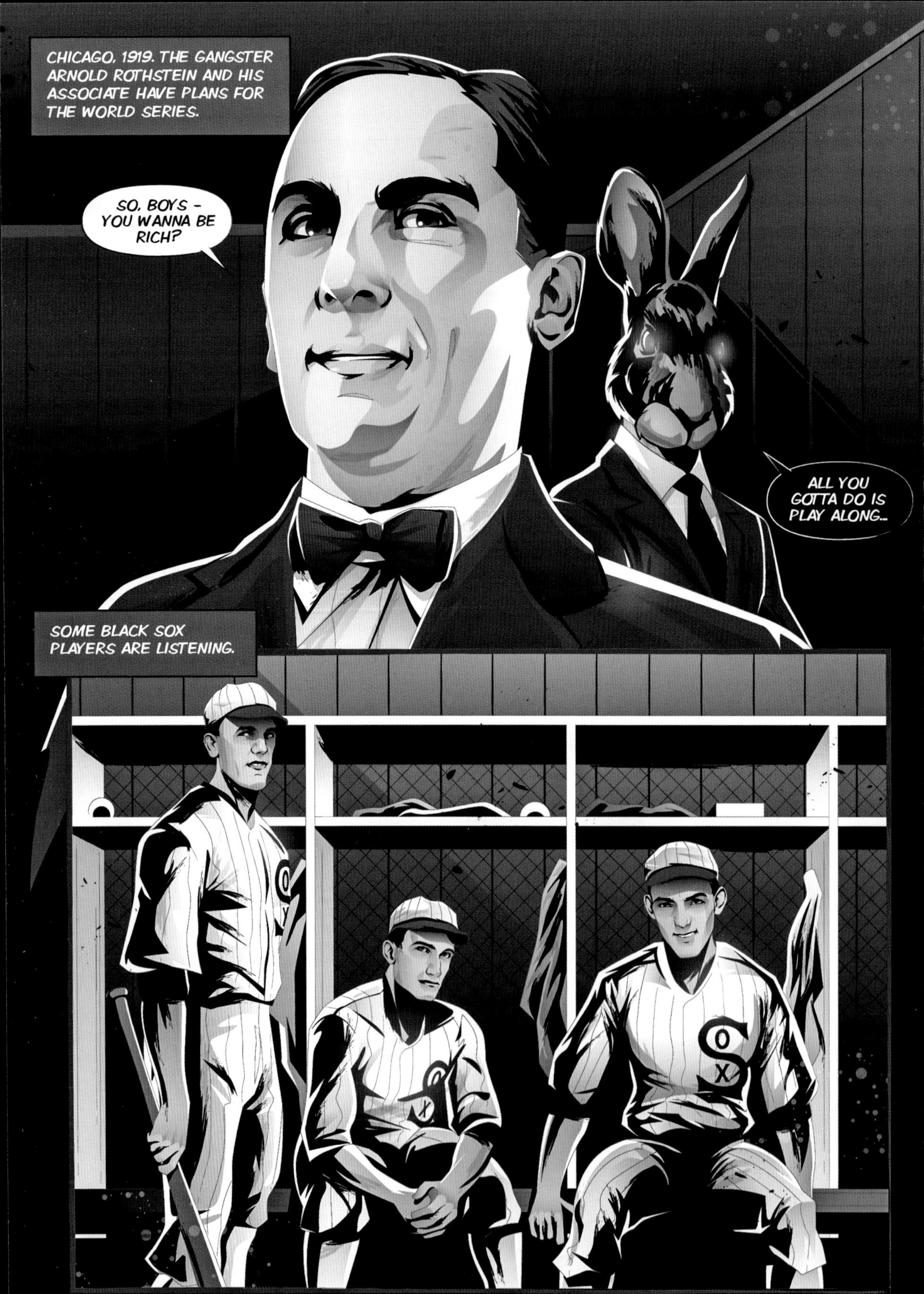
CHICAGO, 1919. THE GANGSTER ARNOLD ROTHSTEIN AND HIS ASSOCIATE HAVE PLANS FOR THE WORLD SERIES.
SO, BOYS - YOU WANNA BE RICH?
ALL YOU GOTTA DO IS PLAY ALONG...
SOME BLACK SOX PLAYERS ARE LISTENING.

COUP D'ETAT

INGREDIENTS

0.25 OZ	Cinnamon Bark Syrup (page 255)
0.25 OZ	Amaro Nonino
0.25 OZ	Yellow Chartreuse
0.5 OZ	Noilly Prat Ambré Vermouth
1 OZ	Novo Fogo Tanager Cachaça
1 OZ	Rémy Martin 1738 Cognac

TOOLS
Jiggers, mixing glass, barspoon, julep strainer, ice pick

METHOD
Stir with ice; strain with julep strainer and serve over large block of ice

GLASSWARE
Old Fashioned

GARNISH
Orange oil (discard peel)

ORIGIN
Gregory Buda

ENDGAME

219.

COUP D'ETAT

GREGORY'S INSPIRATION

I WAS VERY EXCITED ABOUT THE NEW NOVO FOGO TANAGER CACHAÇA – AGED IN ZEBRAWOOD CASKS AND BURSTING WITH CINNAMON AND CLOVE NOTES.

The Coup d'Etat is an Old Fashioned–style drink designed to showcase this beautiful spirit.

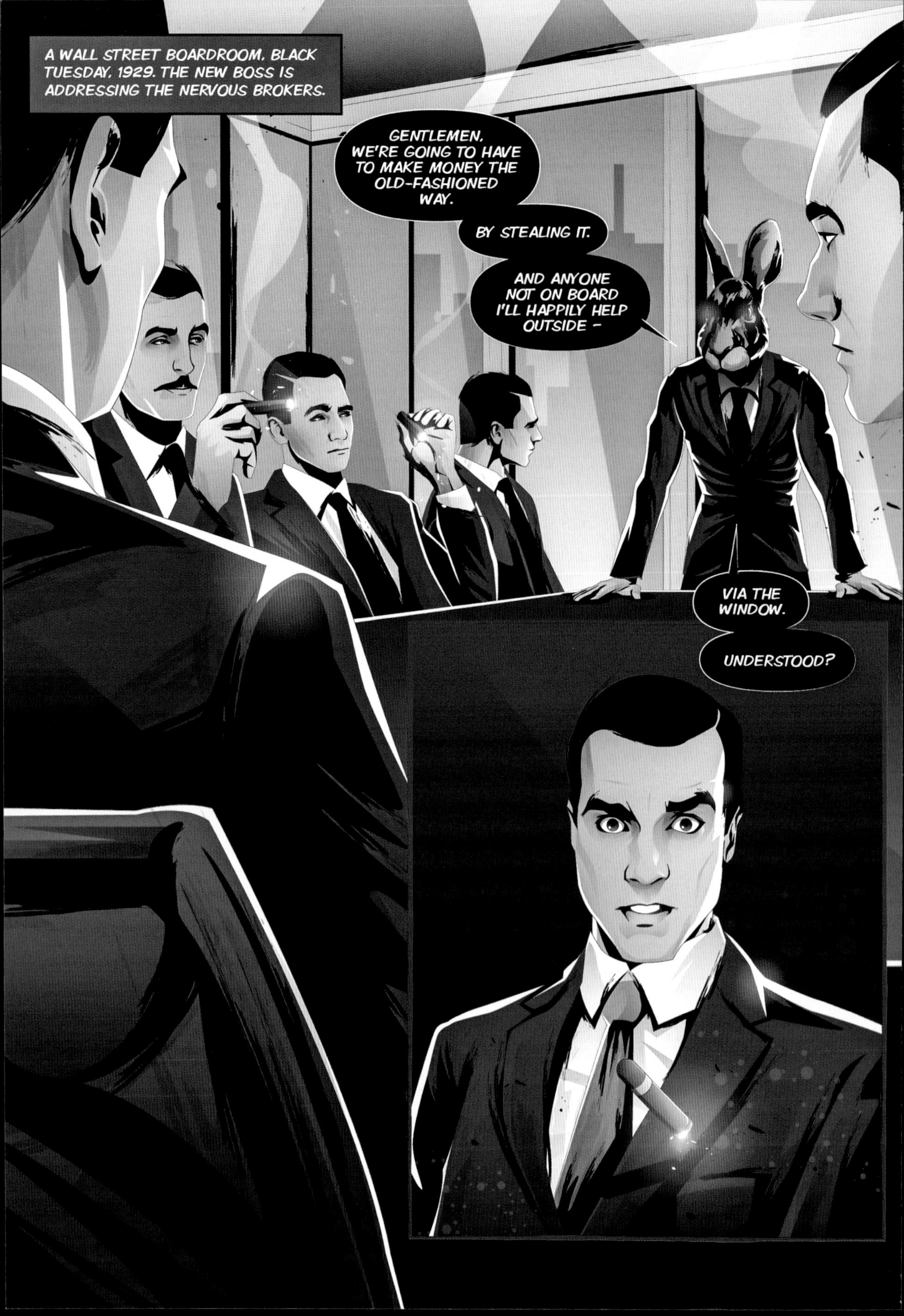
A WALL STREET BOARDROOM, BLACK TUESDAY, 1929. THE NEW BOSS IS ADDRESSING THE NERVOUS BROKERS.
GENTLEMEN, WE'RE GOING TO HAVE TO MAKE MONEY THE OLD-FASHIONED WAY.
BY STEALING IT.
AND ANYONE NOT ON BOARD I'LL HAPPILY HELP OUTSIDE –
VIA THE WINDOW.
UNDERSTOOD?

PALE RIDER

INGREDIENTS

1	Egg white
1 DASH	Dale DeGroff's Pimento Bitters
2 DASHES	Dill Syrup (page 257)
0.75 OZ	Lemon juice
0.5 OZ	Caramel Cane Syrup (page 254)
0.5 OZ	Vanilla Syrup (page 275)
0.75 OZ	Coconut milk
0.5 OZ	Giffard Banane du Brésil
0.5 OZ	Blume Marillen Apricot Eau-de-Vie
1.5 OZ	Old Forester 100 Proof Bourbon
1.5 OZ	Soda water (not to be shaken with other ingredients)

TOOLS
Jiggers, shaker tins, fine strainer, Hawthorne strainer, nutmeg grater

METHOD
Dry shake; long shake with ice; add soda water to glass and fine strain; serve up without ice

GLASSWARE
Highball

GARNISH
Nutmeg

ORIGIN
Jessica Friedman

221.

JESSICA'S INSPIRATION

I LOVE FIZZES BUT SOMETIMES THEY CAN BE TOO RICH, SO I WENT WITH COCONUT MILK TO MAKE IT HEALTHIER AND A BIT MORE DELICATE.

Coconut makes me think of bourbon barrels, so I created this cocktail around the flavors that you would find there.

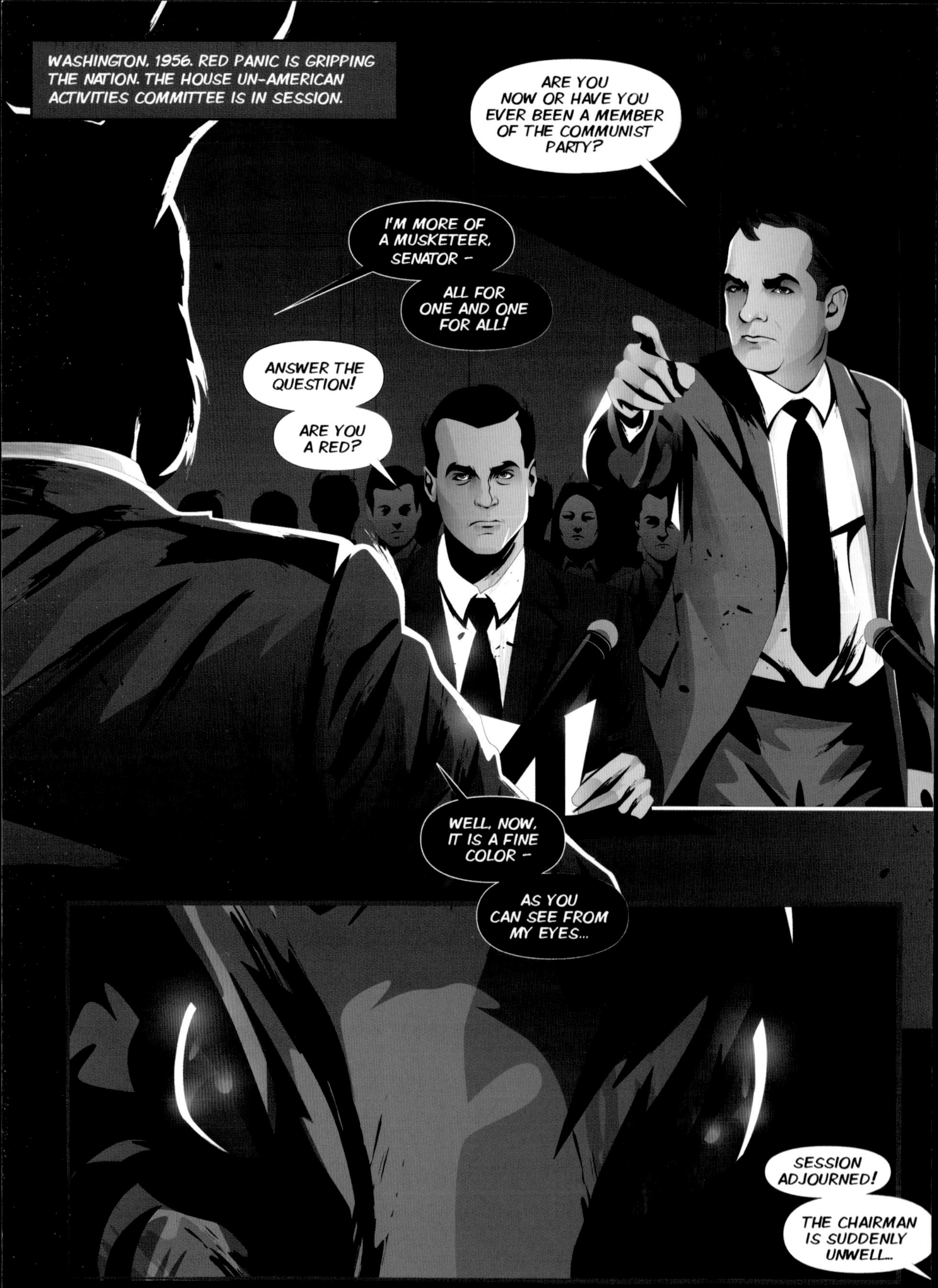
WASHINGTON, 1956. RED PANIC IS GRIPPING THE NATION. THE HOUSE UN-AMERICAN ACTIVITIES COMMITTEE IS IN SESSION.
ARE YOU NOW OR HAVE YOU EVER BEEN A MEMBER OF THE COMMUNIST PARTY?
I'M MORE OF A MUSKETEER, SENATOR -
ALL FOR ONE AND ONE FOR ALL!
ANSWER THE QUESTION!
ARE YOU A RED?
WELL, NOW, IT IS A FINE COLOR -
AS YOU CAN SEE FROM MY EYES...
SESSION ADJOURNED!
THE CHAIRMAN IS SUDDENLY UNWELL...

BEAUTY PARLOR

INGREDIENTS

2	Lemon coins
1 DASH	Bitter Truth Aromatic Bitters
4 DASHES	Peychaud's Bitters
1 TSP	Cane Syrup (page 254)
1 TSP	Giffard Crème de Cacao (white)
1 TSP	Dead Rabbit Jamaican Rum Blend (page 256)
1 OZ	Rémy Martin 1738 Cognac
1 OZ	Torres 15 Year Spanish Brandy
	Absinthe to aromatize glass (not to be mixed in drink)

TOOLS

Jiggers, mixing glass, teaspoon, barspoon, julep strainer

METHOD

Build drink; express lemon oil and drop lemon coins into mixing glass; stir with ice; aromatize small rocks glass with absinthe; strain with julep strainer and serve up without ice

GLASSWARE

Small rocks glass

ORIGIN

Jillian Vose

ENDGAME

223.

BEAUTY PARLOR

JILLIAN'S INSPIRATION

I HAD A SAZERAC IN LONDON THAT WAS THE BEST I'D EVER HAD.

So I set out to make a variation I thought was even better. The Sazerac template is still the same, with the addition of the dark Jamaican rum blend and cacao.

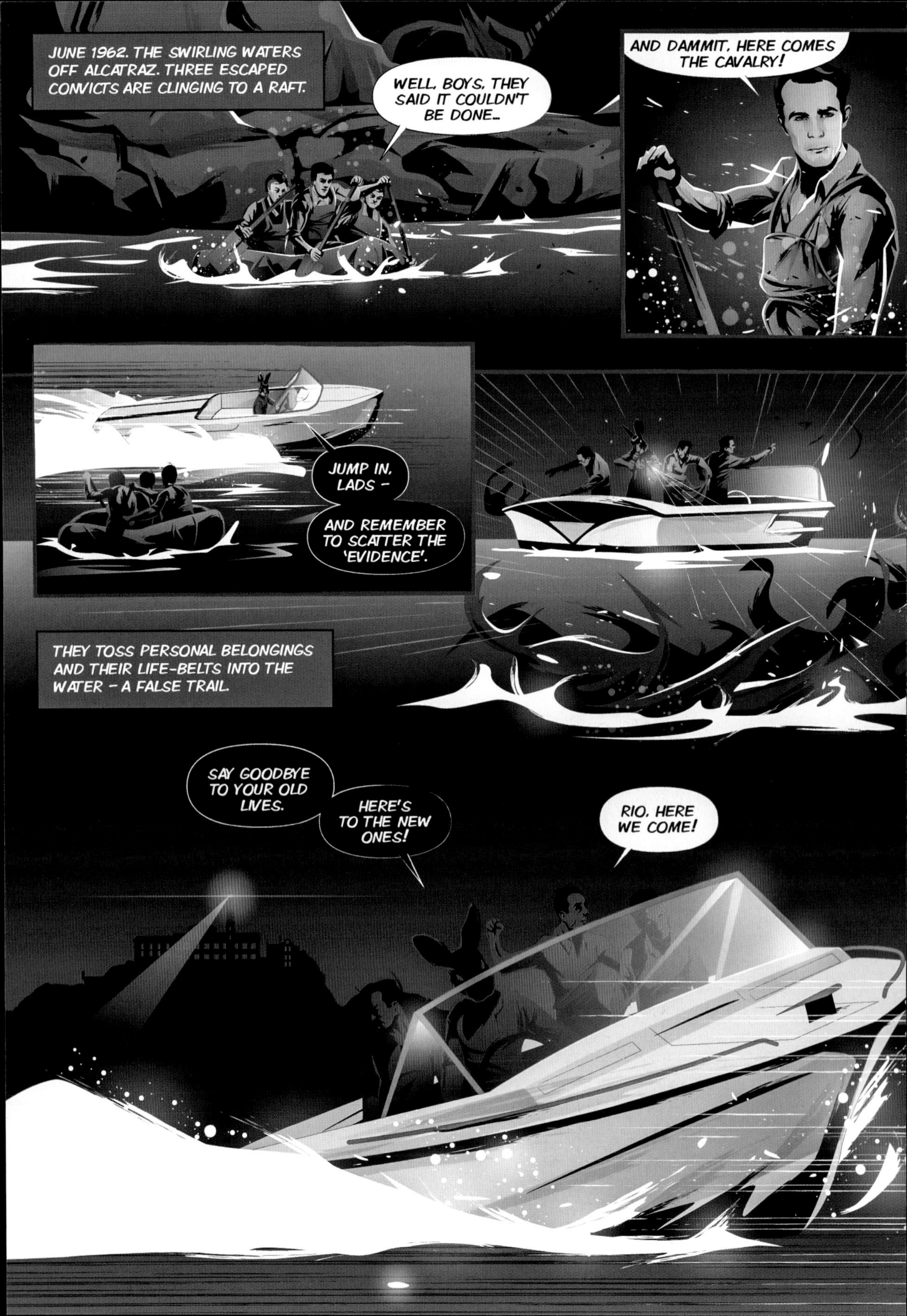
JUNE 1962. THE SWIRLING WATERS OFF ALCATRAZ. THREE ESCAPED CONVICTS ARE CLINGING TO A RAFT.
WELL, BOYS, THEY SAID IT COULDN'T BE DONE...
AND DAMMIT, HERE COMES THE CAVALRY!
JUMP IN, LADS -
AND REMEMBER TO SCATTER THE 'EVIDENCE'.
THEY TOSS PERSONAL BELONGINGS AND THEIR LIFE-BELTS INTO THE WATER - A FALSE TRAIL.
SAY GOODBYE TO YOUR OLD LIVES.
HERE'S TO THE NEW ONES!
RIO, HERE WE COME!

BABY BOOMER

INGREDIENTS

1 DASH	Bitter Truth Aromatic Bitters
1 TSP	Blueberry Cane Syrup (page 253)
0.25 OZ	Becherovka
1 OZ	Ancho Chili–Infused Sweet Vermouth (page 250)
0.5 OZ	Tariquet VS Classique Bas-Armagnac
1.5 OZ	Virgil Kaine Robber Baron Rye Whiskey

TOOLS

Jiggers, mixing glass, teaspoon, barspoon, julep strainer

METHOD

Stir with ice; strain with julep strainer and serve up without ice

GLASSWARE

Nick & Nora

GARNISH

Orange oil (discard peel)

ORIGIN

Jillian Vose

JILLIAN'S INSPIRATION

VIRGIL KAINE RYE WAS THE BASE INSPIRATION.

This has an intensity from its high rye mash bill and 45.5 ABV, so I had to really think about how to balance that out. The citrus, spice and notes of banana and berries made me think of the blueberry component. I now had the basic flavor profile. To modify it to be complex, I thought of Becherovka – a Czech herbal liqueur with a dominant cinnamon note. It needed to be boozier to hit the manhattan style I was after, but more rye made it too hot. I rounded it out with armagnac – yet another split base.

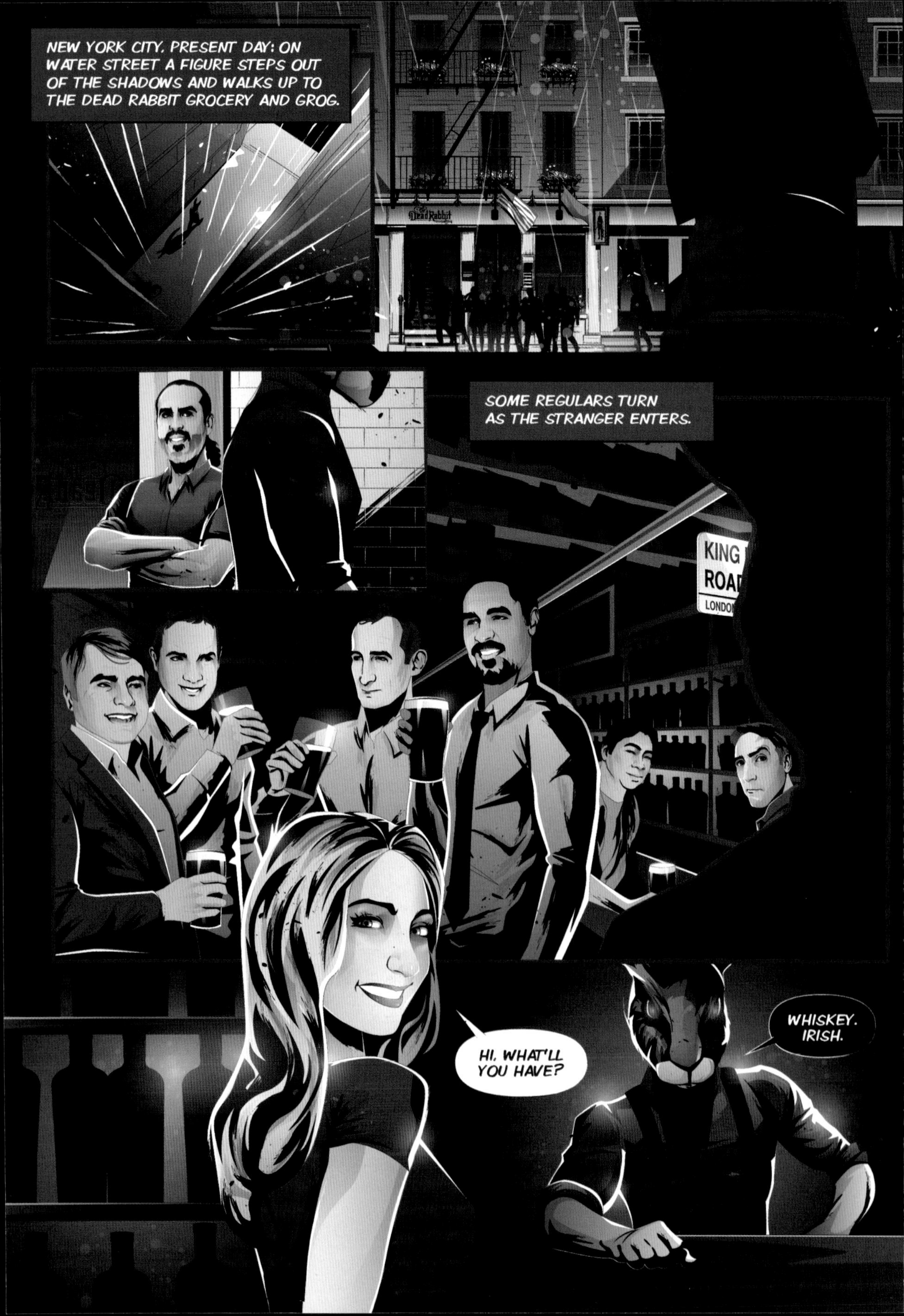
NEW YORK CITY, PRESENT DAY: ON WATER STREET A FIGURE STEPS OUT OF THE SHADOWS AND WALKS UP TO THE DEAD RABBIT GROCERY AND GROG.
Dead Rabbit
SOME REGULARS TURN AS THE STRANGER ENTERS.
KING
ROAD
LONDON
HI, WHAT'LL YOU HAVE?
WHISKEY. IRISH.

SONG AND DANCE

INGREDIENTS

1 DASH	Eucalyptus Tincture (page 258)
1 TSP	Yuzu Cane Syrup (page 277)
0.5 OZ	Lime juice
0.25 OZ	Cucumber juice
0.5 OZ	Fennel Syrup (page 258)
1 OZ	Green Tea–Infused Tanqueray (page 259)
1.5 OZ	Shiso Dry Vermouth (page 270)

TOOLS
Jiggers, teaspoon, shaker tins

METHOD
Whip shake with 15 pieces of pebble ice until ice has melted; serve with pebble ice

GLASSWARE
Nog glass

GARNISH
Top with pebble ice until it's like a snowcone on top

ORIGIN
Harrison Ginsberg

HARRISON'S INSPIRATION

SHISO IS SO AROMATIC AND HERBACEOUS THAT I REALLY WANTED TO HIGHLIGHT IT IN A BRIGHT CLEAN COCKTAIL.

I infused the shiso into dry vermouth and added some green tea–infused London dry gin as a base. I then added fennel and yuzu, rounding everything out with cucumber and lime juice. A dash of eucalyptus really ties everything together.

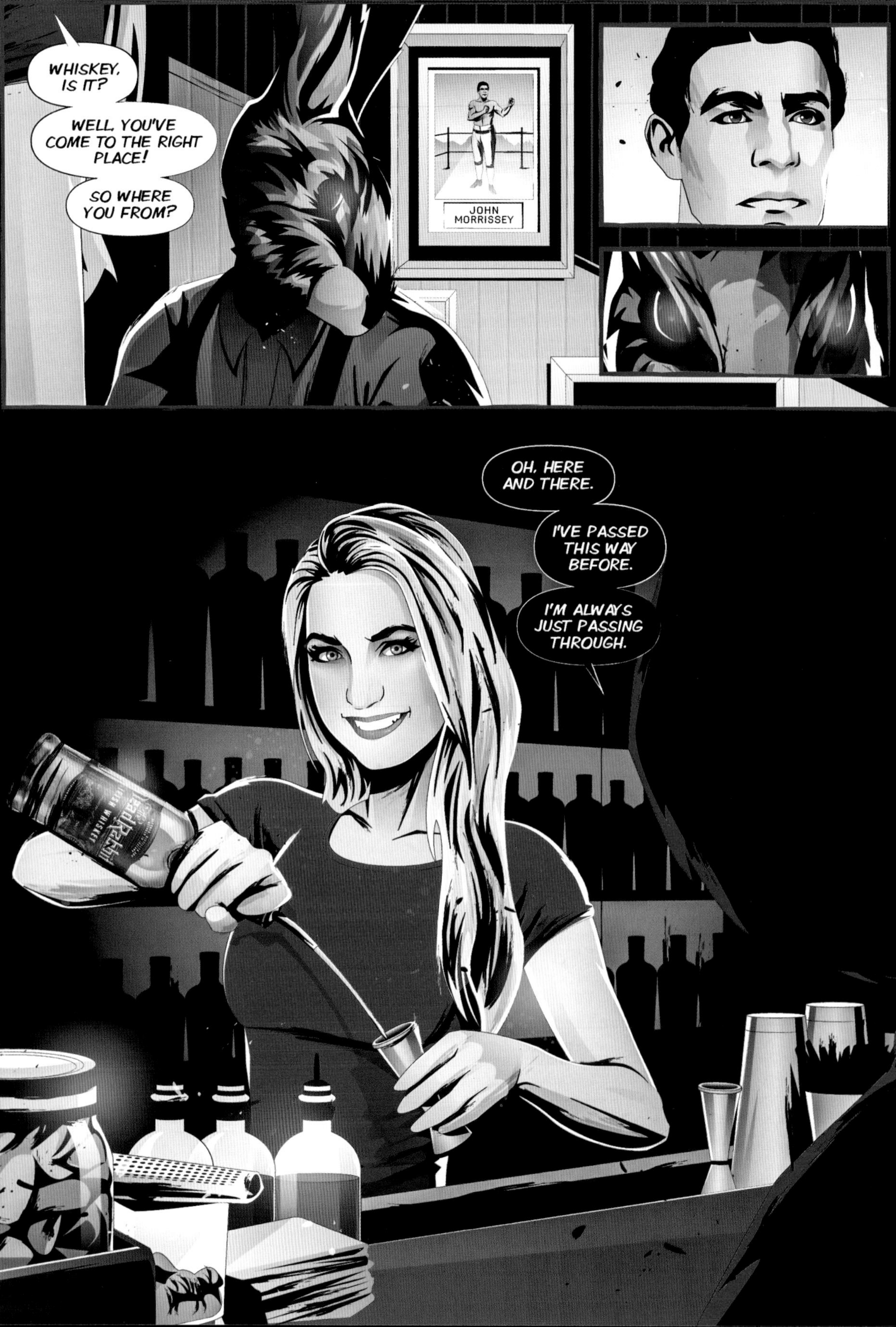

WHISKEY, IS IT?
WELL, YOU'VE COME TO THE RIGHT PLACE!
SO WHERE YOU FROM?
JOHN MORRISSEY
OH, HERE AND THERE.
I'VE PASSED THIS WAY BEFORE.
I'M ALWAYS JUST PASSING THROUGH.

PAY AS YOU GO

INGREDIENTS

1	Egg white
2 DASHES	Bitter Truth Aromatic Bitters
0.5 TSP	Zucca Rabarbaro
1 TSP	Blueberry Cane Syrup (page 253)
0.75 OZ	Lemon juice
0.5 OZ	Lemon Sherbet (page 262)
0.5 OZ	Caffo Amaretto
0.5 OZ	Pierre Ferrand Pineau des Charentes
0.25 OZ	Blume Marillen Apricot Eau-de-Vie
1 OZ	Torres 15 Year Spanish Brandy

TOOLS

Jiggers, ½ teaspoon, teaspoon, shaker tins, fine strainer, Hawthorne shakers

METHOD

Dry shake; shake with ice; fine strain and serve up without ice

GLASSWARE

Punch glass

GARNISH

Lemon oil (discard peel)

ORIGIN

Jessica Friedman

JESSICA'S INSPIRATION

GUESTS ASK FOR AMARETTO SOURS PRETTY OFTEN, BUT I WANTED TO MAKE SOMETHING DIFFERENT, BUT STILL APPEALING TO THE AMARETTO SOUR DRINKER.

I looked at flavors that would pair well with the amaretto while still making it the star of the show . . .

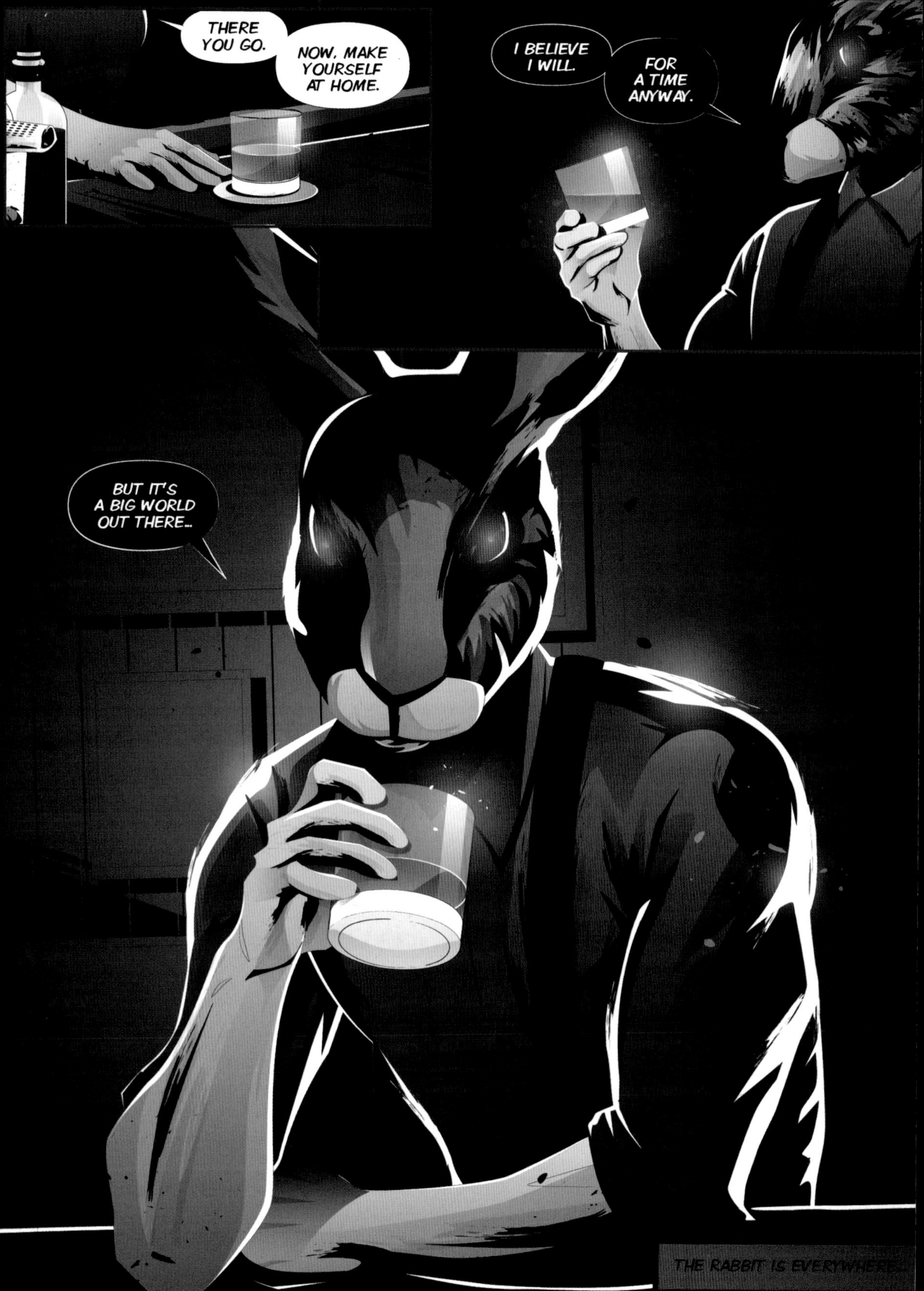
THERE YOU GO.
NOW, MAKE YOURSELF AT HOME.
I BELIEVE I WILL.
FOR A TIME ANYWAY.
BUT IT'S A BIG WORLD OUT THERE...
THE RABBIT IS EVERYWHERE

SNAP DECISION

INGREDIENTS

2 DASHES	House Cardamom Bitters (page 261)
1 TSP	Yellow Chartreuse
0.5 TSP	Combier Liqueur d'Orange
0.25 OZ	Dried Apricot Syrup (page 257)
0.25 OZ	Cocchi Americano
2 OZ	Butternut Squash Seed Oil–Washed Powers Signature (page 253)

TOOLS
Jiggers, mixing glass, teaspoon, ½ teaspoon, barspoon, julep strainer, ice pick

METHOD
Stir with ice; strain with julep strainer and serve over large block of ice

GLASSWARE
Old Fashioned

GARNISH
Lemon oil (discard peel)

ORIGIN
Gregory Buda

231.

GREGORY'S INSPIRATION

THIS OLD FASHIONED VARIATION WAS DESIGNED AROUND AN AMAZING PRODUCT THAT I BOUGHT TO COOK WITH AT HOME: STONY BROOK BUTTERNUT SQUASH SEED OIL.

I wanted to use it as a fat wash in a drink, and selected single pot still Irish Whiskey as a good spirit to try, as it is complex enough to be interesting but soft enough to let the squash shine through. The rest of the ingredients were chosen to complement the butternut squash – apricot, orange, herbs and baking spice – all of which pair nicely with this squash in my kitchen.

ANOTHER

EXTRAS,

TIPS & M

ROUND:
NSIGHTS,
ORE

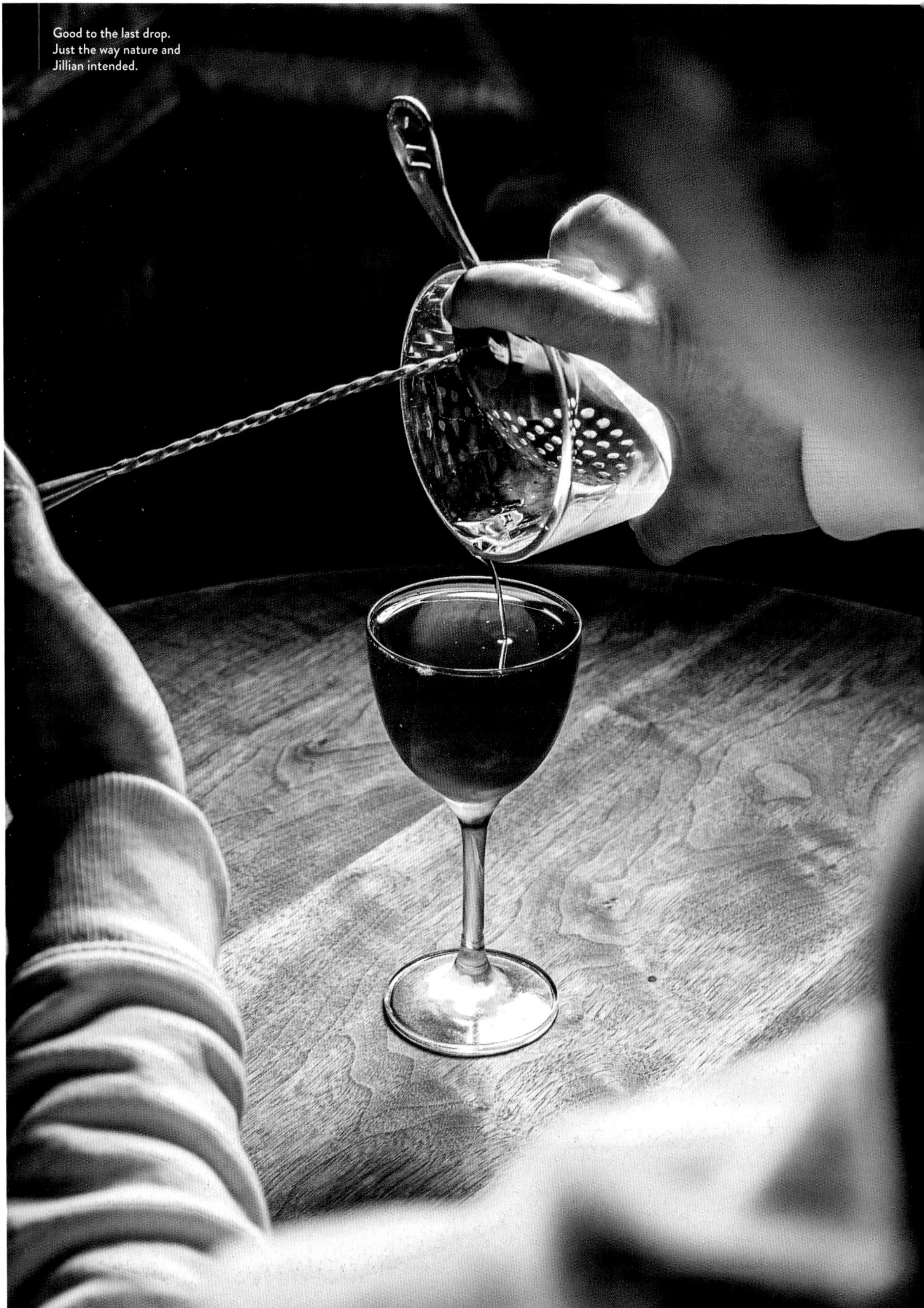

Good to the last drop.
Just the way nature and
Jillian intended.

DESIGNING A COCKTAIL

WHAT MAKES A GOOD ONE?

Here's how we start. This is an overview of the information that all Dead Rabbit staff receive and work with. Think of it as your own personal cocktail master class.

A QUESTION OF BALANCE

Key factors to consider:

— Strength	— Acidity	— Texture	— Aroma
— Bitterness	— Sweetness	— Body	— Aftertaste

Getting the balance of these right is an essential part of designing a great cocktail. It's OK if your drink leans more heavily towards one of these than another, but it shouldn't dominate or be the only element you detect as you drink it.

MAKE IT LOOK AS GOOD AS IT TASTES

Everything – the glassware, garnish and the liquid itself – should be appealing to look at. In practical terms, this means:

— **THE GLASSWARE** is right for the style of drink and the volume of liquid in it.
— **THE LIQUID** shouldn't appear muddy or separated.
— **THE GARNISH** (if there is one) should justify being there.

CREATIVITY COUNTS

The cocktail should bring something new to the party – an experience that's unique or original in some aspect. So, does it?

GOOD TO THE LAST DROP

The drink should be enjoyable from the first sip to the last. It shouldn't quickly become watery or separate, falling apart like a bad sandwich. Because that's unforgivable, right?

WORKING THE INGREDIENTS: THE SOUR AND THE SWEET

ACIDS

We're talking here about fruit and plant acids, of course. What these do is contribute degrees of sharpness to your drink, i.e., dry, tart or sour notes. Let's take a look at the main ones we use.

Lemon is quite soft and works particularly well with other flavors without overpowering them. Lime is sharper and more intense. Grapefruit is sharper still. To add a smooth, mild acid note to a stirred drink, try verjus, which is clear, unsweetened apple juice. For something more assertive, you can consider vinegars and shrubs, which are acidic cordials, but be careful not to use too much. Remember, people: It's all about balance.

You can also use acids in powdered form, such as malic (green apple) or citric (lemon or lime). They're fully soluble but be careful because they can easily overpower a drink. Dry wines and Champagne can also be used to contribute a touch of acid sharpness and, let's face it, a bit of a flourish.

NEUTRAL JUICES

Juices such as orange, pineapple and apple naturally contain both acid as well as sweetness, so you can't depend on them to deliver just a sweet note or just an acid note. (They also discolor and oxidize easily unless you adjust them with citric, malic or tartaric acid.)

SWEETENERS

As with acids, sweetness is a question of degree. White sugar, for example, adds sweetness without flavor, whereas cane sugar has a subtle flavor and brings a little texture and body. When you use demerara sugar, you're going to get body and texture as well as base notes of molasses, coffee and chocolate. Honey delivers moderate sweetness, texture and body, plus a strong flavor. Note that many artisan honeys may also have a floral note – because bees know nothing about cocktails.

BERRIES, FRUIT & HERBS

Berries add fresh, bright flavor, and their pectin means you get a rich texture too. What's not to like? Well, they vary a lot, which is just inconsiderate. And they make a mess of everything they touch. Worth bearing in mind.

Apples, pears, apricots and peaches are tricky to incorporate into a drink, unless they're stirred or mixed in (or muddled, as we cocktail nerds say). Their flavors are quite delicate and can be easily lost, and as with berries, they vary in sweetness and acidity from fruit to fruit. In short, they're often better incorporated as a juice.

Soft green herbs like tarragon, parsley, sage and curry can easily be incorporated into a drink by adding them fresh to the shaker tin – the ice does a good job of extracting the aromatic oils. With tougher herbs like rosemary and lavender, however, a tincture will produce better results.

FORTIFIED WINES

Sherry, port, madeira and vermouth are your flavor friends. (Just ask Gregory Buda. He'll tell you, at great length.) They're flexible and can be excellent modifiers; for example, if you want to thin the texture or intensity of a sour- or old fashioned–style cocktail. They can also add complexity or sophistication, or bind elements of the drink. Need to add body? Bring in the heavy-hitters: PX and Moscatel sherry, Bual and Malmsey madeira, and ports, as well as blanc and sweet vermouths. Job done.

SHERRY

Fino and Manzanilla sherries contribute dry, savory and saline notes. This lets them pair well with gin, vodka, tequila and mezcal, white rum and lighter brown spirits like blended Irish whiskey and scotch.

Amontillado, palo cortado and oloroso bring a savory, nutty, dried-fruit note. Try them with aged spirits like reposado and anejo tequila, aged rum, brandy, American whiskey, pot still Irish whiskey and single malt scotch.

PX and Moscatel sherry can be used in place of – or as part of – the sweetener in your drink, though a little goes a long way.

PORT

Ruby and LBV port can bring some sweetness along with a rich, fruity note. Tawny port adds even more richness, plus hints of chocolate, vanilla and coffee, and even a little nuttiness – which is a good thing once in a while.

MADEIRA

Sercial and Verdelho Madeiras are sharper and higher acid in flavor. However, they're often prohibitively pricey for including in a cocktail. Bual and Malmsey madeiras are richer and contribute sweetness as well as nutty, oxidized notes.

VERMOUTH

Dry vermouth adds body, dryness and herbal flavors, whereas the blanc lends more body, richness and fruitiness. Sweet vermouth contributes a warming spice note.

Bitter vermouths bring both body and, well, bitterness. They also offer a wide range of flavors, depending on the one you choose, such as Cocchi Americano, Bonal, Byrrh, Punt e Mes, etc.

MISTELLE

Mistelle, such as Pineau des Charentes (apple juice and Calvados) and Pommeau de Normandie (grape juice and cognac), are made from a mixture of unfermented juice and alcoholic spirits. They can add subtle sweetness and body, and a rounded, slightly floral fruitiness.

237.

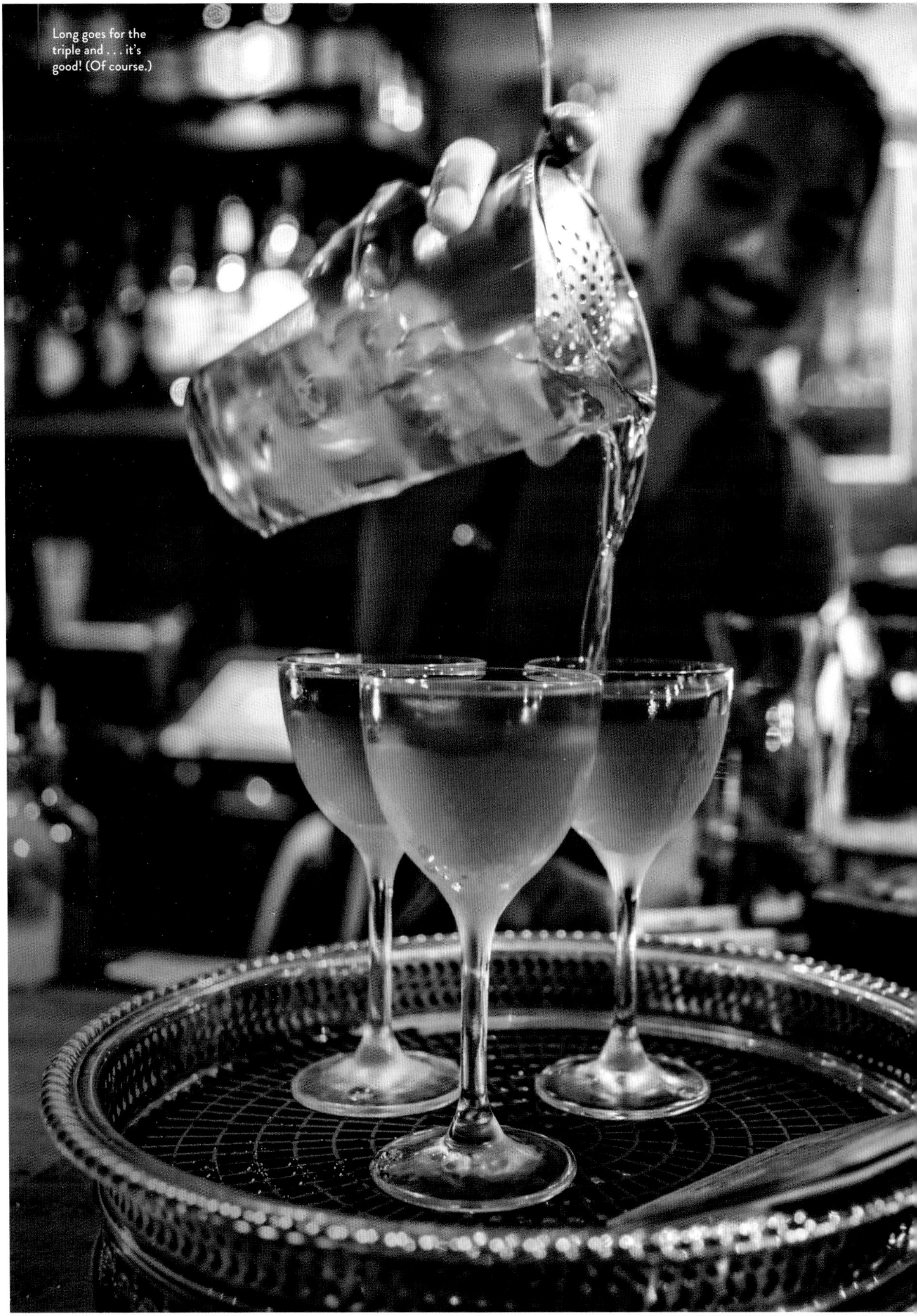

Long goes for the triple and . . . it's good! (Of course.)

DASHING BITTERS

Think of these as the seasoning in your cocktail – the salt and pepper, as it were. As with any seasoning, easy does it, and choose wisely.

Angostura is quite sweet and soft. The Bitter Truth's Aromatic and Jerry Thomas Decanter Bitters are more astringent and savory. Peychaud's Bitters and Creole Bitters bring a bright red fruit flavor with a clear hint of anise; they also affect the color of your drink.

Bittermens' 'Elemkule Tiki and Boston Bittahs; hopped grapefruit; cherry bark and vanilla; and peach all deliver a high note but don't bind flavors together.

Citrus bitters will bring high notes and bitterness to your cocktail, while aromatic bitters add deep bass notes, with hints of cinnamon or clove. Typically these are great for binding flavors and giving an extra layer of complexity.

AMARI & APERITIFS

Used as ingredients, these add complexity, depth and range from sweet to sour via aromatic and floral. For example, amari such as Sibilla or Amaro dell'erborista are very bitter, almost pungent, whereas Montenegro and CioCiaro are more citrus-forward. If you want a warming, cinnamon/clove note, use Meletti or Amargo Vallet. Fernet-Branca, Ramazzotti, Cynar and Amaro Braulio will deliver an herby, vegetal element, while Amaro Nardini and Amaro Nonino are more rich, round and sweet.

Gentian-based aperitif bitters range from Suze (intense) and Aveze (soft and sweet) to Salers, which can be treated as a bitter fortified wine.

Campari is bitter and intense, and pairs well with all types of spirits. Aperol is softer and less bitter, with citrus and rhubarb notes, and works well with white spirits.

ANOTHER ROUND: EXTRAS

239.

DESIGNING A COCKTAIL

INGREDIENTS VS. FLAVOR

ADDING BODY TO A COCKTAIL

If your drink is lacking depth or body, there are a few strategies to deal with this. First, consider a base spirit with a high ABV base. You might also want to consider using a vehicle such as cane syrup or a liqueur to add sweetness plus body. Finally, a fortified wine such as port, oloroso, sweet vermouth or Madeira can do a lot of heavy lifting for you.

ICE ICE, BABY

A big rock will keep a drink cold and dilute the drink slowly. Reserve this for drinks that are richer and sweeter or stronger, as they can handle the dilution without becoming watery. Note: Avoid for thinner, stirred drinks with a high pour of fortified wine.

GETTING A FLAVOR INTO LIQUID FORM

OK kids – here comes the science.

WATER VS. ALCOHOL

Water and alcohol will extract different flavors from the same ingredient. Crazy, right? Well, here's how it breaks down:

— **JUICE / SYRUP** – all water, no alcohol
— **WINE / FORTIFIED WINE** – mainly water, moderate alcohol
— **SPIRITS** – approximately equal water and alcohol
— **OVERPROOF SPIRITS** – moderate water, high alcohol
— **EVERCLEAR** – barely any water, mainly alcohol

THE GREAT CHILI PEPPER CAPER

Capsaicin, the compound that makes peppers spicy, is extremely soluble in fat, fairly soluble in alcohol and not soluble at all in water. However, the compounds that make a pepper taste like a pepper are very water-soluble. Go figure. *Therefore, if you prepare the same chili pepper four different ways, here's what you'll get:*

— **SOUS-VIDE INTO A SYRUP** – all juicy pepper flavor, no heat
— **INFUSED INTO A VERMOUTH** – lots of flavor; soft, muted heat
— **INFUSED INTO A SPIRIT** – moderate flavor, lots of heat
— **MADE INTO A TINCTURE** – very little flavor, extreme heat

Knowing this beforehand can take out some of the guesswork – you just have to ask yourself what you're looking for in terms of heat vs. flavor.

MAKING CUSTOM INGREDIENTS

HARD SPICES *Cinnamon, nutmeg, mace, cloves, coriander, fennel seed, allspice, etc.*

These work very well as tinctures and fairly well as spirit infusions. For syrups, you need to cook these at higher temperatures in order to extract the flavors.

HERBS AND TEA *Tarragon, sage, mint, tansy, chamomile, green tea*

These work well in tinctures that bring out the bright, floral, spicy notes. The flavor is carried in their oils, and is therefore best extracted with alcohol.

Dried herbs and teas work well as infusions, but aren't very stable as syrups due to oxidation. Fresh herbs will have a brighter profile and can often be extracted better and more intensely in alcohol.

BERRIES *Strawberries, blackberries, raspberries, etc.*

The flavors in these are very water-soluble so they do well in syrup form. However, they're very sensitive to heat, so they do better as a sous-vide syrup than a cooked one. Berries don't work as well as spirit infusions or tinctures, as the alcohol tends to extract unpleasant flavors. One last thing: Berries spoil easily, but fortifying your syrup with a spirit can extend its shelf life.

DRIED FRUITS *Dried figs, apricots, dates, etc.*

You tend to need higher temperatures to soften and extract from dried fruits, but the flavor is quite concentrated. However, because their flavor compounds are water-soluble, they don't work very well as spirit infusions or tinctures.

VEGETABLES

As a rule, if they can be juiced, then juice 'em. They work better that way. The juices can be made into a syrup by adding sugar and mixing to dissolve. This works well for beets, ginger and celery. Again, they often don't work well as tinctures or spirit infusions.

TEMPERATURE – TURN IT DOWN, TURN IT UP

Temperature is a controllable factor in how your drink will turn out. For example, refrigeration will slow down processes of extraction, but increase shelf life. You can gently extract flavor at room temperature, but it will often take a long time.

Sous-vide cooking at low temperatures increases extraction and intensity of flavor but doesn't cook, caramelize or burn delicate ingredients, which is great. We sous-vide our infusions and syrups between 45 and 52 degrees Celsius depending on fat and/or water content.

Cooking at high temperatures will change the flavor of what you are extracting by caramelizing the sugars and altering the proteins – science again. This can be good or bad, depending on the ingredient. High temperatures are needed to extract stubborn woody or starchy ingredients like cinnamon, cloves, squash and root vegetables. It's OK, they have it coming.

FAT-WASHING

This unpleasant-sounding technique is actually really useful, and involves using the alcohol of a spirit to extract the flavor from a fat or oil. You can then incorporate that flavor into a drink. Fat-washing also affects the texture of the drink, making it rounder, silkier or heavier. Good examples to try are bacon fat, butter, olive oil, hazelnut oil and pumpkin seed oil.

GARNISHES

We're garnish skeptics around here – they need to earn their keep. A garnish should enhance the experience of a drink visually, aromatically and/or by contributing flavor or texture to the cocktail. And if in doubt, leave it out.

PICKING THE PERFECT TWIST

— **LEMON** – adds brightness and a high note.
— **LIME** – adds brightness and a definite flavor.
— **ORANGE** – adds sweet richness and mild notes; unlike lemon, not a balancing element.
— **GRAPEFRUIT** – adds brightness, richness AND bitterness. Also, don't rub the rim with a grapefruit twist, as it leaves an unpleasant bitter residue.

Choose your twist last. Split your cocktail among several glasses, express all four oils, and blind taste. You'll be surprised.

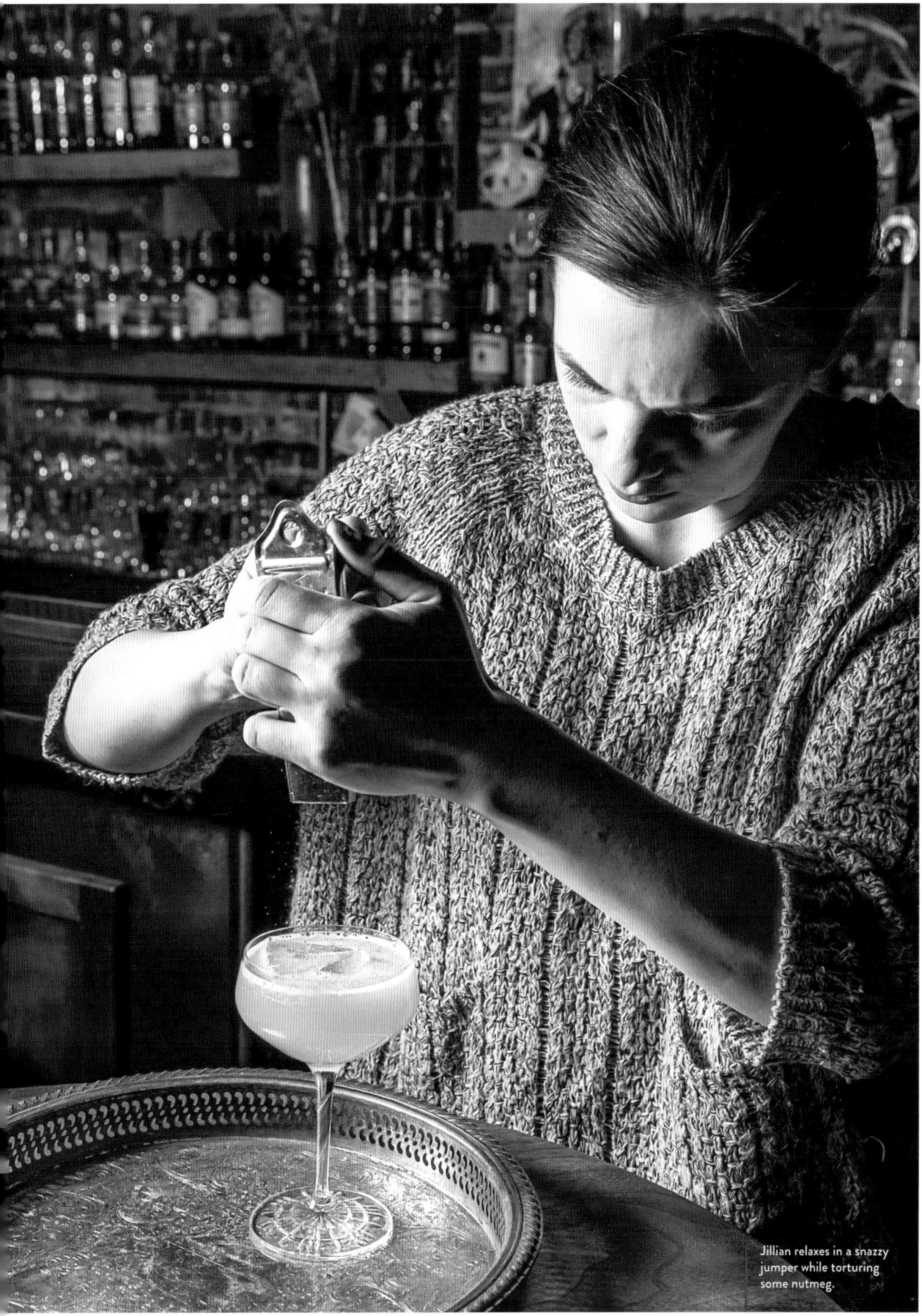

Jillian relaxes in a snazzy jumper while torturing some nutmeg.

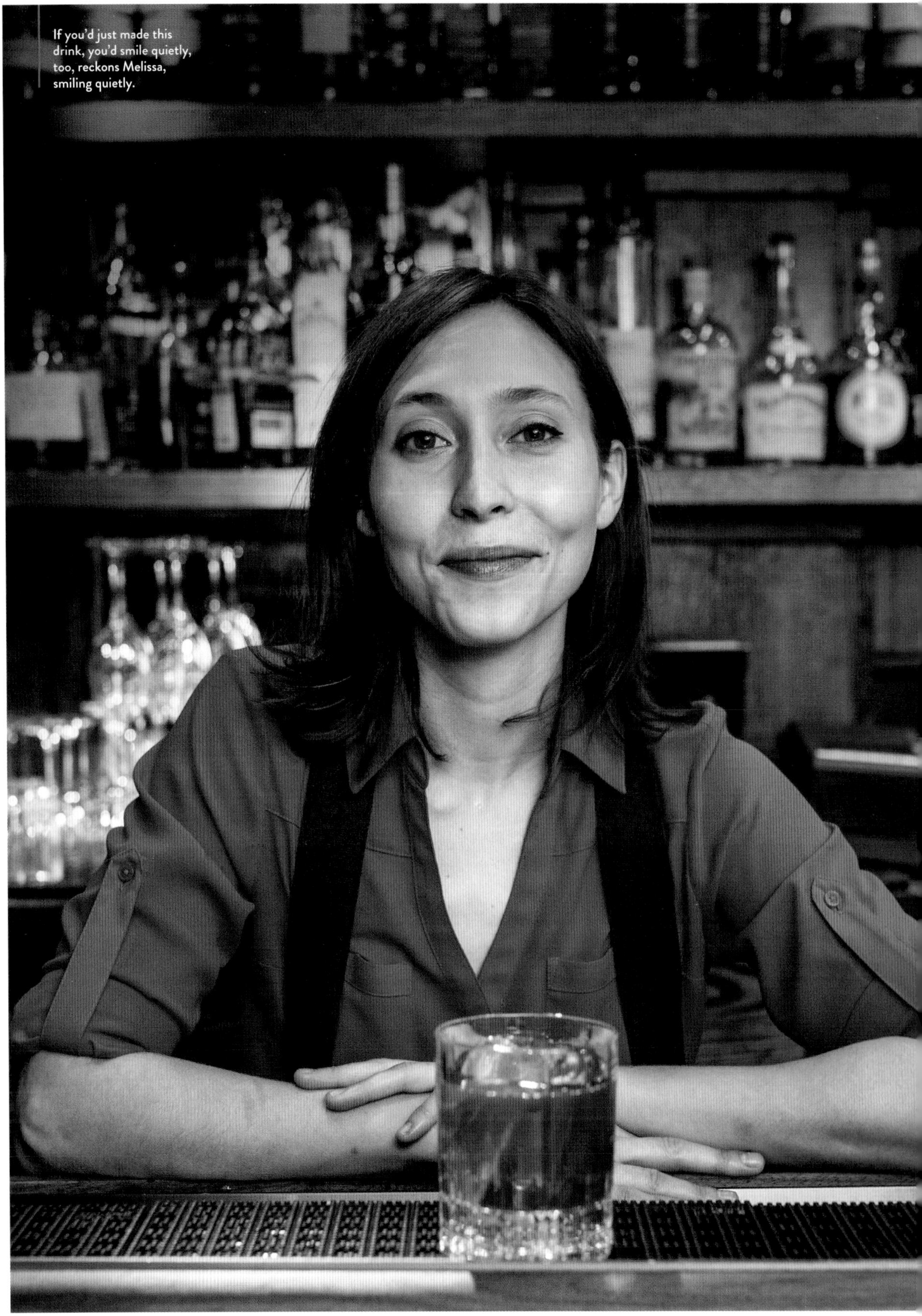

If you'd just made this drink, you'd smile quietly, too, reckons Melissa, smiling quietly.

CREATING KILLER COCKTAILS
SOME GENERAL STRATEGIES & TIPS

Fancy yourself as a would-be Dead Rabbit cocktail-creating ninja? Well, here are a few quick and dirty tips for you. *You're welcome.*

First of all and most obviously: Read everything. We decided against including a bibliography here because it would double the size of the book – there's that many to choose from. Get your hands and eyeballs on as many books you can. Drop hints around your birthday, etc. Build up a collection and never lend any. Seriously.

And don't restrict yourself to just cocktail or bartending books. We're talking about flavor here, so also include a well-chosen cookbook in your reading from time to time.

FLAVOR MAPPING

As you get better and more confident about making drinks, you'll find you can start to design a cocktail on paper. With maybe two or three elements and a style of drink in mind, you can use your vast knowledge of flavors (see pages 236 to 239) to come up with a tree of other flavors, spirits or ingredients that go well with your core set.

EXISTING RECIPES

Take an existing cocktail and use it as inspiration to develop it into a new and better drink. Some established drinks have great flavor pairings that can be incorporated into a new cocktail of a completely different style. Food can also be a great inspiration by giving you ideas for flavor sets that work well together. Several of the recipes in this book were sparked by dishes rather than drinks.

TEMPLATE RECIPES

Certain ratios of ingredients work incredibly well and are used repeatedly in a range of cocktails. *Memorize these:*

— ¾ oz acid, ¾ oz sweetener, 2 oz spirit
— Dashing bitters, 1 oz fortified wine, 2 oz spirit
— Dashing bitters, ½ oz liqueur, 1½ oz fortified wine, 1½ oz spirit
— ¾ oz acid, ½ oz neutral juice, ¾ oz sweetener, 2 oz spirit
— Dashing bitters, ¾ oz acid, ¾ oz sweetener, ¾ oz fortified wine, 1½ oz spirit

KEEP. A. NOTEBOOK. SERIOUSLY.

You think you'll remember that great idea you had. You won't. Write it down. Keep track of ideas for flavor pairings and cocktails – you can always come back to them later. Track the progression of your drinks so you can see where they start and where they finish. It might surprise you.

TIPS TO IMPROVE YOUR DRINKS

Here are some tricks we use for improving our cocktails. Keep them in mind when creating your own.

SPLIT THE BASE

Using two or even three base spirits can add complexity to your cocktail, as well as each one balancing out the other. It's not always necessary, but can work very well.

Examples of pairings that have worked well in many drinks:

— Rye & Cognac
— Irish Whiskey & Rum
— Gin & Pisco
— Tequila & Mezcal
— Tequila & Agricole Rum
— Bourbon & Calvados / Apple Brandy

ADD AN ACCENT SPIRIT

Add a small pour, teaspoon or dash of an accent spirit to add new subtle notes to your drink. They can be more powerful, so a little bit goes a long way. Good accent spirits include absinthe, eau-de-vie, overproof rum, mezcal and peated scotch.

SPLIT YOUR SWEETENERS AND/OR ACIDS

Combining different acids or sweeteners can also add complexity to your drink, as well as round out more assertive flavors. For example, if lime is too assertive and lemon is too soft, consider splitting the acid and adding them both. If a full pour of honey syrup takes over the cocktail, consider combining it with cane or demerara syrup.

TEASPOONS, DASHERS AND ATOMIZERS

If an ingredient is coming across too strongly in your drink at ¼ oz, consider using even smaller measurements, like teaspoons or dashes. Atomizers can coat a glass more efficiently and quickly than a "rinse", and can be used like a garnish to introduce an aroma when sprayed across the drink.

SELECT YOUR SPIRITS WELL, GRASSHOPPER

When picking a particular spirit for a cocktail, you should consider:

—   Style/category (bourbon vs. rye, cognac vs. armagnac) and what each option has to offer
—   Flavor profile and how it fits with the other ingredients of the drink
—   ABV, which affects the body of the drink, as well as how much the alcohol will come through
—   Cost
—   Availability

KEEP FLAVORS SEPARATE

When you are creating homemade ingredients, using too many flavors in one preparation makes it hard to achieve balance and consistency. If one ingredient is too powerful or is inconsistent, it will spoil the whole batch. So instead of making a cinnamon/clove/black pepper tincture, make separate tinctures and adjust the number of dashes in the drink. Smart, right?

AVOID REDUNDANCY

Don't overuse flavors. Rather, consider each ingredient an opportunity to introduce complexity and balance. For example, a cocktail with rhubarb bitters, a rhubarb syrup, a rhubarb-infused spirit and rhubarb for a garnish is ridiculous. Rhubarb could be introduced in one of these forms, say as a syrup, and the bitters, spirit and garnish can all be selected with flavors that pair well with rhubarb and complement one another.

247.

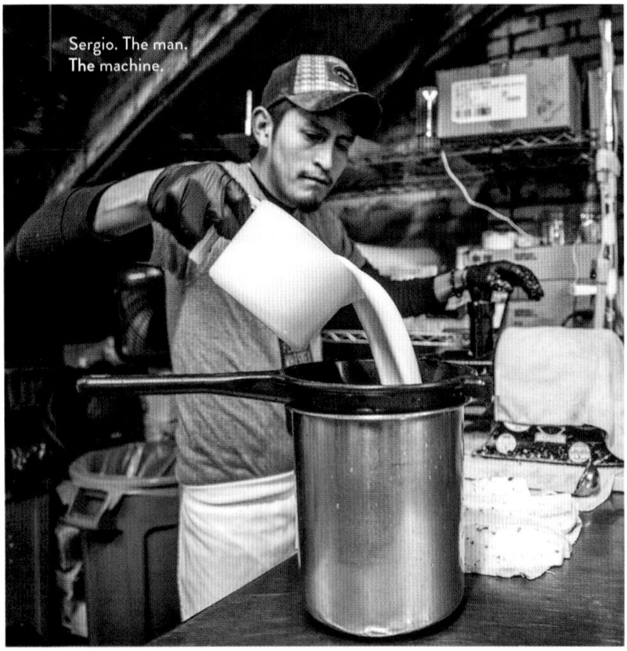

Sergio. The man. The machine.

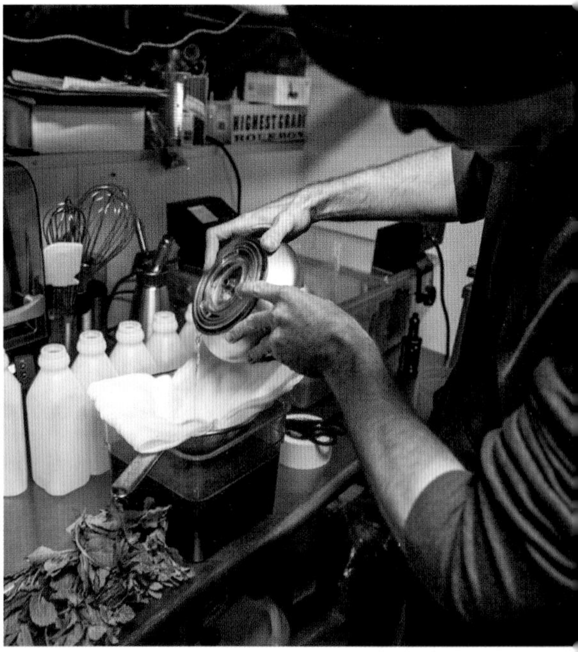
HIGHEST GRADE

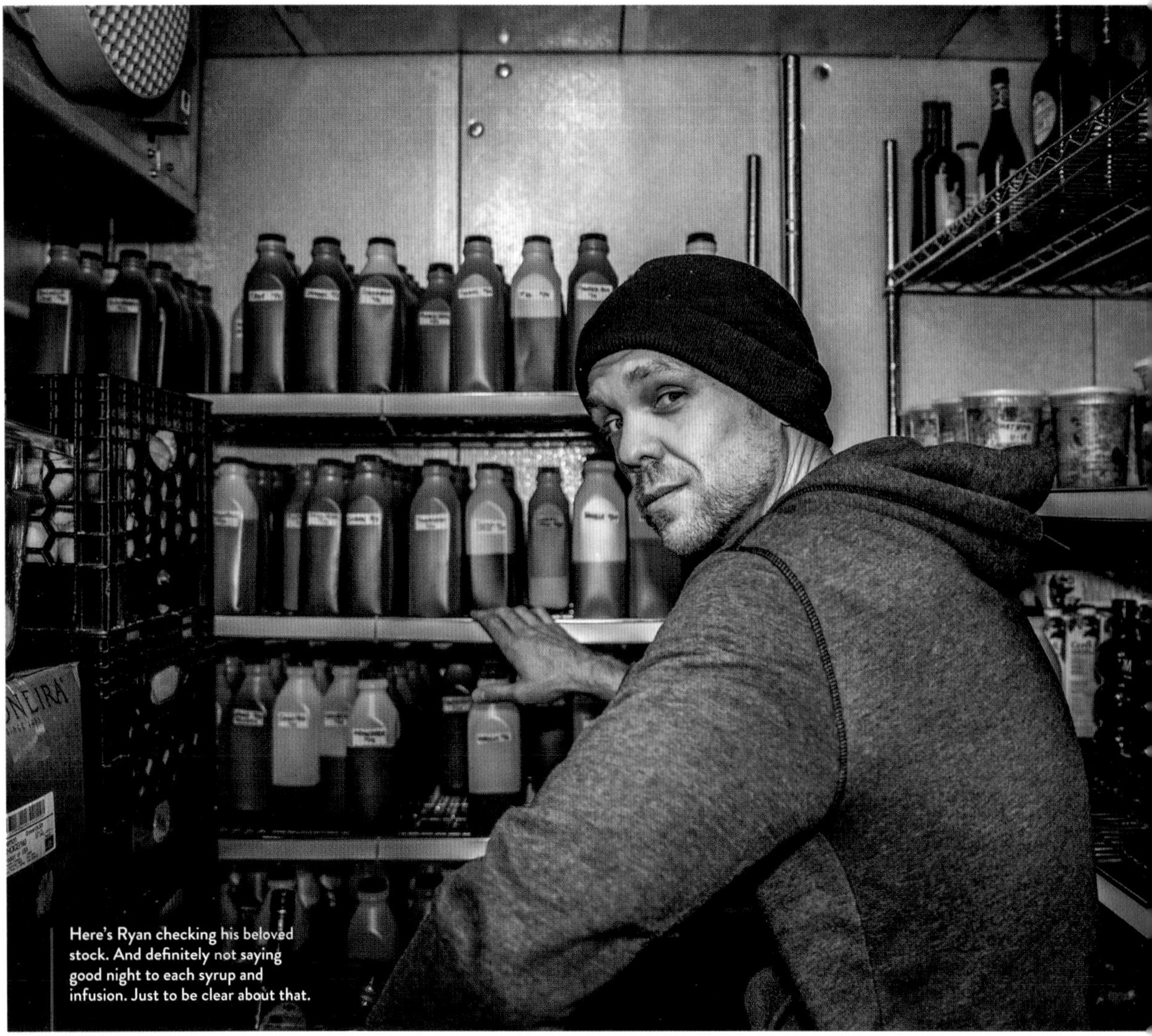

Here's Ryan checking his beloved stock. And definitely not saying good night to each syrup and infusion. Just to be clear about that.

INSTRUCTIONS
SYRUPS & TINCTURES
& WASHES, HOUSE BITTERS, ETC.

It takes several things to make an outstanding cocktail.
A great idea. Fine ingredients. Outstanding technique.
And a secret. These are our secrets, the syrups and
tinctures we painstakingly make in-house.

They're the something-you-can't-quite-put-your-finger-
on when you taste a drink for the first time. Well, now you
know what that special note is, and how to make it yourself.

BUT DON'T TELL EVERYONE, RIGHT?

Note: We have given cooking temperatures in degrees Celsius. If you want to convert temperatures to Fahrenheit, simply multiply the given temperature by 1.8 (or $\frac{9}{5}$) and add 32. You can also find conversion calculators online.

AJI AMARILLO CHILI-INFUSED ORO DE LIDIA REPOSADO TEQUILA

INGREDIENTS	1 liter Oro de Lidia reposado tequila
	4 dried aji amarillo chilis (chopped)
EQUIPMENT	Airtight container, fine mesh strainer
METHOD	Combine the tequila and chilis in an airtight container and let sit at room temperature for 30 minutes. Taste test and continue to test every minute until desired heat level is achieved. Strain through a fine mesh strainer. Bottle, label and store at room temperature.
YIELD	1 liter

ANCHO CHILI-INFUSED SWEET VERMOUTH

INGREDIENTS	4 dried ancho chilis (stemmed and seeded)
	1 liter Martini & Rossi Rosso Vermouth
EQUIPMENT	Plastic gloves, airtight container, cheesecloth
METHOD	Wearing gloves, tear the chilis into strips. Place the chilis and vermouth in an airtight container and let sit at room temperature for 1 hour. Strain through cheesecloth. Bottle, label and refrigerate.
YIELD	1 liter

APPLEWOOD SMOKED SALT SOLUTION

INGREDIENTS	900 ml water
	100 g applewood smoked salt
EQUIPMENT	Scale, airtight container
METHOD	Add the water and salt to a container and shake until the salt is completely dissolved. Seal, label and store at room temperature.
YIELD	1 liter

ARBOL CHILI-INFUSED OLD FORESTER

INGREDIENTS	3 dried Arbol chilis
	1 liter Old Forester 100 Proof Bourbon
EQUIPMENT	Gloves, airtight container, fine mesh strainer
METHOD	Wearing gloves, rip apart the chilis to expose the seeds. Combine the chilis and bourbon in an airtight container and let sit for 5 minutes. Taste test and continue to test a few times until desired heat level is achieved. Strain through a fine mesh strainer. Bottle, label and refrigerate.
YIELD	1 liter

AVOCADO CANE SYRUP

INGREDIENTS	1 liter Cane Syrup (page 254)
	170 g avocado
EQUIPMENT	Scale, vacuum sealer, sous vide, fine strainer, Superbag
METHOD	Seal the cane syrup and avocado in a vacuum bag. Sous-vide at 45°C for 6 hours. Strain through a Superbag. Bottle, label and refrigerate.
YIELD	1 liter

AVOCADO-INFUSED CAÑA BRAVA RUM

INGREDIENTS	1 liter Cana Brava Rum
	170 g avocado
EQUIPMENT	Scale, vacuum sealer, sous vide, fine mesh strainer, cheesecloth
METHOD	Seal the rum and avocado in a vacuum bag. Sous-vide at 45°C for 6 hours. Strain through a fine mesh strainer and then cheesecloth. Bottle, label and refrigerate.
YIELD	1 liter

BANANA SYRUP

INGREDIENTS	1 liter Cane Syrup (page 254)
	170 g bananas, frozen
EQUIPMENT	Scale, vacuum sealer, sous vide, fine mesh strainer
METHOD	Seal the syrup and bananas in a vacuum bag. Sous-vide at 45°C for 12 hours. Strain through a fine mesh strainer. Bottle, label and refrigerate.
YIELD	1 liter

BARLEY ORGEAT

INGREDIENTS	800 ml water
	85 g barley
	800 g sugar
EQUIPMENT	Scale, induction cook-top, stainless steel pot, Superbag, whisk, fine mesh strainer
METHOD	Combine the water and barley in a pot, heat at 80°C and bring to a boil. Remove from heat and cool for 15 minutes. Strain through a Superbag, return the liquid to the pot and boil for about 20 minutes. (The liquid should be reduced to 1200ml, making the final solution a 4:3 ratio.) Add the sugar and heat at 70°C, stirring frequently, until the sugar is completely dissolved. Bottle, label and refrigerate.
YIELD	1 liter

BAY LEAF TINCTURE

INGREDIENTS	500 ml Everclear (or other high-proof neutral spirit)
	10 bay leaves
	500 ml water
EQUIPMENT	Airtight container, Superbag, whisk
METHOD	Combine the Everclear and bay leaves in an airtight container and let sit at room temperature for 72 hours. Strain through a Superbag and mix in water. Bottle, label and store at room temperature.
YIELD	1 liter

BEET SYRUP

INGREDIENTS	500 ml fresh beet juice
	250 ml water
	750 g sugar
EQUIPMENT	Scale, stainless steel pot, induction cook-top, whisk
METHOD	Place all ingredients in the pot and heat at 70°C, stirring frequently, until all the sugar is completely dissolved, about 5 minutes. Pour into a container and cool at room temperature for 10 minutes. Bottle, label and refrigerate.
YIELD	1.25 liters

BLACKBERRY SHRUB

INGREDIENTS	200 g blackberries
	500 g sugar
	Zest of 1 lime
	500 ml apple cider vinegar
EQUIPMENT	Scale, vacuum sealer, stainless steel pot, induction cook-top, whisk, cheesecloth
METHOD	Seal the blackberries, sugar and zest in a vacuum bag. Mash the contents of the bag together and refrigerate overnight. Pour into a pot and add the vinegar. Heat at 80°C, stirring frequently, until the sugar is completely dissolved. Strain through cheesecloth. Bottle, label and refrigerate.
YIELD	750 ml

BLACKBERRY SYRUP

INGREDIENTS	1 liter semi-rich (800 g sugar: 600 ml water) Simple Syrup (page 271)
	200 g blackberries
	0.25 oz Everclear (or other high-proof neutral spirit)
EQUIPMENT	Scale, measuring cup, 0.25 oz jigger, vacuum sealer, sous vide, cheesecloth
METHOD	Seal all the ingredients in a vacuum bag. Sous-vide at 52°C for 4 hours. Strain through cheesecloth. Bottle, label and refrigerate.
YIELD	1 liter

BLACK CARDAMOM TINCTURE

INGREDIENTS 500 ml Everclear (or other high-proof neutral spirit)
1 oz black cardamom (crushed)
500 ml water

EQUIPMENT Scale, measuring cup, airtight container, fine mesh strainer, whisk

METHOD Combine the Everclear and cardamom in an airtight container and let sit at room temperature for 72 hours. Strain through a fine mesh strainer and mix in the water. Bottle, label and store at room temperature.

YIELD 1 liter

BLUEBERRY CANE SYRUP

INGREDIENTS 1 liter Cane Syrup (page 254)
170 g blueberries

EQUIPMENT Scale, vacuum sealer, sous vide, fine mesh strainer

METHOD Seal the cane syrup and blueberries in a vacuum bag. Sous-vide at 52°C for 4 hours. Strain through a fine mesh strainer. Bottle, label and refrigerate.

YIELD 1 liter

BUCKWHEAT ORGEAT

INGREDIENTS 1.6 liters water
170 g buckwheat
1600 g sugar
3 ml orange flower water

EQUIPMENT Measuring cup, scale, ½ teaspoon, stainless steel pot, induction cook-top, whisk, fine strainer

METHOD Combine the water and buckwheat in a pot, heat at 80°C and bring to a boil. Remove from heat and cool for 15 minutes. Strain through a fine mesh strainer, return the liquid to the pot and boil for about 20 minutes. (The liquid should be reduced to 1200 ml, making the final solution a 4:3 ratio.) Add the sugar and heat at 70°C, stirring frequently, until the sugar is completely dissolved. Mix in the orange flower water. Bottle, label and refrigerate.

YIELD 2 liters

BUTTERNUT SQUASH SEED OIL–WASHED POWERS SIGNATURE

INGREDIENTS 1 liter Powers Signature Release Irish Whiskey
2 oz butternut squash seed oil

EQUIPMENT 2 oz jigger, airtight container, coffee filter

METHOD Combine the whiskey and oil in an airtight container. Let sit at room temperature for 4 hours. Place in the freezer. Once the oil has frozen, strain through a coffee filter. Bottle, label and store at room temperature.

YIELD 1 liter

CANE SYRUP

INGREDIENTS	2 parts organic evaporated cane juice
	1 part water
EQUIPMENT	Measuring cup, induction cook-top, stainless steel pot, whisk
METHOD	Cook the sugar and water in a pot over medium heat and stir until the sugar is dissolved. Bring to a rolling boil and then take off heat. Cool and store in the refrigerator.

CARAMEL CANE SYRUP

INGREDIENTS	500 ml caramel sauce (store-bought)
	1 liter Cane Syrup (above)
EQUIPMENT	Measuring cup, hot water bath, blender
METHOD	Place the caramel sauce (in its container) in a hot water bath and let sit until it's pourable. Blend with the cane syrup in a blender for 1 minute. Bottle, label and refrigerate.
YIELD	1.5 liters

CELERY SEED SYRUP

INGREDIENTS	750 g water
	750 ml sugar
	28 g celery seeds (crushed)
EQUIPMENT	Spice grinder, measuring cup, scale, stainless steel pot, induction cook-top, whisk, cheesecloth
METHOD	Add all ingredients to a pot and heat at 80°C; bring to a boil, stirring frequently. Remove from heat and cool at room temperature for 1 hour. Strain through cheesecloth. Bottle, label and refrigerate.
YIELD	1.25 liters

CHAMOMILE TINCTURE

INGREDIENTS	2 oz dried chamomile flowers
	500 ml Everclear (or other high-proof neutral spirit)
	500 ml water
EQUIPMENT	Scale, measuring cup, airtight container, fine mesh strainer, whisk
METHOD	Combine the chamomile and Everclear in an airtight container and let sit at room temperature for 72 hours. Strain and mix in the water. Bottle, label and store at room temperature.
YIELD	1 liter

CHIPOTLE TINCTURE

INGREDIENTS	57 g chipotle chilis
	500 ml Everclear (or other high-proof neutral spirit)
	500 ml water
EQUIPMENT	Scale, plastic gloves, measuring cup, airtight container, fine mesh strainer, whisk
METHOD	Wearing gloves, shred the chilis. Combine with the Everclear in an airtight container and let sit at room temperature for 72 hours. Strain and mix in the water. Bottle, label and store at room temperature.
YIELD	1 liter

CILANTRO TINCTURE

INGREDIENTS	57 g fresh cilantro
	500 ml Everclear (or other high-proof neutral spirit)
	500 ml water
EQUIPMENT	Scale, measuring cup, airtight container, fine mesh strainer, whisk
METHOD	Combine the cilantro and Everclear in an airtight container and let sit at room temperature for 72 hours. Strain and mix in the water. Bottle, label and store at room temperature.
YIELD	1 liter

CINNAMON BARK SYRUP

INGREDIENTS	20 g cassia cinnamon bark
	500 ml water
	500 g fine sugar
EQUIPMENT	Scale, measuring cup, 2 large zipper-top plastic bags, muddler, stainless steel pot, induction cook-top, whisk, fine mesh strainer
METHOD	Double-bag the cinnamon in the plastic bags. On a safe and hard surface, use the muddler to crush the bark. (Even better: Buy it crushed.) Combine all ingredients in the pot. Bring to a boil, stirring frequently. Remove from heat and store in a container at room temperature for 12 hours. Strain. Bottle, label and refrigerate.
YIELD	750 ml

COCONUT-INFUSED PISCO

INGREDIENTS	100 g unsweetened dried coconut flakes (toasted)
	750 ml Pisco Portón
EQUIPMENT	Scale, vacuum sealer, sous vide, coffee filter
METHOD	Seal the coconut and pisco in a vacuum bag and sous-vide at 52°C for 8 hours. Refrigerate overnight. Strain through a coffee filter. Bottle, label and refrigerate.
YIELD	750 ml

255.

COFFEE-CHICORY CANE SYRUP

INGREDIENTS	500 ml black coffee
	1 kg sugar
	2 tbsp chicory root (ground)
EQUIPMENT	Coffee maker, scale, measuring cup, tablespoon, stainless steel pot, induction cook-top, whisk, fine mesh strainer
METHOD	Place all ingredients in a pot and bring to a boil, stirring frequently. Remove from heat and place in an airtight container and cool at room temperature for 1 hour. Strain through a fine mesh strainer. Bottle, label and refrigerate.
YIELD	1 liter

COFFEE-PECAN SYRUP

INGREDIENTS	24 oz Coffee-Chicory Cane Syrup (above)
	8 oz Pecan Orgeat (page 267)
EQUIPMENT	Scale, measuring cup, airtight container, whisk
METHOD	Mix all ingredients together in an airtight container. Seal, label and refrigerate.
YIELD	1 quart

CORIANDER-INFUSED GLENMORANGIE ORIGINAL

INGREDIENTS	1 liter Glenmorangie Original Scotch Whisky
	2 tbsp coriander seed (crushed)
EQUIPMENT	Measuring cup, tablespoon, airtight container, whisk, coffee filter or cheesecloth
METHOD	Mix the Glenmorangie and coriander seed together in an airtight container and let sit at room temperature for 1 hour, stirring occasionally. Strain through a coffee filter or cheesecloth. Bottle, label and store at room temperature.
YIELD	1 liter

DEAD RABBIT JAMAICAN RUM BLEND

INGREDIENTS	3 (750ml) btls Smith and Cross Jamaican Rum
	3 (750 ml) btls Cruzan Black Strap Rum
	2 (750ml) btls Banks 7 Golden Age Blend Rum
EQUIPMENT	Large container, whisk
METHOD	Combine all the rums together and mix well. Bottle, label and store at room temperature.
YIELD	6.75 liters

DEMERARA SYRUP

INGREDIENTS   1 kg demerara sugar (we use Billington's)
500 ml water

EQUIPMENT   Scale, measuring cup, stainless steel pot, induction cook-top, whisk

METHOD   Place the sugar and water in a pot and mix well. Heat at 80°C and continue to stir until the sugar is completely dissolved. Bring to a rolling boil, then remove from heat. Cool. Bottle, label and refrigerate.

YIELD   1 liter

DILL SYRUP

INGREDIENTS   135 g fresh dill
1 liter cold Simple Syrup (page 271)
1 tsp ascorbic acid

EQUIPMENT   Stainless steel pot, induction cook-top, ice bath, blender, tea towel, teaspoon, whisk

METHOD   Bring a pot of water to a boil and prepare an ice bath. Place the dill in boiling water for 15 to 30 seconds, then remove and immediately place in the ice bath for 1 minute. Put the blanched dill in a blender with the cold syrup and pulse on low until the dill is well blended. Strain through a tea towel and whisk in the acid. Bottle, label and refrigerate.

YIELD   1 liter

DRIED APRICOT SYRUP

INGREDIENTS   1 liter water
200 g dried apricots
750 g sugar

EQUIPMENT   Stainless steel pot, induction cook-top, cheesecloth, whisk

METHOD   Place the water and apricots in a pot and bring to a boil. Reduce heat and simmer until the liquid has reduced by one-fourth (750 mls). Remove from heat and cool at room temperature for 30 minutes, then strain through cheesecloth. Return the liquid to the pot, add the sugar and heat at 70°C, stirring frequently, until the sugar is completely dissolved. Bottle, label and store in the refrigerator.

YIELD   1.5 liters

EARL GREY TEA CANE SYRUP

INGREDIENTS   500 ml Earl Grey tea (on the strong side)
1 kg sugar

EQUIPMENT   Scale, stainless steel pot, induction cook-top, whisk

METHOD   Combine the tea and sugar in the pot. Bring the mixture to a boil while stirring frequently. Remove from heat and cool at room temperature for 1 hour. (Caution: Cooling too quickly or unevenly will result in recrystallization.) Bottle, label and refrigerate.

YIELD   1 liter

257.

EUCALYPTUS TINCTURE

INGREDIENTS	250 ml Everclear (or other high-proof neutral spirit) 2 tbsp dried eucalyptus 250 ml water
EQUIPMENT	Measuring cup, tablespoon, airtight container, cheesecloth, whisk
METHOD	Mix the Everclear and eucalyptus in an airtight container and let sit at room temperature for 72 hours. Strain through cheesecloth and mix in water. Bottle, label and store at room temperature.
YIELD	500 ml

EXTRA-VIRGIN OLIVE OIL–WASHED DEL MAGUEY VIDA MEZCAL

INGREDIENTS	750 ml Del Maguey Mezcal Vida 2 oz extra virgin olive oil
EQUIPMENT	2 oz jigger, vacuum sealer, cheesecloth
METHOD	Seal the mezcal and oil in a vacuum bag. Let sit at room temperature for 12 hours, then freeze overnight. Strain through cheesecloth. Bottle, label and store at room temperature.
YIELD	750 ml

FENNEL SYRUP

INGREDIENTS	750 g sugar 750 ml water 28 g fennel seeds (crushed)
EQUIPMENT	Scale, measuring cup, muddler, stainless steel pot, induction cook-top, whisk, cheesecloth
METHOD	Add all ingredients to a pot and heat at 80°C. Bring to a boil, stirring frequently. Remove from heat and cool at room temperature for 1 hour. Strain through cheesecloth. Bottle, label and refrigerate.
YIELD	1 liter

FIG SYRUP

INGREDIENTS	170 g dried Mission figs (stemmed and cut into quarters) 750 ml water 750 g sugar
EQUIPMENT	Knife, scale, measuring cup, stainless steel pot, induction cook-top, whisk, fine mesh strainer
METHOD	Combine the figs and water in a pot, heat at 80°C and bring to a boil. Reduce heat to 60°C and simmer for 1 hour. Strain through a fine mesh strainer, return the liquid to the pot and add the sugar. Heat at 60°C, stirring frequently, until the sugar is completely dissolved. Bottle, label and refrigerate.
YIELD	1 liter

GENMAICHA TEA SYRUP

INGREDIENTS	750 ml water
	750 g sugar
	30 g genmaicha tea
EQUIPMENT	Scale, stainless steel pot, induction cook-top, whisk, fine mesh strainer
METHOD	Combine all ingredients in a pot. Bring to a boil, stirring frequently. Remove from heat and store in a clean container at room temperature for 30 minutes. Strain through a fine mesh strainer. Bottle, label and refrigerate.
YIELD	1 liter

GINGER SYRUP

INGREDIENTS	750 ml fresh ginger juice
	750 g sugar
EQUIPMENT	Juice extractor, scale, measuring cup, stainless steel pot, induction cook-top, cheesecloth
METHOD	Add the ginger juice and sugar to a pot and heat at 70°C for 45 minutes. Remove from heat and cool at room temperature. Strain through cheesecloth. Bottle, label and refrigerate.
YIELD	1 liter

GRANNY SMITH APPLE JUICE

INGREDIENTS	1 liter fresh apple juice
	1 tsp ascorbic acid
EQUIPMENT	Juice extractor, teaspoon, whisk, airtight container
METHOD	Add the acid to the freshly extracted apple juice and mix thoroughly. (It's important to add the acid ASAP to impede the oxidation of the juice.) Transfer to an airtight container, label and refrigerate.
YIELD	1 liter

GREEN TEA-INFUSED TANQUERAY

INGREDIENTS	1 liter Tanqueray No. 10 Gin
	2 g green tea (equivalent to 1 tea bag)
EQUIPMENT	Scale, airtight container, whisk, Superbag
METHOD	Add the gin to an airtight container and mix in the green tea. Let sit at room temperature for 10 to 15 minutes, tasting for the potency every 5 minutes and stirring occasionally. Strain through a Superbag. Bottle, label and store at room temperature.
YIELD	1 liter

ANOTHER ROUND: EXTRAS

259.

SYRUPS & TINCTURES

GREEN TEA-INFUSED TAPATIO BLANCO TEQUILA

INGREDIENTS 1 liter Tapatío Blanco Tequila
2 g green tea (equivalent to 1 tea bag)

EQUIPMENT Scale, airtight container, whisk, Superbag

METHOD Combine the tequila and green tea in an airtight container. Let sit at room temperature for 10 to 15 minutes, tasting for potency every 5 minutes and stirring occasionally. Strain through a Superbag. Bottle, label and refrigerate.

YIELD 1 liter

GRILLED PINEAPPLE-INFUSED BOLS GENEVER

INGREDIENTS ¼ whole pineapple (sliced and grilled)
1 liter unaged Bols Genever

EQUIPMENT Grill, tongs, scale, airtight nonreactive container, cheesecloth

METHOD Place the grilled pineapple and Bols Genever in an airtight nonreactive container and let sit at room temperature overnight. Strain through cheesecloth. Bottle, label and refrigerate.

YIELD 1 liter

GUAVA SYRUP

INGREDIENTS 1 kg guava puree
500 ml water
1.5 kg sugar

EQUIPMENT Scale, stainless steel pot, induction cook-top, whisk, cheesecloth

METHOD Add all ingredients to a pot and heat at 70°C, stirring frequently, until the sugar is completely dissolved. Strain through cheesecloth. Bottle, label and refrigerate.

YIELD 2.5 liters

HONEY SYRUP

INGREDIENTS 20 oz clover honey
10 oz hot water

EQUIPMENT Measuring cup, hot water bath, whisk

METHOD Soften the honey by placing it in a hot water bath. Whisk the honey with the water. Bottle, label and refrigerate.

YIELD 1.25 liters

HONEYDEW AND CUCUMBER-INFUSED BOTANIST GIN

INGREDIENTS	500 g honeydew (thinly sliced)
	750 ml Botanist Gin
	120 g cucumber (thinly sliced)
EQUIPMENT	Knife, scale, nonreactive airtight container, fine mesh strainer
METHOD	Place the honeydew and gin in an airtight container and let sit for 12 hours, agitating occasionally. Add the cucumber and allow to sit for 1 hour more. Strain through a fine mesh strainer. Bottle, label and refrigerate.
YIELD	750 ml

HORCHATA SYRUP

INGREDIENTS	750 ml rice milk
	1 cinnamon stick
	1 vanilla bean (split and scraped)
	½ cup toasted almonds (crushed in food processor)
	750 g sugar
EQUIPMENT	Scale, measuring cup, knife, food processor, stainless steel pot, induction cook-top, whisk, cheesecloth
METHOD	Add all ingredients to the pot and heat at 70°C for 45 minutes, stirring occasionally, until the sugar is completely dissolved. Remove from heat and cool at room temperature for 30 minutes. Strain through cheesecloth. Bottle, label and store at room temperature.
YIELD	1 liter

HOUSE CARDAMOM BITTERS

INGREDIENTS	3 parts Regan's Orange Bitters No. 6
	1 part Scrappy's Cardamom Bitters
EQUIPMENT	Measuring cup or jiggers, airtight container
METHOD	Add both bitters to the container, seal the lid and give it a good shake. Transfer to a dasher bottle, label and store at room temperature.

HOUSE ORANGE BITTERS

INGREDIENTS	1 part Regans' Orange Bitters No. 6
	1 part Angostura Orange Bitters
EQUIPMENT	Measuring cup or jiggers, airtight container
METHOD	Add both bitters to the container, seal the lid and give it a good shake. Transfer to a dasher bottle, label and store at room temperature.

ANOTHER ROUND: EXTRAS

261.

SYRUPS & TINCTURES

KAFFIR LIME LEAF TINCTURE

INGREDIENTS 500 ml Everclear (or other high-proof neutral spirit)
10 fresh kaffir lime leaves
500 ml water

EQUIPMENT Measuring cup, airtight container, whisk

METHOD Combine the Everclear and kaffir leaves in an airtight container and let sit at room temperature for 72 hours. Strain and mix in the water. Bottle, label and store at room temperature.

YIELD 1 liter

LEMON SHERBET

INGREDIENTS 500 g fine sugar
Zest of 4 lemons
500 ml lemon juice

EQUIPMENT Scale, airtight container, stainless steel pot, induction cook-top, whisk, fine mesh strainer (optional: vacuum sealer)

METHOD Combine the sugar and zest in an airtight container, mixing them thoroughly so the oils from the zest begin to express into the sugar. Let sit at room temperature for at least 1 hour. (Alternatively, for faster or more thorough results in less time, vacuum-seal the sugar and zest together.) Transfer to a pot, add the lemon juice and cook at 60°C, stirring regularly, until the sugar is completely dissolved (about 30 minutes). Strain through a fine mesh strainer. Bottle, label and refrigerate.

YIELD 750 ml

LEMONGRASS TINCTURE

INGREDIENTS 500 ml Everclear (or other high-proof neutral spirit)
4 tbsp dried lemongrass
500 ml water

EQUIPMENT Scale, measuring cup, tablespoon, airtight container, whisk, Superbag

METHOD Mix the Everclear and lemongrass in an airtight container and let sit at room temperature for 72 hours. Strain through a Superbag and mix with the water. Bottle, label and store at room temperature.

YIELD 1 liter

MACADAMIA ORGEAT (AKA MACDADDY)

Purchase from **orgeatworks.com**, or use this less clarified recipe.

INGREDIENTS	250 g macadamia nuts
	600 ml hot water
	600 g sugar
	3.5 ml orange flower water
	3.5 oz Everclear (or other high-proof neutral spirit)
EQUIPMENT	Scale, stainless steel pot, induction cook-top, strainer, food processor, cheesecloth, whisk
METHOD	Place the nuts in a pot and add water to cover. Simmer at 60°C for 30 minutes. Strain and process the nuts in a food processor until smooth. Add the hot water and let sit for 2 hours. Strain through cheesecloth and place the resulting "macadamia milk" (approximately 3.6 liters) into a pot with the sugar (adjusted to a 4:3 ratio with macadamia milk) and orange flower water. Cook at 70°C, stirring occasionally, until the sugar is dissolved. Remove from heat and mix in Everclear. Cool at room temperature. Bottle, label and refrigerate.
YIELD	1 liter

MACE TINCTURE

INGREDIENTS	500 ml Everclear (or other high-proof neutral spirit)
	3 tbsp mace blades (crushed)
	500 ml water
EQUIPMENT	Airtight container, whisk, cheesecloth or coffee filter
METHOD	Mix the Everclear and mace in an airtight container and let sit at room temperature for 72 hours. Strain through cheesecloth or a coffee filter and mix with the water. Bottle, label and store at room temperature.
YIELD	1 liter

MANGO-INFUSED PISCO

INGREDIENTS	750 ml Pisco Portón
	1 ripe mango (peeled and pitted)
EQUIPMENT	Vacuum sealer, sous vide, Superbag
METHOD	Seal the pisco and mango in a vacuum bag. Sous-vide at 45°C for 6 hours. Strain through a Superbag. Bottle, label and refrigerate.
YIELD	1 liter

263.

MATCHA GREEN TEA COCO LÓPEZ

INGREDIENTS 15 oz Coco López
1 tsp matcha green tea
EQUIPMENT Measuring cup, teaspoon, blender, airtight container
METHOD Place the Coco López and matcha in a blender and blend on high until the tea is thoroughly incorporated. Pour into an airtight container and refrigerate. In use, hold at room temperature.
YIELD 15 oz

MINT SYRUP

INGREDIENTS 12 oz water
14 fresh mint sprigs
24 oz sugar
EQUIPMENT Measuring cup, stainless steel pot, induction cook-top, ice bath, whisk, blender, cheese-cloth
METHOD Bring a large pot of water to a boil. Meanwhile, prepare an ice bath. Grasping the stem ends of the mint sprigs, completely immerse the leafy ends in the boiling water for 15 seconds, then remove and immediately submerge in the ice bath for 1 minute. Remove, pat dry with paper towels and pick the leaves from the stems. Combine the sugar and water in a pot over medium heat, stirring, until the sugar is dissolved. Cool at room temperature. Blend the blanched mint leaves and cooled syrup in a blender on high speed for 1 minute. Strain through cheesecloth. Bottle, label and refrigerate.
YIELD Roughly 30 oz

NUTMEG SYRUP

INGREDIENTS 1 kg sugar
20 g ground nutmeg
500 ml water
EQUIPMENT Scale, nutmeg grater, stainless steel pot, induction cook-top, whisk, cheesecloth
METHOD Add all ingredients to a pot and heat at 80°C for 30 minutes, stirring occasionally, until the sugar is completely dissolved. Remove from heat and cool at room temperature for 1 hour. Strain through cheesecloth. Bottle, label and refrigerate.
YIELD 1 liter

ORANGE SHERBET

INGREDIENTS	Zest of 3 oranges
	750 g fine sugar
	750 ml orange juice
EQUIPMENT	Scale, airtight container, stainless steel pot, induction cook-top, whisk, fine mesh strainer (optional: vacuum sealer)
METHOD	Combine the zest and sugar in an airtight container, making sure to mix them together thoroughly so the oils from the zest begin to express into the sugar. Let sit at room temperature for 1 hour. (Alternatively, for faster or more thorough results in less time, vacuum-seal the sugar and zest together.) Transfer to a pot, add the orange juice and cook at 60°C, stirring regularly, until the sugar is completely dissolved (about 30 minutes). Strain through a fine mesh strainer. Bottle, label and refrigerate.
YIELD	1 liter

ORGEAT

Purchase from **orgeatworks.com**, or use this less clarified recipe.

INGREDIENTS	250 g blanched almonds
	600 ml hot water
	600 g fine sugar
	1 tsp orange flower water
	0.25 oz Everclear (or other high-proof neutral spirit)
EQUIPMENT	Scale, measuring cup, teaspoon, stainless steel pot, induction cook-top, fine mesh strainer, food processor, airtight container, cheesecloth, whisk
METHOD	Place the almonds in a pot and add water to cover. Simmer at 60°C for 30 minutes. Strain through a fine mesh strainer and process the almonds in a food processor until smooth. Transfer to an airtight container, add the hot water and let sit for 2 hours. Strain through cheesecloth and place the resulting "almond milk" (approximately 450 ml) into the pot with the sugar (adjusted to be a 4:3 ratio to the almond milk) and orange flower water. Cook at 70°C, stirring occasionally, until the sugar is completely dissolved. Remove from heat and mix in the Everclear. Cool at room temperature. Bottle, label and refrigerate.
YIELD	1 liter

PAPRIKA SYRUP

INGREDIENTS	750 g sugar
	50 g smoked ground paprika
	750 ml water
EQUIPMENT	Scale, stainless steel pot, induction cook-top, whisk, cheesecloth
METHOD	Add all ingredients to a pot and heat at 80°C for 30 minutes, stirring occasionally, until the sugar is completely dissolved. Remove from heat and cool at room temperature for 1 hour. Strain through cheesecloth. Bottle, label and refrigerate.
YIELD	1 liter

PASSION BERRY SYRUP

INGREDIENTS	500 g sugar
	20 passion berries
	500 ml water
EQUIPMENT	Scale, stainless steel pot, induction cook-top, cheesecloth
METHOD	Add all ingredients to a pot and heat at 70°C for 1 hour. Remove from heat and cool at room temperature. Strain through cheesecloth. Bottle, label and refrigerate.
YIELD	750 ml

PASSION FRUIT SYRUP

INGREDIENTS	1 kg sugar
	500 ml passion fruit juice (Ceres brand)
EQUIPMENT	Scale, measuring cup, stainless steel pot, induction cook-top, whisk, airtight container
METHOD	Add the sugar and juice to a pot and heat at 80°C, stirring frequently, until it comes to a boil. Remove from heat and cool at room temperature in an airtight container for 1 hour. Bottle, label and refrigerate.
YIELD	1 liter

PEAR SYRUP

INGREDIENTS	2 sweet green pears
	750 g sugar
	750 ml white wine (Viura Rioja)
EQUIPMENT	Knife, scale, stainless steel pot, induction cook-top, whisk, cheesecloth
METHOD	Dice the pears into small pieces. Add all ingredients to a pot and heat at 70°C, stirring frequently, until the sugar is completely dissolved. Remove from heat and cool at room temperature for 1 hour. Strain through cheesecloth. Bottle, label and refrigerate.
YIELD	1 liter

PECAN ORGEAT

INGREDIENTS 250 g pecans, crushed
600 ml hot water
600 g fine sugar
0.25 oz Everclear (or other high-proof neutral spirit)

EQUIPMENT Scale, stainless steel pot, induction cook-top, fine mesh strainer, food processor, Superbag, whisk

METHOD Place the pecans in a pot and add water to cover. Simmer at 60°C for 30 minutes. Strain and process the pecans in a food processor until smooth. Add the hot water and let sit for 2 hours. Strain through a Superbag and place the resulting "pecan milk" (approximately 1.8 liters) into a pot with the sugar (adjusted to be a 4:3 ratio to the pecan milk). Cook at 70°C, stirring occasionally, until the sugar is completely dissolved. Remove from heat and mix in the Everclear. Cool at room temperature. Bottle, label and refrigerate.

YIELD 1 liter

PISTACHIO ORGEAT

INGREDIENTS 250 g pistachios
600 ml hot water
600 g fine sugar
3 ml orange flower water
3 ml Everclear (or other high-proof neutral spirit)

EQUIPMENT Scale, stainless steel pot, induction cook-top, fine strainer, food processor, cheesecloth, whisk

METHOD Place the pistachios in a pot and add water to cover. Simmer at 60°C for 30 minutes. Strain and process the pistachios in a food processor until smooth. Add the hot water and let sit for 2 hours. Strain through cheesecloth and place resulting "pistachio milk" (approximately 3.6 liters) into the pot with the sugar (adjusted to be a 4:3 ratio to the pistachio milk) and orange flower water. Cook at 70°C, stirring occasionally, until the sugar is completely dissolved. Remove from heat and mix in the Everclear. Cool at room temperature. Bottle, label and refrigerate.

YIELD 1 liter

POMEGRANATE SYRUP

INGREDIENTS 1.2 liters pomegranate juice
800 g sugar

EQUIPMENT Scale, stainless steel pot, induction cook-top, whisk, airtight container

METHOD Add the pomegranate juice to a pot and bring to a boil. Reduce heat and simmer until the liquid has reduced by one-third (you should have 800 ml). Add the sugar and whisk until the sugar is completely dissolved. Pour into an airtight container and cool at room temperature for 15 minutes. Bottle, label and refrigerate.

YIELD 1.5 liters

POPPY SEED SYRUP

INGREDIENTS	30 g poppy seeds
	750 ml water
	750 ml sugar
EQUIPMENT	Scale, stainless steel pot, induction cook-top, whisk, cheesecloth
METHOD	Add all ingredients to a pot and heat at 80°C for 30 minutes, stirring occasionally, until the sugar is completely dissolved. Remove from heat and cool at room temperature for 1 hour. Strain through cheesecloth. Bottle, label and refrigerate.
YIELD	1 liter

PUMPKIN SEED–WASHED POWERS GOLD IRISH WHISKEY

INGREDIENTS	1 liter Powers Gold Irish Whiskey
	2 oz pumpkin seed oil
EQUIPMENT	Jigger, measuring cup, airtight container, Superbag
METHOD	Combine the whiskey and oil in an airtight container. Let sit at room temperature for 4 hours. Place in freezer. Once the oil has frozen, strain the whiskey through a Superbag. Bottle, label and store at room temperature.
YIELD	1 liter

PUMPKIN TINCTURE

INGREDIENTS	500 ml Everclear (or other high-proof neutral spirit)
	¼ cup toasted pumpkin seeds
	1 tsp ground cinnamon
	1 tsp ground nutmeg
	1 tsp ground ginger
	1 tsp ground allspice
	¼ tsp ground cloves
	500 ml water
EQUIPMENT	Scale, measuring cup, teaspoon, ½ teaspoon, spice grinder, nutmeg grater, sauté pan, cooktop, whisk, cheesecloth, airtight container
METHOD	Mix the pumpkin seeds and spices into the Everclear. Store in an airtight container at room temperature for at least 72 hours. Strain through cheesecloth and mix in the water. Bottle, label and store at room temperature.
YIELD	1 liter

RASPBERRY-INFUSED BRUTO AMERICANO

INGREDIENTS	255 g (1 standard-size container) raspberries
	750 ml Bruto Americano
EQUIPMENT	Scale, iSi Gourmet Whip, 4 N_2O chargers, fine mesh strainer
METHOD	You will need to do this in two batches. Load an iSi container with half the raspberries and Bruto Americano and charge with 2 nitrous chargers. Allow to infuse at room temperature for 45 minutes. Release pressure and strain. Bottle, label and refrigerate. Repeat with the remaining raspberries and Bruto Americano.
YIELD	750 ml

RASPBERRY SYRUP

INGREDIENTS	1 liter semi-rich Simple Syrup (4 parts sugar to 3 parts water; page 271)
	170 g raspberries
	¼ tsp rose water
	0.25 oz Everclear (or other high-proof neutral spirit)
EQUIPMENT	Scale, ¼ teaspoon, vacuum sealer, sous vide, cheesecloth
METHOD	Seal all ingredients in a vacuum bag. Sous-vide at 45°C for 4 hours. Strain through cheesecloth. Bottle, label and refrigerate.
YIELD	1 liter

RHUBARB SYRUP

INGREDIENTS	1 liter Simple Syrup (page 271)
	0.25 oz rhubarb extract (we buy ours at **terraspice.com**)
EQUIPMENT	Measuring cup, whisk or blender
METHOD	Combine the syrup and extract and whisk or blend thoroughly until completely incorporated. Bottle, label and refrigerate.
YIELD	1 liter

SAGE-INFUSED DOLIN BLANC VERMOUTH

INGREDIENTS	750 ml Dolin Blanc Vermouth
	25 g fresh sage leaves
EQUIPMENT	Scale, airtight container, fine mesh strainer
METHOD	Place all ingredients in an airtight container and let sit at room temperature for 30 minutes. Strain through a fine mesh strainer. Bottle, label and refrigerate.
YIELD	750 ml

269.

SALINE SOLUTION

INGREDIENTS	100 g kosher salt
	30 oz water
EQUIPMENT	Scale, measuring cup, airtight container, whisk
METHOD	Mix the salt and water together in an airtight container and shake until the salt is completely dissolved. Store at room temperature.
YIELD	1 liter

SESAME-INFUSED POWERS GOLD IRISH WHISKEY

INGREDIENTS	3 tsp white sesame seeds
	1 liter Powers Gold Irish Whiskey
EQUIPMENT	Teaspoon, sauté pan, induction cook-top, airtight nonreactive container, whisk, fine mesh strainer
METHOD	Lightly brown the sesame seeds in a pan over medium heat. While still hot, combine with the whiskey in an airtight nonreactive container. Let sit for 10 minutes, stirring often. Strain through a fine mesh strainer. Bottle, label and store at room temperature.
YIELD	1 liter

SHISO DRY VERMOUTH

INGREDIENTS	1 liter Noilly Pratt Dry Vermouth
	20 shiso leaves
EQUIPMENT	iSi Gourmet Whip, 4 N_2O chargers, fine mesh strainer
METHOD	You will need to do this in two batches. Load an iSi container with half the vermouth and shiso leaves and charge with 2 nitrous chargers. Shake and let sit 10 minutes. Release pressure. Strain through a fine mesh strainer. Bottle, label and store at room temperature. Repeat with the remaining vermouth and shiso leaves.
YIELD	1 liter

SILVER NEEDLE TINCTURE

INGREDIENTS	500 ml Everclear (or other high-proof neutral spirit)
	2 tbsp Silver Needle Tea
	500 ml water
EQUIPMENT	Scale, tablespoon, airtight container, whisk, Superbag
METHOD	Mix the Everclear and tea in an airtight container and let sit at room temperature for 72 hours. Strain through a Superbag and mix in the water. Bottle, label and store at room temperature.
YIELD	1 liter

SIMPLE SYRUP

INGREDIENTS	1 part sugar
	1 part water
EQUIPMENT	Saucepan, induction cook-top, whisk, airtight container
METHOD	Combine the sugar and water in saucepan over medium heat, stirring slowly until the sugar is dissolved. Transfer to an airtight container and cool at room temperature. Bottle, label and refrigerate.

SMOKED BLACK PEPPER TINCTURE

INGREDIENTS	500 ml Everclear (or other high-proof neutral spirit)
	3 tbsp ground smoked black peppercorns
	500 ml water
EQUIPMENT	Scale, tablespoon, airtight container, whisk, cheesecloth or coffee filter
METHOD	Mix the Everclear and ground pepper in an airtight container and let sit at room temperature for 72 hours. Strain through cheesecloth or a coffee filter and mix with the water. Bottle, label and store at room temperature.
YIELD	1 liter

SPICED PEAR SYRUP

INGREDIENTS	1 liter Cane Syrup (page 254)
	1 ripe Bartlett pear, cored and chopped
	2 cinnamon sticks
	2 bay leaves
	20 cloves
EQUIPMENT	Vacuum sealer, sous vide, cheesecloth
METHOD	Seal all ingredients in a vacuum bag and sous-vide at 52°C for 6 hours. Strain through cheesecloth. Bottle, label and refrigerate.
YIELD	1 liter

STRAWBERRY SYRUP

INGREDIENTS	1 liter Cane Syrup (page 254)
	170 g frozen strawberries
EQUIPMENT	Scale, vacuum sealer, sous vide, fine mesh strainer
METHOD	Seal the strawberries and cane syrup in a vacuum bag. Sous-vide at 52°C for 4 hours. Strain through a fine mesh strainer. Bottle, label and refrigerate.
YIELD	1 liter

STRAWBERRY TEQUILA CABEZA

INGREDIENTS	1 liter Tequila Cabeza
	500 g strawberries (stemmed and halved)
EQUIPMENT	Scale, vacuum sealer, sous vide, ice bath, fine mesh strainer
METHOD	Seal the tequila and strawberries in a vacuum bag. Sous-vide at 45°C for 2 hours. Submerge in an ice bath for 15 minutes. Strain through a fine mesh strainer. Bottle, label and refrigerate.
YIELD	1 liter

SUGAR SNAP PEA-INFUSED EL TESORO PLATINUM TEQUILA

INGREDIENTS	250 g sugar snap peas (chopped)
	750 ml El Tesoro Blanco Platinum Tequila
EQUIPMENT	Scale, knife, airtight container, whisk, fine mesh strainer
METHOD	Place the peas and tequila in an airtight container and let sit for 4 hours, stirring occasionally. Strain through a fine mesh strainer. Bottle, label and refrigerate.
YIELD	750 ml

SUMAC SYRUP

INGREDIENTS	500 ml water
	2 tbsp ground sumac
	1 kg sugar
EQUIPMENT	Scale, tablespoon, stainless steel pot, induction cook-top, whisk, cheesecloth
METHOD	Add the water and sumac to a pot and heat at 100°C until it comes to a boil. Add the sugar and stir frequently until the sugar is completely dissolved. Strain through cheesecloth and cool at room temperature. Bottle, label and refrigerate.
YIELD	1 liter

SUNFLOWER ORGEAT

INGREDIENTS	250 g sunflower seeds
	600 ml hot water
	600 g fine sugar
	0.25 oz Everclear (or other high-proof neutral spirit)
EQUIPMENT	Scale, measuring cup, stainless steel pot, induction cook-top, fine mesh strainer, food processor, whisk, cheesecloth
METHOD	Place the sunflower seeds in a pot and add water to cover. Simmer at 60°C for 30 minutes. Strain through a fine mesh strainer and process the sunflower seeds in a food processor until smooth. Add the hot water and let sit for 2 hours. Strain through cheesecloth and place the resulting "sunflower milk" (approximately 1800 ml) into the pot with the sugar (adjusted to be a 4:3 ratio to the sunflower milk). Cook at 70°C, stirring occasionally, until the sugar is completely dissolved. Remove from heat and mix in the Everclear. Cool at room temperature. Bottle, label and refrigerate.
YIELD	1 liter

TANSY TINCTURE

INGREDIENTS	28 g tansy leaves
	500 ml Everclear (or other high-proof neutral spirit)
	500 ml water
EQUIPMENT	Scale, airtight container, cheesecloth, whisk
METHOD	Combine the tansy leaves and Everclear in an airtight container and let sit at room temperature for 72 hours. Strain through cheesecloth. Mix in the water. Bottle, label and store at room temperature.
YIELD	1 liter

TARRAGON SYRUP

INGREDIENTS	750 ml water
	2 tbsp dried tarragon
	750 g sugar
EQUIPMENT	Scale, tablespoon, stainless steel pot, induction cook-top, whisk, fine mesh strainer
METHOD	Combine all ingredients in the pot, heat at 80°C and bring to a boil, stirring frequently. Reduce heat to 60°C and simmer for 1 hour. Strain through a fine mesh strainer. Bottle, label and refrigerate.
YIELD	1 liter

TART CHERRY SYRUP

INGREDIENTS	170 g tart cherries, pitted and halved
	800 g sugar
	600 ml water
EQUIPMENT	Scale, measuring cup, cherry pitter, knife, stainless steel pot, induction cook-top, whisk, cheesecloth
METHOD	Combine all ingredients in a pot and heat at 60°C for 2 hours, stirring occasionally, until the sugar is completely dissolved. Remove from heat and cool at room temperature for 15 minutes. Strain through cheesecloth. Bottle, label and refrigerate.
YIELD	1 liter

TOGARASHI SYRUP

INGREDIENTS	750 ml water
	750 g sugar
	30 g togarashi
EQUIPMENT	Scale, stainless steel pot, induction cook-top, whisk, cheesecloth
METHOD	Combine all ingredients in a pot and heat at 80°C for 30 minutes, stirring occasionally, until the sugar is completely dissolved. Remove from heat and cool at room temperature for 1 hour. Strain through cheesecloth. Bottle, label and refrigerate.
YIELD	1 liter

TOMATO SYRUP

INGREDIENTS	500 g cherry tomatoes
	250 ml water
	1 kg sugar
EQUIPMENT	Scale, blender, stainless steel pot, induction cook-top, whisk, cheesecloth
METHOD	Blend tomatoes on high until liquefied. Combine with the water and sugar in a pot and heat at 70°C, stirring occasionally, until the sugar is completely dissolved. Remove from heat and cool at room temperature. Strain through cheesecloth. Bottle, label and refrigerate.
YIELD	1 liter

TONKA BEAN CANE SYRUP

INGREDIENTS	1 whole tonka bean
	500 ml water
	1 kg sugar
EQUIPMENT	Plastic gloves, scale, knife, stainless steel pot, induction cook-top, whisk, cheesecloth, airtight container
METHOD	Wearing gloves, split and gut the tonka bean and add it to a pot with the water. Bring to a boil and reduce to 500 ml. Add the sugar and return to a boil, stirring frequently, until the sugar is completely dissolved. Strain through cheesecloth and cool at room temperature in an airtight container. Bottle, label and refrigerate.
YIELD	1 liter

TURMERIC CITRUS

INGREDIENTS	500 ml water
	3 tbsp ground turmeric
	1 tbsp citric acid
	Zest of 1 lime
EQUIPMENT	Scale, measuring cup, tablespoon, citrus zester, stainless steel pot, induction cook-top, coffee filter
METHOD	Combine all ingredients in a pot and heat at 70°C. Simmer for 10 minutes. Strain through a coffee filter. Bottle, label and refrigerate.
YIELD	500 ml

VANILLA SYRUP

INGREDIENTS	1 Tahitian vanilla bean
	500 g sugar
	500 ml water
EQUIPMENT	Knife, scale, stainless steel pot, induction cook-top, whisk, cheesecloth
METHOD	Split the vanilla bean and scrape the seeds into a pot, then mix in the sugar. Add the water and simmer at 70°C for 1 hour, stirring occasionally, until the sugar is completely dissolved. Remove from heat and cool at room temperature. Strain through cheesecloth. Bottle, label and refrigerate.
YIELD	750 ml

VIURA RIOJA PEAR SYRUP

INGREDIENTS	2 ripe Anjou pears
	750 ml white wine (Viura Rioja)
	750 g sugar
EQUIPMENT	Knife, scale, stainless steel pot, induction cook-top, whisk, cheesecloth
METHOD	Dice the pears into small pieces. Combine all ingredients in the pot and heat at 70°C, stirring frequently, until the sugar is completely dissolved. Remove from heat and cool at room temperature for 1 hour. Strain through cheesecloth. Bottle, label and refrigerate.
YIELD	1 liter

WALNUT ORGEAT

INGREDIENTS	300 g shelled walnuts
	750 ml water
	1 kg sugar
	0.5 oz Everclear (or other high-proof neutral spirit)
EQUIPMENT	Scale, measuring cup, oven, blender, cheesecloth, stainless steel pot, induction cook-top, whisk
METHOD	Roast the walnuts in a 350°F oven for 10 minutes. Blend the walnuts with the water in a blender and let stand for 15 minutes. Strain through cheesecloth and add to a pot with the sugar. Simmer at 70°C for 30 minutes, stirring occasionally, until the sugar is completely dissolved. Cool at room temperature and mix in the Everclear. Bottle, label and refrigerate.
YIELD	1 liter

ANOTHER ROUND: EXTRAS

275.

SYRUPS & TINCTURES

WASABI SYRUP

INGREDIENTS 750 ml water
750 g sugar
50 g wasabi powder

EQUIPMENT Scale, stainless steel pot, induction cook-top, whisk, cheesecloth

METHOD Combine all ingredients in a pot and heat at 80°C for 30 minutes, stirring occasionally, until the sugar is completely dissolved. Remove from heat and cool at room temperature for 1 hour. Strain through cheesecloth. Bottle, label and refrigerate.

YIELD 1 liter

WHITE MISO SYRUP

INGREDIENTS 500 ml water
2 tbsp white miso paste
1 kg sugar

EQUIPMENT Scale, tablespoon, stainless steel pot, induction cook-top, whisk

METHOD Place the water and miso paste in a pot and heat at 80°C, stirring frequently, until the paste is completely dissolved. Add the sugar and increase the temperature to 100°C. Bring to a boil, stirring occasionally. Remove from heat and cool at room temperature for 30 minutes. Bottle, label and refrigerate.

YIELD 1 liter

WHITE PEONY TEA TINCTURE

INGREDIENTS 500 ml Everclear (or other high-proof neutral spirit)
2 tbsp white peony tea
500 ml water

EQUIPMENT Scale, tablespoon, airtight container, whisk, coffee filter

METHOD Mix the Everclear and tea in an airtight container and let sit at room temperature for 72 hours. Strain through a coffee filter and mix in the water. Bottle, label and store at room temperature.

YIELD 1 liter

YUZU CANE SYRUP

INGREDIENTS	750 ml yuzu juice
	1 kg cane sugar
EQUIPMENT	Scale, stainless steel pot, induction cook-top, whisk, airtight container
METHOD	Combine the yuzu juice and sugar in a pot. Cover and heat at 80°C, stirring occasionally. When the liquid comes to a boil, remove from heat and whisk until the sugar is completely dissolved. Cool at room temperature in an airtight container. Bottle, label and refrigerate.
YIELD	1 liter

ZA'ATAR TINCTURE

INGREDIENTS	500 ml Everclear (or other high-proof neutral spirit)
	4 tbsp za'atar
	500 ml water
EQUIPMENT	Scale, tablespoon, airtight container, whisk, cheesecloth or coffee filter
METHOD	Mix the Everclear and za'atar in an airtight container and let sit at room temperature for 48 hours. Strain through cheesecloth or a coffee filter and mix in the water. Bottle, label and store at room temperature.
YIELD	1 liter

277.

INDEX

279.

INDEX

281.

S

T

285.

SEAN MULDOON
DEAD RABBIT COFOUNDER & OPERATING PARTNER

It was while tending bar in Belfast that Sean's passion for traditional Irish pubs met a growing fascination with mixed drinks. Widely respected for his management skills, he was invited to take over the bar at the city's prestigious Merchant Hotel. It was here that his and Jack's paths crossed again.

Soon, the Merchant would scoop a World's Best Cocktail Bar title.

Next came New York and a chance to realize that dream: an Irish bar for the twenty-first century, with amazing cocktails.

JACK McGARRY
DEAD RABBIT COFOUNDER & OPERATING PARTNER

Jack started young, bussing tables back in Belfast, before graduating to tending bar in the city's nascent cocktail scene. Along the way, he also discovered a prodigious instinct for mixed drinks, and quickly accumulated both an encyclopedic knowledge and formidable technique.

He and Sean worked together briefly at a fashionable Belfast bar before being reunited at the city's stylish Merchant Hotel, where their combined talents garnered a World's Best Cocktail Bar title in 2010.

Soon after that, New York came calling.

JILLIAN VOSE
DEAD RABBIT BAR MANAGER & BEVERAGE DIRECTOR

Jillian won the 2013 Rising Stars award from StarChefs and was named one of the 10 Best Bartenders in America at Tales of the Cocktail in 2017 and 2018. Before taking over as Bar Manager and Beverage Director at The Dead Rabbit, she ran the bar program at the highly regarded Death & Co.

Her encyclopedic knowledge and outstanding technical skills ensure Jillian is much in demand for seminars and workshops throughout the world.

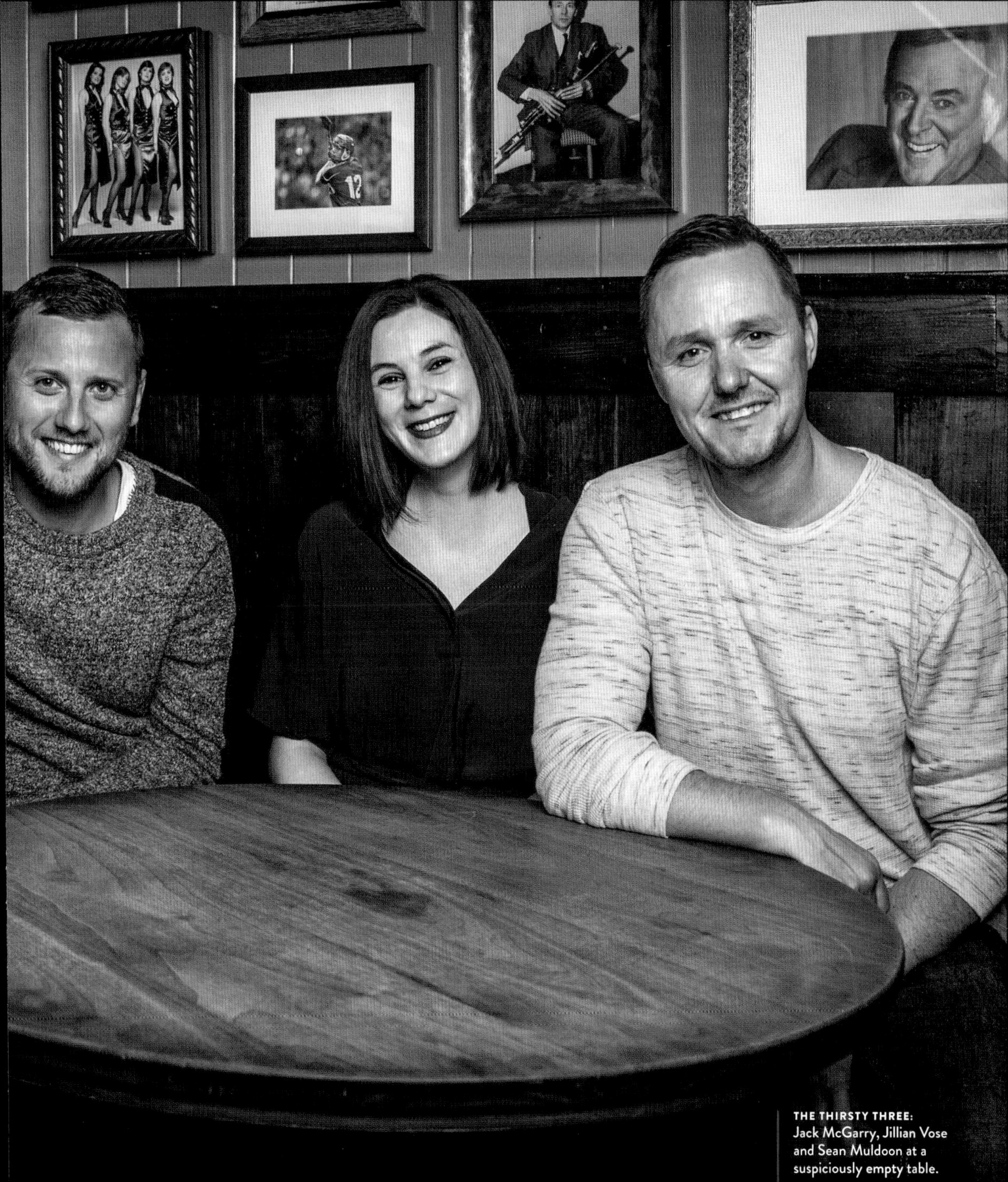
12

THE THIRSTY THREE:
Jack McGarry, Jillian Vose and Sean Muldoon at a suspiciously empty table.

NEW YORK, U.S.A.

THE DEAD RABBIT
GROCERY AND GROG
30 WATER STREET
NEW YORK, NY 10004